MAY 2008

# Reaching Financial Goals

PERSONAL FINANCE SERIES

*First Edition*

# Reaching
# Financial Goals

*Advice from Finance Industry Experts about Saving, Investing, and*
*Managing Money Using Such Financial Tools as Cash Investments,*
*Stocks, Bonds, Mutual Funds, and Annuities, Along with Facts about*
*Researching Investment Opportunities, Tips for Avoiding Fraud, a*
*a Glossary, and Directories of Resources for Additional Help and*
*Information*

*Edited by Karen Bellenir*

P.O. Box 31-1640 • Detroit, MI 48231-1640

Bibliographic Note

Because this page cannot legibly accommodate all the copyright notices, the Bibliographic Note portion of the Preface constitutes an extension of the copyright notice.

Edited by Karen Bellenir

*Personal Finance Series*

Karen Bellenir, *Managing Editor*
Elizabeth Collins, *Research and Permissions Coordinator*
Cherry Stockdale, *Permissions Assistant*
EdIndex, Services for Publishers, *Indexers*

* * *

Omnigraphics, Inc.

Matthew P. Barbour, *Senior Vice President*
Kay Gill, *Vice President—Directories*
Kevin Hayes, *Operations Manager*
David P. Bianco, *Marketing Director*

* * *

Peter E. Ruffner, *Publisher*

Frederick G. Ruffner, Jr., *Chairman*

Copyright © 2007 Omnigraphics, Inc.

ISBN 978-0-7808-0987-1

Library of Congress Cataloging-in-Publication Data

Reaching financial goals : advice from finance industry experts about saving, investing, and managing money using such financial tools as cash investments, stocks, bonds, mutual funds, and annuities, along with facts about researching investment opportunities, tips for avoiding fraud, a glossary, and directories of resources for additional help and information / edited by Karen Bellenir.
  p. cm. -- (Personal finance series)
  Summary: "Provides basic consumer finance information about identifying personal goals and the financial tools to achieve them, managing investments, and avoiding fraud. Includes index, glossary, and related resources"--Provided by publisher.
  Includes bibliographical references and index.
  ISBN 978-0-7808-0987-1 (hardcover : alk. paper) 1. Investments--Handbooks, manuals, etc. 2. Finance, Personal--Handbooks, manuals, etc. 3. Saving and investment--United States--Handbooks, manuals, etc. 4. Financial services industry--Corrupt practices--United States. 5. Advertising, Fradulent--United States. I. Bellenir, Karen.
  HG4521.R35 2007
  332.024--dc22
                                                                              2007028710

Printed in the United States

# Table of Contents

## Part III: Taking Action

## Part IV: Avoiding Fraud and Unscrupulous Practices

## Part V: Additional Help and Information

# *Preface*

## *About This Book*

Some people dream about owning a home and taking a special vacation. Others dream about owning a business and buying a special car. Some people hope to help their children or grandchildren with college expenses, and many hope to enjoy a comfortable retirement. Different people have different financial goals, and those goals often change over the course of a life-time. While the money required to achieve personal financial goals doesn't grow on trees, it does grow when a person learns to save and invest wisely.

*Reaching Financial Goals* describes the process of identifying financial goals and discusses the tools—such as cash investments, stocks, bonds, mutual funds, and annuities—that can be used to achieve them. It explains the differences between planning for short-term and long-term objectives and offers suggestions for working with financial advisors. For people taking their first steps into the world of investing, the book explains how the market for securities functions, and it outlines strategies that can be used to research investment opportunities. For more experienced investors, the book explains the risks and benefits of such practices as margin buying, after-hours trading, and day trading. A special section on fraud and unscrupulous practices provides cautions against some common types of schemes and abusive practices. The book's end section offers a glossary of investment terms and directories of finance information and investor protection resources.

## How to Use This Book

This book is divided into parts and chapters. Parts focus on broad areas of interest. Chapters are devoted to single topics within a part.

*Part I: Identifying Your Financial Goals* discusses the importance of establishing tangible short-term, mid-term, and long-term goals. It provides information about budgeting and describes various savings strategies that may be useful at different stages of life. The unique money-management concerns faced by people who receive a financial windfall from an inheritance, a business, or other source are also addressed.

*Part II: Learning about Financial Tools* explains basic investment principles and describes the types of holdings most commonly used to build wealth, including cash accounts, bonds, certificates of deposit (CDs), stocks, mutual funds, and annuities. It also explains some newer types of investment vehicles, including real estate investment trusts (REITs) and exchange traded funds (ETFs).

*Part III: Taking Action* outlines the steps involved in using financial tools. It discusses the process of working with financial advisers, provides guidance for taking one's first steps into the world of investing, and offers suggestions for staying on course. It explains how to research investment opportunities, how to understand financial information, and how to evaluate the risks associated with practices such as after-hours trading and day trading. The part concludes with information about identifying the difference between taking financial risks and using the financial markets as an outlet for problem gambling.

*Part IV: Avoiding Fraud and Unscrupulous Practices* discusses unrealistic offers, the dissemination of false information, identity theft, and other types of deceptive tactics commonly employed by scam artists. It describes the characteristics of bogus offers and explains how investors can protect themselves from falling victim to dishonest schemes.

*Part V: Additional Help and Information* provides a glossary of investment terms, a directory of finance information resources, and a directory of investor protection services agencies.

## Bibliographic Note

This volume contains documents and excerpts from publications issued by the following U.S. government agencies: Bureau of the Public

Debt; Commodity Futures Trading Commission; Federal Deposit Insurance Corporation (FDIC); Federal Trade Commission (FTC); U.S. Department of Labor; and the U.S. Securities and Exchange Commission (SEC).

In addition, this volume contains copyrighted documents from the following organizations: American Association of Individual Investors; American Institute of Certified Public Accountants; American Stock Exchange; Balance; Cable News Network (CNN); Certified Financial Planner Board of Standards, Inc.; Charles Schwab and Co.; Connecticut Council on Problem Gambling; Federal Reserve Bank of Chicago; Financial Planning Association; Insurance Information Institute; Jump$tart Coalition for Personal Financial Literacy; National Association of Real Estate Investment Trusts; National Futures Association; Ohio State University Extension; Options Industry Council; Rutgers Cooperative Research and Extension; Sudden Money Institute; and the *Wall Street Journal*.

Full citation information is provided on the first page of each chapter or section. Every effort has been made to secure all necessary rights to reprint the copyrighted material. If any omissions have been made, please contact Omnigraphics to make corrections for future editions.

## *Acknowledgements*

In addition to the organizations, agencies, and individuals who have contributed to this book special thanks go to editorial assistants Nicole Salerno and Elizabeth Bellenir, research and permissions coordinator Liz Collins, and permissions assistant Cherry Stockdale.

## *About the* Personal Finance Series

In testimony before the Committee on Banking, Housing, and Urban Affairs, Ben Bernanke, Chairman of the Federal Reserve Board, noted that there seems to be "a significant correlation between the level of financial knowledge and good financial management practices." According to a study he cited, individuals who were familiar with financial concepts and products were more likely to balance their checkbooks every month, budget for savings, and hold investment accounts.

Despite the value of having such financial knowledge, many people do not know how to obtain it. According to a report on financial literacy prepared for the National Conference of State Legislatures, several surveys have demonstrated that many Americans simply do not know how to accomplish basic financial tasks, including balancing their checkbooks, reading contracts, spending money wisely, managing debt, saving for the future, and coping with the money-related problems that accompany losing a job, financing a college education, dealing with a serious illness or injury, or adjusting to other major life events.

Omnigraphics' *Personal Finance Series* addresses these types of concerns and focuses on helping people interact with financial information in a way that helps them meet individual challenges. It covers a wide variety of financial topics focusing on economic decision-making and fiscal responsibility. It helps people understand basic principles about money management, and it describes practical applications of key concepts, including suggestions for making household budgets, instituting spending plans, managing debt, saving and investing, and securing long-term financial well being.

If there is a topic you would like to see addressed in the *Personal Finance Series,* please write to:

Editor
*Personal Finance Series*
Omnigraphics, Inc.
P.O. Box 31-1640
Detroit, MI 48231
E-mail: editorial@omnigraphics.com

# Part One

# Identifying
# Your Financial Goals

# Chapter 1

# *Dream It and Achieve It: How to Set and Attain Financial Goals*

Do you work all day, go home, spend the contents of your paycheck, and wonder where you are really going financially? Vague fantasies of owning your own home, buying new furniture, taking a vacation, or retiring early may pass through your mind—you want something bigger and better, but what exactly? And how do you get there? All too often financial dreams are abandoned in lieu of life's practical obligations. They may seem unachievable, or even silly. After all, you may think, how can a new car be considered when there are bills to pay?

Fortunately the New Year is approaching. An unmarked calendar represents fresh opportunity, and is the ideal time for life-transforming action. You can go from wishing in January to having in December by following the next five steps.

**One:** Identify your goal. Ironically, this is often the most difficult step. You may have suppressed your true desires for so long, you no longer know what you want (outside of an undefined wish for more money). However, a goal should be two things: tangible, so you can track progress and know when you reach the finish line, and exciting, so you are motivated to keep going when you are tempted to give up. This step deserves your utmost attention. As the song says, "If you don't have a dream, how you gonna make a dream come true?"

---

This chapter begins with "Dream It and Achieve It: How to Set and Attain Financial Goals," © 2005 Balance, and also includes "8 Ways to Master Your Money," © 2005 Balance, and "Money Management Planner," © 2004 Balance. Reprinted with permission. For additional information, visit the Balance website at www.balancepro.net or call 888-456-2227.

There are three basic goal types: short-term (under a year), mid-term (one to three years), and long-term (three-plus years). Have multiple goals? Either work towards them simultaneously or narrow your focus to one. The key is to not overwhelm yourself.

**Two:** Look at the numbers. Now that you have a goal, it's time to understand your financial parameters and options. Examine your income and expenses, and determine how much you can save each month. Looks bleak, you say? Consider increasing your cash flow with overtime hours, a part-time job, or even an overdue raise. Omit or reduce unnecessary expenses. Get creative and break out of your box—you'll never reach your dream by saying no.

**Three:** Know when you want it. Assign a time frame for your goal. Mark your calendar with the projected achievement date. If the goal is mid or long-term, allocate progress points ("$500 in my IRA account by June 5th, $1,000 by December 12th"). Keep yourself motivated by flipping to those dates often.

**Four:** Design a savings strategy. Have the allocated savings sum automatically deducted from your paycheck or checking account and deposited into a separate savings account. It's easy, and you'll never miss what you don't see.

A traditional savings account is usually sufficient for short-term goals, but if you have years to build capital, you'll want to move it into an account where your money will really work for you. Once you've accumulated enough to make a minimum deposit in an investment vehicle (amount varies by type), research your options carefully. Remember: the greater the return, the greater the risk. After you've worked so hard to save, you don't want to gamble your goal away.

**Five:** Be flexible. Don't give up—modify! If you simply can't put the $150 into your Maui extravaganza fund this month because your transmission blew, resist the urge to panic. Consider it a temporary setback. With a little extra effort, you may be able to make it up over the next couple of months. Or alter your plans or achievement date slightly.

If you find yourself regularly unable to meet your savings goal, there may be deeper issues to contend with. Were you too optimistic with those overtime hours? Couldn't give up smoking to save the extra $100 per month? Or perhaps the goal really wasn't for you—you thought a new computer was vital to your happiness, but the prospect of owning it just isn't giving you the thrill you anticipated. No matter. Revisit the first four steps and reassess.

There are few greater gifts you can give yourself then pursuing—and achieving—your financial goals. To do so takes strength and courage. So break out that fresh, clean calendar and make this a truly prosperous New Year.

## 8 Ways to Master Your Money

**1. Set specific goals:** Saving tends to be easier when you have a certain purpose in mind: Saving for your first house, retirement at a certain age, a child's college education, or even a trip around the world. The important thing is to be specific.

To develop a sound plan, these goals must have both a time frame and a dollar amount. Once you have listed and quantified your goals, you need to prioritize them. You may find, for example, that saving for a new home is more important than buying a new car.

Whatever your objective, be specific. Figure out how many weeks or months there are between now and when you want to reach your target. Divide the estimated cost by the number of weeks or months. That's how much you'll need to save each week or month to have enough money set aside. Remember, a goal is a dream with a deadline.

**2. Pay yourself first:** Save and invest 5–10% of your gross annual income. Of course, this can be much harder than it sounds. If you're currently living from paycheck to paycheck without any real opportunity to get ahead, begin by creating a solid budget after tracking all monthly expenses.

Once you figure out how you can control your discretionary spending, you can then redirect the money into a savings account. For many people, a good way to start saving regularly is to have a small amount transferred automatically from their paycheck to a savings account or mutual fund. The idea: If you don't see it, you don't miss it.

**3. Maintain an emergency fund:** Before you commit your newfound savings to volatile and hard-to-reach investments, make sure you have at least three to six months' worth of expenses saved in an emergency fund to see yourself through difficult times. Keeping it liquid will ensure that you don't have to sell investments when their prices are down, and guarantee that you can always get to your money quickly.

If you have trouble deciding how much you need to keep on hand, begin by considering the standard expenses you have in a month, and then estimate all the expenses you might have in the future (possible insurance deductibles and other emergencies). Generally, if you spend a larger portion of your income on discretionary expenses that you could cut easily in a financial crisis, the less money you need to keep on hand in your emergency account. If you have dependents, you'd want to keep more money in your emergency fund to offset the greater risk.

**4. Pay off your credit card debt:** If you're trying to save while carrying a large credit card balance at, say, 19.8%, realize that paying off the debt is a guaranteed return of nearly 20%. Once you pay off your credit cards, use them only for convenience, and pay off the balance each month. If you tend to run up credit card charges, get rid of the plastic and go back to using cash.

**5. Insure your family adequately:** A major lawsuit, unexpected illness or accident can be financially devastating if you lack proper insurance. The key to insurance is to cover only financial losses so large that you could not cope with them and remain financially fit. If someone is dependent on your income, you need adequate life insurance. Long-term disability coverage is important as long as you need employment income. Also, be sure to carry adequate liability coverage on your home and auto policies.

To save on annual premiums, it might be feasible for you to raise your insurance deductible, or eliminate dual coverages. And whenever purchasing insurance—life, home, disability, or auto—be sure to shop around, and buy only from a reputable firm.

**6. Take advantage of tax-deferred investments:** If your employer has a tax-deferred investment plan like a 401(k) or 403(b), use it. Often, employers will match your investment. Even if they don't, no taxes are due on your contributions or earnings until you retire and begin withdrawing the funds. Tax-deferred savings means that your investments can grow much faster than they would otherwise. The same is true of IRAs, although the maximum amount you can invest annually in an IRA is substantially less than what you can put in a 401(k) or 403(b).

**7. Diversify your investments:** When it comes to managing risk to maximize your return, it pays to diversify. First you need to diversify among the three major asset classes: cash, stocks, and bonds. Once you have decided on an allocation strategy among these three investment classes, it is important to diversify within each asset. This means buying multiple stocks within a variety of industries and holding bonds of varying maturities. Simply put, don't put all your eggs in one basket. Also, don't make the mistake of putting most or all of your money in "safe" investments like savings accounts, CDs and money market funds. Over the long haul, inflation and taxes will devour the purchasing power of your money in these "safe havens".

All investments involve some trade-off between risk and return. Diversification reduces unnecessary risk by spreading your money among a variety of investments. Aside from diversification, the single most effective strategy is to invest continuously over time, with a long-term perspective.

**8. Write a will:** The simplest way to ensure that your funds, property, and personal effects will be distributed according to your wishes is to prepare a will. A will is a legal document that ensures that your assets will be given to family members or other beneficiaries you designate. Having a will is especially important if you have young children because it gives you the opportunity to designate a guardian for them in the event of your death. Although wills are simple to create, about half of all Americans die intestate, or without a will. With no will to indicate your wishes, the court steps in and distributes your property according to the laws of your state. If you have no apparent heirs and die without a will, it's even possible that the state may claim your estate.

To begin, take an inventory of your assets, outline your objectives and determine to which friends and family you wish to pass your belongings. Then, when drafting a will, be sure to include the following: name a guardian for your children, name an executor, specify an alternate beneficiary, and use a residuary clause which typically reads "I give the remainder of my estate to..." Once your will is drafted, you won't have to think about it again unless your wishes or your financial situation change substantially.

## Money Management Planner

The Money Management Planner is a guide to help you take control of your finances. It will help you determine your net worth, set goals, monitor your cash flow, and track expenses. A sound spending and savings plan is the foundation for your long-term financial success.

Examine your past finances to create a plan for all future spending and savings. In other words, a review of your expenses and spending habits will enable you to design a realistic monthly budget. Be prepared to make some changes, though, if those habits have kept you from achieving your financial goals.

| | Target Date | Total Needed | Current Savings | Additional Savings Needed | Pay Periods Until Target Date | Savings Needed Per Pay Period | Savings Needed Per Month |
|---|---|---|---|---|---|---|---|
| Short Range Goals | | | | | | | |
| Mid Range Goals | | | | | | | |
| Long Range Goals | | | | | | | |

**Figure 1.1.** Financial Goals: Your financial goals are specific things you want to do with your money within a certain time period. Short range goals are accomplished within one year, mid-range goals are accomplished within two to five years, and long range goals generally take more than five years to achieve.

| What You Own | Amount |
|---|---|
| Checking/Saving Accounts | |
| Investment Accounts | |
| Stocks & Bonds | |
| IRA/401(k) | |
| Home/Real Estate | |
| Automobile(s) | |
| Other Assets | |
| **Total Owned** | (A) |

| What You Owe | Amount |
|---|---|
| Mortgage | |
| Credit Cards | |
| Student Loan(s) | |
| Auto Loan(s) | |
| Othe Loan(s) | |
| Income Tax Due | |
| Other Debt(s) | |
| **Total Owed** | (B) |

To figure your net worth, subtract the total owed from the total owned:

| Total Owned (A) | Total Owed (B) | Net Worth |
|---|---|---|
| – | = | |

**Figure 1.2.** Net Worth: In order to evaluate your progress as you work toward your goals, you must determine what your overall financial picture looks like today. Your net worth is simply the difference between what you own and what you owe. To make sure you are staying on track, it's a good idea to calculate your assets and liabilities annually. If you conscientiously follow your plan you should see a gradual, steady increase in your net worth.

| Category | Expense | Average Per Month | Goal Per Month |
|---|---|---|---|
| HOUSING | Rent/Mortgage | | |
| | 2nd Mortgage/Equity Line | | |
| | Homeowner's/Renter's Insurance | | |
| | Condo Fees/HOA Dues | | |
| | Home Maintenance | | |
| | Gas/Electric | | |
| | Water/Sewer/Garbage | | |
| | Telephone | | |
| FOOD | Groceries/Household Items | | |
| | At Work/School | | |
| INSURANCE (Exclude payroll deducted amounts) | Health/Dental/Vision | | |
| | Life/Disability | | |
| MEDICAL CARE (Exclude payroll deducted amounts) | Doctor/Chiropractor | | |
| | Optometrist/Lenses | | |
| | Dentist/Orthodontist | | |
| | Prescriptions | | |
| TRANSPORTATION (Exclude payroll deducted amounts) | Car Payment #1 | | |
| | Car Payment #2 | | |
| | Auto Insurance | | |
| | Registration | | |
| | Gasoline/Oil | | |
| | Maintenance/Repairs | | |
| | Public Transportation/Tolls/Parking | | |
| CHILD CARE (Exclude payroll deducted amounts) | Daycare | | |
| | Child Support/Alimony | | |
| MISCELLANEOUS | Banking Fees | | |
| | Laundry | | |
| | Union Dues | | |
| | Other | | |
| INCOME TAXES | Prior Year | | |
| | Estimated Tax Payments (Self-Employed) | | |
| SAVINGS | Emergency | | |
| | Goals | | |
| TOTALS | | | |

**Figure 1.3.** *Essential Expenses: Household expenses are categorized into essential and discretionary. Since many expenses are variable, such as utilities and groceries, it is important to average these expenses. Other expenses are periodic (such as insurance or vehicle registration). Again, calculate the annual amount and divide by 12.*

| Category | Expense | Average Per Month | Goal Per Month |
|---|---|---|---|
| PERSONAL | Beauty/Barber | | |
| | Clothing/Jewelry | | |
| | Cosmetics/Manicure | | |
| ENTERTAINMENT | Cable/Satellite | | |
| | Movies/Concerts/Theater | | |
| | Books/Magazines | | |
| | CD/Tapes/Videos/DVD | | |
| | Dining Out | | |
| | Sports/Hobbies | | |
| | Vacation/Travel | | |
| MISCELLANEOUS | Internet Service | | |
| | Pet Care | | |
| | Gifts for Holidays/Birthdays | | |
| | Cell Phone/Pager | | |
| | Postage | | |
| | Cigarettes/Alcohol | | |
| | Contributions to Church/Charity | | |
| | Other | | |
| TOTALS | | | |

*Figure 1.4.* Discretionary Expense

| Creditor Name | Interest Rate | Monthly Payment | Balance |
|---|---|---|---|
| 1 | | | |
| 2 | | | |
| 3 | | | |
| 4 | | | |
| 5 | | | |
| 6 | | | |
| 7 | | | |
| 8 | | | |
| 9 | | | |
| 10 | | | |
| 11 | | | |
| 12 | | | |

*Figure 1.5.* Unsecured Debt: List all debts (except auto loans and mortgages) along with the name of the creditor, interest rate, total balance owing, and the required minimum payment. This includes credit and charge cards, installment loans, personal loans, and outstanding medical bills.

| Source | Gross | Net |
|---|---|---|
| Job | | |
| Spouse's job | | |
| Part-time job | | |
| Rental/room & board received | | |
| Commissions/bonuses | | |
| Tax refunds | | |
| Investment income | | |
| Government benefits | | |
| Unemployment insurance | | |
| Child support/alimony | | |
| Support from family/friends | | |
| Other | | |
| **Total** | | |

**Figure 1.6.** *Monthly Income: Enter your gross and net (after taxes) income from all sources. For income received infrequently, such as bonuses or tax returns, calculate the annual income, then divide by 12 to find the monthly amount.*

| Monthly Net Income | Total Essential Expenses | Total Discretionary Expenses | Total Debt Payment | Balance |
|---|---|---|---|---|
| | – | – | – | = |

**Figure 1.7. Bottom Line:** *Once you have determined the total of your take-home pay and expenses you are ready to determine your bottom line. Subtract the total of all expenses including debt payments from your net income. If the result is a positive number, you can add the extra money to your savings to reach your goals sooner. If your expenses exceed your income, you'll need to make some adjustments to bring your finances back into balance.*

## Tracking Day-to-Day Expenses

If you don't know where your money is going, it's time to start tracking your spending. Different methods of tracking work for different people—some like to save receipts while others prefer to jot down all purchases in a small notebook they carry with them. Remember,

| Item | Mon | Tue | Wed | Thu | Fri | Sat | Sun | Total Expenses | Weekly Budget | Over / Under |
|---|---|---|---|---|---|---|---|---|---|---|
| Groceries | | | | | | | | | | |
| Restaurants | | | | | | | | | | |
| Laundry/Dry Cleaning | | | | | | | | | | |
| Medical/Dental | | | | | | | | | | |
| Auto/Gas/Parking | | | | | | | | | | |
| Other Transportation | | | | | | | | | | |
| Child Care | | | | | | | | | | |
| Personal Care | | | | | | | | | | |
| Clothing | | | | | | | | | | |
| Bank Fees/ Postage | | | | | | | | | | |
| Entertainment | | | | | | | | | | |
| Books/Music/ Video | | | | | | | | | | |
| Cigarettes/Alcohol | | | | | | | | | | |
| Gifts/Cards | | | | | | | | | | |
| Home/Garden | | | | | | | | | | |
| Church/Charity Contributions | | | | | | | | | | |
| Other | | | | | | | | | | |
| Other | | | | | | | | | | |
| Other | | | | | | | | | | |
| Other | | | | | | | | | | |
| **Weekly Totals** | | | | | | | | | | |

**Budget Overview:**

Income_____    Expenses_____    Balance (+/-)_____

**Figure 1.8.** Weekly Expenses

tracking is only effective if you count every expense, including the morning newspaper and the 75 cents you put in the office vending machine. Use the sheets on the next two pages to record weekly and monthly spending totals. (We suggest you make copies of the charts shown in Figures 1.8 and 1.9 so that you can track for longer than one week.)

| Item | Week 1 | Week 2 | Week 3 | Week 4 | Week 5 | Total Expenses | Monthly Budget | Over / Under |
|---|---|---|---|---|---|---|---|---|
| Savings | | | | | | | | |
| Groceries | | | | | | | | |
| Restaurants | | | | | | | | |
| Laundry/Dry Cleaning | | | | | | | | |
| Medical/Dental | | | | | | | | |
| Auto/Gas/Parking | | | | | | | | |
| Other Transportation | | | | | | | | |
| Child Care | | | | | | | | |
| Personal Care | | | | | | | | |
| Clothing | | | | | | | | |
| Bank Fees/ Postage | | | | | | | | |
| Entertainment | | | | | | | | |
| Books/Music/ Video | | | | | | | | |
| Cigarettes/Alcohol | | | | | | | | |
| Gifts/Cards | | | | | | | | |
| Home/Garden | | | | | | | | |
| Church/Charity Contributions | | | | | | | | |
| Other | | | | | | | | |
| Other | | | | | | | | |
| Other | | | | | | | | |
| **Monthly Totals** | | | | | | | | |

**Budget Overview:**

Income_____  Expenses_____  Balance (+/-)_____

**Figure 1.9.** *Monthly Expenses*

13

## Budget Guidelines

**Housing:** Spend no more than 35% of net income on housing. Depending on whether you rent or own, that can include: mortgage/rent, utilities, insurance, taxes, and home maintenance.

**Savings:** Save at least 10% of income throughout your working life. Make sure you have 3–6 months income in an emergency fund before you start saving for other goals.

**Transportation:** Spend no more than 15% of net income on transportation. That includes: car payment, auto insurance, tag or license, maintenance, gasoline, and parking.

**Debt:** Spend no more than 15% of net income on all other consumer debt: student loans, retail installment contracts, credit cards, personal loans, tax debts, and medical debts.

**Other:** Spend no more than 25% of net income on all other expenses: food, clothing, entertainment, childcare, medical expenses, tithing/charity, and vacations.

## Adjust Your Plan

If the amount you are now saving falls short of the amount you need to save to reach your goals, here are some questions to ask yourself:

- Are you paying yourself first by putting away at least 10 percent of your after-tax income?
- Could you increase the amount you're saving by earning more or spending less?
- Did you set reasonable, achievable goals?
- Could you delay the target date of any of your goals?

You should reevaluate your spending and savings plan annually, or whenever there is a big change in your financial wants and needs. Remember that a budget is simply a priority list—by following it you are ensuring that your money is used to acquire the things, or reach the goals, that are most important to you.

# Chapter 2

# *How to Budget and Save*

As a consumer, you face many choices on how to manage your money. Knowing how to manage money can help you make smart choices. Your money will work harder for you. You'll be more likely to avoid traps that can undermine your ability to attain your financial goals. You'll be in a better position to pay off debt and build savings.

Being smart about money can help you buy a house, finance higher education, or start a retirement fund. A money management game plan can help you get started and stay with it until you achieve the goals you set for yourself.

### *Establish goals. Where do you want to be?*

Use the following work sheets to help you identify your goals. Without goals, it's difficult to accomplish anything. When you think about your future and what you want to achieve, it's helpful to establish a timeframe.

- Short-term: such as paying off credit card debt, saving for a vacation, or buying new clothes

- Intermediate: such as saving to buy a car

- Long-term: such as saving for education or for retirement

Excerpted and reprinted from "How to Budget and Save," an online financial education publication of the Federal Reserve Bank of Chicago, http://www.chicagofed.org, 2006.

15

Estimate the cost of each goal and the date you want to achieve it. Then figure out how much you need to save each month. Try to set realistic goals and saving requirements.

### Create a budget. Determine your current situation. Where are you today?

Now that you've figured out your financial goals, you are ready to create a budget that will help you attain them. Complete the budget worksheets and write in your budget figures. Start by writing down your expenses (under Current Monthly Expenses, see Figure 2.4).

| Short-term Goals | Cost | Completion Date | Saving Needed per Month |
|---|---|---|---|
| Example: Vacation* | $1,200 | 12 months | $100 |
| *For example, if your goal is to save for a vacation that will cost $1,200, you need to save $100 for 12 months. (Please note that these examples do not include the interest that would accrue over time. | | | |
| | | | |
| | | | |
| | | | |
| | | | |

**Figure 2.1.** *Short-term Goals*

| What You Own | Amount |
|---|---|
| Checking/Saving Accounts | |
| Investment Accounts | |
| Stocks & Bonds | |
| IRA/401(k) | |
| Home/Real Estate | |
| Automobile(s) | |
| Other Assets | |
| **Total Owned** | **(A)** |

| What You Owe | Amount |
|---|---|
| Mortgage | |
| Credit Cards | |
| Student Loan(s) | |
| Auto Loan(s) | |
| Othe Loan(s) | |
| Income Tax Due | |
| Other Debt(s) | |
| **Total Owed** | **(B)** |

To figure your net worth, subtract the total owed from the total owned:

| Total Owned (A) | Total Owed (B) | Net Worth |
|---|---|---|
| | – | = |

**Figure 2.2.** *Intermediate-term Goals*

**Monthly fixed expenses:** Start with monthly fixed expenses such as regular savings, housing, groceries, utilities, and car payments. Put these continuing obligations under the heading: Fixed.

Use checking account statements, credit card statements, receipts and other records to help you complete this estimate. Be realistic— it's better to estimate high than low.

| Category | Expense | Average Per Month | Goal Per Month |
|---|---|---|---|
| HOUSING | Rent/Mortgage | | |
| | 2nd Mortgage/Equity Line | | |
| | Homeowner's/Renter's Insurance | | |
| | Condo Fees/HOA Dues | | |
| | Home Maintenance | | |
| | Gas/Electric | | |
| | Water/Sewer/Garbage | | |
| | Telephone | | |
| FOOD | Groceries/Household Items | | |
| | At Work/School | | |
| INSURANCE (Exclude payroll deducted amounts) | Health/Dental/Vision | | |
| | Life/Disability | | |
| MEDICAL CARE (Exclude payroll deducted amounts) | Doctor/Chiropractor | | |
| | Optometrist/Lenses | | |
| | Dentist/Orthodontist | | |
| | Prescriptions | | |
| TRANSPORTATION (Exclude payroll deducted amounts) | Car Payment #1 | | |
| | Car Payment #2 | | |
| | Auto Insurance | | |
| | Registration | | |
| | Gasoline/Oil | | |
| | Maintenance/Repairs | | |
| | Public Transportation/Tolls/Parking | | |
| CHILD CARE (Exclude payroll deducted amounts) | Daycare | | |
| | Child Support/Alimony | | |
| MISCELLANEOUS | Banking Fees | | |
| | Laundry | | |
| | Union Dues | | |
| | Other | | |
| INCOME TAXES | Prior Year | | |
| | Estimated Tax Payments (Self-Employed) | | |
| SAVINGS | Emergency | | |
| | Goals | | |
| **TOTALS** | | | |

*Figure 2.3.* Long-term Goals

Remember that savings is considered an expense even though you keep the money. You work hard. You deserve to keep some of what you earn every month. Savings is the key to meeting your financial goals.

Make estimates for all money spent—regardless of how you pay: cash, check, credit card, debit card, automatic checking account withdrawals, or savings through work plans such as 401K or 403B plans.

**Monthly variable expenses:** Once you have noted all your fixed expenses, write down your expenses that vary each month such as clothing, vacations, gifts, and personal spending money. Put these

**Current Monthly Expenses**

| Fixed | | | Variable | | |
|---|---|---|---|---|---|
| Savings | $ | | Credit Card Bills | $ | |
| Rent/Mortgage | $ | | Other Loans | $ | |
| Gas (Cooking/Heating) | $ | | Clothing/Shoes | $ | |
| Electric | $ | | Gasoline | $ | |
| Water/Sewer/Trash | $ | | Parking/Tolls | $ | |
| Home Upkeep/Repairs | $ | | Car Maintenance | $ | |
| Home Insurance | $ | | Postage | $ | |
| Life Insurance | $ | | Restaurants | $ | |
| Disability Insurance | $ | | Entertainment | $ | |
| Auto Insurance | $ | | Charity | $ | |
| Telephone | $ | | Gifts | $ | |
| Groceries | $ | | Vacation | $ | |
| Car Loans | $ | | Tobacco/Beverages | $ | |
| Car Stickers/License | $ | | Medical/Dental/Prescriptions | $ | |
| Bus, Train, Cabs | $ | | Eye Glasses/Contacts | $ | |
| Laundry/Dry Cleaning | $ | | Home Cleaning Supplies | $ | |
| Haircuts/Hair Care Cosmetics | $ | | Personal | $ | |
| Newspapers/Publications | $ | | Other | $ | |
| Other | $ | | Other | $ | |
| Other | $ | | Other | $ | |
| Other | $ | | Total Variable Expenses: | $ | |
| Total Fixed Expenses: | $ | | | $ | |
| | | | Total Expenses: | $ | |

**Monthly Income**

| | |
|---|---|
| Wages/Salary | $ |
| (after taxes & deductions) | $ |
| Part-time Work | $ |
| Child Support/Alimony | $ |
| Other | $ |
| Other | $ |
| Other | $ |
| Other | $ |
| Total Net Income: | $ |

**Financial Summary**

| | |
|---|---|
| Total Net Income | $ |
| Minus Total Expenses | $ |
| Surplus or Deficit:* | $ |

*If you are spending less than you are bringing home, you have a surplus; otherwise, you have a deficit.

| | |
|---|---|
| **Your monthly surplus or deficit:** | $ |

**Figure 2.4.** *Monthly Expenses*

expenses under the heading: Variable. You might have these expenses every month, but the amount you spend could change.

Get a handle on variable expenses by writing down every expense for a month—even small purchases. Use a small note book or other informal method to track your spending. This is very important because it's the best way to understand your current spending behavior. Get receipts for all purchases—especially those you make with cash. Record and categorize each transaction. You may be surprised at how much you spend in certain categories.

Use a notebook to write down every purchase you make for one month. This is the best way to understand your current spending behavior.

**List your monthly income:** Now that you have figured out your expenses, write down your monthly income after all taxes and deductions. Write this under the heading: Monthly Income. Make sure this figure reflects the total take-home pay for your household after all taxes and deductions.

**Now compare expenses to income:** One of the advantages of doing a comparison of expenses to income is that it provides a quick reality check. If you are spending more than you're bringing home every month in income, you have a deficit. If you're spending less than you're bringing home, you have a surplus. In either case, it's time to step back and consider some options.

If you have a deficit: Spending more than you're bringing home, ask yourself:

- Can I spend less in some of my variable expenses?

- How much interest am I paying with credit card and other loans?

- Where did my money go? (Consider writing down everything you spend for a month.)

If you have a surplus: Spending less than you're bringing home, ask yourself:

- Am I saving enough to meet my goals?

- Are my spending estimates accurate?

- Have I included all my fixed and variable expenses?

## *Save your way to a more secure future.*

An estimated seventy-five percent of families will experience a major financial setback in any given ten-year period. The economy and the job market are good now, but that could change. It's smart to be prepared for financial thunderstorms.

**Save early, save often:** A consistent, long-term saving program can help you achieve your goals. It also can help you build a financial safety net. Experts recommend that you save from three to six months worth of living expenses for emergencies.

Savings grow beyond what you contribute because of compound interest. Over time, the value of compound interest works to every saver's advantage.

For example, if you save $75 a month for five years and earn five-percent interest, the $4,500 you contributed would grow to $5,122 because of the compounding interest.

It's easy to figure out how long it will take you to double the money you save. It's called the Rule of 72. You take the interest you're earning on your money and divide that number into 72. The result is roughly the number of years it will take your principal to double.

For example, if you're earning 5 percent on your money, you divide 72 by 5 and you get 14.4. Your principal will double in 14.4 years without further contributions.

Keep in mind, however, that inflation reduces the return on your money. For example, five percent-interest, adjusted for three-percent inflation, only nets a two-percent real return.

**What you don't see, you don't spend:** Saving means giving up something now, so you will have more in the future. It's not easy deferring or eliminating purchasing things you want today.

It helps to pay yourself first. Take a portion of savings from every paycheck before you pay any bills. Use your company's payroll deduction plan if available. Arrange for a fixed amount to be taken out so that you never see it. What you don't see, you don't spend. You also can direct automatic checking account withdrawals into a savings account or money market.

Join the company's retirement-savings plan (such as a 401K or 403B). Your contribution avoids current taxes and accumulates tax deferred. Also, companies sometimes match some of your contributions. For example, for every dollar you contribute, the company could contribute 25 cents. That would be a 25-percent return on your money.

Other saving tips:

- When you get a raise, save all or most of it.

- Pay off your credit card balances and save the money you're no longer spending on interest.

- Shift credit card balances to a card with a lower interest rate and use the savings to pay off the balance.

- Keep your car a year or two longer. Do routine maintenance and make regular repairs. Save the money you would have spent on a new car.

- Stop smoking.

- Take $5 from your wallet everyday and put it in a safe place. That will add up to $1,825 in a year.

- Shop with a list and stick to it.

- Don't buy any new clothes until you've paid off your current wardrobe.

- Eat more meals at home.

- Look for inexpensive entertainment: zoos, museums, parks, walks, biking, library books, concerts, movies, and picnics.

- Shop for less expensive insurance.

- Save any tax refund.

- Drop subscriptions to publications you don't read.

- Postpone purchases or consider fewer features on the items you plan to purchase.

The less you spend, the more you can save. And the longer you can consistently save, the faster your savings will grow.

# Chapter 3

# *Financial Security: A Roadmap*

No one is born knowing how to save or to invest. Every successful investor starts with the basics—the information in this chapter.

A few people may stumble into financial security—a wealthy relative may die or a business may take off. But for most people, the only way to attain financial security is to save and invest over a long period of time.

Time after time, people of even modest means who begin the journey reach financial security and all that it promises: buying a home, educational opportunities for their children, and a comfortable retirement. If they can do it, so can you.

## *Your First Step*

What are the things you want to save and invest for? A home, a car, an education, a comfortable retirement, your children, medical or other emergencies, periods of unemployment, caring for parents? Make your own list and then think about which goals are the most important to you. List your most important goals first.

Decide how many years you have to meet each specific goal, because when you save or invest you'll need to find a savings or investment option that fits your time frame for meeting each goal.

---

Excerpted from "Get the Facts on Saving and Investing: A roadmap to start you on a journey to financial security through saving and investing," U.S. Securities and Exchange Commission (www.sec.gov), SEC Pub. 009, June 2006.

Many tools exist to help you put your financial plan together. You'll find a wealth of information, including calculators and links to non-commercial resources, on the U.S. Securities and Exchange Commission (SEC)'s website at www.sec.gov/investor.shtml.

## *Know Your Current Financial Situation*

Sit down and take an honest look at your entire financial situation. You can never take a journey without knowing where you're starting from, and a journey to financial security is no different.

You'll need to figure out on paper your current situation—what you own and what you owe. You'll be creating a "net worth statement." On one side of the page, list what you own. These are your "assets." And on the other side list what you owe other people, your "liabilities" or debts.

Subtract your liabilities from your assets. If your assets are larger than your liabilities, you have a "positive" net worth. If your liabilities are greater than your assets, you have a "negative" net worth.

You'll want to update your "net worth statement" every year to keep track of how you are doing. Don't be discouraged if you have a negative net worth. If you follow a plan to get into a positive position, you're doing the right thing.

## *Know Your Income and Expenses*

The next step is to keep track of your income and your expenses for every month. Write down what you and others in your family earn, and then your monthly expenses.

Include a category for savings and investing. What are you paying yourself every month? Many people get into the habit of saving and investing by following this advice: always pay yourself or your family first. Many people find it easier to pay themselves first if they allow their bank to automatically remove money from their paycheck and deposit it into a savings or investment account.

Likely even better, for tax purposes, is to participate in an employer-sponsored retirement plan such as a 401(k), 403(b), or 457(b). These plans will typically not only automatically deduct money from your paycheck, but will immediately reduce the taxes you are paying. Additionally, in many plans the employer matches some or all of your contribution. When your employer does that, it's offering "free money."

Any time you have automatic deductions made from your paycheck or bank account, you'll increase the chances of being able to stick to your plan and to realize your goals.

## *Pay Off Credit Card or Other High Interest Debt*

There is no investment strategy anywhere that pays off as well as—or with less risk than—merely paying off all high interest debt you may have. Most credit cards charge high interest rates—as much as 18 percent or more—if you don't pay off your balance in full each month. If you owe money on your credit cards, the wisest thing you can do is pay off the balance in full as quickly as possible. (The same advice goes for any other high interest debt—about 8% or above—which does not offer tax advantages.) Virtually no investment will give you the high returns you'll need to keep pace with an 18 percent interest charge.

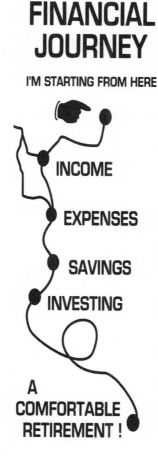

**Figure 3.1.** *Roadmap to financial security.*

25

## Making Money Grow

There are basically two ways to make money:

1.  You work for money. Someone pays you to work for them or you have your own business.

2.  Your money works for you. You take your money and you save or invest it.

Your money can work for you in two ways:

*   **Your money earns money:** When your money goes to work, it may earn a steady paycheck. Someone pays you to use your money for a period of time. When you get your money back, you get it back plus "interest." Or, if you buy stock in a company that pays "dividends" to shareholders, the company may pay you a portion of its earnings on a regular basis. Your money can make an "income," just like you. You can make more money when you and your money work.

*   **You buy something with your money that could increase in value:** You become an owner of something that you hope increases in value over time. When you need your money back, you sell it, hoping someone else will pay you more for it. For instance, you buy a piece of land thinking it will increase in value as more businesses or people move into your town. You expect to sell the land in five, ten, or twenty years when someone will buy it from you for a lot more money than you paid.

And sometimes, your money can do both at the same time—earn a steady paycheck and increase in value.

### The Differences between Saving and Investing

**Saving:** Your "savings" are usually put into the safest places, or products, that allow you access to your money at any time. Savings products include savings accounts, checking accounts, and certificates of deposit. At some banks and savings and loan associations your deposits may be insured by the Federal Deposit Insurance Corporation (FDIC). But there's a tradeoff for security and ready availability. Your money is paid a low wage as it works for you.

After paying off credit cards or other high interest debt, most smart investors put enough money in a savings product to cover an emergency, like sudden unemployment. Some make sure they have up to six months of their income in savings so that they know it will absolutely be there for them when they need it.

But how "safe" is a savings account if you leave all of your money there for a long time, and the interest it earns doesn't keep up with inflation? What if you save a dollar when it can buy a loaf of bread. But years later when you withdraw that dollar plus the interest you earned on it, it can only buy half a loaf? This is why many people put some of their money in savings, but look to investing so they can earn more over long periods of time, say three years or longer.

**Investing:** When you "invest," you have a greater chance of losing your money than when you "save." Unlike FDIC-insured deposits, the money you invest in securities, mutual funds, and other similar investments is not federally insured. You could lose your principal (the amount you've invested). But you also have the opportunity to earn more money.

## The Basic Types of Products

- **Savings:** savings accounts, certificates of deposit, checking accounts

- **Investments:** bonds, stocks, mutual funds, real estate, commodities (gold, silver, etc.)

## A Word about Risk

All investments involve taking on risk. It's important that you go into any investment in stocks, bonds, or mutual funds with a full understanding that you could lose some or all of your money in any one investment. While over the long term the stock market has historically provided around 10% annual returns (closer to 6% or 7% "real" returns when you subtract for the effects of inflation), the long term does sometimes take a rather long, long time to play out. Those who invested all of their money in the stock market at its peak in 1929 (before the stock market crash) had to wait more than 20 years to see the stock market return to the same level.

However, those that kept adding money to the market throughout that time would have done very well for themselves, as the lower cost of stocks in the 1930s made for some hefty gains for those who bought and held over the course of the next twenty years or more.

It is often said that the greater the risk, the greater the potential reward in investing, but taking on unnecessary risk is often avoidable. Investors best protect themselves against risk by spreading their money among various investments, hoping that if one investment loses money, the other investments will more than make up for those losses. This strategy, called "diversification," can be neatly summed up as, "Don't put all your eggs in one basket." Investors also protect themselves from the risk of investing all their money at the wrong time (think 1929) by following a consistent pattern of adding new money to their investments over long periods of time.

Once you've saved money for investing, consider carefully all your options and think about what diversification strategy makes sense for you. While the SEC cannot recommend any particular investment product, you should know that a vast array of investment products exists—including stocks and stock mutual funds, corporate and municipal bonds, bond mutual funds, certificates of deposit, money market funds, and U.S. Treasury securities.

Diversification can't guarantee that your investments won't suffer if the market drops. But it can improve the chances that you won't lose money, or that if you do, it won't be as much as if you weren't diversified.

### Finding the Best Investments

What are the best investments? The answer depends on when you will need the money, your goals, and if you will be able to sleep at night if you purchase a risky investment where you could lose your principal.

For instance, if you are saving for retirement, and you have 35 years before you retire, you may want to consider riskier investment products, knowing that if you stick to only the "savings" products or to less risky investment products, your money will grow too slowly—or, given inflation and taxes, you may lose the purchasing power of your money. A frequent mistake people make is putting money they will not need for a very long time in investments that pay a low amount of interest.

On the other hand, if you are saving for a short-term goal, five years or less, you don't want to choose risky investments, because when it's time to sell, you may have to take a loss. Since investments often move up and down in value rapidly, you want to make sure that you can wait and sell at the best possible time.

When you make an investment, you are giving your money to a company or enterprise, hoping that it will be successful and pay you back with even more money.

**Stocks and bonds:** Many companies offer investors the opportunity to buy either stocks or bonds. The following example shows you how stocks and bonds differ.

Let's say you believe that a company that makes automobiles may be a good investment. Everyone you know is buying one of its cars, and your friends report that the company's cars rarely break down and run well for years. You either have an investment professional investigate the company and read as much as possible about it, or you do it yourself.

After your research, you're convinced it's a solid company that will sell many more cars in the years ahead.

The automobile company offers both stocks and bonds. With the bonds, the company agrees to pay you back your initial investment in ten years, plus pay you interest twice a year at the rate of 8% a year.

If you buy the stock, you take on the risk of potentially losing a portion or all of your initial investment if the company does poorly or the stock market drops in value. But you also may see the stock increase in value beyond what you could earn from the bonds. If you buy the stock, you become an "owner" of the company.

You wrestle with the decision. If you buy the bonds, you will get your money back plus the 8% interest a year. And you think the company will be able to honor its promise to you on the bonds because it has been in business for many years and doesn't look like it could go bankrupt. The company has a long history of making cars and you know that its stock has gone up in price by an average of 9% a year, plus it has typically paid stockholders a dividend of 3% from its profits each year.

Here is an explanation of the main differences between stocks and bonds:

- **Bonds:** The company promises to return money plus interest. Risk: If the company goes bankrupt, your money may be lost. But if there is any money left, you will be paid before stockholders.

- **Stocks:** If the company profits or is perceived as having strong potential, its stock may go up in value and pay dividends. You may make more money than from the bonds. Risk: The company may do poorly, and you'll lose a portion or all of your investment.

You take your time and make a careful decision. Only time will tell if you made the right choice. You'll keep a close eye on the company and keep the stock as long as the company keeps selling a quality car that consumers want to drive, and it can make an acceptable profit from its sales.

**Mutual funds:** Because it is sometimes hard for investors to become experts on various businesses—for example, what are the best steel, automobile, or telephone companies—investors often depend on professionals who are trained to investigate companies and recommend companies that are likely to succeed.

Since it takes work to pick the stocks or bonds of the companies that have the best chance to do well in the future, many investors choose to invest in mutual funds. A mutual fund is a pool of money run by a professional or group of professionals called the "investment adviser." In a managed mutual fund, after investigating the prospects of many companies, the fund's investment adviser will pick the stocks or bonds of companies and put them into a fund. Investors can buy shares of the fund, and their shares rise or fall in value as the values of the stocks and bonds in the fund rise and fall.

Investors may typically pay a fee when they buy or sell their shares in the fund, and those fees in part pay the salaries and expenses of the professionals who manage the fund. Even small fees can and do add up and eat into a significant chunk of the returns a mutual fund is likely to produce, so you need to look carefully at how much a fund costs and think about how much it will cost you over the amount of time you plan to own its shares. If two funds are similar in every way except that one charges a higher fee than the other, you'll make more money by choosing the fund with the lower annual costs.

### *Why Some Investments Make Money and Others Don't*

You can potentially make money in an investment if:

- The company performs better than its competitors.

- Other investors recognize it's a good company, so that when it comes time to sell your investment, others want to buy it.

- The company makes profits, meaning they make enough money to pay you interest for your bond, or maybe dividends on your stock.

You can lose money if:

- The company's competitors are better than it is.

- Consumers don't want to buy the company's products or services.

- The company's officers fail at managing the business well, they spend too much money, and their expenses are larger than their profits.

- Other investors that you would need to sell to think the company's stock is too expensive given its performance and future outlook.

- The people running the company are dishonest. They use your money to buy homes, clothes, and vacations, instead of using your money on the business.

- They lie about any aspect of the business: claim past or future profits that do not exist, claim it has contracts to sell its products when it doesn't, or make up fake numbers on their finances to dupe investors.

- The brokers who sell the company's stock manipulate the price so that it doesn't reflect the true value of the company. After they pump up the price, these brokers dump the stock, the price falls, and investors lose their money.

- For whatever reason, you have to sell your investment when the market is down.

## If You Need Investment Help

Are you the type of person who will read as much as possible about potential investments and ask questions about them? If so, maybe you don't need investment advice. But if you're busy with your job, your children, or other responsibilities, or feel you don't know enough about investing on your own, then you may need professional investment advice.

Investment professionals offer a variety of services at a variety of prices. It pays to comparison shop. You can get investment advice from most financial institutions that sell investments, including brokerages, banks, mutual funds, and insurance companies. You can also hire a broker, an investment adviser, an accountant, a financial planner, or other professional to help you make investment decisions.

Before you invest always the find out answers to these questions with the SEC and your state securities regulator:

- Is the investment registered with securities regulators?

- Have investors complained about the investment in the past?

- Have the people who own or manage the investment been in trouble in the past?

- Is the person selling me this investment licensed in my state?

- Has that person been in trouble in my state, or in any other state?

Some financial planners and investment advisers offer a complete financial plan, assessing every aspect of your financial life and developing a detailed strategy for meeting your financial goals. They may charge you a fee for the plan, a percentage of your assets that they manage, or receive commissions from the companies whose products you buy, or a combination of these. You should know exactly what services you are getting and how much they will cost.

Remember, there is no such thing as a free lunch. Professional financial advisers do not perform their services as an act of charity. If they are working for you, they are getting paid for their efforts. Some of their fees are easier to see immediately than are others. But, in all cases, you should always feel free to ask questions about how and how much your adviser is being paid. And if the fee is quoted to you as a percentage, make sure that you understand what that translates to in dollars.

In contrast to investment advisers, brokers make recommendations about specific investments like stocks, bonds, or mutual funds. While taking into account your overall financial goals, brokers generally do not give you a detailed financial plan. Brokers are generally paid commissions when you buy or sell securities through them. If they sell you mutual funds make sure to ask questions about what fees are included in the mutual fund purchase.

Brokerages vary widely in the quantity and quality of the services they provide for customers. Some have large research staffs, large national operations, and are prepared to service almost any kind of financial transaction you may need. Others are small and may specialize in promoting investments in unproven and very risky companies. And there's everything else in between.

A discount brokerage charges lower fees and commissions for its services than what you'd pay at a full-service brokerage. But generally you have to research and choose investments by yourself.

A full-service brokerage costs more, but the higher fees and commissions pay for a broker's investment advice based on that firm's research.

The best way to choose an investment professional is to start by asking your friends and colleagues who they recommend. Try to get several recommendations, and then meet with potential advisers face-to-face. Make sure you get along. Make sure you understand each other. After all, it's your money.

### *Steer Clear of Trouble*

- **Stop:** Broker not registered with state or SEC
- **Beware:** Promises of quick profits

- **Watch Out:** Pressure to invest
- **Danger:** Broker has been in trouble before

### *Opening a Brokerage Account*

When you open a brokerage account, whether in person or online, you will typically be asked to sign a new account agreement. You should carefully review all the information in this agreement because it determines your legal rights regarding your account.

Do not sign the new account agreement unless you thoroughly understand it and agree with the terms and conditions it imposes on you. Do not rely on statements about your account that are not in this agreement. Ask for a copy of any account documentation prepared for you by your broker.

The broker should ask you about your investment goals and personal financial situation, including your income, net worth, investment experience, and how much risk you are willing to take on. Be honest. The broker relies on this information to determine which investments will best meet your investment goals and tolerance for risk. If a broker tries to sell you an investment before asking you these questions, that's a very bad sign. It signals that the broker has a greater interest in earning a commission than recommending an investment to you that meets your needs. The new account agreement requires that you make three critical decisions:

1. Who will make the final decisions about what you buy and sell in your account? You will have the final say on investment decisions unless you give "discretionary authority" to your broker. Discretionary authority allows your broker to invest your money without consulting you about the price, the type of security, the amount, and when to buy or sell. Do not give discretionary authority to your broker without seriously considering the risks involved in turning control over your money to another person.

2. How will you pay for your investments? Most investors maintain a "cash" account that requires payment in full for each security purchase. But if you open a "margin" account, you can buy securities by borrowing money from your broker for a portion of the purchase price. Be aware of the risks involved with buying stocks on margin. Beginning investors generally should not get started with a margin account. Make sure you understand how a margin account works, and what

happens in the worst case scenario before you agree to buy on margin. Unlike other loans, like for a car or a home, that allow you to pay back a fixed amount every month, when you buy stocks on margin you can be faced with paying back the entire margin loan all at once if the price of the stock drops suddenly and dramatically. The firm has the authority to immediately sell any security in your account, without notice to you, to cover any shortfall resulting from a decline in the value of your securities. You may owe a substantial amount of money even after your securities are sold. The margin account agreement generally provides that the securities in your margin account may be lent out by the brokerage firm at any time without notice or compensation to you.

3.  How much risk should you assume? In a new account agreement, you must specify your overall investment objective in terms of risk. Categories of risk may have labels such as "income," "growth," or "aggressive growth." Be certain that you fully understand the distinctions among these terms, and be certain that the risk level you choose accurately reflects your age, experience, and investment goals. Be sure that the investment products recommended to you reflect the category of risk you have selected.

When opening a new account, the brokerage firm may ask you to sign a legally binding contract to use the arbitration process to settle any future dispute between you and the firm or your sales representative. Signing this agreement means that you give up the right to sue your sales representative and firm in court.

## How Can I Avoid Problems?

Choosing someone to help you with your investments is one of the most important investment decisions you will ever make. While most investment professionals are honest and hardworking, you must watch out for those few unscrupulous individuals. They can make your life's savings disappear in an instant.

Securities regulators and law enforcement officials can and do catch these criminals. But putting them in jail doesn't always get your money back. Too often, the money is gone.

The good news is you can avoid potential problems by protecting yourself.

Let's say you've already met with several investment professionals based on recommendations from friends and others you trust, and you've found someone who clearly understands your investment objectives. Before you hire this person, you still have more homework.

Make sure the investment professional and her firm are registered with the SEC and licensed to do business in your state. And find out from your state's securities regulator whether the investment professional or her firm have ever been disciplined, or whether they have any complaints against them. You'll find contact information for securities regulators in the U.S. by visiting the website of the North American Securities Administrators Association (NASAA) at http://www. nasaa.org or by calling 202-737-0900.

You should also find out as much as you can about any investments that your investment professional recommends. First, make sure the investments are registered. Keep in mind, however, the mere fact that a company has registered and files reports with the SEC doesn't guarantee that the company will be a good investment.

Likewise, the fact that a company hasn't registered and doesn't file reports with the SEC doesn't mean the company is a fraud. Still, you may be asking for serious losses if, for instance, you invest in a small, thinly traded company that isn't widely known solely on the basis of what you may have read online. One simple phone call to your state regulator could prevent you from squandering your money on a scam.

Be wary of promises of quick profits, offers to share "inside information," and pressure to invest before you have an opportunity to investigate. These are all warning signs of fraud. Ask your investment professional for written materials and prospectuses, and read them before you invest. If you have questions, now is the time to ask.

It's always a good idea to write down everything your investment professional tells you. Accurate notes will come in handy if ever there's a problem.

Some investments make money. Others lose money. That's natural, and that's why you need a diversified portfolio to minimize your risk. But if you lose money because you've been cheated, that's not natural, that's a problem.

Sometimes all it takes is a simple phone call to your investment professional to resolve a problem. Maybe there was an honest mistake that can be corrected. If talking to the investment professional doesn't resolve the problem, talk to the firm's manager, and write a letter to confirm your conversation. If that doesn't lead to a resolution, you may have to initiate private legal action. You may need to take action quickly because legal time limits for doing so vary. Your local bar association can provide referrals for attorneys who special-ize in securities law.

At the same time, call or write the SEC to report the problem. In-vestor complaints are very important. You may think you're the only one experiencing a problem, but typically, you're not alone. Sometimes it takes only one investor's complaint to trigger an investigation that exposes a bad broker or an illegal scheme. Complaints can be filed online by going to www.sec.gov/complaint.shtml.

# Chapter 4

# *Insurance Helps Protect Your Assets*

Along the financial road of life arise the inevitable delays, detours, emergencies, and breakdowns. Some are small, which you can pay for out of cash flow, a cash emergency fund, or even investments. But others are major and expensive setbacks. That's when you need insurance.

The purpose of insurance is to shift these major financial risks to insurance companies. Without adequate formal insurance, you are, in reality, self-insuring. You'll pay out of your own pocket the cost of such financial calamities as the loss of a home, an auto accident, or a serious illness—expenses that could demolish your household finances and derail accomplishment of your life's dreams.

Insurance coverage costs money and that cost is rising. So you need to buy insurance wisely: the right kind...the right amount...at the right time...at the best price.

This information, produced by the Financial Planning Association (FPA), the membership organization for the financial planning community, explains what types of insurance are most likely appropriate for the different stages of your life: from first launching out as a young adult to raising a family to retirement. By buying the right mix and amount of insurance—and not buying coverage you don't need—you'll get the best bang for your insurance dollars.

## *Young, Single, and On Your Own*

You are fresh out of high school, college, or a short tour of the military. For the first time, you are truly on your own as a young adult—and you're on your own for insurance, too, as most insurers drop a child from the parents' coverages once the child leaves home or school. Below are some of the insurance coverages you should consider.

**Health:** A medical plan will likely be available at your job, but not all employers provide health benefits, and not all employees join available health plans. You may not have found a job yet out of school, or you may be between jobs. As a consequence, many young people choose to go without coverage. But that's not wise. Even the young can suffer an expensive major illness or accident.

If you are between jobs, and you were covered under the previous employer's plan, you probably can continue that group coverage for up to another 18 months through the federal program COBRA (Consolidated Omnibus Budget Reconciliation Act). But before continuing under COBRA, compare the cost against similar private coverage.

If employer coverage or COBRA isn't available, consider a temporary short-term health care policy (1–12 months) to cover you until you become eligible for a new employer's plan. Or apply for a high-deductible permanent major medical policy. Either of these types of policies can be reasonably priced, but you must qualify medically and they usually don't cover pre-existing conditions.

**Disability:** Your working income is possibly your most precious financial resource at this stage. Yet as a young person, your odds of being disabled by illness or injury at least 90 days or longer before age 65 are higher than your odds of dying, according to the Insurance Information Institute.

Disability insurance, sometimes called income-replacement insurance, pays a portion (typically around 60–80 percent) of lost wages if you're unable to continue your job due to an accident or illness. Any employer disability coverage is usually limited to 6 to 12 months, and what they provide may be insufficient for your wages. State-sponsored worker's compensation programs may provide income, but normally only if you're injured on the job (a few states provide for non-work-related disabilities). Social Security may provide benefits, but only if you're unable to work at virtually any job.

If your employer's coverage doesn't pay at least 60 percent and doesn't last to age 65, you'll likely want to supplement it with private coverage.

**Renter's:** Your personal assets are probably modest, but nonetheless, it could cost you thousands or tens of thousands of dollars to replace clothes, a computer, audio equipment, and other property if stolen or destroyed. Your landlord's insurance does not cover your personal property.

A personal renter's policy is usually quite affordable—$150 to $300 a year will probably buy the coverage you need, though you might need additional coverage for high-valued property such as jewelry. Also see if the policy includes liability coverage in the event you are sued for injuries suffered at your residence.

**Auto:** Once you're no longer a student, you won't be able to insure your vehicle through your parents' policy. Shop around. Rates vary widely for comparable coverage.

**Life:** Because you're single, you probably don't need life insurance yet. It generally is designed to provide income for those whose financial security is tied to you, such as a spouse, child, or dependent parents.

Some financial experts argue, however, that it can be worth buying life insurance while you're young because premiums are relatively low and you're likely in good health.

## Newly Married

Wedding bells ring in the need to revamp the insurance coverage you were carrying when you were single. For example, it may be less expensive for both of you to insure under a single employer's medical plan. You'll probably also want to insure your vehicles with a single carrier. If one of you quits working, you might want to drop that person's disability coverage unless they anticipate returning to work within a couple of years.

**Life:** Now life insurance is more important because someone else is financially tied to you.

Calculate first the amount of coverage you need to replace future lost income, and then decide what type of insurance to buy. You might be able to afford to buy sufficient death benefits through a whole life policy, which has an investment component as well as death benefits. More likely, you'll be better off buying term life insurance, which provides only a "pure" death benefit for a death occurring within a specified time. Generally, term insurance allows you to buy more death benefits for each premium dollar.

**Homeowner's:** You may become a first-time home buyer. If so, it's best (though more expensive) to buy a policy that will pay for the full cost of rebuilding your home and for replacing your personal possessions, versus merely paying for their market value at the time.

Standard policies typically set limits on what they'll pay for higher-end possessions such as jewelry, silverware, and antiques, so you may need a "rider" or "floater" to provide extra coverage.

And be aware that the standard homeowner's policy does not cover flood or earthquake damage. You'll have to buy separate policies for that.

**Liability:** Commonly called umbrella coverage, this provides liability protection above the limited protection offered by standard homeowner's and auto insurance. In this era of lawsuits, liability coverage becomes more important as your net worth grows.

Umbrella coverage is only a few hundred dollars for the typical $1 million policy, especially if bought from the company that insures your car or home.

## Proud Parents

A newborn brings many changes to your household, including insurance.

**Health:** Add your baby to your medical policy within 30 days of birth. Otherwise, many policies require you to wait until the next enrollment period.

**Life:** Boost coverage to take into account the future cost of raising your child, including college. Provide coverage for a stay-at-home parent, too.

Planners differ over whether to buy a small amount of life insurance for children. Some consider it a waste of money, while others recommend coverage for unexpected funeral expenses.

You may want to use your will to create a trust with your children as beneficiaries in order to manage the life insurance proceeds (and other assets) in the event both parents die while the children are still young.

**Other:** Review other existing policies. For example, your auto insurance may cost less if a previously working parent stays home to provide childcare.

## Empty Nesters

As your children strike out on their own, it's time for another major review of your insurance coverage.

**Long-term care insurance:** Now is the time to begin considering one of the most overlooked types of insurance: long-term care. This insurance is designed to pay for custodial care in a nursing home, assisted-living facility, or professional at-home care, any of which can be very expensive.

Many people don't buy this insurance because they assume that the government will pay for it. But Medicare won't pay for long-term custodial nursing home care. And Medicaid, a federal/state program designed for the poor, will pay for it only if you have spent down most of your financial assets in order to qualify. Furthermore, Medicaid benefits are much more limited than private coverage.

The majority of financial planners recommend buying long-term care insurance while you are in your fifties. The premiums are still reasonable at this age and you run less risk of failing to qualify due to deteriorating health. According to a 2003 *Consumer Reports* article, one in four 65-year-olds "flunk the physical." If poor health is a barrier, you may be able to qualify by buying group coverage through work, if it's available.

**Disability:** You'll want to continue this coverage as long as you are working and dependent on the income.

**Life:** With the kids gone, you may not need as much life insurance as before, but it remains critical if you're married and still working.

## Retired

**Health:** Medicare doesn't start until age 65, so if you retire before then, you'll need to bridge the gap with alternative coverage. You may have a retiree medical plan available through your former employer, but many employers are dropping these plans because of costs. If 18 months of COBRA doesn't get you to age 65, you will need to convert your group coverage to individual coverage or venture out into the private coverage market.

Just don't go without as you may have done as a young adult. A Fidelity Investments study, for example, estimated that couples retiring at age 65, with no access to employer-sponsored health insurance,

41

would spend $175,000 out of pocket for medical care over the next 20 years—not including long-term care.

**Medigap:** Medicare generally pays only about 55 percent of retirees' average medical expenses. Consequently, unless you are enrolled in a reliable Medicare HMO program, you either pay the difference out of pocket or you can buy a Medicare supplemental insurance, commonly called Medigap insurance.

Medigap policies come in 10 standardized versions, A through J, with each version offering different degrees of benefits. While the plan benefits are standardized among insurers, prices are not, so shop around carefully.

**Disability:** Once you retire, you don't need disability coverage. Besides, most disability policies won't cover you beyond normal retirement age.

**Long-term care (LTC):** If you haven't already bought LTC insurance, don't wait any longer. You're probably in your sixties now and the cost of coverage climbs rapidly. Your risk of not qualifying because of health reasons also accelerates.

**Life:** You may need minimal or no life insurance at this stage—perhaps just enough to cover any debts you have and to be certain your spouse will be okay financially.

Larger amounts might still be necessary if you want to pass the death benefits on to your adult children or to pay for potential estate taxes. With large amounts, it's often wise to shift ownership of the policy out of your estate in order to reduce any potential tax bite.

**Other:** Retirees often can get a discount for homeowner's coverage, and they may get a discount for auto insurance until they turn 75.

## Don't Skimp on Coverage

Many often view the purchase of insurance—particularly policies such as disability or long-term care—as a "waste" of money. Some see it as money spent on policies they hope or think they will never use.

Yet without adequate insurance, you run the risk of a financial disaster. The key is to buy only the right types and amounts of insurance at the right time. Don't get sidetracked by insurance that may be a waste of money for most people, such as credit, flight, specific disease, car rental, and pet insurance.

# Chapter 5

# *Young Adults:*
# *A To-Do List for Ages and*
# *Stages of Money Management*

To successfully reach your financial goals, a lot depends on what you do and when. Here are just a few ideas young adults can consider at key stages of their life.

### You're in High School

Consider earning money outside of your home, whether it's babysitting, lawn mowing, or working in a movie theater or another "real" business. A job can provide a sense of accomplishment and responsibility. It also can be a good opportunity to learn about careers and to "network" with professionals.

Learn the concept of "paying yourself first"—that is, automatically putting some money into savings or investments before you're tempted to spend it. Start small if you have to and gradually build up.

Consider opening a bank account, either on your own or with a parent or other adult. It's a good way to learn about managing money. You also may want to start using a debit card—you can use it to make purchases but you won't pay interest or get into debt because the money is automatically deducted from your bank account.

Take a personal finance class or join an investment club at school.

From "Ages and Stages of Money Management: A To-Do List," *FDIC Consumer News*, Spring 2005, Federal Deposit Insurance Corporation (FDIC).

If you're planning to go to college, learn about your options for saving or borrowing money for what will be a major expense.

If you (and your parents) are comfortable with getting a credit card, you should know that there are cards designed just for teens. One is a credit card with a low credit limit that can keep you from getting deeply in debt. Another is a pre-paid card that comes with parental controls, including spending limits.

## *You're in College*

Realize that as you pay bills and debts on your own you are building a "credit record" that could be important when you apply for a loan or a job in the future. Pay your bills on time...and borrow only what you can repay.

If you decide to get your own credit card, choose carefully. Take your time, understand the risks as well as the rewards and do some comparison shopping. Don't apply for a credit card just because you received an invitation in the mail or a sales person was offering a free gift on campus.

Protect your Social Security number (SSN), credit card numbers and other personal information from thieves who use someone else's identity to commit fraud. Examples: Use your SSN as identification only if absolutely necessary and never provide it to a stranger. Safeguard your personal information when using the internet or borrowing a computer provided by your school.

Consider a paying job or even an unpaid internship at a workplace related to a career you're considering.

If possible, set aside money into savings and investments.

Try to take a class in personal finance. Read money-related magazine and newspaper articles.

## *You're Starting a Career*

Keep your credit card and other debts manageable. Maintain a good credit record.

Save money for both short-term and long-term goals. Contribute as much as you can to retirement savings, which often can be used for other purposes, including a first-time home purchase. Take advantage of matching contributions that your employer will put into your retirement savings.

Do your best to stick to a budget and control your spending, especially if you're still paying back student loans or working at an entry-level job.

Although insurance sometimes seems like a waste of money, you only need one accident or catastrophe to wipe you out financially. Think about disability insurance (to replace lost income if you become seriously ill) and health insurance (to cover big medical bills). Check into low-cost or free insurance offered through your employer.

## You're Starting a Family

Continue saving and investing money, including in retirement accounts.

If you don't already own your home do some research to see if this is a good option for you. A home purchase can be expensive but it also can be an excellent investment and a source of tax breaks. Check out educational resources for first-time home buyers.

Make sure you are properly insured, including life, health, disability, and home owner's or renter's insurance.

Talk with an attorney about the legal documents you should have to protect your loved ones if you become seriously ill or die. These documents typically include a will, a "durable power of attorney" (giving one or more people the authority to handle personal matters if you become mentally or physically incompetent) and a "living will" (specifying the medical care you want or don't want if you become hopelessly ill and cannot communicate your wishes.)

# Chapter 6

# *Couples and Money*

## *Merging Your Money when You Marry*

Getting married is exciting, but it brings many challenges. One such challenge that you and your spouse will have to face is how to merge your finances. Planning carefully and communicating clearly are important, because the financial decisions that you make now can have a lasting impact on your future.

### *Discuss Your Financial Goals*

The first step in mapping out your financial future together is to discuss your financial goals. Start by making a list of your short-term goals (paying off wedding debt, new car, vacation) and long-term goals (having children, your children's college education, retirement). Then, determine which goals are most important to you. Once you've identified the goals that are a priority, you can focus your energy on achieving them.

---

This chapter includes "Merging Your Money when You Marry," "Financial Tips for Unmarried Couples," and "Dealing with Divorce." Copyright © 2006 by American Institute of Certified Public Accountants. Reproduced with permission. "Remarriage and Prenuptial Agreements," an undated document, is also Copyright © by American Institute of Certified Public Accountants. Reproduced with permission. This information, from the American Institute of Certified Public Accountants' 360 Degrees of Financial Literacy website (http://www.360financialliteracy.org), offers general information for managing personal finances and does not recommend specific financial actions. For financial advice tailored to your situation, please contact an expert such as a certified public accountant (CPA) or a personal financial advisor.

## *Prepare a Budget*

Next, you should prepare a budget that lists all of your income and expenses over a certain time period (monthly, annually). You can designate one spouse to be in charge of managing the budget, or you can take turns keeping records and paying the bills. If both you and your spouse are going to be involved, make sure that you develop a record-keeping system that both of you understand. And remember to keep your records in a joint filing system so that both of you can easily locate important documents.

Begin by listing your sources of income (salaries and wages, interest, dividends). Then, list your expenses (it may be helpful to review several months of entries in your checkbook and credit card bills). Add them up and compare the two totals. Hopefully, you get a positive number, meaning that you spend less than you earn. If not, review your expenses and see where you can cut down on your spending.

## *Bank Accounts—Separate or Joint?*

At some point, you and your spouse will have to decide whether to combine your bank accounts or keep them separate. Maintaining a joint account does have advantages, such as easier record keeping and lower maintenance fees. However, it's sometimes more difficult to keep track of how much money is in a joint account when two individuals have access to it. Of course, you could avoid this problem by making sure that you tell each other every time you write a check or withdraw funds from the account. Or, you could always decide to maintain separate accounts.

## *Credit Cards*

If you're thinking about adding your name to your spouse's credit card accounts, think again. When you and your spouse have joint credit, both of you will become responsible for 100 percent of the credit card debt. In addition, if one of you has poor credit, it will negatively impact the credit rating of the other.

If you or your spouse does not qualify for a card because of poor credit, and you are willing to give your spouse account privileges anyway, you can make your spouse an authorized user of your credit card. An authorized user is not a joint cardholder and is therefore not liable for any amounts charged to the account. Also, the account activity won't show up on the authorized user's credit record. But remember, you remain responsible for the account.

### *Insurance*

If you and your spouse have separate health insurance coverage, you'll want to do a cost/benefit analysis of each plan to see if you should continue to keep your health coverage separate. For example, if your spouse's health plan has a higher deductible or co-payments or fewer benefits than those offered by your plan, he or she may want to join your health plan instead. You'll also want to compare the rate for one family plan against the cost of two single plans.

It's a good idea to examine your auto insurance coverage, too. If you and your spouse own separate cars, you may have different auto insurance carriers. Consider pooling your auto insurance policies with one company; many insurance companies will give you a discount if you insure more than one car with them. If one of you has a poor driving record, however, make sure that changing companies won't mean paying a higher premium.

### *Employer-Sponsored Retirement Plans*

If both you and your spouse participate in an employer-sponsored retirement plan, you should be aware of each plan's characteristics. Review each plan together carefully and determine which plan provides the best benefits. If you can afford it, you should each participate to the maximum in your own plan. If your current cash flow is limited, you can make one plan the focus of your retirement strategy. Here are some helpful tips:

- If both plans match contributions, determine which plan offers the best match and take full advantage of it

- Compare the vesting schedules for the employer's matching contributions

- Compare the investment options offered by each plan—the more options you have, the more likely you are to find an investment mix that suits your needs

- Find out whether the plans offer loans—if you plan to use any of your contributions for certain expenses (your children's college education, a down payment on a house), you may want to participate in the plan that has a loan provision

## *Financial Tips for Unmarried Couples*

More women today are opting for committed relationships that don't include marriage. Those in professional careers and entrepreneurs are financially independent; divorced women may not want to risk another complex marriage dissolution; older women might lose pension or Social Security benefits from a deceased spouse if they remarry.

If you choose a long-term committed relationship, you have many of the same financial concerns as married couples. However, you lack many of the legal protections and advantages that married couples enjoy. Here are some tips that can help you and your partner stay on the road to financial security.

### *Talk about Your Finances*

One of the first financial decisions you'll have to make as an unmarried couple is whether you should handle your finances separately or together. Sit down with your partner and discuss each other's financial values, priorities, and goals. Being open and honest now will help you and your partner avoid the arguments about money that plague most couples, married or unmarried.

How will you handle household expenses: separately or jointly? If you prefer a simple financial arrangement and want to avoid some of the liability associated with joint accounts, you can keep your finances separate. One of you pays the bills and collects money from the other, or you each pay for certain things separately. However, for the sake of convenience, many unmarried couples opt to pay household expenses together, as most married couples do. Keep in mind that if you do open a joint checking account, you'll each be responsible for all checks drawn (or overdrawn) on the account.

What about the rest of your income and other personal expenses? Will you pool all of your finances or keep some income separate for your personal use? Even if you decide to pay your bills together from a joint checking account, you can always keep separate accounts for personal expenses.

Finally, will you hold joint credit cards? You can open joint credit card accounts or add your partner to an existing account as an authorized user. Remember, though, that with a joint account, you are each fully responsible for all charges on the account, including charges that your partner made.

### *Plan for Retirement*

As an unmarried couple, you and your partner don't have to give up on planning for retirement together, but it may be harder for you than for married couples. Neither partner will be eligible for spousal benefits from two key sources of retirement income: Social Security and defined benefit pension plans (traditional pension plans). However, if you're a little creative, there are other ways that you can provide an adequate living for your partner in retirement:

- Designate your partner as the beneficiary of your retirement plan (401(k)s, 403(b)s), if permitted, and of your IRAs.

- Increase your savings now to replace the spousal benefits your partner won't receive from Social Security and your defined benefit pension plan.

- Consider using life insurance to fund your partner's retirement. As long as you can prove that you have an insurable interest, you can purchase an individual policy that names your partner as the beneficiary.

Before you jump into planning jointly for retirement, however, consider all of the possibilities. Although it may seem unlikely now, your relationship could end before you retire, leaving one or both of you with inadequate retirement income. In some cases, it may be wiser for each of you to plan for retirement on your own, even if you plan on being together forever.

## *Make Estate Planning a Priority*

Proper estate planning is essential for unmarried couples. The laws that protect married couples don't apply to you. Without proper protection, your surviving partner could be ordered out of a house that you share, and your next of kin could dispose of your estate however they choose. Your partner could also be left out of financial and medical decisions if you become seriously ill or incapacitated. You owe it to yourself and your partner to ensure that your estate will be handled according to your wishes. Here are some ideas to consider:

- Consult an experienced estate planning attorney to help you protect your assets, your partner, and your family.

- Prepare durable power of attorneys for health care and finances, and name your partner as your representative.

- Execute a will if you want to leave certain property to your partner. Without it, he or she has no legal right to inherit your estate.

- Sign a domestic partner agreement. It won't replace your will, but it can support your will and your partner's right to jointly held property by stating your wishes and intentions.

## *Remarriage and Prenuptial Agreements*

Even if you have never thought about signing a prenuptial agreement, it's wise to consider it now. That's because one or both spouses in a remarriage may have significant assets, business interests, or children to consider. Here are the issues that prenuptial agreements typically address:

- A prenuptial agreement
  - Details the assets and liabilities that each partner brings into the marriage.
  - Spells out a couple's agreement on the division of assets in the event of divorce.

- Assets and liabilities
  - What assets are you each bringing into the marriage, and what is their value?
  - Which assets become marital property, and which ones will continue to be owned individually?
  - Will gifts and inheritances be shared or separate?
  - What liabilities do each of you have?

- If you divorce
  - How will you divide assets?
  - Will either spouse receive a lump-sum settlement or alimony?

- Estate planning
  - What will go to your children from previous marriages?
  - What will go to children you have together?

- Special considerations
  - Will special contributions (limiting a career for the benefit of children or the other spouse) be considered?
  - What if one spouse brings more liabilities to the marriage than the other?
  - Will there be a time limit or condition (10 years of marriage, the birth of a child) that will end the prenuptial agreement?

Writing a prenuptial agreement is not a do-it-yourself project. You and your future spouse should hire separate attorneys. The best prenuptial agreement is one that protects the interests of both spouses without causing mistrust.

## Dealing with Divorce

Divorce can be a lengthy process that may strain your finances and leave you feeling out of control. But with the right preparation, you can protect your interests, take charge of your future, and save yourself time and money. You certainly never expected divorce when you cut the wedding cake—you and your spouse planned on spending the rest of your lives together. Unfortunately, the fairy tale didn't work out, and you're headed for a divorce. So where do you begin?

### Should You Hire an Attorney?

There's no legal requirement that you hire an attorney when divorcing. In fact, going it alone may be a sensible option if you're young and have been married only a short time, are childless, and have few assets. However, most divorcing couples hire attorneys to better protect their interests, even though doing so can be expensive. Divorce attorneys typically charge hourly rates and require you to submit retainers (lump sums) up front. It's not unusual, for example, for an attorney to charge as much as $150 to $200 per hour and require an initial retainer of up to $2,500 to $5,000. The fee depends on the complexity of the case, the reputation and experience of the divorce attorney, and your geographic location.

You should know that if you're a homemaker or earn less income than your spouse, it's still possible to obtain legal representation. You can submit a motion to the court, asking a judge to order your spouse to pay for your attorney's fees.

If you and your spouse can agree on most issues, you may save time and money by filing an uncontested divorce. If you can't agree on significant issues, you may want to meet with a divorce mediator, who can help you resolve issues that the two of you can't resolve alone. To find a mediator, contact your local domestic relations court, ask friends for a referral, or look in the telephone book. Certain attorneys, members of the clergy, psychologists, social workers, marriage counselors, and financial planners may offer their services as mediators.

## *Save Time and Money by Doing Your Homework before Meeting with a Divorce Professional*

To save time and money, compile as much of the following information as you can before meeting with an attorney or other divorce professional:

- Each spouse's date of birth

- Names and birth dates of children, if you have any

- Date and place of marriage and length of time in present state

- Existence of prenuptial agreement

- Information about parties' prior marriages, children, etc.

- Date of separation and grounds for divorce

- Current occupation and name and address of employer for each spouse

- Social Security number for each spouse

- Income of each spouse

- Education, degrees, and training of each spouse

- Extent of employee benefits for each spouse

- Details of retirement plans for each spouse

- Joint assets of the parties

- Liabilities and debts of each spouse

- Life (and other) insurance of each spouse

- Separate or personal assets of each spouse, including trust funds and inheritances

- Financial records

- Family business records

- Collections, artwork, and antiques

If you're uncertain about some of these areas, you can obtain the necessary information through your spouse's financial affidavit or the discovery process, both of which are mandated by the court.

### *Consider the Big Questions, Such as Child Custody and Alimony*

Although your divorce professional will help you work through the big issues, you might want to think about the following questions before meeting with him or her:

- If you have children, what are your wishes regarding custody, visitation, and child support?

- Whose health insurance plan should cover the children?

- Do you earn enough money to adequately support yourself, or should alimony be considered?

- Which assets do you really want, and which are you willing to let your spouse keep?

- How do you feel about the family home? Do you feel strongly about living there, or should it be sold or allotted to your spouse?

- Will you have enough money to pay the outstanding debt on whatever assets you keep?

In addition to an attorney, you may want to see a therapist to help you clarify your wishes, express yourself more clearly, and deal with any child-related issues. Such counseling is typically covered by health insurance.

### *Some Dos and Don'ts when Divorcing*

Keep the following tips in mind:

- Do prepare a budget and a financial plan to sustain you until your divorce is final. Get help if you don't currently have the skills and energy to do this on your own.

- Do review monthly bank and financial statements and make copies for your attorney.

- Do review all tax returns that have been filed jointly or separately by your spouse.

- Do make sure all taxes have been paid to date.

- Do review the contents of any safe-deposit boxes.

- Do get emotional support for yourself—talk to friends, join a support group, or see a therapist.

- Don't make large purchases or create additional debt that might later cause financial hardship.

- Don't quit your job.

- Don't move out of the house before consulting your attorney.

- Don't transfer or give away assets that are owned jointly.

- Don't sign a blank financial statement or any other document without reviewing it with your attorney.

# Chapter 7

# *Financing College*

## *Top Things to Know*

### *1. Saving for your own retirement is more important than saving for college.*

Your children will have more sources of money for college than you will have for your golden years, so don't sacrifice your retirement savings.

### *2. The sooner you start saving, the better.*

Even modest savings can pack a punch if you give them enough time to grow. Investing just $100 a month for 18 years will yield $48,000, assuming an 8 percent average annual return.

### *3. Stocks are best for your college savings portfolio.*

With tuition costs rising faster than inflation, a portfolio tilted toward stocks is the best way to build enough savings in the long term. As your child approaches college age, you can shelter your returns by switching more money into bonds and cash.

---

The text in this chapter is from "Lesson 11: Saving for College," from *Money 101*; reprinted with permission from www.CNNMoney.com. © 2007 Cable News Network. All Rights reserved.

### 4. You don't have to save the entire cost of four years of college.

Federal, state, and private grants and loans can bridge the gap between your savings and tuition bills, even if you think you make too much to qualify.

### 5. With mutual funds, investing for college is simple.

Investing in mutual funds puts a professional in charge of your savings so that you don't have to watch the markets daily.

### 6. 529 savings plans are a good way to save for college and they offer great tax breaks.

Qualified withdrawals are now free of federal tax and most plans let you save between $100,000 and $270,000 per beneficiary. Plus, there are no income limitations or age restrictions, which means you can start a 529 no matter how much you make or how old your beneficiary is.

### 7. Tax breaks are almost as good as grants.

You may be able to take two federal tax credits—the Hope Credit and Lifetime Learning Credit—in the years you pay tuition. Or, if your income is too high to qualify for those credits, you may qualify for a higher education expense deduction.

### 8. The approval process for college loans is more lenient than for other loans.

Late payments on your credit record aren't automatic grounds for refusal of a college loan.

### 9. Lenders can be flexible when it's time to repay.

There are still ways to cut costs after you graduate and begin re-paying your student loans. For instance, if you make 48 consecutive on-time payments, most private lenders will knock two percentage points off your interest rate.

### 10. Taxpayers with student loans get a tax break.

You may deduct the interest you pay up to $2,500 a year if your modified adjusted gross income is less than $65,000 if you're single or less than $130,000 if you're married filing jointly. The deduction can be taken for the life of the loan.

## Getting Started

If you save early and wisely, college may be affordable after all.

Few people question the value of a college education, but the cost is enough to break the bank for a lot of families. With the cost of higher education rising faster than inflation, parents of today's four-year-olds may face college bills of more than $200,000.

Sure, the numbers are scary. But if you start saving regularly while your child is in diapers, you'll put yourself in a good position financially by the time your son or daughter is ready to hit the co-ed bathrooms.

Also, don't forget that the availability of financial aid, loans, and education credits and deductions means you may not have to foot the entire bill yourself.

Indeed, you shouldn't if you're short on retirement savings. As a parent, you might think your most important financial duty is to pay for your children's education. You'd be wrong. Saving enough money for your own retirement is even more crucial.

Your children have a lot of resources besides you to help feed the tuition monster, but no one is going to help you finance your golden years. And, you don't have to worry that socking money into a 401(k) will be held against you if you apply for financial aid. Formulas used to assess need generally don't consider retirement savings as an available asset when determining how much parents can contribute to tuition.

Putting too much money in your child's name, however, might work against you. While it's true that a child's income is usually taxed at a lower rate than a parent's income, keeping funds in a child's name can reduce your financial aid package. Colleges use a formula for aid that assesses a family's need based on up to 5.65 percent of parents' available assets and on 35 percent of assets in a child's name or custodial account.

## What's the Best Way to Invest?

Make sure your investments grow with your children. With college tuition rising faster than inflation, stocks are the best investment to help your education-savings portfolio keep pace long-term.

As your child nears college age, the downside risk of stocks becomes more significant, for the simple reason that university bursars won't defer tuition bills just because you lost money in a crash.

Bonds and cash should begin to play an increasingly significant role when Junior hits high school.

Keep your investments simple, and stick to mutual funds that have solid three- to five-year track records and low expenses. You can even opt to have the fund company make automatic monthly withdrawals from your bank account to force you to save.

Most planners recommend that you base your asset allocation on your child's age. If your child is eight or younger, you can keep 60 to 95 percent of your money in stocks. You can choose a balanced fund, which holds a prescribed ratio, usually 60-40, of stocks to bonds. Or you can choose your own mix of funds and invest proportionately.

When your child is between ages nine and 13, your portfolio should get more conservative, not by moving money out of your earlier investments, but directing more of your new contributions to bond funds and tamer stock funds.

For example, if you were putting 90 percent of your contributions into stock funds, and 10 percent into bond funds, switch to a 50-50 allocation. If you want to curb the volatility that stock funds can create, put your contributions into equity-income funds, which invest in stocks paying high dividends and tend to ride market dips better.

When your child turns 14, start to shelter the returns you've earned so far. You can do this by moving your equity assets into money market and short-term bond funds over the next four years, so that by the time your child enters college, you are out of equities entirely and can cash out quickly.

If the bond portion of your savings has exceeded $10,000, you may consider purchasing government short-term Treasury notes directly from the U.S. Treasury, to avoid paying any management fees to a fund company.

## Tax-Savvy Savings Options

529s, Coverdell IRAs and college savings trusts may work for you.

Saving for college is hard not just because it's a huge expense, but because you can't predict how much, if any, financial aid you'll get.

That's why you need to save what you can now. Fortunately, you have a number of tax-advantaged federal and state college-savings vehicles at your disposal. The best option is the state-sponsored 529 plan, which comes in two flavors: the prepaid tuition plan and the savings plan.

A state's prepaid plan allows you to pay now at today's rates for school tomorrow. In return, your account (or contract as it's often known) is guaranteed to pay for the tuition and fees at the state's public universities and colleges by the time your child graduates from high school. A pre-paid plan often does not, however, cover the costs for room and board.

Your child also may use the pre-paid account to attend a private or out-of-state school but you might risk forfeiting some of its value depending on how the plan values its contracts. Note, too, that most pre-paid plans require that the account owner (you) or the beneficiary (your child) be a resident of the state in which the plan is offered.

At the same time states have been improving their prepaid plans, and private schools have been given the green light to offer their own such deals.

Under the 2001 Tax Relief Act, withdrawals from a private school's prepaid plan were made exempt from federal taxes as of 2004. (Prior to then, you would have been taxed on the increased value of a tuition contract from the date you bought it to the date you redeemed it.)

More than 250 private schools, ranging from tiny liberal arts schools like Ripon College in Wisconsin to well-known universities like the University of Chicago and Wake Forest, have joined forces to offer a prepaid tuition product called Independent 529 Plan. Parents can buy prepaid contracts good for tuition at any of the member schools. To learn more about the plan, call 888-718-7878.

The 529 college savings plan, now offered in most states, is far more flexible than the pre-paid tuition schemes, and perhaps safer. (At times, some states have reported that their pre-paid plans were seriously underfunded.) The money may be used at any school you choose and for all qualified higher education expenses, including room and board.

Each state determines what the lifetime contribution limit or account balance cap will be in its 529 plan, but typically such limits range between $100,000 and $270,000. Investment minimums are low (most plans let you sock away as little as $25 a month), and there is no restriction on how much you may contribute every year unless the account is nearing the lifetime cap.

However, since 529 contributions are treated as gifts subject to gift-tax limitations, if you want to make a tax-free contribution, it shouldn't exceed $12,000 annually ($24,000 if you're contributing with your spouse). There's one exception, however: you may contribute as much as $60,000 tax-free in one year ($120,000 with your spouse), but that contribution will be treated as if it were being made in $12,000 installments over the next five years. That means you can't make other tax-free gifts to the beneficiary during that time.

Most 529 savings plans offer a menu of age-based portfolios, and some also offer a small selection of stock and bond funds. In the former case, your annual contributions get invested in a pre-selected portfolio of stocks and bonds. Early on, the portfolio is tilted toward stocks, and as the time for college nears, the weighting shifts toward bonds. Note, however, that once you choose an investment track, it can be cumbersome to change.

The quality of 529 college savings plans varies by state, but in most instances you may open an account in any state you'd like.

All 529 plans offer generous tax breaks, provided you use the money for qualified expenses. While your contribution is not deductible on your federal taxes, your investment will grow tax-deferred and withdrawals will not be subject to federal tax. In prior years your money had grown tax-deferred and earnings withdrawals were taxed at the student's income tax rate. (Note, however, the federal tax-free provision is set to expire in 2010 unless Congress passes a law to extend it.) What's more, you may get state-tax deductions on contributions or exemptions on withdrawals.

One caveat: Having a 529 is likely to reduce your chances of getting financial aid. Even though the 529 college savings account is considered the parent's asset, and hence is assessed at a much lower rate than if it were the child's. But withdrawals are considered the child's income, which is assessed up to a 50 percent rate for financial aid assessment purposes. A pre-paid tuition plan is treated somewhat differently. The amount in benefits paid out essentially reduces dollar-for-dollar your child's aid eligibility.

Another tax-advantaged option is the Coverdell Education Savings Account (formerly known as the Education IRA). You can contribute up to $2,000 a year and withdrawals are tax-free. To qualify for a full or partial contribution, your adjusted gross income must be less than $110,000 if you're single; $220,000 if you're married and filing jointly.

One of the drawbacks is that the annual contribution cap is per child, meaning if you and your parents want to contribute to an account for your daughter, your combined contributions can't exceed $2,000.

You may now contribute to both a 529 and a Coverdell Education Savings Account on behalf of the same beneficiary in the same year without penalty, but your contributions will be treated as gifts subject to gift-tax limitations. For more on 529 plans, check the website http://www.savingforcollege.com.

## What Kind of Aid Is out There?

Even if you follow a regular savings plan for college, you may still come up short.

Several factors are considered for aid-eligibility, principal among them your income; your non-retirement assets; how many kids you have; and their income and assets.

There are several sources of financial aid for college. Grants and scholarships are the best because the money is usually tax-free and never has to be repaid. These include federal Pell Grants, primarily for low-income families, which offer a maximum of $4,050 per student for the 2005–2006 academic year, based on need.

The federal Supplemental Educational Opportunity Grant, which is administered by colleges, offers need-based awards up to $4,000 a student per year. Most students who receive need-based grants also are expected to participate in the federal Work-Study program, whereby students work part-time jobs to meet the family's remaining financial need.

Finally, there are loans, which come in two basic varieties: need-based, which help families who can't afford college costs; and non-need-based, designed to fill a gap when the family doesn't have available cash, but may have illiquid assets.

The two most common and attractive need-based loans are the Perkins and the Stafford, both federally funded.

The Perkins loan is made directly to students; parents need not co-sign this loan. Students don't need to begin repaying the loan until nine months after they graduate, leave college, or fall below half-time student status; and they have 10 years to repay the loan. With a Perkins, one pays a low interest rate (5 percent), and interest doesn't accrue until repayment begins. A school's financial aid office determines how much a student gets, but the cap on borrowing for undergrads is $4,000 per year, with a cumulative limit of $20,000.

Interest rates for Stafford loans are variable, but the cap is 8.25 percent. With the subsidized Stafford, interest does not accrue until six months after a student graduates, leaves or falls below half-time status. Students can borrow up to maximums that rise the longer a student remains in school, between $2,625 freshman year and $5,500 senior year.

The unsubsidized Stafford is a non-need-based loan for which most students who apply for aid are eligible. Interest accrues immediately, but payment may be postponed until after graduation. Students can borrow up to maximums that rise the longer a student remains in school. As with subsidized Stafford loans, students can borrow up to maximums that rise the longer a student remains in school, between $2,625 freshman year and $5,500 senior year.

Another common, non-need-based loan is the PLUS, or Parent Loans for Undergraduate Students. This loan is made to parents, not students. Parents can borrow up to the annual cost of attending college, minus any financial aid received. This loan is dependent on your credit rating, although the requirements are not as stringent as those for a mortgage.

The drawback of PLUS loans is that interest accrues immediately and repayment begins 60 days after you receive the money, although the repayment period can last 10 years. The interest rate is variable, adjusts once a year and is tied to the 3-month Treasury bill rate. But it can never exceed 9 percent.

## Want Free Money from the IRS?

Take advantage of tuition tax credits and deductions.

Parents who qualify should take advantage of two federal tax credits for tuition costs. The HOPE Credit and Lifetime Learning Credit are almost as good as getting money outright, since they are a dollar-for-dollar reduction of the tax you owe. And you can use these credits against tuition payments that you make using student loans.

The amount of the credit begins to phase out if your modified adjusted gross income (MAGI) is between $41,000 and $51,000 for a single return and between $82,000 and $102,000 for a joint return.

The HOPE Credit lets you slash your taxes by up to $1,500 a year per child for qualified tuition and fees paid during the first two years of college—100 percent of the first $1,000 in tuition, and 50 percent of the next $1,000. That means you need to have at least $2,000 in tuition expenses to get the full credit.

The Lifetime Learning Credit lets you slash your taxes by up to $2,000, regardless of how many children you have in college at one time. You can take 20 percent of up to $10,000 in qualified tuition and fees but you can't claim it in the same year that you take the Hope Credit for the same student.

The education toward which you're applying a federal credit must occur within the tax year in which tuition was paid, or within the first three months of the following year. Since academic years aren't the same as calendar or tax years, you need to be careful how you claim a credit on your tax return.

If you make too much to qualify for the HOPE or Lifetime credits, you may qualify for a new education deduction compliments of the Tax Relief Act of 2001 that's only in effect through 2005—Congress, however, may extend the deduction.

If your income qualifies you to take the HOPE and Lifetime credits as well as the new deduction, you may only take one of them for the same child in the same year. A deduction reduces your taxable income by a percent of every dollar, whereas a credit offers dollar-for-dollar reduction of the tax you owe. If you're in the 25 percent tax bracket, a $100 deduction means you'll pay $25 less in taxes, whereas a $100 credit means you'll pay $100 less.

# Chapter 8

# *Financing Retirement*

Perhaps you've never thought of "buying" your retirement. Yet that is exactly what you do when you put money into a retirement nest egg. You are paying today for the cost of your retirement tomorrow.

The cost of those future years is getting more expensive for most Americans, for two reasons. First, we live longer after we retire—with many of us spending 15, 25, even 30 years in retirement—and we are more active.

Second, you may have to shoulder a greater chunk of the cost of your retirement because fewer companies are providing traditional pension plans and are contributing less to those plans. Many retirement plans today, such as the popular 401(k), are paid for primarily by the employee, not the employer. You may not have a retirement plan available at work or you may be self-employed. This puts the responsibility of choosing retirement investments squarely on your shoulders.

Unfortunately, just about half of all Americans are earning retirement benefits at work, and many are not familiar with the basics of investing. Many people mistakenly believe that Social Security will pay for all or most of their retirement needs. The fact is, since its inception, Social Security has provided a minimum foundation of protection. A

Excerpted and reprinted with permission from "Savings Fitness: A Guide to Your Money and Your Financial Future," created by the U.S. Department of Labor, Employee Benefits Security Administration in partnership with Certified Financial Planner Board of Standards, Inc., September 2005. The full text of this publication and additional information is available online at http://www.cfp.net.

comfortable retirement usually requires Social Security, pensions, personal savings, and investments.

In short, paying for the retirement you truly desire is ultimately your responsibility. You must take charge. You are the architect of your financial future.

## Envision Your Retirement

Retirement is a state of mind as well as a financial issue. You are not so much retiring from work as you are moving into another stage of your life. Some people call retirement a "new career." What do you want to do in that stage? Travel? Relax? Move to a retirement community or to be near grandchildren? Pursue a favorite hobby? Go fishing or join a country club? Work part time or do volunteer work? Go back to school? What is the outlook for your health? Do you expect your family to take care of you if you are unable to care for yourself? Do you want to enter this stage of your life earlier than normal retirement age or later?

The answers to these questions are crucial when determining how much money you will need for the retirement you desire—and how much you'll need to save between now and then. Let's say you plan to retire early, with no plans to work even part time. You'll need to build a larger nest egg than if you retire later because you'll have to depend on it far longer.

### Estimate How Much You Need to Save for Retirement

Now that you have a clearer picture of your retirement goal, it's time to estimate how large your retirement nest egg will need to be and how much you need to save each month to buy that goal. This step is critical! The vast majority of people never take this step, yet it is very difficult to save adequately for retirement if you don't at least have a rough idea of how much you need to save every month.

There are numerous worksheets and software programs that can help you calculate approximately how much you'll need to save. Professional financial planners and other financial advisors can help as well. Regardless of what source you use, here are some of the basic questions and assumptions the calculation needs to answer.

**How much retirement income will I need?** An easy rule of thumb is that you'll need to replace 70 to 90 percent of your pre-retirement income. If you're making $50,000 a year (before taxes), you might need $35,000 to $45,000 a year in retirement income to enjoy the same standard of living you had before retirement. Think of this as your annual "cost" of retirement. The lower your income, generally the higher the portion of it you will need to replace.

However, no rule of thumb fits everyone. Expenses typically decline for retirees: taxes are smaller (though not always), and work-related costs usually disappear. But overall expenses may not decline much if you still have a home and college debts to pay off. Large medical bills may keep your retirement costs high. Much will depend on the kind of retirement you want to enjoy. Someone who plans to live a quiet, modest retirement in a low-cost part of the country will need a lot less money than someone who plans to be active, take expensive vacations, and live in an expensive region.

For younger people in the early stages of their working life, estimating income needs that may be 30 to 40 years in the future is obviously difficult. At least start with a rough estimate and begin saving something—10 percent of your gross income would be a good start. Then every two or three years review your retirement plan and adjust your estimate of retirement income needs as your annual earnings grow and your vision of retirement begins to come into focus.

**How long will I live in retirement?** Based on current estimates, a male retiring at age 55 today can expect to live approximately 23 years in retirement. A female retiring today at age 55 can expect to live approximately 27 years. And the likelihood of living at least 20 years for someone retiring at 55 today is high—over 60 percent for a man and about 75 percent for a woman. These are average figures and how long you can expect to live will depend on factors such as your general health and family history. But using today's average or past history may not give you a complete picture. People are living longer today than they did in the past, and virtually all expert opinion expects the trend toward living longer to continue.

**What other sources of income will I have?** Since October 1999, Social Security has been mailing statements to workers age 25 and older showing all the wages reported and an estimate of retirement, survivors, and disability benefits. You can also request a statement by visiting the Social Security Administration's website at http://www.ssa.gov or by calling 800-772-1213 and requesting a free Personal Earnings and Benefit Estimate Statement.

**Will you have other sources of income?** For instance, will you receive a pension that provides a specific amount of retirement income each month? Is the pension adjusted for inflation?

**What savings do I already have for retirement?** You'll need to build a nest egg sufficient to make up the gap between the total amount of income you will need each year and the amount provided annually by Social Security and any pension income. This nest egg will come from your retirement plan accounts at work, IRAs, annuities, and personal savings.

**What adjustments must be made for inflation?** The cost of retirement will likely go up every year due to inflation—that is, $35,000 won't buy as much in year five of your retirement as it will the first year because the cost of living usually rises. Although Social Security benefits are adjusted for inflation, any other estimates of how much income you need each year—and how much you'll need to save to provide that income—must be adjusted for inflation. The annual inflation rate is 3.0 percent currently, but it varies over time. In 1980, for instance, the annual inflation rate was 13.5 percent; in 1998, it reached a low of 1.6 percent. When planning for your retirement it is always safer to assume a higher, rather than a lower, rate and have your money buy more than you previously thought. Retirement calculators should allow you to make your own estimate for inflation.

**What will my investments return?** Any calculation must take into account what annual rate of return you expect to earn on the savings you've already accumulated and on the savings you intend to make in the future. You also need to determine the rate of return on your savings after you retire. These rates of return will depend in part on whether the money is inside or outside a tax-deferred account.

It's important to choose realistic annual returns when making your estimates. Most financial planners recommend that you stick with the historical rates of return based on the types of investments you choose or even slightly lower.

**How many years do I have left until I retire?** The more years you have, the less you'll have to save each month to reach your goal.

**How much should I save each month?** Once you determine the number of years until you retire and the size of the nest egg you need to "buy" in order to provide the income not provided by other sources, you can calculate the amount to save each month.

It's a good idea to revisit this worksheet at least every two or three years. Your vision of retirement, your earnings, and your financial circumstances may change. You'll also want to check periodically to be sure you are achieving your objectives along the way.

## *Planning for Retirement while You Are Still Young*

Retirement probably seems vague and far off at this stage of your life. Besides, you have other things to buy right now. Yet there are some crucial reasons to start preparing now for retirement.

- **You'll probably have to pay for more of your own retirement** than earlier generations. The sooner you get started, the better.

- **You have one huge ally—time.** Let's say that you put $1,000 at the beginning of each year into an IRA from age 20 through age 30 (11 years) and then never put in another dime. The account earns 7 percent annually. When you retire at age 65 you'll have $168,514 in the account. A friend doesn't start until age 30, but saves the same amount annually for 35 years straight. Despite putting in three times as much money, your friend's account grows to only $147,913.

- **You can start small and grow.** Even setting aside a small portion of your paycheck each month will pay off in big dollars later.

- **You can afford to invest more aggressively.** You have years to overcome the inevitable ups and downs of the stock market.

Developing the habit of saving for retirement is easier when you are young.

## *How to Prepare for Retirement when There's Little Time Left*

What if retirement is just around the corner and you haven't saved enough? Here are some tips. Some are painful, but they'll help you toward your goal.

- It's never too late to start. It's only too late if you don't start at all.

- Sock it away. Pump everything you can into your tax-sheltered retirement plans and personal savings. Try to put away at least 20 percent of your income.

- Reduce expenses. Funnel the savings into your nest egg.

- Take a second job or work extra hours.

- Aim for higher returns. Don't invest in anything you are uncomfortable with, but see if you can't squeeze out better returns.

- Retire later. You may not need to work full time beyond your planned retirement age. Part time may be enough.

- Refine your goal. You may have to live a less expensive lifestyle in retirement.

- Delay taking Social Security. Benefits will be higher when you start taking them.

- Make use of your home. Rent out a room or move to a less expensive home and save the profits.

- Sell assets that are not producing much income or growth, such as undeveloped land or a vacation home, and invest in income-producing assets.

## Facts Women Should Know about Preparing for Retirement

Women face challenges that often make it more difficult for them than men to adequately save for retirement. In light of these challenges, women need to pay special attention to making the most of their money.

- Women tend to earn less than men and work fewer years.

- Women tend to change jobs or work part time more often, and they interrupt their careers to raise children. Consequently, they are less likely to qualify for company-sponsored retirement plans or receive the full benefits of those plans.

- On average, women live five to seven years longer than men, and thus need to build a larger retirement nest egg for themselves.

- Some studies indicate women tend to invest less aggressively than men.

- Women are less likely to be financially informed than men.

- Women tend to lose more income than men following a divorce.

- Women are twice as likely as men during retirement to receive income below the poverty level.

For more information, call the Employee Benefits Security Administration at 866-444-EBSA (3272) and ask for the booklets "Women and Retirement Savings" and "QDROs: The Division of Pensions through Qualified Domestic Relations Orders" (for example, divorce orders). Also call the Social Security Administration at 800-772-1213 for their book-let "Social Security: What Every Woman Should Know," or visit on the web at http://www.ssa.gov.

## Saving for Retirement

Let's look at a few of the places where you might put your money for retirement.

- **Savings accounts, money market mutual funds, certificates of deposit, and U.S. Treasury bills:** These are sometimes referred to as cash or cash equivalents because you can get to them quickly and there's little risk of losing the money you put in.

- **Domestic bonds:** You loan money to a U.S. company or a government body in return for its promise to pay back what you loaned, with interest.

- **Domestic stocks:** You own part of a U.S. company.

- **Mutual funds:** Instead of investing directly in stocks, bonds, or real estate, for example, you can use mutual funds. These pool your money with money of other shareholders and invest it for you. A stock mutual fund, for example, would invest in stocks on behalf of all the fund's shareholders. This makes it easier to invest and to diversify your money.

### Choosing Where to Put Your Money

How do you decide where to put your money? Look back at the short-term goals you wrote down earlier—a family vacation, perhaps, or the down payment for a home. Remember, you should always be saving for retirement. But, for goals you want to happen soon—say within a year—it's best to put your money into one or more of the cash equivalents—a bank account or CD, for example. You'll earn a little interest and the money will be there when you need it.

For goals that are at least five years in the future, however, such as retirement, you may want to put some of your money into stocks, bonds, real estate, foreign investments, mutual funds, or other assets. Unlike savings accounts or bank CDs, these types of investments typically are not insured by the federal government. There is the risk that you can lose some of your money. How much risk depends on the type of investment. Generally, the longer you have until retirement and the greater your other sources of income, the more risk you can afford. For those who will be retiring soon and who will depend on their investment for income during their retirement years, a low-risk investment strategy is more prudent. Only you can decide how much risk to take.

Why take any risk at all? Because the greater the risk, the greater the potential reward. By investing carefully in such things as stocks and bonds, you are likely to earn significantly more money than by keeping all of your retirement money in a savings account, for example.

The differences in the average annual returns of various types of investments over time is dramatic. Since 1926, the average annual return of short-term U.S. Treasury bills, which roughly equals the return of other cash equivalents such as savings accounts, has been 3.7 percent. The annual return of long-term government bonds over the same period has been 5.4 percent. Large-company stocks, on the other hand, while riskier in the short term, have averaged an annual return of 10.4 percent.

Let's put that into dollars. If you had invested $1 in Treasury bills in 1926, that $1 would have grown to approximately $18 today. However, inflation, at an annual average of 3 percent, would have eaten $11 of that gain. If the $1 had been invested in government bonds, it would have grown to $62. But invested in large-company stocks, it would have grown to over $2,532. None of these rates of returns is guaranteed in the future, but they clearly show the relationship between risk and potential reward.

Many financial experts feel it is important to save at least a portion of your retirement money in higher risk—but potentially higher returning—assets. These higher risk assets can help you stay ahead of inflation, which eats away at your nest egg over time.

Which assets you want to invest in, of course, is your decision. Never invest in anything you don't thoroughly understand or don't feel comfortable about.

### Reducing Investment Risk

There are two main ways to reduce risk. First, diversify within each category of investment. You can do this by investing in pooled arrangements, such as mutual funds, index funds, and bank products offered by reliable professionals. These investments typically give you a small share of different individual investments and will allow you to spread your money among many stocks, bonds, and other financial instruments, even if you don't have a lot of money to invest. Your risk of losing money is less than if you buy shares in only a few individual companies. Distributing your investments in this way is called diversification.

Second, you can reduce risk by investing among categories of investments. Generally speaking, you should put some of your money in cash, some in bonds, some in stocks, and some in other investment vehicles. Studies have shown that once you have diversified your investments within each category, the choices you make about how much to put in these major categories is the most important decision you will make and should define your investment strategy.

Why diversify? Because at any given time one investment or type of investment might do better than another. Diversification lets you manage your risk in a particular investment or category of investments and decreases your chances of losing money. In fact, the factors that can cause one investment to do poorly may cause another to do well. Bond prices, for example, often go down when stock prices are up. When stock prices go down, bonds have often increased in value. Over a long time—the time you probably have to save for retirement—the risk of losing money or earning less than you would in a savings account tends to decline.

By diversifying into different types of assets, you are more likely to reduce risk, and actually improve return, than by putting all of your money into one investment or one type of investment. The familiar adage "Don't put all your eggs in one basket" definitely applies to investing.

## Deciding on an Investment Mix

How you diversify—that is, how much you decide to put into each type of investment—is called asset allocation. For example, if you decide to invest in stocks, how much of your retirement nest egg should you put into stocks: 10 percent ... 30 percent ... 75 percent? How much into bonds and cash? Your decision will depend on many factors: how much time you have until retirement, your life expectancy, the size of your current nest egg, other sources of retirement income, how much risk you are willing to take, and how healthy your current financial picture is, among others.

Your asset allocation also may change over time. When you are younger, you might invest more heavily in stocks than bonds and cash. As you get older and enter retirement, you may reduce your exposure to stocks and hold more in bonds and cash. You also might change your asset allocation because your goals, risk tolerance, or financial circumstances have changed.

## *Rebalancing Your Portfolio*

Once you've decided on your investment mix and invested your money, over time some of your investments will go up and others will go down. If this continues, you may eventually have a different investment mix than you intended. Reassessing your mix, or rebalancing as it is commonly called, brings your portfolio back to your original plan. Rebalancing also helps you to make logical, not emotional, investment decisions.

For instance, instead of selling investments in a sector that is declining, you would sell an investment that has made gains and, with that money, purchase more in the declining investment sector. This way, you rebalance your portfolio mix, lessen your risk of loss, and increase you chance for greater returns in the long run.

Here's how rebalancing works: let's say your original investment called for 10 percent in U. S. small company stocks. Because of a stock market decline, they now represent 6 percent of your portfolio. You would sell assets that had increased and purchase enough U. S. small company stocks so they again represent 10 percent of your portfolio.

How do you know when to rebalance? There are two methods of rebalancing: calendar and conditional. Calendar rebalancing means that once a quarter or once a year you will reduce the investments that have gone up and will add to investments that have gone down. Conditional rebalancing is done whenever an asset class goes up or down more than some percentage, such as 25 percent. This method lets the markets tell you when it is time to rebalance.

## *The Power of Compounding*

Regardless of where you choose to put your money—cash, stocks, bonds, real estate, or a combination of places—the key to saving for retirement is to make your money work for you. It does this through the power of compounding. Compounding investment earnings is what can make even small investments become larger given enough time.

You're probably already familiar with the principle of compounding. Money you put into a savings account earns interest. Then you earn interest on the money you originally put in, plus on the interest you've accumulated. As the size of your savings account grows, you earn interest on a bigger and bigger pool of money.

Table 8.1 provides an example of how an investment grows at different annual rates of return over different time periods. Notice how the amount of gain gets bigger each 10-year period. That's because money is being earned on a bigger and bigger pool of money.

**Table 8.1.** Power of Compounding. The value of $1,000 compounded at various rates of return over time is as follows:

| Years | 4% | 6% | 8% | 10% |
|-------|------|------|------|------|
| 10 | $ 1,481 | $ 1,791 | $ 2,159 | $ 2,594 |
| 20 | $ 2,191 | $ 3,207 | $ 4,661 | $ 6,728 |
| 30 | $ 3,243 | $ 5,743 | $10,063 | $17,449 |

Also notice that when you double your rate of return from 4 percent to 8 percent, the end result after 30 years is over three times what you would have accumulated with a 4 percent return. That's the power of compounding!

The real power of compounding comes with time. The earlier you start saving, the more your money can work for you. Look at it another way. For every 10 years you delay before starting to save for retirement, you will need to save three times as much each month to catch up. That's why no matter how young you are, the sooner you begin saving for retirement, the better.

## *Types of Defined Contribution Plans*

The following are some of the most common types of defined contribution plans. For a more detailed description and comparison of some of these plans, go to the website http://www.dol.gov/ebsa and click on the Retirement Savings Education Campaign, then follow the prompt to the Small Business Advisor.

- **401(k) Plan:** This is the most popular of the defined contribution plans and is most commonly offered by larger employers. Employers often match employee contributions.

- **403(b) Tax-Sheltered Annuity Plan:** Think of this as a 401(k) plan for employees of school systems and certain nonprofit organizations. Investments are made in tax-sheltered annuities or mutual funds.

- **SIMPLE IRA:** The Savings Incentive Match Plan for Employees of Small Employers is one of the newest types of employer-based retirement plans. There is also a 401(k) version of the SIMPLE.

- **Profit-Sharing Plan:** The employer shares company profits with employees, usually based on the level of each employee's wages.

- **ESOP:** Employee stock ownership plans are similar to profit-sharing plans, except that an ESOP must invest primarily in company stock. Under an ESOP, the employees share in the ownership of the company.

- **SEP:** Simplified employee pension plans are used by both small employers and the self-employed.

Other retirement plans you may want to learn more about include money purchase plans; 457 plans, which cover state and local government workers; and the Federal Thrift Savings Plan, which covers federal employees. If you are eligible, you may also want to open a Roth IRA.

## Using Employer-Based Retirement Plans

Does your employer provide a retirement plan? If so, say retirement experts . . . grab it! Employer-based plans are the most effective way to save for your future. What's more, you'll gain certain tax benefits. Employer-based plans come in one of two varieties (some employers provide both): defined benefit and defined contribution.

### Defined Benefit Plans

These plans pay a lump sum upon retirement or a guaranteed monthly benefit. The amount of payout is typically based on a set formula, such as the number of years you have worked for the employer times a percentage of your highest earnings on the job. Usually the employer funds the plan—commonly called a pension plan—though in some plans workers also contribute. Most defined benefit plans are insured by the federal government.

### Defined Contribution Plans

The popular 401(k) plan is one type of defined contribution plan. Unlike a defined benefit plan, this type of savings arrangement does not guarantee a specified amount for retirement. Instead, the amount you have available in the plan to help fund your retirement will depend on how long you participate in the plan, how much is invested, and how well the investments do over the years. The federal government does not guarantee how much you accumulate in your account, but it does protect the account assets from misuse by the employer.

In the past 20 years, defined contribution plans have become more common than traditional pension plans. Employers fund some types of defined contribution plans, though the amount of their contributions is not necessarily guaranteed.

Workers with a pension are more likely to be covered by a defined contribution plan, usually a 401(k) plan, rather than the traditional defined benefit plan. In many defined contribution plans, you are offered a choice of investment options, and you must decide where to invest your contributions. This shifts much of the responsibility for retirement planning to workers. Thus, it is critical that you choose to contribute to the plan once you become eligible (usually after working full time for a minimum period) and that you choose your investments wisely.

### *Tax Breaks*

Even though you typically are responsible for funding a defined contribution plan, you receive important tax breaks. The money you invest in the plan and the earnings on those contributions are deferred from income tax until you withdraw the money (hopefully not until retirement). Why is that important? Because postponing taxes on what you earn allows your nest egg to grow faster. Remember the power of compounding? The larger the amount you have to compound, the faster it grows. Even after the withdrawals are taxed, you typically come out ahead.

The tax deduction also means that the decline in your take-home pay, because of your contribution, won't be as large as you might think. For example, let's assume you are thinking about putting $100 into a retirement plan each month and that the rate you pay on income taxes is 15 percent. If you don't put that $100 into a retirement plan, you'll pay $15 in taxes on it. If you put in $100, you postpone the taxes. Thus, your $100 retirement plan contribution would actually reduce your take-home pay by only $85. If you're in the 27 percent tax bracket, the cost of the $100 contribution is only $73. This is like buying your retirement at a discount.

### *Vesting Rules*

Any money you put into a retirement plan out of your pay, and earnings on those contributions, always belong to you. However, contrary to popular belief, employees don't always have immediate access to the money their employer puts into their pension fund or their defined contribution plan. Under some plans, such as a traditional pension plan or a 401(k), you have to work for a certain number of years—say five—before you become "vested" and can receive benefits. Some plans vest in stages. Other defined contribution plans, such as the SEP and the SIMPLE IRA, vest immediately. You have access to the employer's contributions the day the money is deposited. No employer can require you to work longer than seven years before you become vested in your pension benefit.

Be aware of the vesting rules in your employer's plan.

Make sure you know when you're vested. Changing jobs too quickly can mean losing part or all of your pension plan benefits or, at the very least, your employer's matching contributions.

### Retirement Plan Rights

The federal government regulates and monitors company retirement plans. The vast majority of employers does an excellent job in complying with federal law. Unfortunately, a small fraction doesn't. For 10 warning signs and other information on protecting your pension rights, call Employee Benefits Security Administration (EBSA)'s toll-free number at 866-444-3272 and request the booklet "Protect Your Pension."

## Retirement Planning for Employees in Small Companies

Only about two out of every 10 small employers with fewer than 100 employees offer some type of retirement plan or pension to their employees. Many believe their workers prefer higher salaries or other benefits, and they believe the rules are too complex and the costs too high.

If you don't have a plan available at work, encourage your employer to start one. Mention the following benefits:

- A retirement plan can attract and retain valued employees in a competitive labor market, as well as motivate workers.

- Establishing a retirement plan and encouraging employee participation can help employers fund their own retirement. Even after taking into account the cost of establishing an employee plan, employers may still be better off than funding retirement on their own.

- Some plans cost less and have fewer administrative hassles than employers may realize. Alternatives to traditional defined benefit plans and the 401(k) include the SIMPLE and the SEP.

For more information, contact EBSA at 866-444-3272 and request "Savings Incentive Match Plans for Employees of Small Employers," "Simplified Employee Pensions: What Small Businesses Need to Know," and "Choosing a Retirement Solution for Your Small Business."

## *What to Do If You Can't Join an Employer-Based Plan*

You may not be able to join an employer-based retirement plan because you are not eligible or because the employer doesn't offer one. Fortunately, there are steps you can still take to build your retirement strength.

**Take a job with a plan:** If two jobs offer similar pay and working conditions, the job that offers retirement benefits may be the better choice.

**Start your own plan:** If you can't join a company plan, you can save on your own.

You can't put away as much on a tax-deferred basis, and you won't have an employer match. Still, you can build a healthy nest egg if you work at it.

**Open an IRA:** You can put up to $4,000 a year into an individual retirement account on a tax-deductible basis if your spouse isn't covered by a retirement plan at work, or as long as your combined incomes aren't too high. This amount remains the same through 2007 and will increase in 2008 to $5,000. Persons who are 50 or older can contribute an additional $500 for 2005 and an additional $1,000 for 2006 and subsequent years. You also can put the same amount tax-deferred into an IRA for a nonworking spouse if you file your income tax return jointly. (By the way, you don't have to put in the full amount; you can put in less.) With a traditional IRA, you delay income taxes on what you put in and on the earnings until you withdraw the money. With a Roth IRA, the money you put in is already taxed, but you won't ever pay income taxes on the earnings as long as the account is open at least five years.

**Consider an annuity:** An annuity is when you pay money to an insurance company in return for its agreement to pay either a regular fixed amount when you retire or an amount based on how much your investment earns. There is no limit on how much you can invest in a private annuity, and earnings aren't taxed until you withdraw them. However, annuities present complex issues regarding taxes, fees, and withdrawal strategies that may not make them the best investment choice for you. Consider discussing this type of investment first with a financial planner.

**Build your personal savings:** You can always save money on your own, either in mutual funds, stocks, bonds (such as U.S. Savings

Bonds), real estate, CDs, or other assets. It's best to mark these investments as part of your retirement fund and don't use them for anything else unless absolutely necessary.

**Keep your goals in mind:** Investing in an IRA, an annuity, or in personal savings means you are totally responsible for directing your own investments. How conservatively or aggressively you invest is up to you. It will depend in part on how willing you are to take investment risks, your age, the stability of your job, and other financial needs. Learn as much as you can about investing and about specific investments you are considering. You also may want to seek the help of a professional financial planner. Go to www.CFP.net/learn for tips on choosing a financial planner who puts your interests first.

## *Cautions*

- Don't borrow from your retirement plan or permanently withdraw funds before retirement unless absolutely necessary.

- Your retirement plan may allow you to borrow from your account, often at very attractive rates. However, borrowing reduces the account's earnings, leaving you with a smaller nest egg. Also, if you fail to pay back the loan, you could end up paying income taxes and penalties. As an alternative, consider budgeting to save the needed money or pursue other affordable loan options.

- Also avoid permanently withdrawing funds before retirement. This often happens when people change jobs. According to a study by the Employee Benefits Research Institute and Hewitt Associates, only 40 percent of workers changing jobs rolled over into an IRA or a new employer's retirement plan the money they received from their former employer's retirement plan. They spent six out of every 10 dollars, rather than letting it grow in another plan or IRA.

- Pre-retirement withdrawals reduce the ultimate size of your nest egg. In addition, you'll probably pay federal income taxes on the amount you withdraw (10 percent to as high as 39.1 percent) and a 10 percent penalty may be tacked on if you're younger than age 59½. In addition, you may have to pay state taxes. If you're in a SIMPLE IRA plan, that early withdrawal penalty climbs to 25 percent if you take out money during the first two years you're in the plan.

## What to Do If You Are Self-Employed

Many people today work for themselves, either full-time or in addition to their regular job. They have several tax-deferred options from which to choose.

**SEP:** This is the same type of SEP described earlier under employer-based retirement plans. Only here, you're the employer and you fund the SEP from your earnings. You can easily set up a SEP through a bank, mutual fund, or other financial institution.

**Keogh:** Keoghs are more complicated to set up and maintain, but they offer more advantages than a SEP. For one thing, they come in several varieties. Some of the varieties allow you to sock away more money—sometimes a lot more money—than a SEP.

**SIMPLE IRA:** Described earlier under employer-based retirement plans, a SIMPLE IRA can be used by the self-employed. However, generally you can't save as much as you can with a SEP or Keogh.

**IRA:** Usually you are better off funding a SEP or a Keogh unless your self-employment income is small.

**Annuities:** See annuities under the section on "What to Do If You Can't Join an Employer-Based Plan."

## The Bottom Line

Finally, there is only one real key to "buying" that retirement you've dreamed of. It doesn't matter whether you are still young or whether retirement is just around the corner. It doesn't matter whether you're in your first job, trying to save for a home, or putting a child through college. All that matters is that you start saving ... now.

# Chapter 9

# *Receiving a Financial Windfall*

### *Respecting a Windfall*

Last month, 26-year-old Karen Suzanne Daniel was thrilled to receive a check for nearly $5,000 in overdue child support. But then the Maryland resident panicked. "It's a huge amount to suddenly get," she says. "I didn't want to waste it."

Ms. Daniel thought about putting it all in an investment account for her daughter, funding a down payment on a home, paying off some of her debt—or divvying up the surprise sum among those options.

Ultimately she decided that putting the $5,000 toward $20,000 in high-cost credit-card debt made the most sense.

Feelings of anxiety, guilt, and fear are common among those who receive Sudden Money, particularly large sums, say financial planners and accountants. That's in part because the money "presents a new range of possibilities and options" and in some cases could change your life, says Susan Bradley, a financial planner in Palm Beach Gardens, Florida.

For twenty-somethings in particular, an unexpected financial windfall could put your retirement savings on the fast track, jump-start

This chapter begins with "Respecting a Windfall" by Diana Ransom, Copyright 2006 by Dow Jones & Company, Inc. Reproduced with permission of Dow Jones & Company, Inc. via Copyright Clearance Center. The article originally appeared in the *Wall Street Journal Online*, November 12, 2006. Additional text under the heading "Frequently Asked Questions about Sudden Money" is from "Frequently Asked Questions," © 2002 Sudden Money Institute (www.suddenmoney.com). Reprinted with permission.

entrepreneurial ambitions, or simply give you a measure of financial freedom at a time when your salary may be fairly modest.

Here are tips for recipients:

### *Start Off Slowly*

Your first move should be to "do nothing" while you get used to your new financial circumstances and weigh your options, says Ginita Wall, an accountant and financial planner in San Diego. Before making any big decisions, allow yourself anywhere from two weeks, for a modest sum, to one year, for larger amounts.

Of course, that doesn't mean simply holding onto an uncashed check. As soon as possible, Ms. Wall recommends you "get your money working for you" in low-risk holdings such as short-term certificates of deposit, money-market accounts, and Treasury bills.

For help with a large sum, you should consider hiring a financial adviser.

"You need to get financial maturity real fast," Ms. Bradley notes.

### *Check Your Debt*

Paying off high-cost debt should be high on your list of priorities, says Rita Johnson, a financial adviser in Boulder, Colorado, with Raymond James Financial. The average credit-card debt among 25- to 34-year-olds was $5,200 in 2004, according to CardWeb.com, a research firm in Maryland.

But don't rush to pay off lower-interest debt, which is typically student loans and mortgages.

### *Pump Up Your Savings*

An unexpected windfall might allow you to bulk up on your savings for a child's education or a hoped-for home purchase.

Further, putting part of your windfall toward living expenses could allow you to increase your annual contributions to tax-favored retirement accounts such as a 401(k) plan or an individual retirement account.

### *Opportunity Knocking*

A financial windfall could make it easier to make a big life change, such as going back to school, switching careers or even starting a business.

"Usually people have the energy and inclination but not the money," says Ms. Bradley. For young recipients of a windfall, "this money can really accelerate life."

### *Don't Forget Taxes*

Some windfalls don't come with a tax bill attached, but others do.

There's generally no immediate tax on an inheritance, for instance. And child support, as Ms. Daniel received, isn't taxable.

But if you win the lottery, hit it big on a game show, or have a great night in Las Vegas, that's taxable income. If your winnings minus the amount wagered exceed $5,000 in these scenarios, tax will be withheld at a 25% rate.

That's probably better than getting the entire sum, only to face the tax bill later on. "You never see the money, so you don't spend it," says Daniel Silvershein, a tax attorney in New York.

## *Frequently Asked Questions about Sudden Money*

These questions were answered by Susan Bradley, a financial planner, author, and founder of the Sudden Money® Institute.

### *What are some of the unique needs among people who receive Sudden Money?*

The first thing that sets Sudden Money recipients apart from other clients is that their mental and emotional states have been altered by the suddenness of the new money. This creates a fragility and a vulnerability that makes them susceptible to many financial and personal problems.

In order to deal with this reality, it is necessary to postpone financial decisions and concentrate instead on orienting them to their new situation. This time is called the Decision Free Zone (or DFZ), and during it the focus is on education and experiencing emotions. During the DFZ, the client learns about the various aspects of the future planning while allowing their mental and emotional states to naturally evolve. They think about what it means to have more money and how they want to put it to use. They observe the transformation of their feelings, they grieve if they need to, they learn about many financial issues that weren't part of their lives prior to the money, and they observe as many of their relationships go through a process of change.

Sometimes that process and those changes are gradual, and sometimes they are abrupt. The important thing is to create a safe environment for the client where there is no pressure to make decisions and where they can naturally evolve to a place where they can handle what lies ahead for them.

### *What is the most common surprise that recipients of Sudden Money experience?*

In our culture, there is a widely held belief that money solves problems. People think if only they had more money, their troubles would be over. Wealthy people are envied for what they have and what they can afford. But when a family receives Sudden Money, they frequently learn that money can cause as many problems as it solves.

Because we are conditioned to see money as a source of joy, freedom, and empowerment, this can be upsetting and frightening for many people.

The discomfort, fear, and confusion Sudden Money recipients experience can lead to isolation, because family, friends, and advisors may not understand the difficulties involved. It is common for those who receive Sudden Money to feel their emotions are invalid and that they are somehow flawed as people. In time, our culture will probably shift its perception of money as an end-all, be-all commodity. Until then, Sudden Money recipients will continue to experience surprising challenges.

### *What is the best way to handle well-meaning advice from family and friends regarding Sudden Money?*

For many people, Sudden Money can spell disaster. As a result, family and friends want to offer their help. But your first step after learning you will receive the money is to form a team of advisors made up of a financial planner, an attorney, a CPA (certified public accountant), and a "life coach."

It takes time to become oriented to Sudden Money. Work with your team to understand your new financial position, tax consequences, cash flow potential, and the range of lifestyle choices available to you. Let your loved ones know you have established a team and the general path you have chosen. Reassure them you are not giving up control of your money. Discuss details of your plans only with your advisers. Family and friends don't need to know what stocks or bonds you are buying, but they should know you are making informed choices.

You can communicate this without going into details. For example, you can say, "I am putting some of the money into the stock market because I know I need growth. And some of the money will go into bonds because I like the stability and cash that bonds generate." This statement demonstrates knowledge and confidence without the need for giving details.

### When is it best to discuss the new financial position with children?

It is best not to make money a taboo topic. Tell children about the money and let them know having a lot of money is a big responsibility. It's okay to let them know that you will take your time to learn all you can about managing the money. Tell them you will teach them about spending, investing, and sharing money as you learn more about it yourself.

Take time to reevaluate your goals and priorities. Work with your advisors to use the money to support your highest priorities. Decide what you want your children to learn about money and then teach them. If you are clear about what the money means to you and you are intentional in how you use the money, your children will learn by example.

One couple kept their jobs as government workers after winning the lottery. The reason: they did not want their children to think it was okay to sit around and watch television all day just because they were rich. Instead, they planned to work until the children graduated college just to set what they thought was the right example.

Resist the urge to give money to your children right away. There will be plenty of time for that later. Buying them big items right away can send the message that money is for getting things you want.

# Chapter 10

# *Estate Planning*

## *Top Things to Know*

### *1. No matter your net worth, it's important to have a basic estate plan in place.*

Such a plan ensures that your family and financial goals are met after you die.

### *2. An estate plan has several elements.*

They include: a will, assignment of power of attorney, and a living will or health-care proxy (medical power of attorney). For some people, a trust may also make sense. When putting together a plan, you must be mindful of both federal and state laws governing estates.

### *3. Taking inventory of your assets is a good place to start.*

Your assets include your investments, retirement savings, insurance policies, and real estate or business interests. Ask yourself three questions: Whom do you want to inherit your assets? Whom do you want handling your financial affairs if ever you're incapacitated? Whom do you want making medical decisions for you if you become unable to make them for yourself?

---

The text in this chapter is from "Lesson 21: Estate Planning," from *Money 101*; reprinted with permission from www.CNNMoney.com. © 2007 Cable News Network. All Rights reserved.

### 4. Everybody needs a will.

A will tells the world exactly where you want your assets distributed when you die. It's also the best place to name guardians for your children. Dying without a will—also known as dying "intestate"—can be costly to your heirs and leaves you no say over who gets your assets. Even if you have a trust, you still need a will to take care of any holdings outside of that trust when you die.

### 5. Trusts aren't just for the wealthy.

Trusts are legal mechanisms that let you put conditions on how and when your assets will be distributed upon your death. They also allow you to reduce your estate and gift taxes and to distribute assets to your heirs without the cost, delay, and publicity of probate court, which administers wills. Some also offer greater protection of your assets from creditors and lawsuits.

### 6. Discussing your estate plans with your heirs may prevent disputes or confusion.

Inheritance can be a loaded issue. By being clear about your intentions, you help dispel potential conflicts after you're gone.

### 7. The federal estate tax exemption—the amount you may leave to heirs free of federal tax—is rising gradually, from $1.5 million in 2004 to $3.5 million in 2009.

Meanwhile, the top estate tax rate is coming down. The estate tax is scheduled to phase out completely by 2010, but only for a year. Unless Congress passes new laws between now and then, the tax will be reinstated in 2011 and you will only be allowed to leave your heirs $1 million tax-free at that time.

### 8. You may leave an unlimited amount of money to your spouse tax-free, but this isn't always the best tactic.

By leaving all your assets to your spouse, you don't use your estate tax exemption and instead increase your surviving spouse's taxable estate. That means your children are likely to pay more in estate taxes if your spouse leaves them the money when he or she dies. Plus, it defers the tough decisions about the distribution of your assets until your spouse's death.

### 9. There are two easy ways to give gifts tax-free and reduce your estate.

You may give up to $11,000 a year to an individual (or $22,000 if you're married and giving the gift with your spouse). You may also pay an unlimited amount of medical and education bills for someone if you pay the expenses directly to the institutions where they were incurred.

### 10. There are ways to give charitable gifts that keep on giving.

If you donate to a charitable gift fund or community foundation, your investment grows tax-free and you can select the charities to which contributions are given both before and after you die.

## Take Stock

Assessing your assets and goals is groundwork for a good estate plan.
Few people relish estate planning. After all, deciding how you want your assets distributed after you die can serve as an unnerving reminder of your mortality. But there are plenty of reasons to tackle the task with some enthusiasm:

- You get to name the people to whom you wish to give your assets and know that your wishes carry the word of law.

- You can arrange it so that taxes siphon as little from your pot of gold as possible.

- And you have the satisfaction of knowing that your financial affairs are in order and that you're not bequeathing a costly administrative nightmare to your loved ones.

Your first step? Take stock of all your assets. These include your investments, retirement accounts, insurance policies, real estate, and any business interests.

Next, decide what you want to achieve with those assets and who you want to inherit them. This is also the time to think about people you would trust to handle your business affairs and medical care in the event that you become incapacitated.

Once you decide what kinds of bequests you wish to make, be sure to discuss your plans with your heirs. The sooner and more distinctly you outline your intentions to your family and friends, the less chance there will be for disagreements when you're gone. "If you treat your wealth as

93

a hidden kingdom, a box that no one can open until you're gone, you're setting your family up for disaster," says Norman Ross, of the Ross Companies, a New York estate-planning and benefits consulting firm.

In creating your estate plan, keep in mind that the laws governing estate planning are not set in stone. In fact, the Tax Relief Act of 2001 made several sweeping changes that are being phased in over a 10-year period. They include a gradual increase in the estate tax exemption (the amount of money you may leave heirs free from federal tax) and the eventual repeal of the estate tax; a reduction in the estate and gift-tax rates—the top rate will fall as low as 45 percent by 2007, down from 55 percent in 2001; the gradual repeal of the federal credit for estate taxes paid to a state government; and a revision in how the tax basis of inherited assets is calculated.

It's a complex law made more complicated by the fact that it sunsets at the end of 2010. Between now and then, Congress may pass other measures that either extend provisions in the Act or eradicate them.

What that means is estate planning has become far more complicated for people with sizable estates, and having a trusted and competent estate-planning lawyer is essential if you wish to protect as much of your assets from Uncle Sam (and your state tax collector) as possible. Such a lawyer can create legal documents, offer advice, keep your estate plan current with new laws and help administer the disposition of assets.

## Why Do I Need a Will?

If you don't have one, a court decides who gets your assets.

A will is a device that lets you tell the world who you want to get your assets. Die without one, and the state decides who gets what, without regard to your wishes or your heirs' needs.

So-called intestacy laws vary considerably from state to state. In general, though, if you die and leave a spouse and kids, your assets will be split between your surviving mate and children. If you're single with no children, then the state is likely to decide who among your blood relatives will inherit your estate.

Making a will is especially important for people with young children, because wills are the best way to transfer guardianship of minors.

You may amend your will at any time. In fact, it's a good idea to review it periodically and especially when your marital status changes. At the same time, review your beneficiary designations for your 401(k), IRA, pension, and life insurance policy since those accounts will be transferred automatically to your named beneficiaries when you die.

A will is also useful if you have a trust. A trust is a legal mechanism that lets you put conditions on how your assets are distributed after you die and it often lets you minimize gift and estate taxes. But you still need a will since most trusts deal only with specific assets such as life insurance or a piece of property, but not the sum total of your holdings.

Even if you have what's known as a revocable living trust in which you can put the bulk of your assets, you still need what's known as a pour-over will. In addition to letting you name a guardian for your children, a pour-over will ensures that all the assets you intended to put into trust are put there even if you fail to retitle some of them before your death. Any assets that are not retitled in the name of the trust are considered subject to probate. As a result, if you haven't specified in a will who should get those assets, a court may decide to distribute them to heirs whom you may not have chosen.

## Living Wills and Health-Care Proxies

Making known your medical wishes now can save a lot of heartache later.

A living will (also known as an advance medical directive) is a statement of your wishes for the kind of life-sustaining medical intervention you want, or don't want, in the event that you become terminally ill and unable to communicate.

Most states have living will statutes that define when a living will goes into effect (for example, when a person has less than six months to live). State law may also restrict the medical interventions to which such directives apply.

Your condition and the terms of your directive also will be subject to interpretation. Different institutions and doctors may come to different conclusions. As a result, in some instances a living will may not be followed. Nevertheless, a patient's wishes are taken very seriously, and an advance medical directive is one of the best ways to have a say in your medical care when you can't express yourself otherwise.

You increase your chances of enforcing your directive when you have a health-care agent advocating on your behalf.

You can name such an agent by way of a health-care proxy, or by assigning what's called a medical power of attorney. You sign a legal document in which you name someone you trust to make medical decisions on your behalf in the event that you can't do so for yourself.

A health-care proxy applies to all instances when you're incapacitated, not just if you're terminally ill.

Choose your health-care agent carefully. That person should be able to do three key things: understand important medical information regarding your treatment, handle the stress of making tough decisions, and keep your best interests and wishes in mind when making those decisions.

## Why Should I Assign Power of Attorney?

When you can't control your financial life, make sure someone you trust will.

No one is immune from aging or the loss of mental clarity that may come with it. And you're never immune to health crises that may leave you unable to handle the business of your life: paying bills, managing investments, or making key financial decisions.

Granting someone you trust the power of attorney allows that person—known as your "agent" or "attorney in fact"—to manage your financial affairs if you are unable to do so. Your agent is empowered to sign your name and is obligated to be your fiduciary—meaning they must act in your best financial interest at all times and in accordance with your wishes.

There are different kinds of powers of attorney, but in estate planning there are two essential types you should know. The first is the "springing power of attorney," which only goes into effect under circumstances that you specify, the most typical being when you become incapacitated. Often that means your agent cannot act until he or she provides doctors' letters and sometimes court orders to prove you are incapable of making decisions for yourself.

There is also the "durable power of attorney." It is effective immediately, and your agent does not need to prove your incapacity in order to sign your name.

An attorney can help you decide which form makes the best sense for your circumstance. In any case, take care in choosing your agent. That person should be competent, trustworthy, willing to take on the burden of your affairs, and financially secure.

If you choose a relative or friend as your agent, you probably won't have to pay them. But if you name a bank, lawyer, or other outside party, you will have to negotiate compensation, which can range from hourly fees to a percentage of your assets paid annually.

If you do become incapacitated without having assigned power of attorney, the court will step in to appoint a guardian. This process might cost your family well over $1,000, not including the cost of the guardian's annual visits to court to report on your situation. Plus, the person chosen may not be someone you would have picked.

## *Does a Trust Make Sense?*

It's not just for Rockefellers.

The notion of a legal trust may conjure up images of country clubbers cradling gin-and-tonics.

The truth is a trust may be a useful estate-planning tool for your family if you have a net worth of at least $100,000 and meet one of the following conditions, says Mike Janko, executive director of the National Association of Financial and Estate Planning (NAFEP):

- A sizable amount of your assets is in real estate, a business, or an art collection;

- You want to leave your estate to your heirs in a way that is not directly and immediately payable to them upon your death. For example, you may want to stipulate that they receive their inheritance in three parts, or upon certain conditions being met, such as graduating from college;

- You want to support your surviving spouse, but also want to ensure that the principal or remainder of your estate goes to your chosen heirs (your children from a first marriage) after your spouse dies;

- You and your spouse want to maximize your estate-tax exemptions;

- You have a disabled relative whom you would like to provide for without disqualifying him or her from Medicaid or other government assistance.

Among the chief advantages of trusts, they let you:

- Put conditions on how and when your assets are distributed after you die;

- Reduce estate and gift taxes;

- Distribute assets to heirs efficiently without the cost, delay, and publicity of probate court. Probate can cost between 5 percent to 7 percent of your estate;

- Better protect your assets from creditors and lawsuits;

- Name a successor trustee, who not only manages your trust after you die, but is empowered to manage the trust assets if you become unable to do so.

Trusts are flexible, varied, and complex. Each type has advantages and disadvantages, which you should discuss thoroughly with your estate-planning attorney before setting one up.

When it comes to cost, a basic trust plan may run anywhere from $1,600 to $3,000, possibly more depending on the complexity of the trust. Such a plan should include the trust set-up, a will, a living will, and a health-care proxy. You will also pay fees to amend the trust if it's revocable and to administer the trust after you die.

One caveat: Assets you want protected by the trust must be retitled in the name of the trust. Anything that is not so titled when you die will have to be probated and may not go to the heir you intended but to one the probate court chooses. For a trust in which you want to put the majority of your assets—known as a revocable living trust—you also have to have a "pour-over will" to cover any of your holdings that might be outside of your trust if you die unexpectedly. A pour-over will essentially directs that any assets outside of the trust at the time of your death be put into it so they can go to the heirs you choose.

If you'd like to learn about different kinds of trusts, read on.

### *Five Standard Forms of Trusts*

**Credit shelter trust:** With a credit-shelter trust (also called a by-pass or family trust), you write a will bequeathing an amount to the trust up to but not exceeding the estate-tax exemption. Then you pass the rest of your estate to your spouse tax-free. You also specify how you want the trust to be used—for example, you may stipulate that income from the trust after you die goes to your spouse and that when he or she dies, the principal will be distributed tax-free among your children. Since your spouse is also entitled to an estate-tax exemption, the two of you can effectively double (or more than double) that portion of your kids' inheritance that is shielded from estate taxes by using this strategy.

**And there's an added bonus:** Once money is placed in a bypass trust it is forever free of estate tax, even if it grows. So if your surviving spouse invests it wisely, he or she may add to your children's inheritance, says attorney Roger Levine of Levine, Furman & Smeltzer in East Brunswick, N.J. Of course, you can pass an amount equal to the estate-tax exemption directly to your kids when you die, but the reason for a bypass trust is to protect your spouse financially in the event he or she has need for income from the trust or in the event you think your children will squander their inheritance before the surviving parent dies.

**Generation-skipping trust:** A generation-skipping trust (also called a dynasty trust) allows you to transfer a substantial amount of money tax-free to beneficiaries who are at least two generations your junior—typically your grandchildren. The generation-skipping exemption is increasing gradually from $1 million in 2003 to $3.5 million in 2009. You may specify that your children may receive income from the trust and even use its principal for almost anything that would benefit your grandkids, including health care, housing, or tuition bills.

Beware, however. If you leave more than the exemption amount, the bequest will be subject to a generation-skipping transfer tax. This tax is separate from estate taxes, and is designed to stop wealthy seniors from funneling all their money to their grandchildren.

**Qualified personal residence trust:** A qualified personal residence trust (QPRT) can remove the value of your home or vacation dwelling from your estate and is particularly useful if your home is likely to appreciate in value. A QPRT lets you give your home as a gift—most commonly to your children—while you keep control of it for a period that you stipulate, say 10 years. You may continue to live in the home and maintain full control of it during that time.

In valuing the gift, the IRS assumes your home is worth less than its present-day value since your kids won't take possession of it for several years. (The longer the term of the trust, the less the value of the gift.)

Say you put a $675,000 home in a 10-year QPRT. The value of that gift in 10 years will be assumed to be less—say, $400,000—based on IRS calculations that take into account current interest rates, your life expectancy and other factors. Even if the house appreciates in 10 years, the gift will still be valued at $400,000.

Here's the catch: If you don't outlive the trust, the full market value of your house at the time of your death will be counted in your estate. In order for the trust to be valid, you must outlive it, and then either move out of your home or pay your children fair market rent to continue living there, Janko says. While that may not seem ideal, the upside is that the rent you pay will reduce your estate further, Levine notes.

**Irrevocable life insurance trust:** An irrevocable life insurance trust (ILIT) can remove your life insurance from your taxable estate, help pay estate costs and provide your heirs with cash for a variety of purposes. To remove the policy from your estate, you surrender ownership rights, which means you may no longer borrow against it or change beneficiaries. In return, the proceeds from the policy may be used to pay any estate costs after you die and provide your beneficiaries with tax-free income. That can be useful in cases where you leave heirs an illiquid asset such as a business. The business might take awhile to sell, and in the meantime your heirs will have to pay operating expenses. If they don't have cash on hand, they might have to have a fire sale just to meet the bills. But proceeds from an ILIT can help tide them over.

**Qualified terminable interest property trust:** If you're part of a family where there have been divorces, remarriages, and step-children, you may want to direct your assets to particular relatives through a qualified terminable interest property (QTIP) trust. Your surviving spouse will receive income from the trust, and the beneficiaries you specify (your children from a first marriage) will get the principal or remainder after your spouse dies. People typically use QTIP trusts to ensure that a fair portion of their wealth ultimately passes to their own children and not someone else's.

Money in a QTIP trust, unlike that in a bypass trust, is treated as part of the surviving spouse's estate and may be subject to estate tax. That's why you should create a bypass trust first, which shelters assets up to the estate-tax exemption, and then if you have assets left over you can put it in a QTIP, Levine says.

## What's the Best Way to Give Money Now?

Giving gifts to family and charity while you're alive can be a boon to them...and your estate.

Estate planning isn't just about how you want your assets distributed after you die. It's about deciding how much you want to give away while you're still alive. If you plan carefully—so you don't outlive your assets—giving allows you to reduce your taxable estate and provide advance help to your beneficiaries.

There are two easy ways to give gifts without incurring the gift tax:

- You may pay an unlimited amount in medical or educational expenses for another person, if you give the money directly to the institutions where the expenses were incurred.

- You may give up to $11,000 a year in cash or assets to as many people as you like.

Anytime you give more than $11,000 annually to any one person you must file a gift-tax return and the excess amount will be applied toward your lifetime gift-tax exclusion of $1 million. If at any point your gifts exceed that exclusion, you will have to pay gift tax on the excess amount. There is some good news in that regard. The top tax rate on gifts is gradually declining from 55 percent in 2001 to 35 percent by 2010.

Keep in mind, too, gifts you give within three years of your death that exceed the lifetime gift-tax exclusion will reduce the amount of money you may leave to your heirs free of federal estate taxes, according to certified public accountant P. Jeffrey Christakos of First Union Securities in Westfield, N.J. For example, if you give away $100,000 more than your lifetime exclusion within three years of your death, your estate tax exemption will be reduced by $100,000.

If you want to invest in a 529 college savings plan for a beneficiary, contributions are treated as gifts. You may put in as much as $55,000 in one year, but that contribution will be treated as if it were being made in $11,000 installments over five years. That means you can't give any more money to that beneficiary tax-free during that five-year period. Should you die before the five years are up, part of the money you gave will be included in your taxable estate, specifically the $55,000 minus $11,000 for each year you were alive.

The tax consequence of making large gifts can get complicated. So if you have a large estate, consult with your financial or tax planner to see how much giving you can do without triggering a big tax bill.

Charitable donations are another way to reduce your estate. By investing in charitable gift funds and community foundations, those donations can stretch beyond your death.

Charitable gift funds, which are offered by Fidelity, Vanguard, and others, permit you to make a tax-deductible donation, grow your investment tax-free, and then direct a contribution—in your name—to nonprofits of your choosing whenever you like.

Community foundations are regionally based charities that take donations of as little as $5,000 in cash, stock, or property. The foundations invest that money, pool the gains, and allocate grants, usually to local nonprofits. In most cases, you may either have the foundation give money to organizations you choose or ask the foundation to locate a worthy recipient for a cause you like.

You also can set up what's known as a charitable lead trust, from which a charity receives the income and your heirs the principal; or a charitable remainder trust, in which your heirs get the income and the charity gets the principal.

# Part Two

# Learning
# about Financial Tools

# Chapter 11

# *What Determines Interest Rates?*

Interest rates can significantly influence people's behavior. When rates decline, homeowners rush to buy new homes and refinance old mortgages; automobile buyers scramble to buy new cars; the stock market soars, and people tend to feel more optimistic about the future.

But even though individuals respond to changes in rates, they may not fully understand what interest rates represent, or how different rates relate to each other. Why, for example, do interest rates increase or decrease? And in a period of changing rates, why are certain rates higher, while others are lower?

To answer these questions, we must separate movements in the general level of interest rates from differences in individual rates. Interest rates rose steadily from 1979 to 1981 and generally fell after that, with a few upward turns to break the downward trend. Because interest rates tend to move together, we can characterize certain periods as times of high or low interest rates. For example, in 1981 the general level of interest rates was higher than the general level in 1993.

However, individual rates tend to differ, even though they are moving in the same general direction. Thus a 30-year Treasury bond may have a higher rate than a 3-month certificate of deposit. Similarly, a mortgage loan may have a lower rate than an automobile loan.

Reprinted from "Points of Interest: What Determines Interest Rates?" an online financial education publication of the Federal Reserve Bank of Chicago, http://www.chicagofed.org, 2006.

These similarities and differences are not determined by luck, coincidence, a world conspiracy of money barons, or even the Federal Reserve. Rather, they are determined by strong, impersonal economic forces in the marketplace, which reflect the personal choices of millions of individual borrowers and lenders.

This chapter is intended to help you better understand interest rates and how they are influenced by these economic forces. The first section, Levels of Interest, examines the forces that determine the general level of rates. This section discusses basic factors of supply and demand for funds and the function of banks and other similar institutions in meeting the needs of savers and borrowers. It also examines other factors such as fiscal policy and the actions of the Federal Reserve System.

The second section, Different Interests, examines the variations among individual rates, explaining why a 6-month Treasury bill may have one rate, business loans another, and home mortgages still a third. This section discusses the unique characteristics of each credit transaction, such as risk, rights, and tax considerations, and how these factors affect the decision-making process of borrowers and lenders.

## Levels of Interest

### The Price of Credit

To understand the economic forces that drive (and sometimes are driven by) interest rates, we first need to define interest rates. An interest rate is a price, and like any other price, it relates to a transaction or the transfer of a good or service between a buyer and a seller. This special type of transaction is a loan or credit transaction, involving a supplier of surplus funds, usually a lender or saver, and a demander of surplus funds, a borrower.

In a loan transaction, the borrower receives funds to use for a period of time, and the lender receives the borrower's promise to pay at some time in the future.

The borrower receives the benefit of the immediate use of funds. The lender, on the other hand, gives up the immediate use of funds, forgoing any current goods or services those funds could purchase. In other words, lenders loan funds they have saved-surplus funds they do not need for purchasing goods or services today.

Because these lenders/savers sacrifice the immediate use of funds, they ask for compensation in addition to the repayment of the funds loaned. This compensation is interest, the price the borrower must pay for the immediate use of the lender's funds. Put more simply, interest rates are the price of credit.

## Supply and Demand

As with any other price in our market economy, interest rates are determined by the forces of supply and demand, in this case, the supply of and demand for credit. If the supply of credit from lenders rises relative to the demand from borrowers, the price (interest rate) will tend to fall as lenders compete to find use for their funds. If the demand rises relative to the supply, the interest rate will tend to rise as borrowers compete for increasingly scarce funds. The principal source of the demand for credit comes from our desire for current spending and investment opportunities.

The principal source of the supply of credit comes from savings, or the willingness of people, firms, and governments to delay spending. Depository institutions such as banks, thrifts, and credit unions, as well as the Federal Reserve, play important roles in influencing the supply of credit.

## The Source of Demand

**Consumption:** At one time or another, virtually all consumers, businesses, and governments demand credit to purchase goods and services for current use. In these loans, borrowers agree to pay interest to a lender/saver because they prefer to have the goods or services now, rather than waiting until some time in the future when, presumably, they would have saved enough for the purchase. To describe this preference for current consumption, economists say that borrowers have a high rate of time preference. Expressed simply, people with high rates of time preference prefer to purchase goods now, rather than wait to purchase future goods—an automobile now rather than an automobile at some time in the future, a current vacation opportunity rather than a future opportunity, and present goods or services rather than those in the future.

Although lenders/savers generally have lower rates of time preference than borrowers, they too tend to prefer current goods and services. As a result, they ask for the payment of interest to encourage the sacrifice of immediate consumption. As a lender/saver, for example, one would prefer not to spend $100 now only if the money was not needed for a current purchase and one could receive more than $100 in the future.

**Investment:** In the use of funds for investment, on the other hand, time preference is not the sole factor. Here consumers, businesses, and governments borrow funds only if they have an opportunity they believe will earn more—that is, create a larger income stream—than they will have to pay on the loan, or than they will receive in some other activity.

Say, for example, a widget manufacturer sees an opportunity to purchase a new machine that can reasonably be expected to earn a 20 percent return, that is, produce income from the manufacture of widgets equal to 20 percent of the cost of the machine. The manufacturer will borrow funds only if they can be obtained at an interest rate less than 20 percent.

What borrowers are willing to pay, then, depends principally on time preferences for current consumption and on the expected rate of return on an investment.

### The Source of Supply

The supply of credit comes from savings—funds not needed or used for current consumption. When we think of savings, most of us think of money in savings accounts, but this is only part of total savings.

All funds not currently used to purchase goods and services are part of total savings. For example, insurance premiums, contributions to pension funds and social security, funds set aside to purchase stocks and bonds, and even funds in our checking accounts are savings.

Since most of us use funds in checking accounts to pay for current consumption, we may not consider them savings. However, funds in checking accounts at any time are considered savings until we transfer them out to pay for goods and services.

Most of us keep our savings in financial institutions like insurance companies and brokerage houses, and in depository institutions such as banks, savings and loan associations, credit unions, and mutual savings banks. These financial institutions then pool the savings and make them available to people who want to borrow.

This process is called financial intermediation. This process of bringing together borrowers and lenders/savers is one of the most important roles that financial institutions perform.

### Bank's and Deposit Creation

Depository institutions, which for simplicity we will call banks, are different from other financial institutions because they offer transaction accounts and make loans by lending deposits. This deposit creation activity, essentially creating money, affects interest rates because these deposits are part of savings, the source of the supply of credit.

Banks create deposits by making loans. Rather than handing cash to borrowers, banks simply increase balances in borrowers' checking accounts. Borrowers can then draw checks to pay for goods and services. This creation of checking accounts through loans is just as much a deposit as one we might make by pushing a ten-dollar bill through the teller's window.

With all of the nation's banks able to increase the supply of credit in this fashion, credit could conceivably expand without limit. Preventing such uncontrolled expansion is one of the jobs of the Federal Reserve System (the Fed), our central bank and monetary authority. The Fed has the responsibility of monitoring and influencing the total supply of money and credit.

## *The General Level of Rates*

The general level of interest rates is determined by the interaction of the supply and demand for credit. When supply and demand interact, they determine a price (the equilibrium price) that tends to be relatively stable. However, we have seen that the price of credit is not necessarily stable, implying that something shifts the supply, the demand, or both. Let's examine several factors that influence these shifts.

**Expected inflation:** As we have already seen, interest rates state the rate at which borrowers must pay future dollars to receive current dollars. Borrowers and lenders, however, are not as concerned about dollars, present or future, as they are about the goods and services those dollars can buy, the purchasing power of money.

Inflation reduces the purchasing power of money. Each percentage point increase in inflation represents approximately a one percent decrease in the quantity of real goods and services that can be purchased with a given number of dollars in the future. As a result, lenders, seeking to protect their purchasing power, add the expected rate of inflation to the interest rate they demand. Borrowers are willing to pay this higher rate because they expect inflation to enable them to repay the loan with cheaper dollars.

If lenders expect, for example, an eight percent inflation rate for the coming year and otherwise desire a four percent return on their loan, they would likely charge borrowers 12 percent, the so-called nominal interest rate (an eight percent inflation premium plus a four percent "real" rate).

Borrowers and lenders tend to base their inflationary expectations on past experiences which they project into the future. When they have experienced inflation for a long time, they gradually build the inflation premium into their rates. Once people come to expect a certain level of inflation, they may have to experience a fairly long period at a different rate of inflation before they are willing to change the inflation premium.

The effect of an inflation premium can be understood by comparing the consumer price index (or CPI) and the constant maturity 3-year Treasury note rate, although one could use almost any inflation measure and interest rate and discern a similar pattern. As inflation rose through the late 1970s, it came to be "expected" by lenders as well as borrowers. This "inflation expectation" can be seen by the fact that investors in Treasury notes were demanding a relatively high inflation premium in the early 1980s, even after inflation reached its apex. This was partially due to the fact that relatively high levels of inflation were fresh in the memories of borrowers and lenders, and there was uncertainty as to how serious policy-makers would be in pursuing lower levels of inflation. In 1984, for example, it took only a slight increase in inflation to cause a relatively rapid increase in interest rates.

For most of the 1980s, inflation was relatively low and interest rates continued their downward trend with the gap between rates and inflation narrowing. As the memory of high inflation receded, so did pressure for a high inflation premium, as indicated by the relatively modest rise in rates when inflation flared in 1990. Inflationary expectations had been reduced, a goal sought by many monetary policy-makers. Indeed, former Fed Chairman Alan Greenspan has stated that price stability would be achieved when the expectation of future price changes plays no role in the decision-making of businesses and households.

**Economic conditions:** All businesses, governmental bodies, and households that borrow funds affect the demand for credit. This demand tends to vary with general economic conditions.

When economic activity is expanding and the outlook appears favorable, consumers demand substantial amounts of credit to finance homes, automobiles, and other major items, as well as to increase current consumption. With this positive outlook, they expect higher incomes and as a result are generally more willing to take on future obligations. Businesses are also optimistic and seek funds to finance the additional production, plants, and equipment needed to supply this increased consumer demand. All of this makes for a relative scarcity of funds, due to increased demand.

On the other hand, when sales are sluggish and the future looks grim, consumers and businesses tend to reduce their major purchases, and lenders, concerned about the repayment ability of prospective borrowers, become reluctant to lend. As a result, both the supply of and demand for credit may fall. Unless they both fall by the same amount, interest rates are affected.

**Federal Reserve actions:** As we have seen, the Fed acts to influence the availability of money and credit by adjusting the level or price of bank reserves. The Fed affects reserves in three ways: by setting reserve requirements that banks must hold, as we discussed earlier; by buying and selling government securities (usually U.S. Treasury bonds) in open market operations; and by setting the "discount rate," which affects the price of reserves banks borrow from the Fed through the "discount window."

These "tools" of monetary policy influence the supply of credit, but do not directly impact the demand for credit. Because the Fed directly affects only one side of the supply and demand relationship, it cannot totally control interest rates. Nevertheless, monetary policy clearly does affect the general level of interest rates.

**Fiscal policy:** Federal, state, and local governments, through their fiscal policy actions of taxation and spending, can affect either the supply of or the demand for credit. If a governmental unit spends less than it takes in from taxes and other sources of revenue, as many have in recent years, it runs a budget surplus, meaning the government has savings. As we have seen, savings are the source of the supply of credit. On the other hand, if a governmental unit spends more than it takes in, it runs a budget deficit, and must borrow to make up the difference. The borrowing increases the demand for credit, contributing to higher interest rates in general.

### Interest Rate Predictions

The level of interest rates influences people's behavior by affecting economic decisions that determine the well-being of the nation: how much people are willing to save, and how much businesses are willing to invest.

With so many important decisions based on the level of interest rates, it is not surprising that people want to know which way rates are going to move. However, with so many diverse elements influencing rates, it is also not surprising that people are not able to predict the direction of these movements precisely.

Even though we are not able to predict accurately and consistently how interest rates will move, these movements are clearly not random. To the contrary, they are strictly controlled by the most calculating master of all—the economic forces of the market.

## Different Interests

As we have seen, certain factors affect the general level of interest rates. But why do the rates vary for different transactions? For example, on a typical day at a local financial institution, a lending officer might approve a $20,000 loan to the local school board for emergency repairs on the school's furnace and charge the board 8 percent interest for the use of the funds. Later, the banker might approve a used-car loan for $4,000, at 11 percent interest, to be paid in three years, and a small business loan for $17,000, at 8.5 percent interest, for a term of four years.

Meanwhile, the bank's investment officer submits a bid for a two-year Treasury note on which the bank wants to receive 6 percent interest, and purchases a 15-year general obligation municipal bond issued by the local city government. The bank will receive 8 percent interest on this bond. At the next desk, the new accounts officer opens an interest-paying checking account, which will pay a customer 1.5 percent interest.

### Credit Transactions

As different as all these transactions may at first appear, they are the same in one respect—they all involve borrowing and lending funds. Each transaction has a lender, who exchanges funds for an asset in the form of an IOU or credit, and a borrower who exchanges the IOU for funds. Because credit, the IOU, is being bought and sold, these are called credit transactions. Most of us can easily see that the loan officer is providing credit—the bank is lending money to the school board, the person buying the used car, and the businessperson.

The other transactions are also credit transactions, although we generally think of them in different terms. We usually refer to the purchase of a Treasury note or a municipal bond as making an investment, but they are credit transactions because the bank is loaning money to the federal and city governments. By investing in the note and bond, the bank makes funds available directly to the government (or indirectly by replacing the previous holder of the government's debt). The bank, in return, receives interest payments from the government.

When the new accounts officer opened the checking account for the customer, the bank gained the use of funds. This, too, is a credit transaction in which the customer is the lender and the bank is the borrower. To compensate for the use of funds, the bank pays interest.

112

### Degrees of Interest

Although all the transactions at the bank that morning were credit transactions, they all involved different interest rates, different prices of credit. As with other prices in a free market system, interest rates are determined by many factors. As we've seen, some factors are more or less the same for all credit transactions. General economic conditions, for example, cause all interest rates to move in the same direction over time.

Other factors vary for different kinds of credit transactions, causing their interest rates to differ at any one time. Here is a list of some of the most important of these factors:

- Different levels and kinds of risk

- Different rights granted to borrowers and lenders

- Different tax considerations

- Let's examine each of these

### Levels of Risk

Risk refers to the chance that something unfavorable may happen. If you go skydiving, the risks you assume are obvious. When you purchase a financial asset, say by lending funds to a corporation by purchasing one of its bonds, you also take a risk—a financial risk. Something unfavorable could happen to your money—you could lose all of it if the company issuing the security goes bankrupt, or you could lose part of it if the asset's price goes down and you have to sell before maturity.

Different people are willing to accept different levels of risk. Some people will not go skydiving under any circumstances, while others will go at the drop of a hat. In credit transactions, too, people are willing to accept different levels of risk. However, most people risk averse; that is, they prefer not to increase risks with their money unless they receive increased compensation.

To illustrate, let's say we have choice of buying two debt securities, which are bonds or IOUs issued by corporations or governments seeking to borrow funds. One security pays (meaning, we will receive) a certain five percent interest, while the other has a 50 percent chance of paying eight percent interest and a 50 percent chance of paying two percent. Which security should we buy? If we risk averse investors/lenders, we would choose the security paying the certain five percent, because would not view the uncertainty return on the second security as advantage.

If, on the other hand, the second security has a 50 percent chance paying 15 percent interest and 50 percent chance of paying two percent, we might be inclined to buy it because we might consider the higher potential return to be worth the risk.

Even though lenders are willing to accept different levels of risk, they want to be compensated for taking the risk. Therefore, as securities differ in level of risk, their interest rates tend to differ. Generally, interest rates on debt securities are affected by three kinds of risk:

- Default risk

- Liquidity risk

- Maturity risk

### *Default Risk*

For any number of reasons, even the most well-intentioned borrowers may not be able to make interest payments or repay borrowed funds on time. If borrowers do not make timely payments, they are said to have defaulted on loans. When borrowers do not make interest payments, lenders' returns (the interest they receive) are reduced or wiped out completely; when borrowers do not repay all or part of the principal, the lenders' return is actually negative.

All loans are subject to default risk since borrowers may die, go bankrupt, or be faced with unforeseen problems that prevent payments. Of course, default risk varies with different people and companies; nevertheless, no one is free from risk of default.

While investors/lenders accept this risk when they loan funds, they prefer to reduce the risk. As a result, many borrowers are compelled to secure their loans; meaning, they give the lender some assurances against default. Frequently, these assurances are in the form of collateral, some physical object the lender can possess and then sell in the event of default. For automobile loans, for example, the car usually serves as collateral. Other assurances could include a cosigner, another person willing to make payment if the original borrower defaults. Generally speaking, because secured loans are comparatively less risky, they carry a lower interest rate than unsecured loans.

As a borrower, the federal government offers firm assurances against default. As a result of the power to tax and authority to coin money, payments of principal and interest on loans made to (or securities purchased from) the U.S. government are, for all practical purposes, never in doubt, making U.S. government securities virtually default-risk free. Since investors tend to be risk averse and U.S. government securities are all but free from default risk, they generally carry a lower interest rate than securities from corporations.

Similarly, other types of borrowers represent different levels of risk to the lender. In each case, the lender needs to evaluate what are commonly called "the three Cs" of character, capital, and capacity. Character represents the borrower's history with previous loans. A history containing bankruptcies, repossessions, consistently late or missed payments, and court judgments may indicate a higher risk potential for the lender. Capital represents current financial condition. Is the borrower currently debt-free, or relatively so in comparison with assets? They may represent a party with "thrifty" habits, who can take on additional debt without imposing an undue burden on other assets. Capacity represents the future ability to service the loan, that is, make principal and interest payments. Income, job stability, regular promotions, and raises are all indicators to be considered.

### Liquidity Risk

In addition to default risk, liquidity risk affects interest rates. If a security can be quickly sold at close to its original purchase price, it is highly liquid; meaning, it is less costly to convert into money than one that cannot be sold at a price close to its purchase price. Therefore, it is less risky than one with a wide spread between its purchase price and its selling price.

To illustrate, let's say that we have a choice between purchasing an infrequently traded security of an obscure company, and a broadly traded security of a well-known company, which we know we can sell easily at a price close to our purchase price. If we are risk averse, we would choose the security from the well-known company if both were paying the same interest rate.

To encourage us to buy its security, the obscure company must pay a higher rate to compensate us for the difficulty we will experience if we want to sell.

### Maturity Risk

Credit transactions usually involve lending/borrowing funds for an agreed upon period of time. At the end of that time the loan is said to have matured and must be repaid. The length of maturity is a source of another kind of risk-maturity risk.

Long-term securities are subject to more risk than short-term securities because the future is uncertain and more problems can arise the longer the security is outstanding. These greater risks usually, but not always, result in higher rates for long-term securities than for short-term securities.

To illustrate, let's examine U.S. government securities—Treasury bills (with original maturities of one year or less), Treasury notes (with original maturities of two to ten years), and Treasury bonds (with original maturities of over ten years). These securities are quite similar, except in length of maturity. As we have seen, U.S. government securities are virtually default-risk free, and because there is such a large and active market for them, they are also virtually liquidity-risk free.

If default and liquidity were the only kinds of risk in holding government securities, we would be inclined to think that they all would have the same interest rate. However, because of maturity risk, short-term Treasury bills usually pay less (have a lower interest rate) than longer-term Treasury notes and bonds.

### Tax Considerations

In addition to the level and kinds of risk and the different rights granted by different debt securities, taxes also play a significant role in affecting rates of return.

To illustrate, let's say you borrow $1,000 for a year at 10 percent interest. At the end of the year, you pay the $1,000 principal plus $100 interest. However, if the lender is in a 25 percent tax bracket, the lender will pay $25 in taxes on that $100. Thus, the lender's actual after-tax yield is reduced from 10 percent to 7.5 percent.

Different debt securities carry different tax considerations. Corporate bonds (loans to corporations) are subject to local, state, and federal taxes. U.S. government securities are subject to federal taxes, but exempt from local and state taxes. Municipal bonds are exempt from federal taxes, and in some states, exempt from local taxes.

Taking taxes into consideration, a lender will receive more after-tax interest income from a municipal bond paying 10 percent than from a corporate bond paying the same rate. This special tax-exempt status of municipal bonds enables state and local governments to raise funds at a relatively lower interest cost.

On the other hand, for corporations to attract lenders, they must pay a higher rate of interest to compensate for taxes.

## Different Rights

Risk is not the only reason credit transactions can have different rates of interest. As we have seen, certain assurances, such as securing loans, also affect rates. Typically, borrowers write these assurances into their debt securities specifying the rights of both borrower and lender. Because these rights differ, debt securities tend to pay different rates of interest. Let's look at some of these rights in the more common debt securities.

**Coupon and zero-coupon bonds:** Most debt securities promise to repay the amount borrowed (the principal) at the end of the length of the loan, and also pay interest at specified times, such as every six months, throughout the term of the loan. Some of these bonds are issued with attached coupons, which lenders can clip and send every six months or year to collect the interest that is due.

Zero-coupon bonds, however, make no interest payments throughout the life of the loan. Rather than pay interest, these bonds are sold at a price well below their stated face value. Although not usually thought of in such terms, a savings bond is like a zero-coupon bond in that it renders one payment at maturity.

Even though zero-coupon bonds make no interest payments, investors/lenders still need to know the return on these bonds so they can compare it to the return on a coupon bond or other alternative investment. To figure the return, or yield, investors compare the difference between their purchase price and selling price.

Since zero-coupon bonds provide lenders no compensation until the end of the loan period, borrowers issuing these bonds tend to pay a higher rate than borrowers issuing coupon bonds.

**Convertible bonds:** Some borrowers sell bonds that can be converted into a fixed number of shares of common stock. With convertible bonds, a lender (bondholder) can become a part owner (stockholder) of the company by converting the bond into the company's stock. Because investors generally view this right as desirable, borrowers can sell convertible bonds at a lower interest rate than they would otherwise have to pay for a similar bond that was not convertible.

**Call provisions:** Some bonds are callable after a specified date; that is, the borrower has the right to pay off part or all of it before the scheduled maturity date. Unlike convertible bonds which give certain rights to the lenders, call provisions give borrowers certain rights, the right to call the bond. As a result, borrowers must pay a higher interest rate than on similar securities without a call provision.

Of course, borrowers will call (redeem) only when it is to their benefit. For example, when the general level of interest rates falls, the borrower can call the bonds paying high rates of interest and re-borrow funds at the lower rate.

As partial compensation to the lender, the borrower often has to pay a penalty to call a bond. Naturally, a borrower will call a bond only if the advantages of doing so outweigh the penalty. In other words, interest rates would have to fall sufficiently to compensate for the penalty before a borrower would call a bond.

**Municipal bonds:** Municipal bonds are debt securities issued by local and state governments. Usually these governmental bodies issue either general obligation bonds or revenue bonds.

General obligation bonds, the more common type, are issued for a wide variety of reasons, such as building schools and providing social services. They are secured by the general taxing power of the issuing government.

Revenue bonds, on the other hand, are issued to finance a specific project-building a tollway, for example. The interest and principal are paid exclusively out of the receipts that the project generates.

Both kinds of municipal bonds are considered safe. However, because general obligation bonds are secured by the assets of the issuing government and the power of that government to tax, they are usually considered safer than revenue bonds, whose payments must come out of receipts of the specific project for which the bond is issued. As a result, general obligation bonds usually pay a lower rate of interest than revenue bonds.

### *Efficient Allocation*

With so many different interest rates and so many different factors affecting them, it may seem that borrowing and lending would be hopelessly complicated and inefficient. In reality, however, the variety of interest rates reflects the efficiency of the market in allocating funds.

In analyzing investment opportunities, lenders look for an interest rate high enough to account for all their risks, rights, and taxes, as we have discussed. If the project will not pay that rate, they will look for other investments. For their part, borrowers will undertake only projects with returns high enough to cover at least the cost of borrowed funds.

The market, then, serves to assure that only worthwhile projects will be funded with borrowed funds. In other words, market forces and differences in interest rates work together to foster the efficient allocation of funds.

# Chapter 12

# *Cash Investments*

At times, depending on what's going on with the markets, the economy and interest rates, you might hear some financial gurus warn, "Cash is trash!" Other times, these market mavens might proclaim, "Cash is king!" In fact, it's not unusual to hear both points of view at the same time.

One thing's for sure right now—after years of relentless tightening by the Federal Reserve, money market yields are more attractive than they've been in a long, long time. So, is cash royalty or refuse—or neither? As usual, the answer depends on your situation and financial goals.

### What is cash?

In an investment context, cash usually means cash equivalents such as money market funds, Treasury bills (T-bills), short-term corporate commercial paper, and overnight government repurchase agreements. There are also near-cash investments such as short-term certificates of deposit (CDs), ultra-short bond funds, and stable value funds.

### Why hold cash?

Let's look at three broad reasons for maintaining a cash position as part of your financial plan.

"What about Cash?" by Rande Spiegleman. Copyright 2007 Charles Schwab & Co., Inc. Reprinted with permission.

**Reason No. 1: Liquidity.** Apart from day-to-day expenses, which you typically pay from current cash flow, the need for liquidity generally falls into two categories:

- Emergencies (health problems, you lose your job, etc.)
- Known obligations coming due in the next one to three years

For emergency funds, we recommend setting aside cash equal to three to six months of after-tax income. The amount that's right for you depends on your job outlook and other sources of income and credit.

Once you decide how much to set aside for emergencies, including that cash in your portfolio allocation is up to you. Your emergency cash reserve may be larger than your portfolio's targeted cash allocation, in which case you'll need to keep at least some cash outside your investment portfolio. On the other hand, if your portfolio is big enough, you could choose to include your emergency reserve within your targeted cash allocation. Either way, the key is safety and liquidity in case of emergency.

Unlike your emergency reserve, which you maintain "just in case," think about cash set aside to cover known obligations as money that's already spent. Known obligations that you might pay from cash reserves (instead of current salary or other monthly income) can include quarterly estimated income taxes, property taxes, a down payment on a home, your child's wedding, college bills, a vacation, and so on.

Liquidity is extremely important here—don't invest money reserved for short-term obligations in the market. Instead, keep it in cash or near-cash investments.

*Liquidity for retirees:* Retirees typically have special liquidity needs. For example, the need for emergency funds may go away—if you're no longer working, there's no need to plan for the possibility of losing your job. However, you may want to set aside enough cash to cover at least 12 months' living expenses. Think of it as a "known obligation."

Beyond that, it's not a bad idea to keep another two to four years' worth of expenses in near-cash investments (short-term bonds, ultra-short bond funds, CDs, etc.) as part of the fixed income portion of your retirement portfolio. That way, when a bear market comes along, you could avoid having to liquidate other assets during the worst possible time, assuming the bear market doesn't last more than a few years.

**Reason No. 2: Flexibility.** By holding a percentage of your portfolio in cash, you can take advantage of investment opportunities as they arise. For example, a cash allocation may come in handy if you wish to slightly overweight or underweight certain asset classes in your portfolio based on your outlook for the markets.

We're not talking about market timing or even large, tactical shifts between stocks, bonds, and cash. The odds against being consistently right are too great to make such a huge bet. However, by shifting your asset allocation 5% to 10% one way or the other, you may be able to add value when you're right—without derailing your long-term goals if you're wrong.

In addition, a cash allocation can provide flexibility when it's time to rebalance your portfolio and/or pay investment fees.

**Reason No. 3: Stability.** Bonds have been the traditional choice for reducing a portfolio's overall risk. Bonds tend to perform differently than stocks in the same market conditions—sometimes moving in the opposite direction.

Historically, however, cash is even less correlated with stocks. What's more, cash is far less volatile than bonds on average. The big advantage of bonds, of course, is the potential for higher income. That said, in the appropriate proportion, cash can stabilize your portfolio over time.

### *Where should you keep your cash?*

Whatever your reasons for holding cash, you need a good place to park it. That does NOT include under the mattress or in a big safe. Physical cash earns no interest and can be stolen or destroyed.

Table 12.1 summarizes various ways to invest your cash, from lowest to highest generally expected yield.

## *The Bottom Line*

- **Checking, savings,** and **money market accounts** are good for day-to-day expenses as well as your emergency reserve.

- **Shorter-term CDs** and **T-bills** can be used as part of your strategic cash allocation and are also good for known obligations coming due in the next three to 12 months.

- **Longer-term CDs, ultra-short bond funds** and **stable value funds** can be used as part of your strategic cash allocation and are good for known obligations coming due within one to three years.

121

**Table 12.1.** Smart ways to invest your cash

| Investment | Liquidity | Value | Credit quality |
|---|---|---|---|
| Checking and savings accounts | Immediate | Stable | FDIC insured |
| Money market funds | Immediate (may be limits on writing checks) | Stable | Not FDIC insured |
| Position-traded money market funds | Generally available day after sale | Stable | Not FDIC insured |
| T-bills | Available at maturity | Fluctuates prior to maturity | Backed by U.S. Treasury |
| Certificates of Deposit (CDs) | Penalties for early withdrawal | Stable | FDIC insured |
| Ultra-short bond funds | Generally available day after sale | Fluctuates | Subject to bonds in portfolio (look for overall credit rating of A or better) |
| Stable value funds* | Generally available day after sale, may have short-term redemption fees | Stable | Subject to bonds in portfolio and insurance provider (look for companies rated A or better) |

*Stable value funds (sometimes called capital preservation funds) are found in many 401(k) plans. These funds typically invest in high-quality bonds with short-term maturities, and seek to maintain a stable net asset value through the use of insurance contracts. Therefore, all else being equal, it's reasonable to expect this type of fund to have a yield less than bonds of similar quality and duration (you're paying for protection against price volatility), but higher than what you might expect from an average money market fund. Typically, stable value funds have a short-term redemption fee similar to the premature withdrawal penalty on CDs.

The right choices for you, and the extent to which you include some or all of your cash in your portfolio, will depend on your particular situation and preferences.

In any event, try not to take the perennial debate over whether cash is "king" or "trash" too seriously. Cash is simply a tool—one that comes in pretty handy when you need it, so manage it with care.

## *About Information from Charles Schwab*

Investors should consider carefully information contained in the prospectus, including investment objectives, risks, charges, and expenses. You can request a prospectus by calling Schwab at 800-435-4000. Please read the prospectus carefully before investing.

Investment value will fluctuate, and shares, when redeemed, may be worth more or less than original cost.

An investment in a money market fund is not insured or guaranteed by the FDIC (Federal Deposit Insurance Corporation) or any other government agency. Although money market funds seek to preserve the value of your investment at $1 per share, it is possible to lose money by investing in these funds.

A stable value fund is not a mutual fund and its units are not registered under the Securities Act of 1933 or the Investment Company Act of 1940, as amended, or other applicable law, and unit holders are not entitled to the protection of these Acts. Stable value funds are not FDIC insured. The unit value of these funds may fluctuate and investors may lose money.

The information presented does not consider your particular investment objectives or financial situation and does not make personalized recommendations. This information should not be construed as an offer to sell or a solicitation of an offer to buy any security. The investment strategies and the securities shown may not be suitable for you. We believe the information provided is reliable, but Charles Schwab & Co., Inc. ("Schwab") and its affiliates do not guarantee its accuracy, timeliness, or completeness. Any opinions expressed herein are subject to change without notice.

# Chapter 13

# *Investing in Bonds*

Generally, "savers" and "investors" have different objectives for their money. "Savers" plan to use their money in the next 3–5 years, while "investors" won't need their money for five years or longer. Many "savers" want liquidity or quick access to their money without penalty. Bonds provide a desirable saving or investment vehicle for many reasons. Bonds tend to be safer than stocks because if you hold bonds until the maturity date, you don't risk the principal. Plus, bonds can provide a regular, steady source of income (typically, interest payments are received every six months). For the long term, investors need to be willing to "tie up" money when investing in bonds. However, bonds tend to have a lower return than stocks over the long term.

## *Owner vs. Loaner*

Investment securities usually involve two types of securities—those where the investor is an owner or those where the investor is a loaner. Owner securities include stocks, real estate, equity unit investment trusts, equity mutual funds, collectibles, business ownership, and commodities.

Loaner assets are certificates of deposit, U.S. Treasury securities, municipal bonds, corporate bonds, convertible bonds, zero-coupon bonds, bond unit investment trusts, bond mutual funds, mortgage-backed

---

"All About Money: Investing in Bonds," by Ruth Anne Mears. © 2001 Ohio State University Extension. Reprinted with permission.

securities, collateralized mortgage obligations, fixed annuities, preferred stock, and guaranteed investment contracts.[1]

## What Is a Bond?

A bond represents a loan obligation of the bond issuer (government, corporation, or individual) to the bondholder or investor. In essence, the investor loans funds to the bond issuer in exchange for interest payments for a set period of time. At the end of this time the borrower (bond issuer) pays the investor (bond holder/loaner) back the money loaned. A certificate of deposit is an example of a bond. A consumer goes to the bank and gives the bank money. In turn, the bank pays the consumer interest for the use of that money for a specified period. Then, the bank uses that money to invest in other projects, such as, small businesses or home mortgages.

## Bond Terminology

Face value or par value is the value of the bond (amount of principal) printed on the certificate and received at maturity. If interest rates change and you need to sell Bond A before maturity, the value you receive may change. If interest rates increase, Bond A may sell at a discount or less than the face value. In this case, investors can buy Bond B paying higher rates so they are not as interested in this Bond A. If interest rates decrease, Bond A may sell at a premium because other investors would be willing to pay more for the higher interest rate on Bond A. See the example at the end of this chapter.

Coupon rate (also known as coupon, coupon yield, stated interest rate) is the interest rate printed on the bond certificate when the bond is issued. It usually is stated as an annual fixed rate typically paid every six months to the investor.

Maturity date is the day when the face amount of the bond must be repaid and the debt retired. The coupon rate remains the same until the maturity date. Bond maturities may run from a few months to 40 years.

A call feature allows the issuing agency to pay the investor the face amount for the bond and buy back the bond before maturity. This allows the issuer to then reissue the bond at lower interest rates. In the event a bond is called, investors may then need to reinvest their money at lower interest rates as well. This results in reinvestment rate risk.

Default is the failure of the issuer of the bond to make payment on the interest or money borrowed. Thus, the investor can lose money.

Tax-equivalent yield—If you are buying municipal bonds for the state in which you live, the interest may be free of federal, state, and local income taxes. (You still may have to pay capital gain taxes if you sell the bonds at a premium.) These income tax-exempt bonds are appropriate for investors with marginal tax rates of 28% or higher. There are charts that compare taxable and tax-free yields for different marginal tax rates. Refer to the following website for this type of chart: http://www.bondmarkets.com.

## Different Types of Bonds

The following bonds are listed in order of risk. Those listed first have the least risk.

**U.S. government bonds:** The United States Treasury sells bonds to finance the federal government. Because the U.S. government has never failed to pay its debt, these bonds are considered to be some of the safest you can buy. Savings bonds can be bought with small dollar amounts ($25) and new inflation-indexed bonds (I-bonds) help protect against inflation. Information about these bonds can be found on the following website: http://www.savingsbonds.gov or call 800-722-2678. Consumers can also purchase some U.S. bonds through brokers and banks or directly through the Federal Reserve Banks.

**Mortgage-backed securities:** Government agencies also sell bonds. Listed in order of safety, Ginnie Mae, Freddie Macs, and Fannie Maes are federal government agency home mortgages, which are lower risk but not as low risk as U.S. Treasuries. These bonds have uncertain maturities because people pay back mortgages before the end of the mortgage. All have irregular monthly payments that may include both interest and principal.

**Municipal bonds:** State and local governments and government-related agencies (schools, water, bridge, highway authorities) sell bonds to raise money for a variety of purposes. After U.S. Treasuries, municipal bonds are considered the safest. Depending on the reason for selling bonds, there are different types of municipal bonds. In order of safety, these bonds are: general obligation, revenue, equipment, debenture. Bonds for private purposes (sports stadiums, airports, hospitals, industrial parks) may not be income tax-exempt.

**Corporate bonds:** Corporations sell bonds to raise money for major projects. Corporate bonds pay higher interest because corporations cannot tax to raise money. Corporate bonds have no income tax advantages, thus, usually have higher yields; whereas, U.S. Treasuries are not taxed by state and local government. Some municipal bonds are free from federal income tax and may not be taxed by state and local governments.

**Specialty bonds:** Variable rate bonds, CMOs (collateralized mortgage obligations),[2] convertible bonds, and zero-coupon bonds are some examples of specialty bonds. Zero-coupon bonds are bought at a discount. At maturity the face value of a zero-coupon bond is more than the issued purchased price. However, there are no interest payments made to the investor. The value of the bond increases each year. Even if the interest is not received by the investor, the interest is taxable as current income (unless zeros qualify as tax-free bonds).

## How to Buy Bonds

When buying bonds, consider five factors: your investment objective, laddering of bond (spreading out maturity), diversification, bond yield, and bond risks. Bonds provide income through interest and some safety of the principal invested.

### Investment Objective

Bonds should fit your investment objective which is income and safety of principal. If you are looking for long-term growth, bonds do not match your objective. However, if your objective is safety of principal and you want to earn current income from your money, bonds would match your objective. For example, a major objective of someone over 70 is to live off his/her investments and not lose money in case he/she may need money for health care. Although this individual may live 30 more years, a portion of his/her retirement money might be invested for growth in stocks but a majority should probably be invested for income in bonds that mature at different times so the principal would be available without loss.

### Laddering

When buying several bonds, buy at different maturity levels. This is known as laddering. For example, buy a 2-year bond maturing in 2008, a 3-year bond maturing in 2009, 4-year bond maturing in 2010, and a 5-year bond maturing in 2011. When the 2-year bond matures in 2008, buy another bond maturing in 2012. That way you will have a bond maturing in each year and if you need money, you won't need to sell a bond at a reduced price (discount) before maturity.

## *Diversification*

Bonds can provide diversification to an investor's holdings. Stocks and bonds tend to move in opposite directions. When the stock prices go up, bonds go down; when bonds go up, stocks go down. Over the long haul, this low correlation between stocks and bonds permits a portfolio to even out the highs and lows and can result in an overall higher return.

## *Bond Yield*

Compare the yields of bonds to see the best return.

- **Yield to maturity** is one way to compare bonds on the basis of time. This yield measures the bond's return when purchased (at par, discounted, premium) and held to maturity. The change in current income generated by the bond (interest) and as well as any change in its principal when it is held to maturity is "yield to maturity." However, this yield does not indicate which bonds are more likely to have price fluctuations and may not provide the best comparison of bonds with different maturities and different coupons. (See "duration" below.)

- **Yield to call** expresses the return to the call date considering any premium paid for the bond when called and the premium or discount paid for bonds when purchased. It may be higher or lower than the yield to maturity. As an investor, you are required to return bonds when called. A bond might be recalled if the bond issuer could refinance the debt at lower interest rates.

- **Duration** will compare bonds with different coupons and different terms to maturity. It reflects the average time it takes to collect a bond's interest and principal repayment. This is a weighted average that encompasses the total amount of the bond's payments and their timing and then standardizes for the bond's price.[3] Higher duration indicates bonds more sensitive to interest rate changes. Bonds with shorter duration reduce risk associated with interest rates. If Bond A has a duration of 5.4 years and Bond B has a duration of 6.2 years, the second bond has more risk. So, a conservative investor will want Bond A with the lower duration and a more aggressive investor, interested in capitalizing on the bond's price fluctuations, will desire Bond B with the higher duration. Durations can be used to compare bond mutual funds to see which funds will have more volatility if interest rates change.

## Bond Risks

The risks associated with bonds are tied to several factors. There are interest-rate risk, credit risk, callability risk, reinvestment rate risk, and inflation risk. The safest bonds are short-term (less than 5 years) Treasury Bills followed by other short-term government bonds. The riskiest bonds are long-term bonds (12–40 years), junk bonds, and high yield, or high return bonds.

**The longer the maturity of bonds, the greater the interest (coupon) rate risk** while shorter term bonds have less risk but lower returns.

- Short-term bonds mature in 5 years or less.

- Intermediate bonds mature between 5 and 12 years.

- Long-term bonds have maturity dates of more than 12 years.

Investors need to consider their time frame to choose bonds that fit their needs. If an 80-year-old buys a 30-year bond, she faces interest rate risk. Within 30 years interest rates could change dramatically. If the bond pays 6% interest, and interest rates climb to 12%, chances are you could lose money to inflation and could be making more money elsewhere over 30 years.

**Risk is also associated with the coupon or interest rate** on the bond. Bonds with lower interest rates will experience more fluctuations in bond prices than bonds with higher interest rates. If you have two bonds maturing in 30 years and Bond A pays 5% in interest and Bond B pays 15% in interest, Bond A's price will change more dramatically than Bond B's price. The principal value will have wider swings in its price if sold before the maturity date. Junk bonds and zero-coupon bonds will experience wider changes in prices. These changes in a bond's price will be reflected on broker statements, but are only realized if the bond is sold.

**Ratings on bonds also reflect assumed risk.** Credit rating systems help consumers make more informed bond purchases from firms, individuals, and state and local governments. Higher rated bonds carry less risk while lower rated bonds (for example, junk bonds or high yield/high return bonds) have more risk. During good economic times, junk bonds are safer than during poor economic conditions. Moody's Bond Ratings and Standard & Poor's Bond Ratings include investment grade or safer bonds as anything rated triple-B or above—(Aaa,AAA; Aa,AA; A,A; Bbb,BBB) while those ratings below the triple-B—(Ba,BB; B,B; Ccc,CCC; Cc,CC; C,C; D) carry higher risk of default. Junk bonds and high-yield securities are below the triple-B ratings and have higher risk.

**Bonds can be called.** Bonds may have call dates that protect the issuer from paying high interest rates if they can refinance and pay lower rates. If you hold a bond, it can be called back by the company issuing it. The company will pay you a predetermined amount to do this. You run the risk of having to reinvest your money at lower interest rates. This is a type of reinvestment rate risk.

## Individual Bonds vs. Bond Mutual Funds

Investors have the choice of buying individual or bond mutual funds. There are advantages and disadvantages of each way of adding bonds to your portfolio.

**Individual bonds:** Many investors purchase U.S. Savings Bonds. These are a very safe investment but sometimes they do not keep up with the cost of inflation. When buying municipal or corporate bonds, you need to purchase several different individual bonds to protect against business and financial risk. This requires a large sum of money for a beginning investor. If you hold bonds to maturity, you won't lose the principal of individual bonds. For the beginning investor, a bond mutual fund or a balance mutual fund (which holds both stock and bonds) is a good place to start.

**Bond mutual funds:** Risk in bond funds is determined by the credit ratings of the bonds held, the duration of the bonds held (or the average maturity), and the variability of interest rates. The longer the average maturity, the more risky the fund is or the higher the duration, then the riskier the fund. Advantages of buying bond mutual funds are that they:

- can reinvest dividends which can't be done with individual bonds,

- can invest small sums of money and make small, regular contributions,

- can withdraw portions of invested money if forced to sell bonds before maturity,

- can help investors speculate on a decline in interest rates, and

- can achieve diversification for a small amount of money.

Bond funds provide flexibility in buying and selling for small investors. If you want all your capital back, then buy individual bonds. Fees are a factor in bond mutual funds, so carefully read the mutual fund prospectus to identify the fees charged. Bond mutual funds do not guarantee a return of the money invested.

## *Advantages and Disadvantages of Investing in Bonds[4]*

*Advantages of Bonds*

- Bonds pay higher interest rates than savings accounts.

- Bonds usually offer a relatively safe return of principal.

- Bonds often have less volatility (price fluctuations) than stocks, especially short-term bonds.

- Bonds offer regular income.

- Bonds are sold in small dollar amounts (U.S. Savings Bonds— $25, $50).

- Bonds need less careful attention in management than other alternative investments.

- Bond interest from municipal bonds can be exempt from federal income taxes and possibly from state and local income taxes.

*Disadvantages of Bonds*

- Bonds offer no hedge against inflation because inflation causes interest rates to rise which then causes bond prices to fall.

- Bond prices can be quite volatile because market interest rates vary after a bond is issued.

- Bonds over the long term have lower returns than stocks.

- Bond prices may swing 20% or more if selling bonds before maturity. Speculators might see this as an opportunity but conservative investors will need to ignore price changes if planning to hold to maturity.

- Individual bonds do not compound their interest. However, this is possible with bond mutual funds.

- Taxes will be owed on capital gains/losses (selling before maturity) and interest unless the bonds are tax-exempt.

- Diversification is hard to achieve (unless investing in bond mutual funds) because at $1,000 for each bond, many different types of bonds would be needed.

In conclusion, bonds are a good way to diversify a portfolio and help to meet investors' income objectives.

## Example

See how much you understand by trying to answer the questions about the example given in Table 13.1. Choose which bond to buy. It is now the year 2001.

**Table 13.1.** Example Bonds

| Description | Price | Callable | YTM or YTC | Rating |
|---|---|---|---|---|
| **Bond A** 7.75% due 04/15/24 Semiannual Interest Payments MBIA Insured (Min. $5,000 principal) | $997.50 | 04/15/04 @103.751 | 7.773% YTM | AAA/Aaa |
| **Bond B** 8.625% Due 08/01/20 Semiannual Interest Payments (Min. $5,000 principal) | $1016.25 | 08/01/05 @100.00 | 8.116% YTC | A/A |

Comparing the two bonds in Table 13.1:

1. How much would you receive in interest payments for the year for Bond A and Bond B?

2. What are the maturity dates of Bond A and Bond B?

3. Which bonds are insured—Bond A and/or Bond B?

4. Which bond is selling at a premium and which bond is selling at a discount?

5. Can these bonds be called and if so, when? When they are called, do you get the face value?

6. If the coupon rate on Bond A is 7.75%, why is the yield to maturity (YTM) 7.773%?

7. If the coupon rate on Bond B is 8.625%, and it sold for a premium, why is the yield to call (YTC) 8.116%?

8. Which bond would you buy?

### Answers to Questions

1. Bond A will pay $77.50 yearly for every $1,000 purchased. With a minimum investment of $5,000 you would receive $387.50. If you purchased bonds worth $10,000 you would receive $775 divided into two semiannual payments. For Bond B the interest would be $86.25 for every $1,000 owned. For the minimum of $5,000, an investor would receive $431.25 a year.

2. Bond A matures on April 15, 2024, while Bond B matures on August 1, 2020. Both are long-term bonds which are considered more risky than short-term bonds (matures in 5 years or less).

3. Bond A indicates it is insured and Bond B does not indicate any insurance. This insurance means if the company issuing Bond A goes bankrupt, you will receive your principal back from the insurer.

4. Bond B is selling at a premium of $16.25 over a face value of $1,000. Bond A is selling at a discount of $2.50 under a face value of $1,000. The reason for this is the interest rate or coupons on Bonds A and B. B pays a higher interest rate while A is paying a rate lower than market rates. These are not newly issued bonds which sell at the face value.

5. Yes, both bonds can be called. Bond B can be called in 2005 at face value or $1,000 for each $1,000 invested. Bond A can be called in 2004 at more than face value $1,037.51 for each $1000 owned.

6. Yield to Maturity (YTM) on Bond A is 7.773% or more than the 7.75% interest paid. The reason for this is you bought the bond at a discount so you paid less than $1,000 and the $2.50 increase in value of the bond is added to the interest you have received since that time. That discount increases the yield you will receive.

7. When this bond is called you will receive the face value of $1,000 yet you paid a premium of $1,016.25 so you have lost $16.25. That loss is added to the interest paid 8.625% and it lowers your return to 8.116%.

8. It depends on how much risk you are willing to assume. Bond A is the safer bond, is insured, is highly rated, but has a lower interest rate. It is a long-term bond and it is callable within a few years. Bond B has a lower credit rating, is not insured, but has a higher interest payment. If interest rates rise, the face value of this bond will drop. If interest rates drop, this bond will sell at an even higher premium. Conservative investors will probably like Bond A, while aggressive investors thinking that rates will drop within the next 4 years might speculate on Bond B hoping to sell at an even higher premium.

## Notes

1. *Investing for Your Future*, A Cooperative Extension System Basic Investing Home Study Course, February 2000, Rutgers Cooperative Extension.

2. CMOs are collateralized mortgage obligations and will pay back interest and a portion of principle. These are sometimes included in retirement plan options.

3. Mayo, Herbert. *Investments: An Introduction*. The Dryden Press, 1993.

4. Quinn, Jane Bryant. *Making the Most of Your Money*. Simon & Schuster, 1997, Chapter 25, How to Use Bonds.

# Chapter 14

# *Certificates of Deposit (CDs)*

Investors searching for relatively low-risk investments that can easily be converted into cash often turn to certificates of deposit (CDs). A CD is a special type of deposit account with a bank or thrift institution that typically offers a higher rate of interest than a regular savings account. Unlike other investments, CDs feature federal deposit insurance up to $100,000.

Here's how CDs work: When you purchase a CD, you invest a fixed sum of money for fixed period of time—six months, one year, five years, or more—and, in exchange, the issuing bank pays you interest, typically at regular intervals. When you cash in or redeem your CD, you receive the money you originally invested plus any accrued interest. But if you redeem your CD before it matures, you may have to pay an "early withdrawal" penalty or forfeit a portion of the interest you earned.

Although most investors have traditionally purchased CDs through local banks, many brokerage firms and independent salespeople now offer CDs. These individuals and entities—known as "deposit brokers"—can sometimes negotiate a higher rate of interest for a CD by promising to bring a certain amount of deposits to the institution. The deposit broker can then offer these "brokered CDs" to their customers.

At one time, most CDs paid a fixed interest rate until they reached maturity. But, like many other products in today's markets, CDs have become more complicated. Investors may now choose among variable rate CDs, long-term CDs, and CDs with other special features.

"Certificates of Deposit: Tips for Investors," U.S. Securities and Exchange Commission (www.sec.gov), June 2005.

Some long-term, high-yield CDs have "call" features, meaning that the issuing bank may choose to terminate—or call—the CD after only one year or some other fixed period of time. Only the issuing bank may call a CD, not the investor. For example, a bank might decide to call its high-yield CDs if interest rates fall. But if you've invested in a long-term CD and interest rates subsequently rise, you'll be locked in at the lower rate.

Before you consider purchasing a CD from your bank or brokerage firm, make sure you fully understand all of its terms. Carefully read the disclosure statements, including any fine print. And don't be dazzled by high yields. Ask questions—and demand answers—before you invest. These tips can help you assess what features make sense for you:

- **Find out when the CD matures:** As simple as this sounds, many investors fail to confirm the maturity dates for their CDs and are later shocked to learn that they've tied up their money for five, ten, or even twenty years. Before you purchase a CD, ask to see the maturity date in writing.

- **Investigate any call features:** Callable CDs give the issuing bank the right to terminate—or "call"—the CD after a set period of time. But they do not give you that same right. If interest rates fall, the issuing bank might call the CD. In that case, you should receive the full amount of your original deposit plus any unpaid accrued interest. But you'll have to shop for a new one with a lower rate of return. Unlike the bank, you can never "call" the CD and get your principal back. So if interest rates rise, you'll be stuck in a long-term CD paying below-market rates. In that case, if you want to cash out, you will lose some of your principal. That's because your broker will have to sell your CD at a discount to attract a buyer. Few buyers would be willing to pay full price for a CD with a below-market interest rate.

- **Understand the difference between call features and maturity:** Don't assume that a "federally insured one-year non-callable" CD matures in one year. It doesn't. These words mean the bank cannot redeem the CD during the first year, but they have nothing to do with the CD's maturity date. A "one-year non-callable" CD may still have a maturity date 15 or 20 years in the future. If you have any doubt, ask the sales representative at your bank or brokerage firm to explain the CD's call features and to confirm when it matures.

- **For brokered CDs, identify the issuer:** Because federal deposit insurance is limited to a total aggregate amount of $100,000 for each depositor in each bank or thrift institution, it is very important that you know which bank or thrift issued your CD. Your broker may plan to put your money in a bank or thrift where you already have other CDs or deposits. You risk not being fully insured if the brokered CD would push your total deposits at the institution over the $100,000 insurance limit. (If you think that might happen, contact the institution to explore potential options for remaining fully insured, or call the Federal Deposit Insurance Corporation, FDIC.) For more information about federal deposit insurance, visit the Federal Deposit Insurance Corporation's website and read its publication "Your Insured Deposit" or call the FDIC's Consumer Information Center at 877-275-3342. The phone numbers for the hearing impaired are 800-925-4618 or (202) 942-3147.

- **Find out how the CD is held:** Unlike traditional bank CDs, brokered CDs are sometimes held by a group of unrelated investors. Instead of owning the entire CD, each investor owns a piece. Confirm with your broker how your CD is held, and be sure to ask for a copy of the exact title of the CD. If several investors own the CD, the deposit broker will probably not list each person's name in the title. But you should make sure that the account records reflect that the broker is merely acting as an agent for you and the other owners (for example, "XYZ Brokerage as Custodian for Customers"). This will ensure that your portion of the CD qualifies for up to $100,000 of FDIC coverage.

- **Research any penalties for early withdrawal:** Deposit brokers often tout the fact that their CDs have no penalty for early withdrawal. While technically true, these claims can be misleading. Be sure to find out how much you'll have to pay if you cash in your CD before maturity and whether you risk losing any portion of your principal. If you are the sole owner of a brokered CD, you may be able to pay an early withdrawal penalty to the bank that issued the CD to get your money back. But if you share the CD with other customers, your broker will have to find a buyer for your portion. If interest rates have fallen since you purchased your CD and the bank hasn't called it, your broker may be able to sell your portion for a profit. But if interest rates have risen, there may be less demand for your lower-yielding CD. That means you would have to sell the CD at a discount and lose some of your original deposit—despite no "penalty" for early withdrawal.

- **Thoroughly check out the broker:** Deposit brokers do not have to go through any licensing or certification procedures, and no state or federal agency licenses, examines, or approves them. Since anyone can claim to be a deposit broker, you should always check whether your broker or the company he or she works for has a history of complaints or fraud. You can do this by calling your state securities regulator or by checking with the National Association of Securities Dealers' "Central Registration Depository" at 800-289-9999.

- **Confirm the interest rate you'll receive and how you'll be paid:** You should receive a disclosure document that tells you the interest rate on your CD and whether the rate is fixed or variable. Be sure to ask how often the bank pays interest—for example, monthly or semi-annually. And confirm how you'll be paid—for example, by check or by an electronic transfer of funds.

- **Ask whether the interest rate ever changes:** If you're considering investing in a variable-rate CD, make sure you understand when and how the rate can change. Some variable-rate CDs feature a "multi-step" or "bonus rate" structure in which interest rates increase or decrease over time according to a pre-set schedule. Other variable-rate CDs pay interest rates that track the performance of a specified market index, such as the S&P 500 or the Dow Jones Industrial Average.

The bottom-line question you should always ask yourself is: Does this investment make sense for me? A high-yield, long-term CD with a maturity date of 15 to 20 years may make sense for many younger investors who want to diversify their financial holdings. But it might not make sense for elderly investors.

Don't be embarrassed if you invested in a long-term, brokered CD in the mistaken belief that it was a shorter-term instrument—you are not alone. Instead, you should complain promptly to the broker who sold you the CD. By complaining early you may improve your chances of getting your money back. Here are the steps you should take:

1. Talk to the broker who sold you the CD, and explain the problem fully, especially if you misunderstood any of the CD's terms. Tell your broker how you want the problem resolved.

2. If your broker can't resolve your problem, then talk to his or her branch manager.

3. If that doesn't work, then write a letter to the compliance department at the firm's main office. The branch manager should be able to provide with contact information for that department. Explain your problem clearly, and tell the firm how you want it resolved. Ask the compliance office to respond to you in writing within 30 days.

4. If you're still not satisfied, then send The Securities and Exchange Commission (SEC) your complaint using their online complaint form. Be sure to attach copies of any letters you've sent already to the firm. If you don't have access to the internet, write to them at the address below:

Office of Investor Education and Assistance
U.S. Securities and Exchange Commission
100 F Street, N.E.
Washington, DC 20549-0213

The SEC will forward your complaint to the firm's compliance department and ask that they look into the problem and respond to you in writing.

Please note that sometimes a complaint can be successfully resolved. But in many cases, the firm denies wrongdoing, and it comes down to one person's word against another's. In that case, the SEC cannot do anything more to help resolve the complaint. They cannot act as a judge or an arbitrator to establish wrongdoing and force the firm to satisfy your claim. And the SEC cannot act as your lawyer.

You should also contact the banking regulator that oversees the bank that issued the CD:

- The Board of Governors of the Federal Reserve System oversees state-chartered banks and trust companies that belong to the Federal Reserve System.

- The Federal Deposit Insurance Corporation regulates state-chartered banks that do not belong to the Federal Reserve System.

- The Office of the Controller of the Currency regulates banks that have the word "National" in or the letters "N.A." after their names.

- The National Credit Union Administration regulates federally charted credit unions.
- The Office of Thrift Supervision oversees federal savings and loans and federal savings banks.

# Chapter 15

# *U.S. Treasury Securities*

### *What are U.S. Treasury securities?*

U.S. Treasury securities are debt instruments. The U.S. Treasury issues securities to raise the money needed to operate the Federal Government and to pay off maturing obligations—its debt, in other words.

### *Why should I buy a Treasury security?*

Treasury securities are a safe and secure investment option because the full faith and credit of the United States government guarantees that interest and principal payments will be paid on time. Also, most Treasury securities are liquid, which means they can easily be sold for cash.

### *What types of securities are sold to individual investors?*

The U.S. Treasury sells Treasury bills, notes, bonds, TIPS, and U.S. savings bonds to individual investors.

### *What are Treasury bills?*

Treasury bills (or T-bills) are short-term securities that mature in one year or less from their issue date. You buy T-bills for a price less than their par (face) value, and when they mature you are paid their

---

"The Basics of Treasury Securities," U.S. Department of the Treasury, Bureau of the Public Debt, 2005.

par value. Your interest is the difference between the purchase price of the security and what you are paid at maturity (or what you get if you sell the bill before it matures). For example, if you bought a $10,000 26-week Treasury bill for $9,750 and held it until maturity, your interest would be $250.

## What are Treasury notes, bonds, and TIPS?

Treasury notes and bonds are securities that pay a fixed rate of interest every six months until your security matures, which is when you are paid their par value. The only difference between them is their length until maturity. Treasury notes mature in more than a year, but not more than 10 years from their issue date. Bonds, on the other hand, mature in more than 10 years from their issue date.

The U.S. Treasury also sells Treasury inflation-protected securities (TIPS). They pay interest twice a year and the principal value of TIPS is adjusted to reflect inflation as measured by the Consumer Price Index—the Bureau of Labor Statistics' Consumer Price Index for All Urban Consumers (CPI-U). With TIPS, your semiannual interest payments and maturity payment are calculated based on the inflation-adjusted principal value of your security.

## What are U.S. savings bonds?

Savings bonds are Treasury securities that are payable only to the person to whom they are registered. Savings bonds can earn interest for up to 30 years, but you can cash them after six months if purchased before February 1, 2003 or 12 months if purchased on or after February 1, 2003.

## What types of savings bonds are available?

You can buy two types of savings bonds for cash: the Series EE bond or the Series I bond. For more information on these types of securities and how to purchase them, visit the U.S. Treasury Department's Savings Bonds website at http://www.savingsbonds.gov.

## How do Treasury bills, notes, bonds, and TIPS differ from savings bonds?

Unlike savings bonds, Treasury bills, notes, bonds and TIPS are transferable, so you can buy or sell them in the securities market. Also, bills, notes, bonds, and TIPS are electronic—they're not paper securities like savings bonds. You can buy Treasury bills, notes, bonds and TIPS for a minimum of $1,000, and you can buy savings bonds for as little as $25.

### How can I buy a Treasury bill, note, bond, or TIPS?

It's easy. Buy Treasury bills, notes, bonds, or TIPS either at one of the auctions we conduct or in the securities market. If you want to buy a Treasury security at auction, contact the U.S. Treasury Department, a Federal Reserve Bank, a financial institution, or a government securities broker or dealer. If you want to buy a Treasury security in the securities market, contact your financial institution, broker, or dealer for more information.

### What is a Treasury auction?

Each Treasury bill, note, bond or TIPS (except savings bonds, of course) is sold at a public auction. In Treasury's auctions, all successful bidders (bids are discussed below) are awarded securities at the same price, which is the price equal to the highest rate or yield of the competitive bids accepted. You can find a complete explanation of the auction process in the Uniform Offering Circular, which is in the Code of Federal Regulations (CFR) at 31 CFR Part 356 (see http://www.treasurydirect.gov/instit/statreg/auctreg/auctreg.htm).

### How can I find out when an auction will be held?

Usually a couple days before each auction, the U.S. Treasury Department issues a press release announcing the security being sold, the amount it is selling, the auction date, and other pertinent information. This information is available from the Treasury Department and from your financial institution, broker, or dealer. Many newspapers also report Treasury auction schedules in their financial sections.

### How can I participate in an auction?

Simply submit a bid for the security you want to buy. You can bid either noncompetitively or competitively, but not both in the same auction.

If you bid noncompetitively, you'll receive the full amount of the security you want at the return determined at that auction. Therefore, you don't have to specify the return you'd like to receive. You can't bid for more than $5 million in a bill, note, bond or TIPS auction. Most individual investors bid noncompetitively.

If you bid competitively, on the other hand, you have to specify the return—the rate for bills or the yield for notes, bonds and TIPS—that you would like to receive. If the return you specify is too high, you might not receive any securities, or just a portion of what you bid for. However, you can bid competitively for much larger amounts than you can noncompetitively.

### How do I submit my bid?

Once the auction of a security is announced, you can submit a bid for an auction directly to the Treasury Department's Bureau of Public Debt, to a Federal Reserve Bank, or through a financial institution, broker, or dealer. Bids are accepted by mail or, for current customers, over the internet and by touch-tone phone. A financial institution, government securities broker, or dealer can also submit bids on your behalf. Although there are no fees to process a bid, some financial institutions, brokers, and dealers may charge for that service.

### What is the minimum purchase amount for Treasury securities?

The minimum amount that you can purchase of any given Treasury bill, note, bond, or TIPS is $1,000. Additional amounts must be in multiples of $1,000.

### Do I have a choice as to where my Treasury securities are kept?

All Treasury securities are issued in what is called "book-entry" form—an entry in a central electronic ledger. You can hold your Treasury securities in one of three systems: TreasuryDirect, Legacy Treasury Direct, or the commercial book-entry system. TreasuryDirect and Legacy Treasury Direct are direct holding systems where you have a direct relationship with the Treasury Department. The commercial book-entry system is an indirect holding system where you hold your securities with your financial institution, government securities broker, or dealer. The commercial book-entry system is a multi-level arrangement that involves the Treasury, the Federal Reserve System (acting as Treasury's agent), banks, brokers, dealers, and other financial institutions. So, in the commercial book-entry system, there can be one or more entities between you (the ultimate owner of the security) and Treasury.

## What features does TreasuryDirect offer?

TreasuryDirect provides a completely online environment for buying and holding Treasury bills, notes, bonds, and TIPS, as well as savings bonds. You use the TreasuryDirect website (http://www.treasurydirect.gov) to open an account, conduct transactions, and access account information. All services are available 24 hours a day, seven days a week. You designate the financial account or accounts into which payments and withdrawals are made. There are no fees when you open an account or buy securities. Interested? Take the TreasuryDirect guided tour at http://www.treasurydirect.gov/indiv/TDTour/default.htm.

## What features does Legacy Treasury Direct offer?

Legacy Treasury Direct allows you to conduct transactions online, over the phone, and by paper and mail. In this program, you can buy Treasury bills, notes, bonds, and TIPS, and hold those securities. You designate the financial account into which payments and withdrawals are made. Account statements are sent to you by mail. There are no fees when you open an account or buy securities (except for an annual maintenance fee, if your account has a total par amount of more than $100,000.) You can reinvest most maturing securities. Although you have a direct relationship with the Treasury Department, your financial institution, government securities broker, or dealer can submit a bid for a security to be delivered to Legacy Treasury Direct for you. For more information on Legacy Treasury Direct, please visit http://www.publicdebt.treas.gov/sec/sectrdir.htm.

## What features does the commercial book-entry system offer?

In the commercial book-entry system, you'll maintain your relationship with your financial institution, broker, or dealer and potentially pay fees for their services. The commercial book-entry system allows you to easily buy and sell securities as well as (unlike Legacy Treasury Direct) use them for collateral. You can also hold Treasury securities in stripped form, known as STRIPS or zero-coupon Treasuries, in the commercial book-entry system.

## What are STRIPS or zero-coupon Treasuries?

STRIPS, also known as zero-coupon securities, are Treasury securities that don't make periodic interest payments. Market participants create

147

STRIPS by separating the interest and principal parts of a Treasury note, bond, or TIPS. For example, a 10-year Treasury note consists of 20 interest payments—one every six months for 10 years—and a principal payment payable at maturity. When this security is "stripped," each of the 20 interest payments and the principal payment become separate securities and can be held and transferred separately. STRIPS can only be bought and sold through a financial institution, broker, or dealer and held in the commercial book-entry system.

### How can I sell my Treasury security before maturity?

If you hold your security in the commercial book-entry system, contact your financial institution, government securities dealer, broker, or investment advisor. Normally there is a fee for this service. If you hold your security in TreasuryDirect or Legacy Treasury Direct, you can transfer it to an account in the commercial book-entry system or let the Treasury Department sell your security through our Sell Direct program for a modest fee.

### How do I receive my interest and principal payments in each system?

In the TreasuryDirect and Legacy Treasury Direct, Treasury makes interest and principal payments directly to the financial account you choose. In the commercial book-entry system, Treasury's interest and principal payments may flow through several institutions on their way to you. For example, a payment could go from the Federal Reserve to a large bank to a smaller bank to your bank or broker before it gets to you.

### What happens when my security matures?

When your security matures, the principal and the final interest payment are made through TreasuryDirect, Legacy Treasury Direct, or the commercial book-entry system. Rather than take payment of the principal, customers of TreasuryDirect and Legacy Treasury Direct can choose to roll the principal into another security. In TreasuryDirect you do this by scheduling a repeat purchase. In Legacy Treasury Direct, you do it by scheduling a reinvestment. Legacy Treasury Direct allows you to reinvest any securities except TIPS, and to schedule reinvestments by mail, phone, or over the internet.

## *How can I get more information about Treasury securities?*

You can get information about Treasury securities on the Treasury Department's website (http://www.treasurydirect.gov) or your financial institution, broker, or dealer. If you're interested in Legacy Treasury Direct, ask the Treasury Department for Investor Kit (PD P 009).

# Chapter 16

# *Municipal Bonds*

Municipal bonds, "munis" for short, are issued by city, county, and state governments, as well as by enterprises with a public purpose, such as certain electric utilities, universities, and hospitals.

Municipal bonds are the only sector of the bond market where the primary buyers are individual investors. The chief attraction of munis is that they are exempt from federal taxes. If you are a resident of the state issuing the bonds, they are also exempt from state taxes.

Overwhelmingly, munis deserve their popularity among individual investors. Even though there are thousands of issues outstanding, munis are sound and relatively uncomplicated instruments. Nonetheless, buying individual municipal bonds is not quite as simple as buying Treasuries. The buyer of municipal bonds must be aware of a number of issues: The first one is whether or not you would earn more by buying munis than by buying taxable bonds; second, you need to understand credit quality; and finally, commission costs can be high—particularly if you need to sell a bond before it matures. However, commission costs are hidden.

## *Should I Buy Munis?*

No one likes to pay taxes. But it does not always pay to buy tax-exempt bonds rather than taxable bonds.

"What You Need to Know about Investing in Municipal Bonds," by Annette Thau, *AAII Journal*, October 2002. © 2002 American Association of Individual Investors. All Rights reserved. Reprinted with permission.

If you are considering buying munis, your first step should be to determine whether you will earn more by buying munis or by buying taxable instruments. The method used most often is to calculate how much you would have to earn on taxable investments to earn as much as you net on municipal bonds. This is called the taxable-equivalent yield.

This is easy to do. First, determine your exact tax bracket. Then, use the following formula:

Taxable-equivalent yield = tax-exempt yield/(1 − tax bracket)

For example, suppose you are in the 35% tax bracket and you are considering the purchase of a muni with a 5% yield to maturity. To obtain the taxable-equivalent yield, convert percentages to decimals. Your calculation looks like this:

Taxable-equivalent yield = 0.05/(1 − 0.35) = 0.0769 = 7.69%

This tells you that in your tax bracket (35%), a municipal bond yield of 5% is equivalent to a taxable bond yield of 7.69%. If you were in the 15% tax bracket, on the other hand, the same formula would result in a tax-equivalent yield of 5.88%. This changes the picture considerably: You might actually earn more by buying a taxable instrument.

You can use the same formula to determine whether an in-state bond, on which you pay no state tax, would net you more than an out-of-state bond on which you would have to pay state taxes. For example, if your state tax is 5%, add that amount to your federal tax (35% in the preceding example) and substitute the resulting number (40%) in the above formula.

Note that your tax bracket is not the only factor to consider when comparing taxable and tax-exempt yields. You need to compare fixed-income instruments that are comparable in credit quality and maturity length. In the world of bonds, you can always get a higher yield by taking on more risk. That could be interest rate risk (buying bonds with longer maturities) or credit risk (buying bonds with lower credit quality). That does not mean you should not be taking on higher risk, but rather that you need to understand the risk you are taking and be comfortable with it. It also means that you should be compensated adequately for the additional risk. But when comparing bond yields, the first step is to start by comparing bonds whose risk profiles are similar.

Also, be sure that you are comparing the same quoted yields. For individual bonds, you will normally be quoted a yield to maturity.

As a rule, taxpayers in the highest tax brackets benefit from buying tax-exempt bonds; those in the lowest do not. But these relationships are not constant. That is partly because tax laws change. In addition, demand for municipal bonds varies over time. Also, the yield curve [the graph of yields at different maturities for bonds of the same credit quality] in the municipal bond market is typically more steep than that of the Treasury market. In the early 1990s, typically, the yield of munis with long maturities (20 to 30 years) was somewhere between 80% and 85% of Treasuries with comparable maturities. In the first few years of the 2000s, munis with comparable maturities were yielding 95% (or higher) of Treasuries. That means that munis were a screaming buy, even for investors in the 15% tax bracket. Therefore, it always pays to recalculate.

## *Credit Quality: Ratings*

Few investors have either the time or the access to information to perform extensive credit analyses. If you buy individual bonds, you would, like most individual investors, rely on the ratings assigned by the major rating agencies. Table 16.1 lists the main ratings of the rating agencies, along with a translation (in plain English) of what these ratings mean.

The lowest investment-grade rating is Baa (Moody's), which is equivalent to BBB (both Standard & Poor's and Fitch). The wording "investment grade" indicates that bank trust funds are allowed to invest in securities bearing these grades, but it does not denote high credit quality.

Ratings convey information about credit quality: that is, the likelihood that the issuer of a bond will have sufficient money to pay interest on time and repay principal when a bond matures. The highest rated bonds are those issued by the United States Treasury. Treasuries actually do not carry a rating because it is assumed that a default on the part of the U.S. Treasury is not conceivable. The credit quality of municipal bonds, in the aggregate, is high. Nonetheless, defaults do occur from time to time, and credit rating downgrades occur frequently.

If you are buying bonds, you need to understand the relationship between ratings and yield. Higher ratings come at a cost: The higher the rating, the stronger the credit quality, the lower the yield. On the other hand, and particularly because ratings change over time, if you are buying bonds that have very long maturities, say 20 to 30 years, credit quality is important. You want to know that you will receive interest payments on time and that you will receive principal in full when the bond matures. Also, bonds with very strong credit quality are more liquid: That is, they are bought, and sold, with lower mark-ups than bonds with lower credit quality.

There are a lot of misconceptions concerning ratings and credit quality. What follows is a discussion of some essential points that should clarify these issues.

**Table 16.1.** Credit Quality Ratings and What They Mean

| Moody's | Standard & Poor's | Fitch | Interpretation |
|---------|-------------------|-------|----------------|
| Aaa | AAA | AAA | Gilt-edged. If everything that can go wrong does go wrong, they can still service debt. |
| Aa | AA | AA | Very high-quality by all standards. |
| A | A | A | Investment grade: good quality. |
| Baa | BBB | BBB | Lowest investment grade rating: satisfactory, but needs to be monitored. |
| Ba | BB | BB | Somewhat speculative: low grade. |
| B | B | B | Very speculative. |
| Caa | CCC | CCC | Even more speculative; substantial risk. |
| Ca | CC | CC | Wildly speculative; may be in default. |
| C | C | C | In default. |

## *'Go' and Revenue Bonds*

Municipal bonds come in two varieties: general obligation and revenue. General obligation bonds (also called GOs) are issued by states, cities, or counties to raise money for schools, sewers, road improvements, and the like. Moneys to pay interest to bondholders are raised through taxes and some user fees.

Revenue bonds are issued by a variety of enterprises that perform a public function, such as electric utilities, toll roads, airports, hospitals, universities, and other specially created "authorities." Money to pay interest to bondholders is generated by the enterprise of the issuer.

Electric utilities depend on the fees paid by users of electricity; hospitals depend on patient revenues; toll roads depend on tolls and so on.

One misconception concerning municipal bonds is that GOs are safer than revenue bonds. There are strong and weak credits in each sector. The supposed safety of GOs is ascribed to the fact that they are backed by the taxing power of the issuer. Theoretically, that power is "unlimited." That's because bond indentures state that general obligation bonds are backed by the "unlimited taxing power" of the issuer. In the real world, however, the power to tax is limited by political and economic considerations. The classic question any rating analyst has to ask is: In the event there is an economic crunch, who will the issuer pay, its teachers, police and fire department, or the bondholders? If municipalities could tax at will, all GOs would be AAA, and as we know, this is not the case.

Similarly, the supposed lower safety of revenue bonds is based on the fact that issuers run businesses whose revenues cannot be predicted with certainty. Again, that bears no relationship to what goes on in the real world. Most electric utilities and toll roads can, and do, raise rates to pay for increasing costs. Consequently, many revenue bonds, particularly those issued for essential services such as electric power, sewer, or water are high-quality credits. So are many toll roads or state "authorities."

The ratings of revenue bonds revolve around an analysis of revenues generated by sales, compared to money needed to cover interest payments (debt service). In practice, the rating is determined by a key ratio known as the debt service coverage ratio. This is defined as the amount of money specifically available for payment of debt service divided by the amount of debt service to be paid. This ratio is calculated for the past. How much money was actually available for debt service last year, or for the past five years? It is also estimated for the future. How much money is going to be available next year, and the year after, and so on, for debt service? The past ratio is called "the historical debt service ratio."

A historical debt service ratio of at least two is generally required for an "A" rating. That ratio indicates that moneys reserved for payment of debt service were equal to twice the amount needed for debt service. A historical ratio of five or six times debt service is considered fantastic. A historical ratio below one—indicating there wasn't enough money in the till to cover debt service—would almost guarantee a below investment-grade rating. Nonetheless, no matter how sound their management or how strong debt service coverage has been, revenue bonds are almost never rated AAA on their own merit.

This does not make them unattractive investments—just the opposite. They yield more than GOs.

Also, in practice, the boundary lines between revenue and general obligation bonds are sometimes fuzzy. For example, some counties and cities own hospitals and/or electric revenue plants, sometimes both. Therefore, the revenue bonds they issue have both general obligation and revenue backing. These bonds are sometimes called "double barreled" credits.

Among GOs, the weakest credits are found in two groups: GOs of large cities with deteriorating downtown cores and large social outlays; and older, small cities or districts with shrinking populations, a shrinking tax base, and deteriorating economies.

Among revenue bonds, the riskiest bonds have been hospitals with strong dependence on government reimbursement (government programs do not cover hospital expenses in full); bonds issued by developers of nursing homes (many of these are highly speculative); and so-called private-purpose bonds (also called industrial development bonds, or IDBs). These are issued by specially constituted authorities on behalf of private businesses.

Finally, keep in mind that, inevitably, ratings change. When the economy prospers, generally bond ratings improve. When the economy undergoes stresses, bond ratings deteriorate. At the current time, many state and local governments are experiencing revenue shortfalls and as a result, many bond ratings are being downgraded.

How concerned should you be about these downgrades? This is a difficult question to answer. Downgrades from a high quality rating (strong AA or AAA) to one or even two notches below may mean that the price of the bond would go down slightly. But that is not a concern unless you need to sell the bond before it matures. Also, issuers (such as states or cities) that issue a lot of bonds and come to the market often simply cannot afford to default.

On the other hand, defaults can and do occur. Some have been highly publicized (for example, in the 1970s, the defaults of Washington Public Power and the near default of New York City, as well as the more recent default of Orange County in California). But other less publicized defaults have occurred as well, mainly in the speculative areas discussed above. One indication is yield. If an issue sports a much higher yield than other issues with comparable maturities, that is an indication that credit risk is high. Therefore, if you have a small portfolio, it is best to limit purchases of individual munis to issuers that are large, well known, and have high credit quality—even if that means a lower yield.

## Municipal Bond Insurance

Insurance is purchased by an issuer when bonds are brought to market. The insurance guarantees that in the event the issuer experiences financial problems, the insurer will step in and take over payment of both interest and principal. Generally, an entire bond issue is insured, and it is insured for the life of the bond. Occasionally, only part of an issue is covered, perhaps only specific maturities (the longest term bonds), or perhaps the reserve fund only.

There are a number of firms that insure municipal bonds. The oldest and best known bond insurance firms are Municipal Bond Insurance Association (MBIA), Financial Guaranty Insurance Company (FGIC), and American Municipal Bond Assurance Co. (AMBAC).

A fourth firm, Financial Security Assurance (FSA) entered the market in the early 1990s. All of these firms are rated AAA by the major rating agencies, and the bonds they insure are consequently rated AAA as well. The AAA rating of the major bond insurance firms indicates that, in the opinion of the rating agencies, the insurers have sufficient reserves to back up their guarantee—even under a simulated severe depression scenario. As in any other industry, however, changes occur. One major change is that several new firms have appeared on the scene. And unlike the older firms, these firms are not rated AAA: Asset Guaranty (AG), is rated AA; and therefore, so are the bonds it insures.

Another firm, American Capital Access (ACA) is rated only A. It insures mainly lower quality credits; those are also rated A, based on the rating of that insurer.

Issuers who have a strong credit history (A+ or better) generally come to market without insurance. Issuers who need "enhancements" in order to attract buyers are most likely to insure their bonds. These would include credits that are marginally investment grade, that are not well-known, or that may be undergoing temporary difficulties.

In effect, bond insurance transforms a potential lemon into lemonade. Instead of coming to market with a rating that may be barely investment grade, the bond comes to market with a AAA rating, based, however, on the rating of the insurance firm.

For municipal bond insurers, municipal bond insurance has proved a dream product. These companies screen bonds very carefully. Only issuers deemed unlikely to default are granted insurance. Some minor defaults have occurred, but to date, no major bond insurance firm has taken a hit that has been significant enough to threaten its rating.

For individual investors, there are a number of pluses to bond insurance. For starters, the insurance does confer a layer of protection against default. As a result, the bonds are more liquid. If a major issuer is downgraded, the insured bonds of that issuer decline less in price than the uninsured bonds of the same issuer. Also, bond insurance functions as a second opinion on credit quality. Someone other than the rating agencies—who moreover has money on the line—has carefully screened a possibly marginal issuer for credit quality.

On the minus side, however, insurance protects only against default risk. It does not protect against fluctuations in the price of a bond due to changes in interest rates. Also, insurance comes at a cost—a somewhat lower yield than the issuer would have to pay based on its own rating.

Nor is there any guarantee that the rating of the bond insurance firms will not be downgraded. As noted earlier, changes have already occurred in the industry. More are likely to occur. Insurers may continue to prosper, and they may not. In the event that a bond insurance firm is downgraded (certainly a possibility), then all the bonds guaranteed by that firm would be downgraded as well to reflect the new rating of the insurer. This, in turn, would result in some decline in the price of the bond due to the downgrade.

There may also be a misconception concerning the relative safety of insured bonds. Many individual investors consider bonds that are insured to be safer than bonds rated AAA on their own merit, but the opposite is true. In the bond market, insured bonds rated AAA are not considered quite as gilt-edged as bonds that are rated AAA on their own merit. The yield of bonds rated AAA based on the rating of an insurer tends to track AA credits, and not, as their rating would suggest, AAA credits. To an individual investor, this means that insured bonds yield somewhat more than AAA bonds, and that may be considered a plus. The yield (and therefore the price) of an insured bond is actually based both on the insurance and on the underlying credit of the issuer. For that reason, you should find out how the bonds would be rated if they were not insured. To check the rating of the issuer, find out, if you can, how uninsured bonds of the same issuer are rated.

If a broker offers you a AAA credit, be sure to inquire if the bond is rated AAA on its own, or if that AAA rating is based on bond insurance. Many brokers do not differentiate between the two. However, the distinction is important.

## *Is bond insurance a good deal for the individual investor?*

On balance, for most individuals, the answer is yes. The main advantage is that bond insurance adds a layer of protection against totally unforeseeable risks. This is particularly true for bonds with maturities of longer than 10 years, or if you are buying riskier credits such as hospitals, or if you have a relatively undiversified portfolio (any portfolio consisting of a few individual issues).

## *Other Quality Indicators*

If you want to be sure that you are buying high-quality credits, there are possibilities other than insured bonds.

Any bond rated A to AAA on its own is a sound investment. The strongest credits, however, are those of "refunded" bonds. These are high-coupon bonds, usually selling at a premium. They are backed by U.S. Treasury bonds held in escrow. How can that be?

Well, suppose a municipality issued bonds five years ago when interest rates were much higher than current rates, say 8%. Suppose also that, due to the original call provisions, the municipality cannot just call the bonds. How can that municipality lower its interest costs?

The answer is that the municipality may "refinance" by issuing new bonds at the current lower coupon rate (say 5½%). The newly issued bonds are known as "refunding" bonds. The municipality issues an amount of bonds sufficient to cover interest payments and to redeem principal of the older bonds (the 8% bonds) at the first call date. The proceeds from the sale of the refunding bonds (the 5½% bonds) are used to purchase U. S. Treasury securities, which are then placed in an escrow account. The coupons of the Treasury bonds are used to pay the coupon payments on the older bonds (the 8% bonds), now called the "refunded" bonds. At the first call date, the remaining assets in the escrow account are used to redeem the refunded bonds.

The refunded bonds are totally free of default risk since moneys to pay the bondholders are held in escrow and invested in Treasuries. Whatever the initial rating of the bonds may have been, it now jumps to AAA. This is not automatic, however. Technically, the issuer has to apply for a new rating-because the rating agencies want their fee. In the event the refunded bonds are not re-rated, they will generally trade like AAA bonds. The refunding bonds (that is, the newly issued 5½% bonds), on the other hand, trade with the rating of the issuer.

Note that another advantage of "refunded" bonds is that maturities for such bonds are short to intermediate. Therefore, interest rate risk is low.

A number of states, such as Maine and Virginia, issue bonds for small localities through very well-run and highly rated "bond banks." Other states (including New York and New Jersey) add a layer of protection to the bonds of local school districts by reserving state aid payments for debt service if the school district is in financial difficulty.

Many other possibilities will no doubt continue to turn up as the markets and economic conditions change. This is one reason for dealing with a knowledgeable specialist who can assist you in uncovering new opportunities.

## To Summarize

Here are some important points to keep in mind concerning municipal bond investments:

- Before buying any bond, first determine whether you will earn more by buying a taxable or a tax-exempt bond;

- Be aware that ratings may change, and monitor credit ratings of the bonds you own; and

- The longer the maturity of the bond, the higher the rating you should require.

## About the Author

Annette Thau, Ph.D., is author of *The Bond Book: Everything Investors Need to Know About Treasuries, Municipals, GNMAs, Corporates, Zeros, Bond Funds, Money Market Funds, and More*, (© 2001, published by McGraw-Hill). Ms. Thau is a former municipal bond analyst for Chase Manhattan Bank and former visiting scholar at the Columbia University Graduate School of Business.

# Chapter 17

# *Investing in Stocks*

Savers and investors have different objectives for their money. Typically, savers have objectives to use their money in the next three to five years, while investors won't need their money in the next three to five years. Therefore, stocks are not an appropriate security for a saving objective. People who invest in stocks need a long time frame for their investment objectives. Over the long haul, stocks have out-performed other investment options by a wide margin. Because of the volatility of stock prices, you should not have any money in stocks that you will need to use in the next three to five years.

## Owner vs. Loaner

Investment securities usually involve two types of securities. Those where the investor is an owner or those where the investor is a loaner. Owner securities include stocks, real estate, equity unit investment trusts, equity mutual funds, collectibles, business ownership, and com-modities. Common stocks are an owner asset.

Loaner assets for an investor are certificates of deposit, U.S. Trea-sury securities, municipal bonds, corporate bonds, convertible bonds, zero-coupon bonds, bond unit investment trusts, bond mutual funds, mortgage-backed securities, collateralized mortgage obligations, fixed annuities, preferred stock, and guaranteed investment contracts.[1]

---

"All About Money: Investing in Stocks," by Ruth Anne Mears. © 2001 Ohio State University Extension. Reprinted with permission.

161

## What Is a Stock?

Stock comes in two types: common and preferred. This chapter will focus on common stock. Preferred stock is more similar to a loaner asset and will not be discussed here.

When you buy common stock, you become part owner of a company. Common stock owners elect directors, who hire the people that manage the company on a day-to-day basis. Owners vote on issues at a stockholders meeting, online, or over the phone.

When a company makes money, the board of directors determines what is done with the profit. They can reinvest the profit back into the company or share the profit with the owners via dividends. Dividends are paid quarterly, annually, or not at all. The dividend amount can be adjusted within a year and thus is not a steady source of income. For the stockholder, dividends are current income and are reported on each year's tax return.

## Risks Associated with Stocks

There are several risks associated with stocks. Market risk, business risk, and financial risk are all part of owning stocks. Although you assume risk in owning stock, the potential returns are higher than other investments.

Stock is generally owned for its growth potential. This potential growth is obtained through changes in the price of a share of stock. If the stock increases in value, the investor makes money when the stock is sold and has a capital gain. However, stock prices can go down in value and the investor can lose money if the stock is sold at that time. This change in market price of stock is considered market risk.

"Beta" is a measurement of market risk. The greater the beta over 1, the greater the risk of price changes. For betas under 1, there may be less swings in share price.

Other types of risk associated with stock ownership are business risk and financial risk. These risks have to do with the type of company and its ability to manage the balance sheet and to make money. These types of risk can be managed by diversification (owning several different types of companies in different sectors). Different sectors of businesses perform differently in good and poor economic times. During periods of economic contractions, large cost items (housing, large machinery) do not perform as well as during times of economic expansion.

Financial risk is associated with companies managing their income and expenses. Owning stock in a variety of different companies allows an investor to spread out the risk of a company they own going bankrupt. Thus, diversification helps to spread out business and financial risks.

## Classification of Stocks

Stocks are grouped according to size, investment objective, and type of company. Having different sizes of companies, different types of investment objectives, and different sectors results in diversification thus reducing risks. Investors also need to match their investment objective with the appropriate investment.

Companies are grouped according to size—small capitalization, medium capitalization, and large capitalization. The assets listed on the financial statement determine the size of the company. Small companies over time have more growth potential but also have the largest potential risk of loss. Large companies tend to pay more in dividends than small companies and their stock prices do not tend to fluctuate as much. The New York Stock Exchange (NYSE) trades large and medium sized companies, while smaller companies tend to be traded over the National Association of Securities Dealers Automated Quotation System (NASDAQ).

Investment objectives may be growth, aggressive growth, value, or income. Growth and aggressive growth companies anticipate good sales and expansion that will result in profits and higher share prices. Value companies are businesses which may be in a downturn, but the future prospects look good so their share prices are undervalued or priced lower than usual. Income stocks pay good dividends compared to other companies but there are no guarantees that these dividends will continue.

Stocks are often grouped by sectors. Holding different sectors helps ensure an investor is diversified in different types of industries. If you own individual stocks, all your holdings should not be in the same sector because if the economy swings in a particular direction, you will be affected more strongly than if your holdings were spread out among sectors.

Morningstar, which is a company that researches mutual funds, uses the following sectors in analyzing mutual funds. The list below is in order of risk with the safest sectors listed first to the most risky but highest-growth rate sectors last.

### *Stock Sectors*

- Utilities: telephones, electric utilities, gas utilities

- Energy: oil, natural gas

- Financials: banks, brokers, thrifts, insurance, real estate

- Industrial Cyclicals: aerospace, construction, machinery, machine tools, chemicals, metals, papers, building materials

- Consumer Durable: autos, housewares, recreation/luxury, multi-industry

- Consumer Staples: food, beverages, tobacco, household goods

- Services: media, entertainment, personal and business services, waste management, transportation

- Retail: all retail (except drug wholesalers)

- Health: pharmaceuticals, health-care services, medical devices, drug wholesalers

- Technology: computer hardware, software, electronics, electrical equipment, wireless communications

When investing in individual stocks, how many do you need? Most people recommend that you hold at least 6–8 individual stocks representing different sectors.

## Owning a Share of Stock

Owning a share of stock entitles you to any dividend distributed, voting privilege (if common stock), and annual reports of the company. Some companies will automatically reinvest dividends for their shareholders to purchase more stock. The costs of these dividend reinvestment programs are usually lower than buying more stock through a broker but the investor should check costs. This is a convenient way to buy additional shares on a continual basis. Some companies allow investors to buy directly from them so a broker is not used. However, check the costs and remember you are not getting financial advice that a broker might provide. So, you will need to do your own research.

When buying stock through a broker, buying round lots (100 shares) is usually cheaper than buying odd lots (for example, 30 shares, 5 shares, or 76 shares) or shares not divided evenly by 100. A full service broker, a discount broker, over the internet, and direct from the company are all ways to purchase stock.

## *Deciding which Stock to Buy*

**Price/earning ratio:** Price earnings ratios are one statistic often reported in newspapers. This ratio takes the price per share of an individual stock and the earnings the company makes on a per share basis. So, if a share of Company A was $50 and the earnings were $1.99 per share, the price/earnings ratio would be 25 ($50/1.99). If Company B had a price of $75 a share and had earnings of $2.25 per share, the price/earnings ratio for Company B would be 33 ($75/2.25). This means that Company A stock may be undervalued compared to Company B or Company B is overpriced compared to Company A. To compare two companies' price/earnings ratios, they must be comparable industries. You do not want to compare price/earnings ratios of health care companies to technology companies.

**Yearly high and yearly low:** Newspapers often report on the yearly high price and the yearly low price of stocks. This provides an indication of how the current price compares to the yearly high and low prices. If the stock price is close to the high for the year or close to the low for the year, you can compare the current price to these figures.

**Yield:** Yield is reported as a percentage and reports the dividends paid as compared to the price of a share of stock. Stocks that do not pay dividends do not have a yield reported. So, if a company's stock was $45 a share and paid $.60 in dividends, the yield would be 1.3% (dividend divided by share price = yield or $.60/$45 = 1.3%). A yield is similar to the interest paid on a bank account, however, companies do not guarantee dividends so the yield changes daily based on share price and dividends paid. Investors looking for growth and income should consider purchasing stocks with higher yields.

**Splits:** Sometimes, companies will split their shares. So, if you own 50 shares, you now have 100 shares if there is a 2-for-1 split. Your cost basis per share will be cut in half so if you had 50 shares worth $102 a share you now have 100 shares worth $51 a share. Your value in this company is still the same ($5,100). Because your cost basis is reduced by one-half for each share, a record of splits needs to be kept for future tax records. Generally, there is no taxable event when this occurs.

**Taxes and stocks:** There are three types of taxes that are paid on stocks in non-retirement accounts. Individual Retirement Accounts and Pension Plans are not taxed until withdrawn and then the money taxed is taxed as ordinary income (except for Roth IRAs where the earnings are never taxed). Dividends are taxed each year at the same rate as your income. Those federal tax rates can be 15%, 28%, 31%, etc., plus any applicable state and local income taxes.

The other type of tax on stock is capital gains/loss tax. This tax is incurred when you sell a stock. Let's say you purchased a stock at $10 a share and sold it 6 months later at $15 a share. You have a profit of $5 a share and, because you held the stock for less than 1 year, you have a short-term capital gain that is taxed as regular income. If you held this stock for 12 months or 3 years, for example, you have long-term capital gain which is taxed at a lower rate. See your tax advisor for the details of capital gains/losses.

## Determining Cost Basis

There are two different ways to determine your cost basis when selling stocks, FIFO and specific identification. A third method, average cost method, is only used for selling mutual fund shares.

- First in first out, or FIFO, uses the first shares purchased as your cost basis. This is a good method when the first shares you purchased were the most expensive.

- Specific identification is a second method of determining cost basis. In this method you identify the particular shares you are selling. Before selling shares, you instruct the broker or fund company which shares you plan to sell. This method allows you control over the capital gains taxes you pay because you determine how much will be paid by the shares you select to sell. Long-term or short-term gains can also be controlled.

- Average cost is the third method and is only used with mutual funds. In this method the average cost is determined by dividing the total cost of all shares purchased, including any invested dividends, by the total number of shares held. If you start with this method you must continue to use it each time you sell shares in a mutual fund. This works well when the shares you have owned the longest have the lowest cost basis.

## Record Keeping

Keep track of all confirmations when you buy or sell stock. If your year-end statement includes these confirmations, you can throw individual confirmations away and keep all of the year-end statements, including reinvestment purchases. These are used to determine cost basis of your stock when selling. Having a separate folder for each company owned allows you to file a copy of the most recent annual report, a listing of reasons why you bought this stock, and research reports about the company.

## Conclusion

Stocks are a growth investment. Diversification is an important consideration when investing in stocks. At least six to eight different companies in different sectors helps to reduce risk. As with all investments, accurate records need to be kept to determine cost basis when individual stocks are sold.

## Note

1. *Investing for Your Future*, A Cooperative Extension System Basic Investing Home Study Course, February 2000, Rutgers Cooperative Extension (http://www.investing.rutgers.edu).

# Chapter 18

# *Microcap Stocks*

## *Introduction*

Information is the investor's best tool when it comes to investing wisely. But accurate information about "microcap stocks" (low-priced stocks issued by the smallest of companies) may be difficult to find. Many microcap companies do not file financial reports with the U.S. Securities and Exchange Commission (SEC), so it's hard for investors to get the facts about the company's management, products, services, and finances. When reliable information is scarce, fraudsters can easily spread false information about microcap companies, making profits while creating losses for unsuspecting investors.

### *What is a microcap stock?*

The term "microcap stock" applies to companies with low or "micro" capitalizations, meaning the total value of the company's stock. Microcap companies typically have limited assets. For example, in cases where the SEC suspended trading in microcap stocks, the average company had only $6 million in net tangible assets—and nearly half had less than $1.25 million. Microcap stocks tend to be low priced and trade in low volumes.

Excerpted from "Microcap Stock: A Guide for Investors," U.S. Securities and Exchange Commission, February 2006. The complete text of this document is available online at http://www.sec.gov/investor/pubs/ microcapstock.htm.

## *Where do microcap stocks trade?*

Many microcap stocks trade in the "over-the-counter" (OTC) market and are quoted on OTC systems, such as the OTC Bulletin Board (OTCBB) or the "Pink Sheets."

**OTC Bulletin Board:** The OTCBB is an electronic quotation system that displays real-time quotes, last-sale prices, and volume information for many OTC securities that are not listed on the NASDAQ Stock Market or a national securities exchange. Brokers who subscribe to the system can use the OTCBB to look up prices or enter quotes for OTC securities. Although the National Association of Securities Dealers (NASD) oversees the OTCBB, the OTCBB is not part of the NASDAQ Stock Market. Fraudsters often claim that an OTCBB company is a NASDAQ company to mislead investors into thinking that the company is bigger than it is.

**The "Pink Sheets":** The Pink Sheets—named for the color of paper on which they've historically been printed—are listings of price quotes for companies that trade in the over-the-counter market (OTC market). "Market makers" (the brokers who commit to buying and selling the securities of OTC issuers) can use the pink sheets to publish bid and ask prices. A company named Pink Sheets LLC, formerly known as the National Quotation Bureau, publishes the pink sheets in both hard copy and electronic format. Pink Sheets LLC is not registered with the SEC as a stock exchange, nor does the SEC regulate its activities.

## *How are microcap stocks different from other stocks?*

**Lack of public information:** The biggest difference between a microcap stock and other stocks is the amount of reliable, publicly available information about the company. Larger public companies file reports with the SEC that any investor can get for free from the SEC's website. Professional stock analysts regularly research and write about larger public companies, and it's easy to find their stock prices in the newspaper. In contrast, information about microcap companies can be extremely difficult to find, making them more vulnerable to investment fraud schemes.

**No minimum listing standards:** Companies that trade their stocks on major exchanges and in the NASDAQ Stock Market must meet minimum listing standards. For example, they must have

170

minimum amounts of net assets and minimum numbers of share-holders. In contrast, companies on the OTCBB or the Pink Sheets do not have to meet any minimum standards.

**Risk:** While all investments involve risk, microcap stocks are among the most risky. Many microcap companies tend to be new and have no proven track record. Some of these companies have no assets or operations. Others have products and services that are still in de-velopment or have yet to be tested in the market. Another risk that pertains to microcap stocks involves the low volumes of trades. Be-cause microcap stocks trade in low volumes, any size of trade can have a large percentage impact on the price of the stock.

### Which companies file reports with the SEC?

In general, the federal securities laws require all but the smallest of public companies to file reports with the SEC. A company can be-come "public" in one of two ways—by issuing securities in an offering or transaction that's registered with the SEC or by registering the company and its outstanding securities with the SEC. Both types of registration trigger ongoing reporting obligations, meaning the com-pany must file periodic reports that disclose important information to investors about its business, financial condition, and management.

All OTCBB companies must file updated financial reports with the SEC or with their banking or insurance regulators. Any company that does not file timely reports with the SEC or their banking or insur-ance regulators is removed from the OTCBB.

When an OTCBB company fails to file its reports on time, the NASD will add a fifth letter "E" to its four-letter stock symbol. The company then has 30 days to file with the SEC or 60 days to file with its banking or insurance regulator. If it's still delinquent after the grace period, the company will be removed from the OTCBB. You'll find a list of securities that have been removed from the OTCBB at http:// www.otcbb.com.

### Which companies don't have to file reports with the SEC?

Smaller companies—those with less than $10 million in assets—generally do not have to file reports with the SEC. But some smaller companies, including microcap companies, may choose voluntarily to register their securities with the SEC. Any company that wants to offer or sell securities to the public must either register with the SEC

171

or meet an exemption. Here are two of the most common exemptions that many microcap companies use:

- **"Reg A" offerings:** Companies raising less than $5 million in a 12-month period may be exempt from registering their securities under a rule known as Regulation A. Instead of filing a registration statement through EDGAR (EDGAR stands for electronic data gathering and retrieval; the EDGAR database is available on the SEC's website at http://www.sec.gov), these companies need only file a printed copy of an "offering circular" with the SEC containing financial statements and other information.

- **"Reg D" offerings:** Regulation D exempts from registration companies that seek to raise less than $1 million dollars in a twelve-month period. It also exempts companies seeking to raise up to $5 million, as long as the companies sell only to 35 or fewer individuals or any number of "accredited investors" who must meet high net worth or income standards. In addition, Reg D exempts some larger private offerings of securities.

Unless they otherwise file reports with the SEC, companies that are exempt from registration under Reg A, Reg D, or another offering exemption do not have to file reports with the SEC.

### *What's so important about public information?*

Many of the microcap companies that don't file reports with the SEC are legitimate businesses with real products or services. But the lack of reliable, readily available information about some microcap companies can open the door to fraud. It's easier for fraudsters to manipulate a stock when there's little or no information available about the company.

### *How do I get information about microcap companies?*

If you're working with a broker or an investment adviser, you can ask your investment professional if the company files reports with the SEC and to get you written information about the company and its business, finances, and management. Be sure to carefully read the prospectus and the company's latest financial reports. Remember that unsolicited e-mails, message board postings, and company news releases should never be used as the sole basis for your investment decisions. You can also get information on your own from these sources:

**From the company:** Ask the company if it is registered with the SEC and files reports. If the company is small and unknown to most people, you should also call your state securities regulator to get information about the company, its management, and the brokers or promoters who've encouraged you to invest in the company.

**From the SEC:** Using the EDGAR database, you can find out whether a company files with the SEC and get any reports in which you're interested. For companies that do not file on EDGAR, check with the SEC's Public Reference Room to see whether the company has filed an offering circular under Reg A.

**From your state securities regulator:** The SEC strongly urges you to contact your state securities regulator to find out whether they have information about a company and the people behind it. Look in the government section of your phone book or visit the website of the North American Securities Administrators Association (http://www.nasaa.org) to get the name and phone number. Even though the company does not have to register its securities with the SEC, it may have to register them with your state. Your regulator will tell you whether the company has been legally cleared to sell securities in your state. Too many investors could easily have avoided heavy and painful financial losses if they only called their state securities regulator before they bought stock.

**From other government regulators:** Many companies, such as banks, do not have to file reports with the SEC. But banks must file updated financial information with their banking regulators. Visit the Federal Reserve System's National Information Center of Banking Information site at www.ffiec.gov/nicpubweb/nicweb/nichome.aspx, the Office of the Comptroller of the Currency at http://www.occ.treas.gov, or the Federal Deposit Insurance Corporation at http://www.fdic.gov.

**From reference books and commercial databases:** Visit your local public library or the nearest law or business school library. You'll find many reference materials containing information about companies. You can also access commercial databases for more information about the company's history, management, products or services, revenues, and credit ratings. The SEC cannot recommend or endorse any particular research firm, its personnel, or its products. But there are a number of commercial resources you may consult, including: Bloomberg, Dun & Bradstreet, Hoover's Profiles, Lexis-Nexis, and Standard & Poor's Corporate Profiles. Ask your librarian about additional resources.

**The Secretary of State where the company is incorporated:**
Contact the secretary of state where the company is incorporated
to find out whether the company is a corporation in good standing.
You may also be able to obtain copies of the company's incorporation papers and any annual reports it files with the state. Please visit
the National Association of Secretaries of State website at http://
www.nass.org for contact information regarding a particular Secretary of State.

**Caution:** If you've been asked to invest in a company but you can't
find any record that the company has registered its securities with
the SEC or your state, or that it's exempt from registration, call or
write your state's securities regulator or the SEC immediately with
all the details. You may have come face to face with a scam.

## What if I want to invest in microcap stocks?

To invest wisely and avoid investment scams, research each investment opportunity thoroughly and ask questions. These simple steps
can make the difference between profits and losses:

- Find out whether the company has registered its securities with
  the SEC or your state's securities regulators.

- Make sure you understand the company's business and its products or services.

- Read carefully the most recent reports the company has filed
  with its regulators and pay attention to the company's financial
  statements, particularly if they are not audited or not certified
  by an accountant. If the company does not file reports with the
  SEC, be sure to ask your broker for what's called the "Rule 15c2-
  11 file" on the company. That file will contain important information about the company.

- Check out the people running the company with your state securities regulator, and find out if they've ever made money for
  investors before. Also ask whether the people running the company have had run-ins with the regulators or other investors.

- Make sure the broker and his or her firm are registered with
  the SEC and licensed to do business in your state. And ask your
  state securities regulator whether the broker and the firm have
  ever been disciplined or have complaints against them.

Also, watch out for these "red flags":

- **SEC trading suspensions:** The SEC has the power to suspend trading in any stock for up to 10 days when it believes that information about the company is inaccurate or unreliable. Think twice before investing in a company that's been the subject of an SEC trading suspension. You'll find information about trading suspensions on the SEC's website.

- **High pressure sales tactics:** Beware of brokers who pressure you to buy before you have a chance to think about and investigate the "opportunity." Dishonest brokers may try to tell you about a "once-in-a-lifetime" opportunity or one that's based on "inside" or "confidential" information. Don't fall for brokers who promise spectacular profits or "guaranteed" returns. These are the hallmarks of fraud. If the deal sounds too good to be true, then it probably is.

- **Assets are large but revenues are small:** Microcap companies sometimes assign high values on their financial statements to assets that have nothing to do with their business. Find out whether there's a valid explanation for low revenues, especially when the company claims to have large assets.

- **Odd items in the footnotes to the financial statements:** Many microcap fraud schemes involve unusual transactions among individuals connected to the company. These can be unusual loans or the exchange of questionable assets for company stock that may be discussed in the footnotes.

- **Unusual auditing issues:** Be wary when a company's auditors have refused to certify the company's financial statements or if they've stated that the company may not have enough money to continue operating. Also question any change of accountants.

- **Insiders own large amounts of the stock:** In many microcap fraud cases—especially "pump and dump" schemes—the company's officers and promoters own significant amounts of the stock. When one person or group controls most of the stock, they can more easily manipulate the stock's price at your expense. You can ask your broker or the company whether one person or group controls most of the company's stock, but if the company is the subject of a scam, you may not get an honest answer.

- **Additional red flags:** Don't deal with brokers who refuse to provide you with written information about the investments they're promoting. Never tell a cold caller your social security number or numbers for your banking and securities accounts. And be extra wary if someone you don't know and trust recommends foreign investments.

# Chapter 19

# *Initial Public Offerings (IPOs)*

IPO stands for initial public offering and occurs when a company first sells its shares to the public.

## *Initial Public Offerings: Why Individuals Have Difficulty Getting Shares*

The underwriters and the company that issues the shares control the IPO process. They have wide latitude in allocating IPO shares. The U.S. Securities and Exchange Commission (SEC) does not regulate the business decision of how IPO shares are allocated.

While smaller or individual investors are finding it easier to buy IPO shares through online brokerage firms, they may still find it difficult to buy IPO shares for a number of reasons:

### *The Underwriting Process*

The IPOs of all but the smallest of companies are usually offered to the public through an "underwriting syndicate," a group of underwriters who agree to purchase the shares from the issuer and then sell the shares to investors. Only a limited number of broker-dealers

This chapter includes the following publications of the U.S. Securities and Exchange Commission (www.sec.gov): "Initial Public Offerings (IPO)," May 2000; "Initial Public Offerings: Why Individuals Have Difficulty Getting Shares," November 1999; "Initial Public Offerings, Pricing Differences," May 2000; and "Risky Business: Pre-IPO Investing," January 2005.

are invited into the syndicate as underwriters and some of them may not have individual investors as clients. Moreover, syndicate members themselves do not receive equal allocations of securities for sale to their clients.

The underwriters in consultation with the company decide on the basic terms and structure of the offering well before trading starts, including the percentage of shares going to institutions and to individual investors. Most underwriters target institutional or wealthy investors in IPO distributions. Underwriters believe that institutional and wealthy investors are better able to buy large blocks of IPO shares, assume the financial risk, and hold the investment for the long term.

### Hot IPOs

When an IPO is "hot," appealing to many investors, the demand for the securities far exceeds the supply of shares. The excess demand can only be satisfied once trading in the IPO shares begins. It is unclear how "hot" the offering will be until close to the time when the shares start trading. Since "hot" IPOs are in high demand, underwriters usually offer those shares to their most valued clients.

Underwriting firms that have a high percentage of individual investors as clients are more likely to allocate portions of IPO shares to individuals. Several online brokers offer IPOs, but these firms often have only a small allotment of shares to sell to the public. As a result, individual investors' ability to buy these shares may be limited no matter which firm they do business with.

### Eligibility Requirements

By their nature, investing in an IPO is a risky and speculative investment. Brokerage firms must consider if the IPO is appropriate for individual investors in light of their income and net worth, investment objectives, other securities holdings, risk tolerance, and other factors. A firm may not sell IPO shares to an individual investor unless it has determined the investment is suitable for that particular investor.

### Other Restrictions

Even if the firm decides that an IPO is an appropriate investment for an individual investor, the brokerage firm may sell the IPO only to selected clients. For example, before you can purchase an IPO, some firms require that you have a minimum cash balance in your account, are an active trader with the firm, or subscribe to one of their more expensive or "premium" services. In addition, some firms impose restrictions on investors who "flip" or sell their IPO shares soon after the first day of trading to make a quick profit. If you flip your IPO shares, your firm may refuse to sell you other IPOs altogether or prevent you from buying an IPO for several months. You can often find these restrictions on the firm's website.

## Initial Public Offerings: Pricing Differences

You may have found that there can be a large difference between the price of an initial public offering (IPO) and the price when the IPO shares start trading in the secondary market.

The pricing disparities occur most often when an IPO is "hot" or appeals to many investors. When an IPO is "hot," the demand for the securities far exceeds the supply of shares. The excess demand can only be satisfied once trading in the IPO shares begins. This imbalance between supply and demand generally causes the price of each share to rise dramatically in the first hours or days of trading. Many times the price falls after this initial flurry of trading subsides.

## Risky Business: "Pre-IPO" Investing

"Pre-IPO" investing involves buying a stake in a company before the company makes its initial public offering of securities. Many companies and stock promoters entice investors by promising an opportunity to make high returns by investing in a start-up enterprise at the ground floor level—often a new company that claims to be related to the internet or e-commerce.

But investing at the pre-IPO stage can involve significant risk for investors. And pre-IPO offerings targeted at the general public—especially those that are publicized through "spam" e-mails—are often fraudulent and illegal. Consider the following:

- **The offering may be illegal:** Any company that wants to offer or sell securities to the public must either register the transaction with the SEC or meet an exemption. Otherwise the offering is illegal, and you may lose every penny you invest. The most common exemptions include those found in Regulation D of the Securities Act. But to meet these exemptions, the company and its promoters generally cannot advertise the offering or make solicitations to the general public.

179

- **You're buying unregistered securities:** That means you may have an extremely difficult time selling your securities if you want to liquidate before the company goes public. You may also have a difficult time obtaining current, reliable information about the company. In addition, if you purchase or acquire restricted securities, you cannot sell those securities for at least one year—even if the company goes public in the meantime.

- **The company may never go public:** In a growing number of cases, fraudsters have focused on the predicted value and imminence of an alleged IPO to lure—and pressure—investors. But don't be taken in by such false promises. While some IPOs yield double- and even triple-digit returns, many others don't or quickly fall back to levels far below the IPO price. In any event, the fact remains that the company may never go public. And if that's the case, you may never recoup your investment.

Before you even think about investing in any pre-IPO opportunity, be sure to do your homework. At a minimum, you'll want to know:

1. **Details about the offering:** Is the securities offering subject to an exemption? Remember, if it's neither registered nor exempt, it's illegal. Check with your state securities regulator to find out whether they have any information about the company, the offering, and the people promoting the deal. You can also check with the SEC's (Securities and Exchange Commission) Public Reference Room to see whether the company has filed an offering circular under Regulation A or a Form D under Regulation D. If you ultimately decide to invest, find out whether your stock will be restricted in any way. And be sure to ask how, if at all, you can liquidate your investment if the company does not go public.

2. **Information on the company:** What are its products and services? Who are its customers? Does it have the physical plant, contracts, or inventory it claims to have? Are audited financials available? If so, ask for copies and review them carefully. We've seen over the years that the most successful frauds typically start out with plausible lies. That's why you should always independently verify claims about any company in which you plan to invest.

180

3. **Management's background:** Who runs the company? Have they made money for investors in the past? Have any of them violated the law, including any of the federal securities laws? Your state securities regulator may be able to tell you whether the company and the people who run it have previously defrauded investors.

4. **The existence and identity of the underwriter:** Has the company retained an investment banking firm to underwrite the offering? If so, which firm? Contact your state securities regulator to find out whether the firm has a history of complaints or fraud.

5. **The identity and disciplinary history of the promoter:** How did you find out about the offering? If you heard about it from a stranger or saw a general advertisement, exercise extreme caution. Unscrupulous promoters typically try to lure in as many unwitting investors as possible to maximize their returns. Be sure to check out the disciplinary history of any promoters with your state securities regulator.

**Remember:** The people and companies that promote fraudulent pre-IPO offerings often use impressive-looking websites, bulletin board postings, and e-mail spam to exploit investors who scour the internet looking for e-businesses in which to invest. To lure you in, they make unfounded comparisons between their company and other established, successful internet companies. But these and other claims that sound so believable at first often turn out to be false or misleading. Always be skeptical when considering any offer you hear about through the internet.

# Chapter 20

# *Exchange Traded Options*

## *What Is an Option?*

A stock option is a contract which conveys to its holder the right, but not the obligation, to buy or sell shares of the underlying security at a specified price on or before a given date. This right is granted by the seller of the option.

There are two types of options, *calls* and *puts*. A call option gives its holder the right to buy an underlying security, whereas a put option conveys the right to sell an underlying security. For example, an American-style XYZ Corp. May 60 call entitles the buyer to purchase 100 shares of XYZ Corp. common stock at $60 per share at any time prior to the option's expiration date in May. Likewise, an American-style XYZ Corp. May 60 put entitles the buyer to sell 100 shares of XYZ Corp. common stock at $60 per share at any time prior to the option's expiration date in May.

## Underlying Security

The specific stock on which an option contract is based is commonly referred to as the underlying security. Options are categorized as derivative securities because their value is derived in part from the value and characteristics of the underlying security. A stock option contract's unit of trade is the number of shares of underlying stock which are represented by that option. Generally speaking, stock options have a unit of trade of 100 shares. This means that one option contract represents the right to buy or sell 100 shares of the underlying security.

## Strike Price

The *strike price,* or *exercise price,* of an option is the specified share price at which the shares of stock can be bought or sold by the *holder,* or buyer, of the option contract if he *exercises* his right against a *writer,* or seller, of the option. To exercise your option is to exercise your right to buy (in the case of a call) or sell (in the case of a put) the underlying shares at the specified strike price of the option.

The strike price for an option is initially set at a price which is reasonably close to the current share price of the underlying security. Additional or subsequent strike prices are set at the following intervals: 2½-points when the strike price to be set is $30 or less; 5-points when the strike price to be set is over $30 through $200; and 10-points when the strike price to be set is over $200. New strike prices are introduced when the price of the underlying security rises to the highest, or falls to the lowest, strike price currently available. The strike price, a fixed specification of an option contract, should not be confused with the *premium,* the price at which the contract trades, which fluctuates daily.

If the strike price of a call option is less than the current market price of the underlying security, the call is said to be *in-the-money* because the holder of this call has the right to buy the stock at a price which is less than the price he would have to pay to buy the stock in the stock market. Likewise, if a put option has a strike price that is greater than the current market price of the underlying security, it is also said to be *in-the-money* because the holder of this put has the right to sell the stock at a price which is greater than the price he would receive selling the stock in the stock market. The converse of in-the-money is, not surprisingly, *out-of-the-money.* If the strike price equals the current market price, the option is said to be *at-the-money.*

## Premium

Option buyers pay a price for the right to buy or sell the underlying security. This price is called the option *premium*. The premium is paid to the *writer,* or seller, of the option. In return, the writer of a call option is obligated to deliver the underlying security (in return for the strike price per share) to a call option buyer if the call is *exercised.* Likewise, the writer of a put option is obligated to take delivery of the underlying security (at a cost of the strike price per share) from a put option buyer if the put is exercised. Whether or not an option is ever exercised, the writer keeps the premium. Premiums are quoted on a per share basis. Thus, a premium of .80 represents a premium payment of $80.00 per option contract ($0.80 x 100 shares).

## American, European, and Capped Styles

There are three *styles* of options: American, European, and Capped. In the case of an *American* option, the holder of an option has the right to exercise his option on or before the expiration date of the option; otherwise, the option will expire worthless and cease to exist as a financial instrument. At the present time, all exchange-traded stock options are American-style. A *European* option is an option which can only be exercised during a specified period of time prior to its expiration. A *Capped* option gives the holder the right to exercise that option only during a specified period of time prior to its expiration, unless the option reaches the cap value prior to expiration, in which case the option is automatically exercised. The holder or writer of any style of option can close out his position at any time simply by making an offsetting, or closing, transaction. A *closing transaction* is a transaction in which, at some point prior to expiration, the buyer of an option makes an offsetting sale of an identical option, or the writer of an option makes an offsetting purchase of an identical option. A closing transaction cancels out an investor's previous position as the holder or writer of the option.

## The Option Contract

An option contract is defined by the following elements: type (put or call), style (American, European, or Capped), underlying security, unit of trade (number of shares), strike price, and expiration date. All option contracts that are of the same type and style and cover the same underlying security are referred to as a *class* of options. All options of the same class that also have the same unit of trade at the same strike price and expiration date are referred to as an option *series*.

185

If a person's interest in a particular series of options is as a net holder (that is, if the number of contracts bought exceeds the number of contracts sold), then this person is said to have a *long* position in the series. Likewise, if a person's interest in a particular series of options is as a net writer (if the number of contracts sold exceeds the number of contracts bought), he is said to have a *short* position in the series.

### Exercising the Option

If the holder of an option decides to exercise his right to buy (in the case of a call) or to sell (in the case of a put) the underlying shares of stock, the holder must direct his broker to submit an *exercise notice* to the Options Clearing Corporation (OCC). In order to ensure that an option is exercised on a particular day, the holder must notify his broker before the broker's cut-off time for accepting exercise instructions on that day. Different firms may have different cut-off times for accepting exercise instructions from customers, and those cut-off times may be different for different classes of options.

Upon receipt of an exercise notice, OCC will then *assign* this exercise notice to one or more Clearing Members with short positions in the same series in accordance with its established procedures. The Clearing Member will, in turn, assign one or more of its customers (either randomly or on a first in first out basis) who hold short positions in that series. The assigned Clearing Member will then be obligated to sell (in the case of a call) or buy (in the case of a put) the underlying shares of stock at the specified strike price. OCC then arranges with a stock clearing corporation designated by the Clearing Member of the holder who exercises the option for delivery of shares of stock (in the case of a call) or delivery of the settlement amount (in the case of a put) to be made through the facilities of a correspondent clearing corporation.

### The Expiration Process

A stock option usually begins trading about eight months before its expiration date. The exception is LEAPS® or long-term options, discussed below. However, as a result of the sequential nature of the expiration cycles, some options have a life of only one to two months. A stock option trades on one of three expiration cycles. At any given time, an option can be bought or sold with one of four expiration dates as designated in the expiration cycle tables.

186

The *expiration date* is the last day an option exists. For listed stock options, this is the Saturday following the third Friday of the expiration month. Please note that this is the deadline by which brokerage firms must submit exercise notices to OCC; however, the exchanges and brokerage firms have rules and procedures regarding deadlines for an option holder to notify his brokerage firm of his intention to exercise. Please contact your broker for specific deadlines.

OCC has developed a procedure known as *Exercise By Exception* to expedite its processing of exercises of expiring options by certain brokerage firms that are Clearing Members of OCC. Under this procedure, which is sometimes referred to as "ex-by-ex", OCC has established in-the-money thresholds and every contract at or above its in-the-money threshold will be exercised unless OCC's Clearing Member specifically instructs OCC to the contrary. Conversely, a contract under its in-the-money threshold will not be exercised unless OCC's Clearing Member specifically instructs OCC to do so. OCC does have discretion as to which securities are subject to, and may exclude other securities from, the ex-by-ex procedure. *You should also note that ex-by-ex is not intended to dictate which customer positions should or should not be exercised and that ex-by-ex does not relieve a holder of his obligation to tender an exercise notice to his firm if the holder desires to exercise his option. Thus, most firms require their customers to notify the firm of the customer's intention to exercise even if an option is in-the-money. You should ask your firm to explain its exercise procedures including any deadline the firm may have for exercise instructions on the last trading day before expiration.*

## LEAPS®/Long-Term Options

Long-term Equity AnticiPation Securities® (LEAPS®)/long-term stock options provide the owner the right to purchase or sell shares of a stock at a specified price on or before a given date up to three years in the future. As with other options, LEAPS® are available in two types, calls and puts. Like other exchange-traded stock options, LEAPS® are American-style options.

LEAPS® calls provide an opportunity to benefit from a stock price increase without making an outright stock purchase for those investors with a longer term view of the stock market. An initial LEAPS® position does not require an investor to manage each position daily. Purchase of LEAPS® puts provides a hedge for stock owners against substantial declines in their stocks. Current options users will also find LEAPS® appealing if they desire to take a longer term position of up to three years in some of the same options they currently trade.

Like other stock options, the expiration date for LEAPS® is the Saturday following the third Friday of the expiration month. All equity LEAPS® expire in January.

## The Pricing of Options

There are several factors which contribute value to an option contract and thereby influence the premium or price at which it is traded. The most important of these factors are the price of the underlying stock, time remaining until expiration, the volatility of the underlying stock price, cash dividends, and interest rates.

### Underlying Stock Price

The value of an option depends heavily upon the price of its underlying stock. As previously explained, if the price of the stock is above a call option's strike price, the call option is said to be in-the-money. Likewise, if the stock price is below a put option's strike price, the put option is in-the-money. The difference between an in-the-money option's strike price and the current market price of a share of its underlying security is referred to as the option's *intrinsic value*. Only in-the-money options have intrinsic value.

For example, if a call option's strike price is $45 and the underlying shares are trading at $60, the option has intrinsic value of $15 because the holder of that option could exercise the option and buy the shares at $45. The buyer could then immediately sell these shares on the stock market for $60, yielding a profit of $15 per share, or $1,500 per option contract.

When the underlying share price is equal to the strike price, the option (either call or put) is *at-the-money*. An option which is not in-the-money or at-the-money is said to be *out-of-the-money*. An at-the-money or out-of-the-money option has no intrinsic value, but this does not mean it can be obtained at no cost. There are other factors which give options value and therefore affect the premium at which they are traded. Together, these factors are termed *time value*. The primary components of time value are time remaining until expiration, volatility, dividends, and interest rates. Time value is the amount by which the option premium exceeds the intrinsic value.

*Option Premium = Intrinsic Value + Time Value*

For in-the-money options, the time value is the excess portion over intrinsic value. For at-the-money and out-of-the-money options, the time value is the total option premium.

### Time Remaining until Expiration

Generally, the longer the time remaining until an option's expiration date, the higher the option premium because there is a greater possibility that the underlying share price might move so as to make the option in-the-money. Time value drops rapidly in the last several weeks of an option's life.

### Volatility

Volatility is the propensity of the underlying security's market price to fluctuate either up or down. Therefore, volatility of the underlying share price influences the option premium. The higher the volatility of the stock, the higher the premium because there is, again, a greater possibility that the option will move in-the-money.

**Table 20.1.** Illustration of a typical newspaper listing for exchange-traded options

| Option & NY Close | Strike Price | Calls-Last | | | Puts-Last | | |
|---|---|---|---|---|---|---|---|
| | | May[5] | Jun[5] | Jul[5] | May[5] | Jun[5] | Jul[5] |
| XYZ[1] | 105[3] | 7.50[4] | 9.25[4] | 10.15[4] | .25[4] | .60[4] | 1.15[4] |
| 112.35[2] | 110[3] | 3[4] | 4.75[4] | 6.25[4] | 1.20[4] | 1.90[4] | 2.65[4] |
| 112.35[2] | 115[3] | .85[4] | 2.15[4] | 3.50[4] | 4[4] | 4.65[4] | 5[4] |
| 112.35[2] | 120[3] | .80[4] | .90[4] | 1.75[4] | 8.15[4] | 8.40[4] | 8.75[4] |
| 112.35[2] | 125[3] | .05[4] | s | .80[4] | r | s | r |
| 112.35[2] | 130[3] | s | s | .40[4] | s | s | 18.75[4] |

1. stock identification
2. stock closing price
3. option strike prices
4. closing option prices
5. option expiration months
r = not traded
s = no option listed

189

## Dividends

Regular cash dividends are paid to the stock owner. Therefore, cash dividends affect option premiums through their effect on the underlying share price. Because the stock price is expected to fall by the amount of the cash dividend, higher cash dividends tend to imply lower call premiums and higher put premiums.

Options customarily reflect the influences of stock dividends (for example, additional shares of stock) and stock splits because the number of shares represented by each option is adjusted to take these changes into consideration.

### Interest Rates

Historically, higher interest rates have tended to result in higher call premiums and lower put premiums.

### Understanding Option Premium Tables

Premiums (prices) for exchange-traded options are published daily in a large number of newspapers. A typical newspaper listing is illustrated in Table 20.1. In the example, the out-of-the-money XYZ July 115 calls closed at 3.50, or $350 per contract, while XYZ stock closed at 112.35. The in-the-money July 120 puts closed at 8.75, or $875 per contract.

# Chapter 21

# *Convertible Securities*

A "convertible security" is a security—usually a bond or a preferred stock—that can be converted into a different security—typically shares of the company's common stock. In most cases, the holder of the convertible determines whether and when a conversion occurs. In other cases, the company may retain the right to determine when the conversion occurs.

Companies generally issue convertible securities to raise money. Companies that have access to conventional means of raising capital (such as public offerings and bank financings) might offer convertible securities for particular business reasons. Companies that may be unable to tap conventional sources of funding sometimes offer convertible securities as a way to raise money more quickly. In a conventional convertible security financing, the conversion formula is generally fixed—meaning that the convertible security converts into common stock based on a fixed price. The convertible security financing arrangements might also include caps or other provisions to limit dilution (the reduction in earnings per share and proportional ownership that occurs when, for example, holders of convertible securities convert those securities into common stock).

By contrast, in less conventional convertible security financings, the conversion ratio may be based on fluctuating market prices to determine the number of shares of common stock to be issued on conversion.

"Convertible Securities," U.S. Securities and Exchange Commission (www.sec.gov), February 2003.

A market price based conversion formula protects the holders of the convertibles against price declines, while subjecting both the company and the holders of its common stock to certain risks. Because a market price based conversion formula can lead to dramatic stock price reductions and corresponding negative effects on both the company and its shareholders, convertible security financings with market price based conversion ratios have colloquially been called "floorless," "toxic," "death spiral," and "ratchet" convertibles.

Both investors and companies should understand that market price based convertible security deals can affect the company and possibly lower the value of its securities. Here's how these deals tend to work and the risks they pose:

- The company issues convertible securities that allow the holders to convert their securities to common stock at a discount to the market price at the time of conversion. That means that the lower the stock price, the more shares the company must issue on conversion.

- The more shares the company issues on conversion, the greater the dilution to the company's shareholders will be. The company will have more shares outstanding after the conversion, revenues per share will be lower, and individual investors will own proportionally less of the company. While dilution can occur with either fixed or market price based conversion formulas, the risk of potential adverse effects increases with a market price based conversion formula.

- The greater the dilution, the greater the potential that the stock price per share will fall. The more the stock price falls, the greater the number of shares the company may have to issue in future conversions and the harder it might be for the company to obtain other financing.

Before you decide to invest in a company, you should find out what types of financings the company has engaged in—including convertible security deals—and make sure that you understand the effects those financings might have on the company and the value of its securities. You can do this by researching the company in the SEC's (U.S. Securities and Exchange Commission) EDGAR (Electronic Data Gathering, Analysis, and Retrieval) database and looking at the company's registration statements and other filings. Even if the company sells convertible securities in a private, unregistered transaction (or "private placement"), the company and the purchaser normally agree that the company will register the underlying common stock for the purchaser's resale prior to conversion. You'll also find disclosures about these and other financings in the company's annual and quarterly reports on Forms 10-K and 10-Q, respectively, and in any interim reports on Form 8-K that announce the financing transaction.

If the company has engaged in convertible security financings, be sure to ascertain the nature of the convertible financing arrangement— fixed versus market price based conversion ratios. Be sure you fully understand the terms of the convertible security financing arrangement, including the circumstances of its issuance and how the conversion formula works. You should also understand the risks and the possible effects on the company and its outstanding securities arising from the below market price conversions and potentially significant additional share issuances and sales, including dilution to shareholders. You should be aware of the risks arising from the effects of the purchasers and other parties trading strategies, such as short selling activities, on the market price for the company's securities, which may affect the amount of shares issued on future conversions.

Companies should also understand the terms and risks of convertible security arrangements so that they can appropriately evaluate the issues that arise. Companies entering into these types of convertible securities transactions should understand fully the effects that the market price based conversion ratio may have on the company and the market for its securities. Companies should also consider the effect that significant share issuances and below market conversions have on a company's ability to obtain other financing.

Companies or investors seeking to learn more about the SEC's registration requirements for common stock issuable upon conversion of unregistered convertible securities, including the timing of the filing of the resale registration statement and the appropriate form that the company may use to register the resale, should consult the Division of Corporation Finance's manual of publicly available telephone interpretations.

# Chapter 22

# *Mutual Funds*

Over the past decade, American investors increasingly have turned to mutual funds to save for retirement and other financial goals. Mutual funds can offer the advantages of diversification and professional management. But, as with other investment choices, investing in mutual funds involves risk. And fees and taxes will diminish a fund's returns. It pays to understand both the upsides and the downsides of mutual fund investing and how to choose products that match your goals and tolerance for risk.

## *Key Points to Remember*

- Mutual funds are not guaranteed or insured by the Federal Deposit Insurance Corporation (FDIC) or any other government agency—even if you buy through a bank and the fund carries the bank's name. You can lose money investing in mutual funds.

- Past performance is not a reliable indicator of future performance. So don't be dazzled by last year's high returns. But past performance can help you assess a fund's volatility over time.

- All mutual funds have costs that lower your investment returns. Shop around, and use a mutual fund cost calculator at http://www.sec.gov/investor/tools.shtml to compare many of the costs of owning different funds before you buy.

Excerpted from "Invest Wisely: An Introduction to Mutual Funds," U.S. Securities and Exchange Commission, March 2006. The complete text of this document is available online at http://www.sec.gov/investor/pubs/inwsmf.htm.

## *How Mutual Funds Work*

A mutual fund is a company that pools money from many investors and invests the money in stocks, bonds, short-term money-market instruments, other securities or assets, or some combination of these investments. The combined holdings the mutual fund owns are known as its portfolio. Each share represents an investor's proportionate ownership of the fund's holdings and the income those holdings generate.

Some of the traditional, distinguishing characteristics of mutual funds include the following:

- Investors purchase mutual fund shares from the fund itself (or through a broker for the fund) instead of from other investors on a secondary market, such as the New York Stock Exchange or NASDAQ Stock Market.

- The price that investors pay for mutual fund shares is the fund's per share net asset value (NAV) plus any shareholder fees that the fund imposes at the time of purchase (such as sales loads).

- Mutual fund shares are "redeemable," meaning investors can sell their shares back to the fund (or to a broker acting for the fund).

- Mutual funds generally create and sell new shares to accommodate new investors. In other words, they sell their shares on a continuous basis, although some funds stop selling when, for example, they become too large.

- The investment portfolios of mutual funds typically are managed by separate entities known as "investment advisers" that are registered with the U.S. Securities and Exchange Commission (SEC).

### *Other Types of Investment Companies*

Legally known as an "open-end company," a mutual fund is one of three basic types of investment companies. While this chapter discusses only mutual funds, you should be aware that other pooled investment vehicles exist and may offer features that you desire. The two other basic types of investment companies are:

- **Closed-end funds:** which, unlike mutual funds, sell a fixed number of shares at one time (in an initial public offering) that later trade on a secondary market; and

- **Unit investment trusts (UITs):** which make a one-time public offering of only a specific, fixed number of redeemable securities called "units" and which will terminate and dissolve on a date specified at the creation of the UIT.

"Exchange-traded funds" (ETFs) are a type of investment company that aims to achieve the same return as a particular market index. They can be either open-end companies or UITs. But ETFs are not considered to be, and are not permitted to call themselves, mutual funds.

## A Word about Hedge Funds and "Funds of Hedge Funds"

"Hedge fund" is a general, non-legal term used to describe private, unregistered investment pools that traditionally have been limited to sophisticated, wealthy investors. Hedge funds are not mutual funds and, as such, are not subject to the numerous regulations that apply to mutual funds for the protection of investors—including regulations requiring a certain degree of liquidity, regulations requiring that mutual fund shares be redeemable at any time, regulations protecting against conflicts of interest, regulations to assure fairness in the pricing of fund shares, disclosure regulations, regulations limiting the use of leverage, and more.

"Funds of hedge funds," a relatively new type of investment product, are investment companies that invest in hedge funds. Some, but not all, register with the SEC and file semi-annual reports. They often have lower minimum investment thresholds than traditional, unregistered hedge funds and can sell their shares to a larger number of investors. Like hedge funds, funds of hedge funds are not mutual funds. Unlike open-end mutual funds, funds of hedge funds offer very limited rights of redemption. And, unlike ETFs, their shares are not typically listed on an exchange.

## Advantages and Disadvantages of Mutual Funds

Every investment has advantages and disadvantages. But it's important to remember that features that matter to one investor may not be important to you. Whether any particular feature is an advantage for you will depend on your unique circumstances. For some investors, mutual funds provide an attractive investment choice because they generally offer the following features:

- **Professional management:** Professional money managers research, select, and monitor the performance of the securities the fund purchases.

- **Diversification:** Diversification is an investing strategy that can be neatly summed up as "Don't put all your eggs in one basket." Spreading your investments across a wide range of companies and industry sectors can help lower your risk if a company or sector fails. Some investors find it easier to achieve diversification through ownership of mutual funds rather than through ownership of individual stocks or bonds.

- **Affordability:** Some mutual funds accommodate investors who don't have a lot of money to invest by setting relatively low dollar amounts for initial purchases, subsequent monthly purchases, or both.

- **Liquidity:** Mutual fund investors can readily redeem their shares at the current NAV—plus any fees and charges assessed on redemption—at any time.

But mutual funds also have features that some investors might view as disadvantages, such as the following:

- **Costs despite negative returns:** Investors must pay sales charges, annual fees, and other expenses (which will be discussed below) regardless of how the fund performs. And, depending on the timing of their investment, investors may also have to pay taxes on any capital gains distribution they receive—even if the fund went on to perform poorly after they bought shares.

- **Lack of control:** Investors typically cannot ascertain the exact make-up of a fund's portfolio at any given time, nor can they directly influence which securities the fund manager buys and sells or the timing of those trades.

- **Price uncertainty:** With an individual stock, you can obtain real-time (or close to real-time) pricing information with relative ease by checking financial websites or by calling your broker. You can also monitor how a stock's price changes from hour to hour—or even second to second. By contrast, with a mutual fund, the price at which you purchase or redeem shares will typically depend on the fund's NAV, which the fund might not calculate until many hours after you've placed your order. In general, mutual funds must calculate their NAV at least once every business day, typically after the major U.S. exchanges close.

## *Different Types of Funds*

When it comes to investing in mutual funds, investors have literally thousands of choices. Before you invest in any given fund, decide whether the investment strategy and risks of the fund are a good fit for you. The first step to successful investing is figuring out your financial goals and risk tolerance—either on your own or with the help of a financial professional. Once you know what you're saving for, when you'll need the money, and how much risk you can tolerate, you can more easily narrow your choices.

Most mutual funds fall into one of three main categories—money market funds, bond funds (also called "fixed income" funds), and stock funds (also called "equity" funds). Each type has different features and different risks and rewards. Generally, the higher the potential return, the higher the risk of loss.

**Money market funds:** Money market funds have relatively low risks, compared to other mutual funds (and most other investments). By law, they can invest in only certain high-quality, short-term investments issued by the U.S. government, U.S. corporations, and state and local governments. Money market funds try to keep their net asset value (NAV)—which represents the value of one share in a fund—at a stable $1.00 per share. But the NAV may fall below $1.00 if the fund's investments perform poorly. Investor losses have been rare, but they are possible.

Money market funds pay dividends that generally reflect short-term interest rates, and historically the returns for money market funds have been lower than for either bond or stock funds. That's why "inflation risk" (the risk that inflation will outpace and erode investment returns over time) can be a potential concern for investors in money market funds.

**Bond funds:** Bond funds generally have higher risks than money market funds, largely because they typically pursue strategies aimed at producing higher yields. Unlike money market funds, the SEC's rules do not restrict bond funds to high-quality or short-term investments. Because there are many different types of bonds, bond funds can vary dramatically in their risks and rewards. Some of the risks associated with bond funds include: credit risk (the possibility that companies or other issuers whose bonds are owned by the fund may fail to pay their debts); interest rate risk (the risk that the market value of the bonds will go down when interest rates go up); and prepayment risk (the chance that a bond will be paid off early).

**Stock funds:** Although a stock fund's value can rise and fall quickly (and dramatically) over the short term, historically stocks have performed better over the long term than other types of investments—including corporate bonds, government bonds, and treasury securities.

Overall "market risk" poses the greatest potential danger for investors in stocks funds. Stock prices can fluctuate for a broad range of reasons—such as the overall strength of the economy or demand for particular products or services.

Not all stock funds are the same. For example:

- Growth funds focus on stocks that may not pay a regular dividend but have the potential for large capital gains.

- Income funds invest in stocks that pay regular dividends.

- Index funds aim to achieve the same return as a particular market index, such as the S&P 500 Composite Stock Price Index, by investing in all—or perhaps a representative sample—of the companies included in an index.

- Sector funds may specialize in a particular industry segment, such as technology or consumer products stocks.

## How to Buy and Sell Shares

You can purchase shares in some mutual funds by contacting the fund directly. Other mutual fund shares are sold mainly through brokers, banks, financial planners, or insurance agents. All mutual funds will redeem (buy back) your shares on any business day and must send you the payment within seven days.

The easiest way to determine the value of your shares is to call the fund's toll-free number or visit its website. The financial pages of major newspapers sometimes print the NAVs for various mutual funds. When you buy shares, you pay the current NAV per share plus any fee the fund assesses at the time of purchase, such as a purchase sales load or other type of purchase fee. When you sell your shares, the fund will pay you the NAV minus any fee the fund assesses at the time of redemption, such as a deferred (or back-end) sales load or redemption fee. A fund's NAV goes up or down daily as its holdings change in value.

### How Funds Can Earn Money for You

You can earn money from your investment in three ways:

- **Dividend payments:** A fund may earn income in the form of dividends and interest on the securities in its portfolio. The fund then pays its shareholders nearly all of the income (minus disclosed expenses) it has earned in the form of dividends.

- **Capital gains distributions:** The price of the securities a fund owns may increase. When a fund sells a security that has increased in price, the fund has a capital gain. At the end of the year, most funds distribute these capital gains (minus any capital losses) to investors.

- **Increased NAV:** If the market value of a fund's portfolio increases after deduction of expenses and liabilities, then the value (NAV) of the fund and its shares increases. The higher NAV reflects the higher value of your investment.

With respect to dividend payments and capital gains distributions, funds usually will give you a choice: the fund can send you a check or other form of payment, or you can have your dividends or distributions reinvested in the fund to buy more shares (often without paying an additional sales load).

## Factors to Consider before Buying Mutual Funds

Thinking about your long-term investment strategies and tolerance for risk can help you decide what type of fund is best suited for you. But you should also consider the effect that fees and taxes will have on your returns over time.

### Degrees of Risk

All funds carry some level of risk. You may lose some or all of the money you invest (your principal) because the securities held by a fund go up and down in value. Dividend or interest payments may also fluctuate as market conditions change.

Before you invest, be sure to read a fund's prospectus and shareholder reports to learn about its investment strategy and the potential risks. Funds with higher rates of return may take risks that are beyond your comfort level and are inconsistent with your financial goals.

### Fees and Expenses

As with any business, running a mutual fund involves costs—including shareholder transaction costs, investment advisory fees, and marketing and distribution expenses. Funds pass along these costs to investors by imposing fees and expenses. It is important that you understand these charges because they lower your returns.

Some funds impose "shareholder fees" directly on investors whenever they buy or sell shares. In addition, every fund has regular, recurring, fund-wide "operating expenses." Funds typically pay their operating expenses out of fund assets—which means that investors indirectly pay these costs.

SEC rules require funds to disclose both shareholder fees and operating expenses in a "fee table" near the front of a fund's prospectus. The lists below will help you decode the fee table and understand the various fees a fund may impose:

**Shareholder fees:** The following are fees imposed directly on investors:

- **Sales charge (load) on purchases:** The amount you pay when you buy shares in a mutual fund. Also known as a "front-end load," this fee typically goes to the brokers that sell the fund's shares. Front-end loads reduce the amount of your investment. For example, let's say you have $1,000 and want to invest it in a mutual fund with a 5% front-end load. The $50 sales load you must pay comes off the top, and the remaining $950 will be invested in the fund. According to National Association of Securities Dealers (NASD) rules, a front-end load cannot be higher than 8.5% of your investment.

- **Purchase fee:** Another type of fee that some funds charge their shareholders when they buy shares. Unlike a front-end sales load, a purchase fee is paid to the fund (not to a broker) and is typically imposed to defray some of the fund's costs associated with the purchase.

- **Deferred sales charge (load):** A fee you pay when you sell your shares. Also known as a "back-end load," this fee typically goes to the brokers that sell the fund's shares. The most common type of back-end sales load is the "contingent deferred sales load" (also known as a "CDSC" or "CDSL"). The amount of this type of load will depend on how long the investor holds his or her shares and typically decreases to zero if the investor holds his or her shares long enough.

- **Redemption fee:** Another type of fee that some funds charge their shareholders when they sell or redeem shares. Unlike a deferred sales load, a redemption fee is paid to the fund (not to a broker) and is typically used to defray fund costs associated with a shareholder's redemption.

- **Exchange fee:** A fee that some funds impose on shareholders if they exchange (transfer) to another fund within the same fund group or "family of funds."

- **Account fee:** A fee that some funds separately impose on investors in connection with the maintenance of their accounts. For example, some funds impose an account maintenance fee on accounts whose value is less than a certain dollar amount.

**Annual fund operating expenses:** The following fees are typically paid out of fund assets (this means that investors pay them indirectly):

- **Management fees:** Fees that are paid out of fund assets to the fund's investment adviser for investment portfolio management, any other management fees payable to the fund's investment adviser or its affiliates, and administrative fees payable to the investment adviser that are not included in the "other expenses" category (discussed below).

- **Distribution [and/or service] fees ("12b-1" fees):** Fees paid by the fund out of fund assets to cover the costs of marketing and selling fund shares and sometimes to cover the costs of providing shareholder services. "Distribution fees" include fees to compensate brokers and others who sell fund shares and to pay for advertising, the printing and mailing of prospectuses to new investors, and the printing and mailing of sales literature. "Shareholder service fees" are fees paid to persons to respond to investor inquiries and provide investors with information about their investments.

- **Other expenses:** Expenses not included under "management fees" or "distribution or service (12b-1) fees," such as any shareholder service expenses that are not already included in the 12b-1 fees, custodial expenses, legal and accounting expenses, transfer agent expenses, and other administrative expenses.

- **Total annual fund operating expenses ("expense ratio"):** The line of the fee table that represents the total of all of a fund's annual fund operating expenses, expressed as a percentage of the fund's average net assets. Looking at the expense ratio can help you make comparisons among funds.

## A Word about "No-Load" Funds

Some funds call themselves "no-load." As the name implies, this means that the fund does not charge any type of sales load. But, as discussed above, not every type of shareholder fee is a "sales load." A no-load fund may charge fees that are not sales loads, such as purchase fees, redemption fees, exchange fees, and account fees. No-load funds will also have operating expenses.

Be sure to review carefully the fee tables of any funds you're considering, including no-load funds. Even small differences in fees can translate into large differences in returns over time. For example, if you invested $10,000 in a fund that produced a 10% annual return before expenses and had annual operating expenses of 1.5%, then after 20 years you would have roughly $49,725. But if the fund had expenses of only 0.5%, then you would end up with $60,858—an 18% difference.

A mutual fund cost calculator can help you understand the impact that many types of fees and expenses can have over time. It takes only minutes to compare the costs of different mutual funds.

## Classes of Funds

Many mutual funds offer more than one class of shares. For example, you may have seen a fund that offers "Class A" and "Class B" shares. Each class will invest in the same "pool" (or investment portfolio) of securities and will have the same investment objectives and policies. But each class will have different shareholder services and/ or distribution arrangements with different fees and expenses. As a result, each class will likely have different performance results.

## Tax Consequences

When you buy and hold an individual stock or bond, you must pay income tax each year on the dividends or interest you receive. But you won't have to pay any capital gains tax until you actually sell and unless you make a profit.

Mutual funds are different. When you buy and hold mutual fund shares, you will owe income tax on any ordinary dividends in the year you receive or reinvest them. And, in addition to owing taxes on any personal capital gains when you sell your shares, you may also have to pay taxes each year on the fund's capital gains. That's because the law requires mutual funds to distribute capital gains to shareholders if they sell securities for a profit that can't be offset by a loss.

Bear in mind that if you receive a capital gains distribution, you will likely owe taxes—even if the fund has had a negative return from the point during the year when you purchased your shares. For this reason, you should call the fund to find out when it makes distributions so you won't pay more than your fair share of taxes. Some funds post that information on their websites.

SEC rules require mutual funds to disclose in their prospectuses after-tax returns. In calculating after-tax returns, mutual funds must use standardized formulas similar to the ones used to calculate before-tax average annual total returns. You'll find a fund's after-tax returns in the "Risk/Return Summary" section of the prospectus. When comparing funds, be sure to take taxes into account.

**Tax exempt funds:** If you invest in a tax-exempt fund—such as a municipal bond fund—some or all of your dividends will be exempt from federal (and sometimes state and local) income tax. You will, however, owe taxes on any capital gains.

## Avoiding Common Mutual Fund Pitfalls

If you decide to invest in mutual funds, be sure to obtain as much information about the fund before you invest. And don't make assumptions about the soundness of the fund based solely on its past performance or its name.

### Sources of Information

**Prospectus:** When you purchase shares of a mutual fund, the fund must provide you with a prospectus. But you can—and should—request and read a fund's prospectus before you invest. The prospectus is the fund's selling document and contains valuable information, such as the fund's investment objectives or goals, principal strategies for achieving those goals, principal risks of investing in the fund, fees and expenses, and past performance. The prospectus also identifies the fund's managers and advisers and describes how to purchase and redeem fund shares.

While they may seem daunting at first, mutual fund prospectuses contain a treasure trove of valuable information. The SEC requires funds to include specific categories of information in their prospectuses and to present key data (such as fees and past performance) in a standard format so that investors can more easily compare different funds.

205

Here's some of what you'll find in mutual fund prospectuses:

- **Date of issue:** The date of the prospectus should appear on the front cover. Mutual funds must update their prospectuses at least once a year, so always check to make sure you're looking at the most recent version.

- **Risk/return bar chart and table:** Near the front of the pro-spectus, right after the fund's narrative description of its invest-ment objectives or goals, strategies, and risks, you'll find a bar chart showing the fund's annual total returns for each of the last 10 years (or for the life of the fund if it is less than 10 years old). All funds that have had annual returns for at least one cal-endar year must include this chart. Except in limited circum-stances, funds also must include a table that sets forth returns (both before and after taxes) for the past 1-, 5-, and 10-year peri-ods. The table will also include the returns of an appropriate broad-based index for comparison purposes. Be sure to read any footnotes or accompanying explanations to make sure that you fully understand the data the fund provides in the bar chart and table. Also, bear in mind that the bar chart and table for a multiple-class fund (that offers more than one class of fund shares in the prospectus) will typically show performance data and returns for only one class.

- **Fee table:** Following the performance bar chart and annual re-turns table, you'll find a table that describes the fund's fees and expenses. These include the shareholder fees and annual fund op-erating expenses described in greater detail above. The fee table includes an example that will help you compare costs among dif-ferent funds by showing you the costs associated with investing a hypothetical $10,000 over a 1-, 3-, 5-, and 10-year period.

- **Financial highlights:** This section, which generally appears to-wards the back of the prospectus, contains audited data concern-ing the fund's financial performance for each of the past 5 years. Here you'll find net asset values (for both the beginning and end of each period), total returns, and various ratios, including the ra-tio of expenses to average net assets, the ratio of net income to average net assets, and the portfolio turnover rate.

- **Profile:** Some mutual funds also furnish investors with a "profile," which summarizes key information contained in the fund's prospectus, such as the fund's investment objectives, principal investment strategies, principal risks, performance, fees and expenses, after-tax returns, identity of the fund's investment adviser, investment requirements, and other information.

**Statement of additional information ("SAI"):** Also known as "Part B" of the registration statement, the SAI explains a fund's operations in greater detail than the prospectus—including the fund's financial statements and details about the history of the fund, fund policies on borrowing and concentration, the identity of officers, directors, and persons who control the fund, investment advisory and other services, brokerage commissions, tax matters, and performance such as yield and average annual total return information. If you ask, the fund must send you an SAI. The back cover of the fund's prospectus should contain information on how to obtain the SAI.

**Shareholder reports:** A mutual fund also must provide shareholders with annual and semi-annual reports within 60 days after the end of the fund's fiscal year and 60 days after the fund's fiscal mid-year. These reports contain a variety of updated financial information, a list of the fund's portfolio securities, and other information. The information in the shareholder reports will be current as of the date of the particular report (that is, the last day of the fund's fiscal year for the annual report, and the last day of the fund's fiscal mid-year for the semi-annual report).

Investors can obtain all of these documents by:

- Calling or writing to the fund (all mutual funds have toll-free telephone numbers);

- Visiting the fund's website;

- Contacting a broker that sells the fund's shares;

- Searching the SEC's EDGAR database (EDGAR stands for Electronic Data Gathering, Analysis, and Retrieval; the EDGAR database is available on the SEC's website at http://www.sec.gov), and downloading the documents for free; or

- Contacting the SEC's Office of Public Reference by telephone at 202-551-8090, by fax at 202-942-9001, or by e-mail at publicinfo@sec.gov. Please be aware that there is a per page charge for photocopying; be sure to ask about current fees.

## *Past Performance*

A fund's past performance is not as important as you might think. Advertisements, rankings, and ratings often emphasize how well a fund has performed in the past. But studies show that the future is often different. This year's "number one" fund can easily become next year's below average fund.

Be sure to find out how long the fund has been in existence. Newly created or small funds sometimes have excellent short-term performance records. Because these funds may invest in only a small number of stocks, a few successful stocks can have a large impact on their performance. But as these funds grow larger and increase the number of stocks they own, each stock has less impact on performance. This may make it more difficult to sustain initial results.

While past performance does not necessarily predict future returns, it can tell you how volatile (or stable) a fund has been over a period of time. Generally, the more volatile a fund, the higher the investment risk. If you'll need your money to meet a financial goal in the near-term, you probably can't afford the risk of investing in a fund with a volatile history because you will not have enough time to ride out any declines in the stock market.

## *Looking Beyond a Fund's Name*

Don't assume that a fund called the "XYZ Stock Fund" invests only in stocks or that the "Martian High-Yield Fund" invests only in the securities of companies headquartered on the planet Mars. The SEC requires that any mutual fund with a name suggesting that it focuses on a particular type of investment must invest at least 80% of its assets in the type of investment suggested by its name. But funds can still invest up to one-fifth of their holdings in other types of securities— including securities that you might consider too risky or perhaps not aggressive enough.

## *Bank Products versus Mutual Funds*

Many banks now sell mutual funds, some of which carry the bank's name. But mutual funds sold in banks, including money market funds, are not bank deposits. As a result, they are not federally insured by the Federal Deposit Insurance Corporation (FDIC).

**Money market matters:** Don't confuse a "money market fund" with a "money market deposit account." The names are similar, but they are completely different:

- A money market fund is a type of mutual fund. It is not guaranteed or FDIC insured. When you buy shares in a money market fund, you should receive a prospectus.

- A money market deposit account is a bank deposit. It is guaranteed and FDIC insured. When you deposit money in a money market deposit account, you should receive a Truth in Savings form.

## *If You Have Problems*

If you encounter a problem with your mutual fund, you can send a complaint to the SEC using its online complaint form (http://www.sec.gov). You can also contact the SEC by regular mail at:

**Securities and Exchange Commission**
Office of Investor Education and Assistance
100 F Street, N.E.
Washington, DC 20549-0213

# Chapter 23

# *Exchange Traded Funds (ETFs)*

Exchange traded funds (ETFs) are index funds or trusts that are listed on an exchange and can be traded intraday. Investors can buy or sell shares in the collective performance of an entire portfolio as a single security. Exchange traded funds add the flexibility, ease, and liquidity of stock trading to the benefits of traditional index fund investing.

In recent years, these unique features and benefits have helped exchange traded funds explode in popularity and emerge as one of the most flexible, multi-purpose investment vehicles available. Ever since the American Stock Exchange pioneered the concept of a tradable basket of stocks with the creation of the Standard & Poor's Depository Receipt (SPDR) in 1993, exchange traded funds have evolved into an entirely new investment category. Today, the number of exchange traded funds (ETFs) listed and traded at the American Stock Exchange (Amex) has grown to more than 352 and continues to grow—not only in the number of products and their variety—but also in terms of assets and market value.

The American Stock Exchange lists exchange traded funds (ETFs) on more than 352 broad stock market, stock industry sector, international stock, U.S. Treasury, and corporate bond indexes and commodities, providing a wide array of investment opportunities. Exchange traded funds (ETFs) provide a simple and effective way to invest in markets worldwide. Investors can establish long-term investments in the market performance of the leading companies in the leading industries in the United States or abroad, or tailor asset allocations using diversified investments in stocks in particular industries or countries or in U.S. bonds or commodities.

## The Advantages of ETFs

**Tax efficiency:** ETFs, like index funds in general, tend to offer greater tax benefits because they generate fewer capital gains due to low turnover of the securities that comprise the portfolio. Generally, an ETF only sells securities to reflect changes in its underlying index. Exchange trading of ETFs further enhances their tax efficiency. Investors who want to liquidate shares in an ETF simply sell them to other investors through exchange trading. Because of this unique structure, ETFs are not required to sell securities to meet investor cash redemptions, potentially generating capital gains tax liability for remaining investors. Keep in mind that the sale of an ETF will generate capital gains/losses for the investor liquidating shares.

**Lower costs:** Expenses can have a significant impact on returns for investors. ETFs, in general, have significantly lower annual expense ratios than other investment products. ETFs are less likely to experience high management fees because they are index-based, not "actively" managed. And, since they trade on an exchange, ETFs are insulated from the costs of having to buy and sell securities to accommodate shareholder purchases and redemptions. Of course, an investor selling ETF shares may realize capital gains or losses, as with common stocks. Purchases or sales of exchange traded funds are subject to brokerage commissions.

**Transparency:** ETFs generally are designed to correspond to the performance of their underlying index or commodity.

**Buying and selling flexibility:** Because they are exchange traded, ETFs can be:

- bought and sold at intraday market prices;
- purchased on margin;
- sold short, even on a downtick (unlike common stocks);
- traded using stop orders and limit orders, which allow investors to specify the price points at which they are willing to trade.

**All day tracking and trading:** ETFs are priced and traded throughout the day, and are not restricted to once-a-day trading at the end of the day. And because the pricing of ETFs is continuous during trading hours, investors will always be able to obtain up-to-the-minute share prices from their broker or financial adviser.

**Diversification:** Because each ETF is comprised of a basket of securities, it inherently provides diversification across an entire index. Additionally, the expanding universe of ETFs offers exposure to a diverse variety of markets, including:

- broad-based equity indexes (such as total market, large-cap growth, and small-cap value);
- broad-based international and country-specific equity indexes (such as Europe, EAFE [Europe, Australasia, Far East], and Japan);
- industry sector-specific equity indexes (such as healthcare, energy, and real estate);
- U.S. bond indexes (such as long-term Treasury bonds and corporate bonds);
- commodities (such as gold, silver, and oil).

**Dividend opportunities:** Dividends paid by companies and interest paid on bonds held in an ETF are distributed to ETF holders, less expenses, on a pro rata basis. Of course, not all companies will pay dividends. Based on past performance, few, if any, distributions can be expected from certain ETFs. There may also be opportunities for reinvestment of distributions.

**Wide array of investment strategies:** Investors can capitalize on the convenience and flexibility of ETFs to pursue a wide variety of investment strategies.

- **Core investment:** Investors can use ETFs as a core investment for their portfolio. The purchase of shares in a single ETF can provide broad market exposure for long-term holding that is easy to establish, easy to track, inexpensive, and tax efficient.
- **Portfolio diversification:** ETFs cover virtually every segment of the equity market and several segments of the U.S. bond market and commodities, providing an easy and convenient way to adjust the investment mix of a core portfolio.

- **Hedging:** Exchange traded funds can be purchased on margin and sold short (even on a downtick), which has opened up risk management strategies for individual investors that were once available only to large institutions. For example, ETFs can be sold short to hedge a core stock portfolio or interest rate fluctuations. This allows investors to keep their portfolio intact while protecting them from market losses. In a declining stock market or rising interest rate environment, profits from a short position can offset some of the losses in a portfolio. (Investors are required to make arrangements to borrow securities before selling short.) Listed options, available on some ETFs, also offer opportunities for additional hedging or to increase income. Investors should contact their broker regarding initial and maintenance margin requirements.

- **Cash management:** ETFs have often been used to "equitize" cash, providing a way for investors to put cash to work in the market or maintain allocation targets while determining where to invest for the longer term.

- **Rebalancing:** Investors can adjust ETF positions at any time throughout the trading day, without redemption fees or short-term restrictions. Again, usual brokerage commissions will apply.

- **Tax loss strategy:** An investor can sell a security that is underperforming and claim a tax loss but retain exposure to its sector by investing in an ETF. Consult a tax advisor about a tax loss strategy.

**Risks and other considerations:** ETF shareholders are subject to risks similar to those of holders of other diversified portfolios. A primary consideration is that the general level of securities or commodities may decline, thus affecting the value of an exchange traded fund because ETFs represent interest in securities or commodities. When interest rates rise, bond prices generally will decline, which will adversely affect the value of fixed income ETFs. Moreover, the overall depth and liquidity of the secondary market may also fluctuate.

An exchange traded sector fund may also be adversely affected by the performance of that specific sector or group of industries on which it is based.

International investments may involve risk of capital loss from unfavorable fluctuations in currency values, differences in generally accepted accounting principles, or economic or political instability in other nations.

Although exchange traded funds are designed to provide investment results that generally correspond to the price and yield performance of their respective underlying indexes or commodities, the trusts may not be able to exactly replicate that performance because of trust expenses and other factors.

## Questions and Answers about ETFs

### How can I buy or sell exchange traded funds?

Investors can buy or sell exchange traded funds through a broker, the same as stocks.

### How easily can I buy or sell exchange traded funds?

As easily as buying or selling shares of stock. Exchange traded funds are listed on an exchange and can be traded intraday, making it easy for investors to buy or sell exchange traded funds (ETFs).

### What is the minimum size purchase of an exchange traded fund?

Investors can purchase as little as one share.

### Why invest in an index?

Indexing, often called "passive management," involves investing in a group of securities that represent the composition of a broad stock market, stock industry sector, international stock, or U.S. bond index. Index funds offer "market level" performance; they aim to generally match the performance of a specific index. Index funds generally have lower management fees and operating expenses than actively managed funds.

### How does the performance of an exchange traded fund compare with the performance of its underlying index?

Exchange traded funds are designed to provide investment results that generally correspond to their underlying benchmark index by holding a portfolio of securities designed to give similar price and yield performance. In the secondary market, one mechanism that helps to keep an exchange traded fund (ETF) trading on the exchange at a price close to the value of its underlying portfolio is arbitrage. Because

215

exchange traded funds are both created from the securities of an underlying portfolio and can be redeemed into the securities of an underlying portfolio on any day, arbitrage traders may move to profit from any price discrepancies between an exchange traded fund and the portfolio, which in turn helps to close the price gap between the two. Exchange traded funds (ETFs) creations and redemptions are restricted to large transactions, typically in multiples of 50,000 shares but ranging from 25,000 to 600,000 shares, usually transacted by large investors and institutions.) Of course, because of the forces of supply and demand and other market factors, there may be times when shares of an exchange traded fund trade at a premium or discount to its underlying portfolio value.

### Where do exchange traded funds initially come from?

Exchange traded funds are "created" by large investors and institutions in block-sized units of shares (or multiples thereof) known as "creation units" of a respective exchange traded funds (ETFs). A creation requires a deposit with the trustee for a specified number of shares of a portfolio of securities closely approximating the composition of the specific index and a specific amount of cash in return for shares of a specific exchange traded fund. Similarly, block-sized units of exchange traded fund shares can be redeemed in return for a portfolio of securities approximating the index and a specified amount of cash.

### Where can I find exchange traded funds listed in the newspaper?

Investors can find exchange traded funds listed in the financial section of many newspapers under the heading "American Stock Exchange Listed Stocks." They are also listed under "Exchange Traded Portfolios" in the financial section of *The Wall Street Journal*. Many financial information websites have daily pricing information and introductory exchange traded fund information (for example, Yahoo, MSNBC, Seeking Alpha, Index Universe, and *Wall Street Journal Online*).

### Is the value of an exchange traded fund equivalent to the value of the underlying index?

Not necessarily. The share price of many exchange traded funds is initially set at a percentage of the index upon which they are based, but may differ over time due to costs and other factors.

### *Where can I get up-to-date price information on exchange traded funds (ETFs)?*

The pricing of exchange traded funds is continuous on the American Stock Exchange during normal trading hours. Investors can obtain this information from their brokers or stock quotation systems. The closing prices are also published in major newspapers on the following business day. Issuers of exchange traded funds generally have the most up to date daily pricing and performance percentage returns on their family of exchange traded funds. Each issuers home page has multiple links to detailed exchange traded fund information.

### *What are the risks of investing in exchange traded funds (ETFs)?*

Equity-based exchange traded funds are subject to risks similar to those of stocks; fixed income-based exchange traded funds (ETFs) are subject to risks similar to those of bonds. Investment returns will fluctuate and are subject to market volatility, so that an investor's shares, when redeemed or sold, may be worth more or less than their original cost. Foreign investments have unique and greater risks than domestic investments. Past performance is no guarantee of future results.

## ETFs: Terms You Should Know

**authorized participants:** An authorized participant is usually an institutional investor, specialist, or market maker who has signed a participant agreement with a particular exchange traded fund (ETF) sponsor or distributor. Becoming an authorized participant allows an investor to transact directly with the fund or trust on an "in kind" basis in a process known as creations/redemptions.

**creation unit:** The unit size aggregation in which an authorized participant can create or redeem exchange traded fund (ETF) shares with the fund or trust. The creation unit size can vary by fund and ranges from 25,000 to 600,000 shares. Exchange traded funds (ETFs) typically issue shares in creation unit size in exchange for a predefined basket of the underlying index securities. Authorized participants engaging in the creation and redemption process will typically be charged a creation or redemption fee that varies from fund to fund. The fees for creations and redemptions can be found in the prospectus of each exchange traded fund (ETF).

**creations/redemptions:** The process by which authorized participants transact directly with the fund on an "in kind" basis. Creations/redemptions occur in creation unit aggregations or multiples thereof and involve delivering a specified basket of securities to the fund in exchange for exchange traded fund (ETF) shares and vice versa. Creations/redemptions occur at the end-of-day net asset value (NAV) of the fund to avoid dilution of existing fund shares. Creations/redemptions involve an "in kind" transfer of securities, a transaction that is not a taxable event for the fund. This allows imbalances between supply and demand for exchange traded fund (ETF) shares to be satisfied without having an adverse taxable effect upon existing exchange traded fund (ETF) shareholders.

**equal dollar weighted index:** In an equal dollar weighted index, share quantities for each of the component stocks in the index are determined as if one were buying an equal dollar amount of each stock in the index. Equal dollar weighted indexes are usually rebalanced to equal weightings either quarterly, semiannually, or annually.

**exchange traded fund(s):** Exchange traded fund(s) are open-ended registered investment companies under the Investment Company Act of 1940, which have received certain exemptive relief from the U.S. Securities and Exchange Commission (SEC) to allow secondary market trading in the exchange traded fund (ETF) shares. Exchange traded funds (ETFs) are index-based products, in that each exchange traded fund (ETF) holds a portfolio of securities that is intended to provide investment results that, before fees and expenses, generally correspond to the price and yield performance of the underlying benchmark index.

**modified market capitalization index:** This index is set up much like a market capitalization weighted index; however, there has been an adjustment to the weights of one or more of the components. This is typically done to avoid having an index that has one or a few stocks representing a disproportionate amount of the index value.

**net asset value (NAV):** The NAV of an exchange traded funds (ETFs) is determined in a manner consistent with other mutual funds. The NAV is calculated by taking the total assets of the exchange traded fund (ETF), less liabilities, divided by the number of exchange traded fund (ETF) shares outstanding.

**portfolio composition file:** This is a file created by the exchange traded fund (ETF) fund manager or trustee each day after the market close. Its purpose is to tell authorized participants the securities and share quantities that would be required to effect a creation or redemption on the next trading day.

**premium/discount:** The amount (stated in dollars or percent) by which the selling or purchase price of an exchange traded fund (ETF) is greater than (premium) or less than (discount) its face amount/value or net asset value (NAV). See also net asset value (NAV).

**price weighted average:** A price weighted average is computed by taking the average of the market prices of the stocks that make up a particular index. Since the value of the index is based on averaging the prices of the components of the index, the index must have equal share quantities of each of the stocks.

# Chapter 24

# *Closed-End Funds and Unit Investment Trusts*

## *Investment Companies*

Generally, an "investment company" is a company (corporation, business trust, partnership, or limited liability company) that issues securities and is primarily engaged in the business of investing in securities.

An investment company invests the money it receives from investors on a collective basis, and each investor shares in the profits and losses in proportion to the investor's interest in the investment company. The performance of the investment company will be based on (but it won't be identical to) the performance of the securities and other assets that the investment company owns.

The federal securities laws categorize investment companies into three basic types:

- Mutual funds (legally known as open-end companies)

- Closed-end funds (legally known as closed-end companies)

- UITs (legally known as unit investment trusts)

---

This chapter includes text from the following publications of the U.S. Securities and Exchange Commission (www.sec.gov): "Investment Companies," March 2007; "Closed-End Funds," October 2000; "Interval Funds," March 2007; and "Unit Investment Trusts (UITs)," October 2000.

Each type has its own unique features. For example, mutual fund and UIT shares are "redeemable" (meaning that when investors want to sell their shares, they sell them back to the fund or trust, or to a broker acting for the fund or trust, at their approximate net asset value). Closed-end fund shares, on the other hand, generally are not redeemable. Instead, when closed-end fund investors want to sell their shares, they generally sell them to other investors on the secondary market, at a price determined by the market. In addition, there are variations within each type of investment company, such as stock funds, bond funds, money market funds, index funds, interval funds, and exchange-traded funds (ETFs).

Some types of companies that might initially appear to be investment companies may actually be excluded under the federal securities laws. For example, private investment funds with no more than 100 investors and private investment funds whose investors each have a substantial amount of investment assets are not considered to be investment companies—even though they issue securities and are primarily engaged in the business of investing in securities. This may be because of the private nature of their offerings or the financial means and sophistication of their investors.

Before purchasing shares of an investment company, you should carefully read all of a fund's available information, including its prospectus and most recent shareholder report.

Investment companies are regulated primarily under the Investment Company Act of 1940 and the rules and registration forms adopted under that Act. Investment companies are also subject to the Securities Act of 1933 and the Securities Exchange Act of 1934. For the definition of "investment company," you should refer to Section 3 of the Investment Company Act of 1940 and the rules under that section.

## Closed-End Funds

A "closed-end fund," legally known as a "closed-end company," is one of three basic types of investment company. The two other basic types of investment companies are mutual funds and Unit Investments Trusts (UITs).

Here are some of the traditional and distinguishing characteristics of closed-end funds:

- Closed-end funds generally do not continuously offer their shares for sale. Rather, they sell a fixed number of shares at one time (in the initial public offering), after which the shares typically trade on a secondary market, such as the New York Stock Exchange or the NASDAQ Stock Market.

- The price of closed-end fund shares that trade on a secondary market after their initial public offering is determined by the market and may be greater or less than the shares' net asset value (NAV).

- Closed-end fund shares generally are not redeemable. That is, a closed-end fund is not required to buy its shares back from investors upon request. Some closed-end funds, commonly referred to as interval funds, offer to repurchase their shares at specified intervals.

- The investment portfolios of closed-end funds generally are managed by separate entities known as "investment advisers" that are registered with the SEC.

- Closed-end funds also are permitted to invest in a greater amount of "illiquid" securities than mutual funds. (An "illiquid" security generally is considered to be a security that can't be sold within seven days at the approximate price used by the fund in determining NAV.) Because of this feature, funds that seek to invest in markets where the securities tend to be more illiquid are typically organized as closed-end funds.

Closed-end funds come in many varieties. They can have different investment objectives, strategies, and investment portfolios. They also can be subject to different risks, volatility, and fees and expenses.

Keep in mind that just because a fund had excellent performance last year does not necessarily mean that it will duplicate that performance. For example, market conditions can change and this year's winning fund could be next year's loser. You should carefully read all of a fund's available information, including its prospectus and most recent shareholder report before purchasing mutual fund shares.

Closed-end funds are subject to SEC registration and regulation, and are subject to numerous requirements imposed for the protection of investors. Closed-end funds are regulated primarily under the Investment Company Act of 1940 and the rules adopted under that Act. Closed-end funds are also subject to the Securities Act of 1933 and the Securities Exchange Act of 1934. You can find the definition of "closed-end company" in Section 5 of the Investment Company Act.

## Interval Funds

An interval fund is a type of investment company that periodically offers to repurchase its shares from shareholders. That is, the fund periodically offers to buy back a stated portion of its shares from shareholders. Shareholders are not required to accept these offers and sell their shares back to the fund.

Legally, interval funds are classified as closed-end funds, but they are very different from traditional closed-end funds in that:

- Their shares typically do not trade on the secondary market. Instead, their shares are subject to periodic repurchase offers by the fund at a price based on net asset value.

- They are permitted to (and many interval funds do) continuously offer their shares at a priced based on the fund's net asset value.

An interval fund will make periodic repurchase offers to its shareholders, generally every three, six, or twelve months, as disclosed in the fund's prospectus and annual report. The interval fund also will periodically notify its shareholders of the upcoming repurchase dates. When the fund makes a repurchase offer to its shareholders, it will specify a date by which shareholders must accept the repurchase offer. The actual repurchase will occur at a later, specified date.

The price that shareholders will receive on a repurchase will be based on the per share NAV determined as of a specified (and disclosed) date. This date will occur sometime after the close of business on the date that shareholders must submit their acceptances of the repurchase offer (but generally not more than 14 days after the acceptance date).

Note that interval funds are permitted to deduct a redemption fee from the repurchase proceeds, not to exceed 2% of the proceeds. The fee is paid to the fund, and generally is intended to compensate the fund for expenses directly related to the repurchase. Interval funds may charge other fees as well.

An interval fund's prospectus and annual report will disclose the various details of the repurchase offer. Before investing in an interval fund, you should carefully read all of the fund's available information, including its prospectus and most recent shareholder report.

Interval funds are regulated primarily under the Investment Company Act of 1940 and the rules adopted under that Act, in particular Rule 23c-3. Interval funds are also subject to the Securities Act of 1933 and the Securities Exchange Act of 1934.

## Unit Investment Trusts (UITs)

A "unit investment trust," commonly referred to as a "UIT," is one of three basic types of investment company. The other two types are mutual funds and closed-end funds.

Here are some of the traditional and distinguishing characteristics of UITs:

- A UIT typically issues redeemable securities (or "units"), like a mutual fund, which means that the UIT will buy back an investor's "units," at the investor's request, at their approximate net asset value (or NAV). Some exchange-traded funds (ETFs) are structured as UITs. Under SEC exemptive orders, shares of ETFs are only redeemable in very large blocks (blocks of 50,000 shares, for example) and are traded on a secondary market.

- A UIT typically will make a one-time "public offering" of only a specific, fixed number of units (like closed-end funds). Many UIT sponsors, however, will maintain a secondary market that allows owners of UIT units to sell them back to the sponsors and allows other investors to buy UIT units from the sponsors.

- A UIT will have a termination date (a date when the UIT will terminate and dissolve) that is established when the UIT is created (although some may terminate more than fifty years after they are created). In the case of a UIT investing in bonds, for example, the termination date may be determined by the maturity date of the bond investments. When a UIT terminates, any remaining investment portfolio securities are sold and the proceeds are paid to the investors.

- A UIT does not actively trade its investment portfolio. That is, a UIT buys a relatively fixed portfolio of securities (for example, five, ten, or twenty specific stocks or bonds), and holds them with little or no change for the life of the UIT. Because the investment portfolio of a UIT generally is fixed, investors know more or less what they are investing in for the duration of their investment. Investors will find the portfolio securities held by the UIT listed in its prospectus.

- A UIT does not have a board of directors, corporate officers, or an investment adviser to render advice during the life of the trust.

Keep in mind that just because a UIT had excellent performance last year does not necessarily mean that it will duplicate that performance. For example, market conditions can change, and this year's winning UIT could be next year's loser. That is why the SEC requires funds to tell investors that a fund's past performance does not necessarily predict future results. Before investing in a UIT, you should carefully read all of the UIT's available information, including its prospectus.

UITs are regulated primarily under the Investment Company Act of 1940 and the rules adopted under that Act, in particular Section 4 and Section 26.

# Chapter 25

# *Real Estate Investment Trusts (REITs)*

Real estate investment trusts (REITs) are an efficient way for many investors to invest in commercial and residential real estate businesses. As an investment, REITs combine the best features of real estate and stocks. They give an investor a practical and effective means to include professionally managed real estate in a diversified investment portfolio.

The REIT industry began its fifth decade in 2000. Because of the industry's overall maturity and performance over the last four decades, REITs can be viewed as "all-weather" investments.

Here are answers to fundamental questions about REITs for investors, financial planners, stock brokers, the media, and the general public.

### *What is a REIT?*

A REIT is a company that owns, and in most cases, operates income-producing real estate such as apartments, shopping centers, offices, hotels, and warehouses. Some REITs also engage in financing real estate. The shares of many REITs are freely traded, usually on a major stock exchange.

To qualify as a REIT, a company must distribute at least 90 percent of its taxable income to its shareholders annually. A company that

---

Excerpted from "Frequently Asked Questions about REITs," © National Association of Real Estate Investment Trusts. Reprinted with permission. Available online at http://www.investinreits.com/learn/faq.cfm; accessed October 2006.

qualifies as a REIT is permitted to deduct dividends paid to its shareholders from its corporate taxable income. As a result, most REITs remit at least 100 percent of their taxable income to their shareholders and therefore owe no corporate tax. Taxes are paid by shareholders on the dividends received and any capital gains. Most states honor this federal treatment and also do not require REITs to pay state income tax. Like other businesses, but unlike partnerships, a REIT cannot pass any tax losses through to its investors.

### Why were REITs created?

Congress created REITs in 1960 to make investments in large-scale, income-producing real estate accessible to smaller investors. Congress decided that a way for average investors to invest in large scale commercial properties was the same way they invest in other industries, through the purchase of equity. In the same way as shareholders benefit by owning stocks of other corporations, the stockholders of a REIT earn a pro-rata share of the economic benefits that are derived from the production of income through commercial real estate ownership. REITs offer distinct advantages for investors: greater diversification through investing in a portfolio of properties rather than a single building and management by experienced real estate professionals.

### How does a company qualify as a REIT?

In order for a company to qualify as a REIT, it must comply with certain provisions within the Internal Revenue Code. As required by the tax code, a REIT must:

- Be an entity that is taxable as a corporation;
- Be managed by a board of directors or trustees;
- Have shares that are fully transferable;
- Have a minimum of 100 shareholders;
- Have no more than 50 percent of its shares held by five or fewer individuals during the last half of the taxable year;
- Invest at least 75 percent of its total assets in real estate assets;
- Derive at least 75 percent of its gross income from rents from real estate property or interest on mortgages on real property;
- Have no more than 20 percent of its assets consist of stocks in taxable REIT subsidiaries;

- Pay annually at least 90 percent of its taxable income in the form of shareholder dividends.

## How many REITs are there?

There are about 190 REITs registered with the Securities and Exchange Commission (SEC) in the United States that trade on one of the major stock exchanges—the majority on the New York Stock Exchange. Total assets of these listed REITs exceed $400 billion.

About 20 REITs are registered with the SEC but are not publicly traded. Approximately 800 REITs are not registered with the SEC and are not traded on a stock exchange.

## What types of REITs are there?

The REIT industry has a diverse profile, which offers many alternative investment opportunities to investors. REITs often are classified in one of three categories: equity, mortgage or hybrid.

**Equity REITs:** Equity REITs own and operate income-producing real estate. Equity REITs increasingly have become primarily real estate operating companies that engage in a wide range of real estate activities, including leasing, development of real property, and tenant services. One major distinction between REITs and other real estate companies is that a REIT must acquire and develop its properties primarily to operate them as part of its own portfolio rather than to resell them once they are developed.

**Mortgage REITs:** Mortgage REITs lend money directly to real estate owners and operators or extend credit indirectly through the acquisition of loans or mortgage-backed securities. Today's mortgage REITs generally extend mortgage credit only on existing properties. Many modern mortgage REITs also manage their interest rate risk using securitized mortgage investments and dynamic hedging techniques.

**Hybrid REITs:** As the name suggests, a hybrid REIT both owns properties and makes loans to real estate owners and operators.

## How are REITs structured?

REITs are typically structured in one of three ways: Traditional, UPREIT, and DownREIT. A traditional REIT is one that owns its assets directly rather than through an operating partnership.

In the typical UPREIT, the partners of an existing partnership and a REIT become partners in a new partnership termed the operating partnership. For their respective interests in the operating partnership (units), the partners contribute the properties from the existing partnership and the REIT contributes the cash. The REIT typically is the general partner and the majority owner of the operating partnership units.

After a period of time (often one year), the partners may enjoy the same liquidity of the REIT shareholders by tendering their units for either cash or REIT shares (at the option of the REIT or operating partnership). This conversion may result in the partners incurring the tax deferred at the UPREIT's formation. The unitholders may tender their units over a period of time, thereby spreading out such tax. In addition, when a partner holds the units until death, the estate tax rules operate in such a way as to provide that the beneficiaries may tender the units for cash or REIT shares without paying income taxes.

A DownREIT is structured much like an UPREIT, but the REIT owns and operates properties other than its interest in a controlled partnership that owns and operates separate properties.

### *What types of properties do REITs invest in?*

REITs invest in a variety of property types: shopping centers, apartments, warehouses, office buildings, hotels, and others. Most REITs specialize in one property type only, such as shopping malls, self-storage facilities, or factory outlet stores. Health care REITs specialize in health care facilities, including acute care, rehabilitation and psychiatric hospitals, medical office buildings, nursing homes, and assisted living centers.

Some REITs invest throughout the country or in certain other countries. Others specialize in one region only, or even a single metropolitan area.

### *Who determines a REIT's investments?*

A REIT's investments are determined by its board of directors or trustees. Like other publicly traded companies, a REIT's directors are elected by, and responsible to, the shareholders. In turn, the directors appoint the management personnel. As with other corporations, REIT directors are typically well-known and respected members of the real estate, business, and professional communities.

## *How are REITs managed?*

Like other public companies, the corporate officers and professionals that manage REITs are accountable to both their boards of directors as well as their shareholders and creditors. Many REITs became public companies within the past 10 years, often transforming to public ownership what previously had been private enterprises. In many cases, the majority owners of these private enterprises became the senior officers of the REIT and rolled their ownership positions into shares of the new public companies. Thus, the senior management teams of many REITs have ownership interests which are aligned with the interests of shareholders.

## *How do REITs measure financial performance?*

Like the rest of corporate America, the REIT industry uses net income as defined under generally accepted accounting principles (GAAP) as the primary operating performance measure for real estate companies.

The REIT industry also uses funds from operations (FFO) as a supplemental measure of a REIT's operating performance. The National Association of Real Estate Investment Trusts (NAREIT) defines FFO as net income (computed in accordance with GAAP) excluding gains or losses from sales of most property and depreciation of real estate. When real estate companies use FFO in public releases or SEC filings, the law requires them to reconcile FFO to GAAP net income.

Many real estate professionals as well as investors believe that commercial real estate maintains residual value to a much greater extent than machinery, computers, or other personal property. Therefore, they view the depreciation measure used to arrive at GAAP net income as generally overstating the economic depreciation of REIT property assets and the actual cost to maintain and replace these assets over time, which may in fact be appreciating. Thus, FFO excludes real estate depreciation charges from periodic operating performance. Many securities analysts judge a REIT's performance according to its adjusted FFO (AFFO), thereby deducting certain recurring capital expenses from FFO.

NAREIT's April 2002 "White Paper" on FFO discusses the definition in detail, advises REITs to adopt certain computational and disclosure practices, and recommends that REITs disclose additional information about other financial calculations such as details on capital expenditures.

## *How do shareholders treat REIT distributions for tax purposes?*

REITs are required by law to distribute each year to their shareholders at least 90 percent of their taxable income. Thus, as investments, REITs tend to be among those companies paying the highest dividends. The dividends come primarily from the relatively stable and predictable stream of contractual rents paid by the tenants who occupy the REIT's properties. Since rental rates tend to rise during periods of inflation, REIT dividends tend to be protected from the long-term corrosive effect of rising prices.

For REITs, dividend distributions for tax purposes are allocated to ordinary income, capital gains, and return of capital, each of which may be taxed at a different rate. All public companies, including REITs, are required to provide their shareholders early in the year with information clarifying how the prior year's dividends should be allocated for tax purposes. This information is distributed by each company to its list of shareholders on IRS Form 1099-DIV. An historical record of the allocation of REIT distributions between ordinary income, return of capital and capital gains can be found at NAREIT's website, http://www.nareit.com. A return of capital distribution is defined as that part of the dividend that exceeds the REIT's taxable income. Because real estate depreciation is such a large non-cash expense that may overstate any decline in property values, the dividend rate divided by funds from operations (FFO) or adjusted funds from operations (AFFO) is used by many as a measure of the REIT's ability to pay dividends.

A return of capital distribution is not taxed as ordinary income. Rather, the investor's cost basis in the stock is reduced by the amount of the distribution. When shares are sold, the excess of the net sales price over the reduced tax basis is treated as a capital gain for tax purposes. So long as the appropriate capital gains rate is less than the investor's marginal ordinary income tax rate, a high return of capital distribution may be especially attractive to investors in higher tax brackets.

## *Are REIT dividends subject to the new 15 percent maximum tax rate?*

In May 2003, the U.S. Congress passed the Jobs and Growth Tax Relief Reconciliation Act, which cut income tax rates on most dividends and capital gains to a 15 percent maximum. Because REITs do not generally pay corporate taxes, the majority of REIT dividends continue to be taxed as ordinary income at the maximum new rate of 35 percent (down from 38.6 percent).

However, REIT dividends will qualify for a lower tax rate in the following instances:

- When the individual taxpayer is subject to a lower scheduled income tax rate;

- When a REIT makes a capital gains distribution (15 percent maximum tax rate);

- When a REIT distributes dividends received from a taxable REIT subsidiary or other corporation (15 percent maximum tax rate); and

- When permitted, a REIT pays corporate taxes and retains earnings (15 percent maximum tax rate).

In addition, the maximum 15 percent capital gains rate applies generally to the sale of REIT stock.

Available data indicate that about 44 percent of REIT dividends qualified for the lower 15 percent capital gains rate in 2005. Of this amount, 36 percent represented capital gain distributions and 64 percent represented return of capital, which is taxed at a capital gain rate when the stock is sold.

## What real estate fundamentals should I consider before investing?

REIT investors often compare current stock prices to the net asset value (NAV) of a company's assets. NAV is the per share measure of the market value of a company's net assets. At times, the stock price of a REIT may be more or less than its NAV. Investors should understand some of the fundamental factors that influence the value of a REIT's real estate holdings. One critical factor is how well balanced the supply of new buildings is with the demand for new space. When construction adds new space into a market more rapidly than it can be absorbed, building vacancy rates increase, rents can weaken, and property values decline, thereby depressing net asset values.

In a strong economy, growth in employment, capital investment, and household spending increase the demand for new office buildings, apartments, industrial facilities, and retail stores. Population growth also boosts the demand for apartments. However, the economy is not always equally strong in all geographic regions, and economic growth may not increase the demand for all property types at the same time. Thus, investors should compare the locations of properties of different companies with the relative strength or weakness of real estate markets in those locations.

Information on company properties is available at their internet sites, while information on local and regional real estate markets is available in the financial press or at research sites on the internet such as http://www.lendlease.com or http://www.tortowheatonresearch.com.

### How has real estate financing changed over time?

Historically, income-producing commercial real estate often was financed with high levels of debt. Properties provided tangible security for mortgage financing, and the rental income from those properties was a clear source of revenue to pay the interest expense on the loan. Property markets often were dominated by developers or entrepreneurial businessmen who were attempting to build personal fortunes and who were willing to take on huge risks to do so. Prior to the real estate recession of the early 1990s, it was not uncommon for individual properties to carry mortgages that represented over 90 percent of the properties' estimated market value or cost of construction. Occasionally, loan-to-value ratios went even higher. The severe real estate recession of the early 1990s forced many real estate lenders, developers and owners to reconsider the appropriate use of debt financing on real estate projects.

Today, properties owned by REITs are financed on a much more conservative basis. On average, REITs are financing their projects with about half debt and half equity, which significantly reduces interest rate exposure and creates a much stronger and less volatile business operation. Two-thirds of the REITs with senior unsecured debt ratings are investment grade.

### How are REIT stocks valued?

Like all companies whose stocks are publicly traded, REIT shares are priced every day in the market and give investors an opportunity to value their portfolios daily. To assess the investment value of REIT shares, typical analysis involves one or more of the following criteria:

- Management quality and corporate structure

- Anticipated total return from the stock, estimated from the expected price change and the prevailing dividend yield

- Current dividend yields relative to other yield-oriented investments (for example, bonds, utility stocks, and other high-income investments)
- Dividend payout ratios as a percent of REIT FFO
- Anticipated growth in earnings per share
- Underlying asset values of the real estate and/or mortgages, and other assets

Stock of REITs that are registered with the SEC but not publicly traded on an exchange should be valued in consultation with a qualified financial advisor.

## What factors contribute to REIT earnings?

Growth in earnings typically comes from several sources, including higher revenues, lower costs, and new business opportunities. The most immediate sources of revenue growth are higher rates of building occupancy and increasing rents. As long as the demand for new properties remains well balanced with the available supply, market rents tend to rise as the economy expands. Low occupancy in underutilized buildings can be increased when skilled owners upgrade facilities, enhance building services, and more effectively market properties to new types of tenants. Property acquisition and development programs also create growth opportunities, provided the economic returns from these investments exceed the cost of financing. Like other public companies, REITs and publicly traded real estate companies also increase earnings by improving efficiency and taking advantage of new business opportunities.

The REIT Modernization Act (RMA), which took effect on January 1, 2001, provides REITs with other opportunities to increase earnings. Prior to the enactment of the RMA, REITs were limited to providing only those services that were long accepted as being "usual and customary" landlord services, and were restricted from offering more cutting-edge services provided by other landlords. The RMA allows REITs to create subsidiaries that can provide the competitive services that many of today's tenants desire.

## What should I look for when investing in a REIT?

The market usually rewards companies that demonstrate consistent earnings and dividend growth with higher price-earnings multiples. Thus, investors should look for REITs and publicly traded real estate companies with the following characteristics:

- A demonstrated ability to increase earnings in a reliable manner. For example, look for companies with properties in which rents are below current market levels. Such properties provide upside potential in equilibrium markets and downside protection when economic growth slows.

- Management teams able to quickly and effectively reinvest available cash flow. The ability to consistently complete new projects on time and within budget.

- Creative management teams with sound strategies for developing new revenue opportunities under the REIT Modernization Act.

- Strong operating characteristics, including effective corporate governance procedures, conservative leverage, widely accepted accounting practices, strong tenant relationships, and a clearly defined operating strategy for succeeding in competitive markets.

### *How do I invest in a REIT?*

An individual may invest in a publicly traded REIT, which is listed on a major stock exchange, by purchasing shares through a stockbroker. As with other publicly traded securities, investors may purchase common stock, preferred stock, or debt securities. An investor can enlist the services of a broker, investment advisor, or financial planner to help analyze his or her financial objectives. These professionals may be able to recommend appropriate REIT investments for the investor. An investor may also contact a REIT directly for a copy of the company's annual report, prospectus, and other financial information. Much of this information is available on a company's website. The NAREIT website, http://www.nareit.com, also lists all publicly traded REITs with their exchange symbols. Many local libraries offer a wide range of publications which provide investment research and information on public companies such as REITs.

Another alternative is to diversify your investment further by buying shares in a mutual fund that specializes in investing in real estate securities. A list of such mutual funds is available at the NAREIT website. Investors can compare and evaluate the performance of mutual funds through public information sources such as Morningstar, Inc., which can also be found in many local libraries. These sources can offer detailed information on past performance, current portfolio holdings, and information dealing with the various costs of investing in funds. There are also a number of real estate and REIT exchange traded funds and closed end funds.

# Chapter 26

# *Annuities*

## *What are the different types of annuities?*

**Fixed vs. variable annuities:** In a fixed annuity, the insurance company guarantees the principal and a minimum rate of interest. In other words, as long as the insurance company is financially sound, the money you have in a fixed annuity will grow and will not drop in value. The growth of the annuity's value and/or the benefits paid may be fixed at a dollar amount or by an interest rate, or they may grow by a specified formula. The growth of the annuity's value and/or the benefits paid does not depend directly or entirely on the performance of the investments the insurance company makes to support the annuity. Some fixed annuities credit a higher interest rate than the minimum, via a policy dividend that may be declared by the company's board of directors, if the company's actual investment, expense, and mortality experience is more favorable than was expected. Fixed annuities are regulated by state insurance departments.

Money in a variable annuity is invested in a fund—like a mutual fund but one open only to investors in the insurance company's variable life insurance and variable annuities. The fund has a particular investment objective, and the value of your money in a variable annuity—and the amount of money to be paid out to you—is determined by the investment performance (net of expenses) of that fund. Most variable annuities are structured to offer investors many different fund alternatives. Variable annuities are regulated by state insurance departments and the federal Securities and Exchange Commission (SEC).

**Types of fixed annuities:** An equity-indexed annuity is a type of fixed annuity, but looks like a hybrid. It credits a minimum rate of interest, just as a fixed annuity does, but its value is also based on the performance of a specified stock index—usually computed as a fraction of that index's total return.

A market-value-adjusted annuity is one that combines two desirable features—the ability to select and fix the time period and interest rate over which your annuity will grow, and the flexibility to withdraw money from the annuity before the end of the time period selected. This withdrawal flexibility is achieved by adjusting the annuity's value, up or down, to reflect the change in the interest rate "market" (that is, the general level of interest rates) from the start of the selected time period to the time of withdrawal.

**Other types of annuities:** All of the following types of annuities are available in fixed or variable forms.

*Deferred vs. immediate annuities:* A deferred annuity receives premiums and investment changes for payout at a later time. The payout might be a very long time; deferred annuities for retirement can remain in the deferred stage for decades.

An immediate annuity is designed to pay an income one time-period after the immediate annuity is bought. The time period depends on how often the income is to be paid. For example, if the income is monthly, the first payment comes one month after the immediate annuity is bought.

*Fixed period vs. lifetime annuities:* A fixed period annuity pays an income for a specified period of time, such as ten years. The amount that is paid doesn't depend on the age (or continued life) of the person who buys the annuity; the payments depend instead on the amount paid into the annuity, the length of the payout period, and (if it's a fixed annuity) an interest rate that the insurance company believes it can support for the length of the pay-out period.

A lifetime annuity provides income for the remaining life of a person (called the "annuitant"). A variation of lifetime annuities continues income until the second one of two annuitants dies. No other type of financial product can promise to do this. The amount that is paid depends on the age of the annuitant (or ages, if it's a two-life annuity), the amount paid into the annuity, and (if it's a fixed annuity) an interest rate that the insurance company believes it can support for the length of the expected pay-out period.

With a "pure" lifetime annuity, the payments stop when the annuitant dies, even if that's a very short time after they began. Many annuity buyers are uncomfortable at this possibility, so they add a guaranteed period—essentially a fixed period annuity—to their lifetime annuity. With this combination, if you die before the fixed period ends, the income continues to your beneficiaries until the end of that period.

*Qualified vs. nonqualified annuities:* A qualified annuity is one used to invest and disburse money in a tax-favored retirement plan, such as an IRA or Keogh plan or plans governed by Internal Revenue Code sections, 401(k), 403(b), or 457. Under the terms of the plan, money paid into the annuity (called "premiums" or "contributions") is not included in taxable income for the year in which it is paid in. All other tax provisions that apply to nonqualified annuities also apply to qualified annuities.

A nonqualified annuity is one purchased separately from, or "outside of," a tax-favored retirement plan. Investment earnings of all annuities, qualified and non-qualified, are tax-deferred until they are withdrawn; at that point they are treated as taxable income (regardless of whether they came from selling capital at a gain or from dividends).

*Single premium vs. flexible premium annuities:* A single premium annuity is an annuity funded by a single payment. The payment might be invested for growth for a long period of time—a single premium deferred annuity—or invested for a short time, after which payout begins—a single premium immediate annuity. Single premium annuities are often funded by rollovers or from the sale of an appreciated asset.

A flexible premium annuity is an annuity that is intended to be funded by a series of payments. Flexible premium annuities are only deferred annuities; that is, they are designed to have a significant period of payments into the annuity plus investment growth before any money is withdrawn from them.

## What is the difference between a fixed and variable annuity?

Fixed annuities pay a "fixed" rate of return. When you receive payments, the monthly payout is a set amount and is guaranteed. Fixed annuities may be a good choice for:

- Conservative investors who value safety and stability.

- Those nearing retirement who want to shelter their assets from the volatility of the stock or bond market.

With variable annuities, you can invest in a variety of securities including stock and bond funds. Stock market performance determines the annuity's value and the return you will get from the money you invest. The amount of risk you are willing to assume should influence the kind of funds you select.

You may want to consider a variable annuity if you are:

- Comfortable with fluctuations in the stock market and want your investments to keep pace with inflation over a long period of time.

- Young and want to prepare financially for retirement by reaping the gains in the stock or bond market over the long term.

### What are deferred and immediate annuities?

**Deferred annuity:** This type of annuity is good for long-term retirement planning for the following reasons:

- Payments on income taxes are deferred until you withdraw the money.

- Unlike a 401(k) or an IRA, there are no limits on your annual annuity contributions.

- There is a death benefit. If you die before collecting on the annuity, your heirs get the amount you contributed, plus investment earnings, minus whatever cash withdrawals you made.

**Immediate annuity:** This allows you to convert a lump sum of money into an annuity so that you can immediately receive income. Payments generally start about a month after you purchase the annuity. This type of annuity offers financial security in the form of income payments for the rest of your life. In other words, you cannot outlive it.

Immediate annuities allow you to:

- Supplement your current income. If you are nearing retirement, you may consider transferring another savings or investment account into an immediate annuity. You can also move the proceeds from a deferred annuity into an immediate annuity.

- Pay taxes only on the portion of your immediate annuity payments that is considered earnings. You are not taxed on the portion that is principal. The principal is the initial deposit made with funds that have already been taxed.

Like deferred annuities, immediate annuities can be fixed or variable. Fixed immediate annuity income payments are pegged to the amount you contribute, your age, and the interest rate at the time of purchase. Those payments to you will not go up or down. Variable immediate annuity payments vary with the investments you chose.

## *What is a lifetime annuity?*

You can think of a lifetime annuity as investment vehicle that functions as a personal pension plan. Sometimes referred to as "single life," "straight life," or "non-refund," these are a form of immediate annuity that provides income for your entire life. The payments can be increased to cover a second person. This is called a "Joint and Survivor" annuity. While most provide income for life, some may offer the option of payments for a fixed number of years.

A lifetime annuity could serve as a retirement income supplement to Social Security checks, 401(k) retirement plans, company pension funds, etc. Lifetime annuities provide income for as long as you live—even after all the money you contributed is exhausted. They can be useful for those who want the certainty and security of establishing a regular and guaranteed income stream. If, however, you die before all the funds in your account have been used up, the payment option to your beneficiaries will be determined by the choice you made when you purchased the annuity. In some cases, no payouts will be made to your dependents or other beneficiaries. Instead, you will be getting an income that you can't outlive.

A straight life annuity makes sense for someone who needs the most retirement income possible and does not plan to use the money invested for dependents or other beneficiaries.

## *How are annuities different from life insurance?*

Both annuities and life insurance can be considered in your long-term financial plan. While both include death benefits, you buy life insurance in the event you die too soon and an annuity in case you live too long. In other words, life insurance provides economic protection to your loved ones if you die before your financial obligations to them are met, while annuities guard against outliving your assets.

241

**Table 26.1.** Life Insurance versus Annuities

| | **Life Insurance** | |
|---|---|---|
| | Term life | Whole life |
| **Main reason for buying it** | Provide income for dependents | Provide income for dependents or meetd estate planning needs |
| **Pays out when** | You die | You die, borrow the cash value, or surrender the policy |
| **Typical form of payment** | Single sum | Single sum |
| **Buyer's age when it is typically bought** | 25–50 | 30–60 |
| **Accumulates money tax-deferred?** | No | Yes |
| **Pays a death benefit?** | Yes | Yes |
| **Are benefits taxable income when received?** | No | No, unless a cash value withdrawal exceeds the sum of premiums |

**Annuities**

| | Deferred annuities | Immediate annuities |
|---|---|---|
| **Main reason for buying it** | To accumulate money in a tax-deferred product | To assure you don't "outlive your income" |
| **Pays out when** | You make withdrawals | One period after you buy the annuity, stops paying when you die (payments continue if the annuity has a guaranteed-period option that hasn't expired at the annuitant's death) |
| **Typical form of payment** | Single sum or income | Lifetime income |
| **Buyer's age when it is typically bought** | 40–65 | 55–80 |
| **Accumulates money tax-deferred?** | Yes | Yes, but only in the early payout years |
| **Pays a death benefit?** | Yes | Payments continueif the annuity has a guaranteed-period option that hasn't expired at the annuitant's death) |
| **Are benefits taxable income when received?** | Yes, but only the part derived from investment income | Yes, but only the part derived from investment income |

243

There are two main types of annuities—deferred and immediate— and two main types of life insurance—term and whole life. Table 26.1 compares them.

### *How are annuities sold?*

Annuities can be purchased through insurance agents, financial planners, banks, and life insurance carriers. However, only life insurance companies issue policies.

Here is a closer look:

**Agents:** Agents are insurance professionals who are licensed by your state insurance department. Some agents work exclusively for one insurance company, while others represent several.

If you decide to use an insurance agent, find one who is knowledgeable about annuities and has a reputation for excellent customer service. The agent should be able to advise you and answer all your questions. If you are thinking about buying a variable annuity, the agent should also have a license to sell variable annuity products. Since variable annuities are considered securities, you should receive a prospectus describing the investment alternatives available to you.

**Banks and brokerage firms:** Products developed by life insurance companies are often marketed through banks and stock brokerage firms. Make sure the person who sells you the annuity is a licensed life insurance agent. In the case of a variable annuity, the agent should also be a licensed securities dealer. If you buy an annuity through a bank or brokerage firm, you should ask about the types of annuities the insurer issues and the financial strength of the insurance company.

## *About the Insurance Information Institute*

The mission of the Insurance Information Institute (I.I.I.) is to improve public understanding of all forms of insurance including auto, home, life, health, annuities, long-term care, disability, and business. For complete information, including a list of available brochures and other publications, visit www.iii.org.

# Chapter 27

# *Hedge Funds*

## *What are hedge funds?*

Like mutual funds, hedge funds pool investors' money and invest those funds in financial instruments in an effort to make a positive return. Many hedge funds seek to profit in all kinds of markets by pursuing leveraging and other speculative investment practices that may increase the risk of investment loss.

Unlike mutual funds, however, hedge funds are not required to register with the U.S. Securities and Exchange Commission (SEC). This means that hedge funds are subject to very few regulatory controls. Because of this lack of regulatory oversight, hedge funds historically have generally been available solely to accredited investors and large institutions. Most hedge funds also have voluntarily restricted investment to wealthy investors through high investment minimums (for example, $1 million).

Historically, most hedge fund managers have not been required to register with the SEC and therefore have not been subject to regular SEC oversight. However, in December 2004, the SEC issued a final rule and rule amendments that require certain hedge fund managers to register with the SEC as investment advisers under the Investment Advisers Act by February 1, 2006.

---

"Hedging Your Bets: A Heads Up on Hedge Funds and Funds of Hedge Funds," U.S. Securities and Exchange Commission (www.sec.gov), May 2006.

## *What are "funds of hedge funds?"*

A fund of hedge funds is an investment company that invests in hedge funds—rather than investing in individual securities. Some funds of hedge funds register their securities with the SEC. These funds of hedge funds must provide investors with a prospectus and must file certain reports quarterly with the SEC.

Note: Not all funds of hedge funds register with the SEC.

Many registered funds of hedge funds have much lower investment minimums ($25,000) than individual hedge funds. Thus, some investors that would be unable to invest in a hedge fund directly may be able to purchase shares of registered funds of hedge funds.

## *What information should I seek if I am considering investing in a hedge fund or a fund of hedge funds?*

Read a fund's prospectus or offering memorandum and related materials. Make sure you understand the level of risk involved in the fund's investment strategies and ensure that they are suitable to your personal investing goals, time horizons, and risk tolerance. As with any investment, the higher the potential returns, the higher the risks you must assume.

Understand how a fund's assets are valued. Funds of hedge funds and hedge funds may invest in highly illiquid securities that may be difficult to value. Moreover, many hedge funds give themselves significant discretion in valuing securities. You should understand a fund's valuation process and know the extent to which a fund's securities are valued by independent sources.

Ask questions about fees. Fees impact your return on investment. Hedge funds typically charge an asset management fee of 1–2% of assets, plus a "performance fee" of 20% of a hedge fund's profits. A performance fee could motivate a hedge fund manager to take greater risks in the hope of generating a larger return. Funds of hedge funds typically charge a fee for managing your assets, and some may also include a performance fee based on profits. These fees are charged in addition to any fees paid to the underlying hedge funds.

Tip: If you invest in hedge funds through a fund of hedge funds, you will pay two layers of fees: the fees of the fund of hedge funds and the fees charged by the underlying hedge funds.

- Understand any limitations on your right to redeem your shares. Hedge funds typically limit opportunities to redeem, or cash in, your shares (for example, to four times a year), and often impose a "lock-up" period of one year or more, during which you cannot cash in your shares.

- Research the backgrounds of hedge fund managers. Know with whom you are investing. Make sure hedge fund managers are qualified to manage your money, and find out whether they have a disciplinary history within the securities industry. You can get this information (and more) by reviewing the adviser's Form ADV. You can search for and view a firm's Form ADV using the SEC's Investment Adviser Public Disclosure (IAPD) website (http://www.adviserinfo.sec.gov). You also can get copies of Form ADV for individual advisers and firms from the investment adviser, the SEC's Public Reference Room, or (for advisers with less than $25 million in assets under management) the state securities regulator where the adviser's principal place of business is located. If you don't find the investment adviser firm in the SEC's IAPD database, be sure to call your state securities regulator or search the National Association of Securities Dealers (NASD)'s BrokerCheck database (available through a link at http://www.nasd.com) for any information they may have.

- Don't be afraid to ask questions. You are entrusting your money to someone else. You should know where your money is going, who is managing it, how it is being invested, how you can get it back, what protections are placed on your investment and what your rights are as an investor. In addition, you may wish to read NASD's investor alert, which describes some of the high costs and risks of investing in funds of hedge funds.

### *What protections do I have if I purchase a hedge fund?*

Hedge fund investors do not receive all of the federal and state law protections that commonly apply to most registered investments. For example, you won't get the same level of disclosures from a hedge fund that you'll get from registered investments. Without the disclosures that the securities laws require for most registered investments, it can be quite difficult to verify representations you may receive from a hedge fund. You should also be aware that, while the SEC may conduct examinations of any hedge fund manager that is registered as an investment adviser under the Investment Advisers Act, the SEC and other securities regulators generally have limited ability to check routinely on hedge fund activities.

The SEC can take action against a hedge fund that defrauds investors, and the agency has pursued a number of fraud cases involving hedge funds. Commonly in these cases, hedge fund advisers misrepresented their experience and the fund's track record. Other cases were classic "Ponzi schemes," where early investors were paid off to make the scheme look legitimate. In some of the cases we have brought, the hedge funds sent phony account statements to investors to camouflage the fact that their money had been stolen. That's why it is extremely important to thoroughly check out every aspect of any hedge fund you might consider as an investment.

### What should I do if I have a complaint about a hedge fund or a fund of hedge funds?

If you encounter a problem with your hedge fund or fund of hedge funds, you can send the SEC your complaint using their online complaint form at www.sec.gov/complaint.shtml. You can also reach them by regular mail at:

Securities and Exchange Commission
Office of Investor Education and Assistance
100 F Street, NE
Washington, DC 20549-0213

# Chapter 28

# *Speculation in Futures Contracts: Opportunity and Risk*

## *Futures Contracts*

A futures contract is a legally binding agreement to buy or sell a commodity or financial instrument at a later date. Futures contracts are standardized according to the quality, quantity, and delivery time and location for each commodity. The only variable is price.

There are two types of futures contracts, those that provide for physical delivery of a particular commodity or item and those which call for a cash settlement. The month during which delivery or settlement is to occur is specified. For example, a July futures contract is one providing for delivery or settlement in July.

It should be noted that even in the case of delivery-type futures contracts very few actually result in delivery. Not many speculators have the desire to take or make delivery of 5,000 bushels of wheat or 112,000 pounds of sugar. Rather, the vast majority of speculators in futures markets choose to realize their gains or losses by buying or selling offsetting futures contracts prior to the delivery date.

Selling a contract that was previously purchased liquidates a futures position in exactly the same way, for example, that selling 100 shares of IBM stock liquidates an earlier purchase of 100 shares of IBM stock. Similarly, a futures contract that was initially sold can be liquidated by an offsetting purchase. In either case, the resulting gain or loss is the difference between the buying price and the selling price less transaction costs (commissions and fees).

Since delivery on futures contracts is the exception rather than the rule, why do most contracts even have a delivery provision? There are two reasons. One is that it offers buyers and sellers the opportunity to take or make delivery of the physical commodity if they so choose. More importantly, however, the fact that buyers and sellers can take or make delivery helps to assure that futures prices will accurately reflect the cash market value of the commodity at the time the contract expires—that is, that futures and cash prices will eventually converge. It is convergence that makes hedging an effective way to obtain protection against an adverse price movement in the cash market.

Cash settlement futures contracts are precisely that, contracts which are settled in cash rather than by delivery at the time the contract expires. Stock index futures contracts, for example, are settled in cash on the basis of the index number used for the final settlement. There is no provision for delivery of the shares of stock that make up the various indexes. That would be impractical. With a cash settlement contract, convergence is automatic.

Futures prices are established through competitive bidding and are immediately and continuously relayed around the world by wire and satellite. A farmer in Nebraska, a merchant in Amsterdam, an importer in Tokyo and a speculator in Ohio have simultaneous access to the latest market-derived price quotations. And, should they choose, they can establish a price level for future delivery—or for speculative purposes—simply by having their broker buy or sell the appropriate contracts.

## How Prices Are Quoted

Futures prices are usually quoted the same way prices are quoted in the underlying cash market. That is, in dollars, cents, and sometimes fractions of a cent, per bushel, pound, or ounce; also in dollars, cents,

**FUTURES**

| Future | Exchange | Monetary units per quantity | Lifetime High | Lifetime Low | Date | Open | High | Low | Settle | Change | Open Interest |
|---|---|---|---|---|---|---|---|---|---|---|---|
| AGRICULTURAL | | | | | | | | | | | |
| Corn | CBT | ¢ / bushel | 302 ¾ | 217 ¼ | Jul 06 | 238 ¼ | 243 | 238 ¼ | 240 | + 2 | 576,182 |
| Soybeans | CBT | ¢ / bushel | 736 | 485 | Jul 06 | 606 | 612 | 604 ¾ | 606 | + 1 ½ | 225,894 |
| Soybean Meal | CBT | $ / ton | 227.00 | 158.70 | Jul 06 | 180.00 | 181.50 | 178.20 | 178.80 | – .70 | 93,312 |
| Soybean Oil | CBT | ¢ / lb | 26.57 | 19.61 | Jul 06 | 25.10 | 25.35 | 25.01 | 25.28 | + .20 | 162,452 |
| Wheat | CBT | ¢ / bushel | 418 ¼ | 268 ¾ | Jul 06 | 384 ¾ | 389 ½ | 383 ½ | 384 ½ | – ¼ | 240,326 |
| Winter Wheat | KC | ¢ / bushel | 474 ½ | 342 | Jul 06 | 468 ½ | 472 ½ | 465 | 465 ¼ | – 2 ¾ | 83,750 |
| Oats | CBT | ¢ / bushel | 270 ½ | 133 ¼ | Jul 06 | 189 | 190 ¼ | 187 ½ | 189 | – ¼ | 8,505 |
| Rough Rice | CBT | $ / CWT | 9.210 | 6.900 | Jul 06 | 8.460 | 8.560 | 8.450 | 8.545 | + .085 | 5,695 |

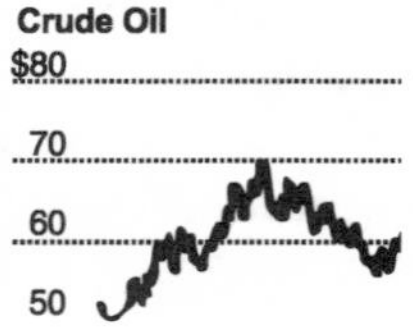
Crude Oil
$80
70
60
50

***Figure 28.1.*** *How futures prices are reported in newspaper financial sections.*

and increments of a cent for foreign currencies; and in points and percentages of a point for financial instruments. Cash settled index contract prices are quoted in terms of an index number, usually stated to two decimal points. Be certain you understand the price quotation system for the particular futures contract you are considering.

SOYBEANS Delayed Futures -09:20 - Monday, 8 May
( Go to Daily ) ( Profile ) (Click on Contract for Chart)

| Contract | Last | Change | Open | High | Low | Prev. Stl. | Time |
|---|---|---|---|---|---|---|---|
| May '06 (SK06) | 594-4 | +3-6 | 597-0 | 601-4 | 593-0 | 590-6 | 05/05/06 |
| Jul '06 (SN06) | 606-4 | +2-6 | 609-4 | 614-4 | 605-0 | 603-6 | 05/05/06 |
| Aug '06 (SQ06) | 612-0 | +3-0 | 615-0 | 619-0 | 611-0 | 609-0 | 05/05/06 |
| Sep '06 (SU06) | 615-4 | +2-2 | 620-0 | 622-0 | 614-0 | 613-2 | 05/05/06 |
| Nov '06 (SX06) | 625-2 | +3-0 | 627-4 | 631-0 | 623-4 | 622-2 | 05/05/06 |
| Jan '07 (SF07) | 632-2 | +3-0 | 636-0 | 636-0 | 632-0 | 629-2 | 05/05/06 |
| Mar '07 (SH07) | 639-0 | +4-0 | 641-0 | 644-0 | 636-0 | 635-0 | 05/05/06 |
| May '07 (SK07) | 640-0 | +3-0 | 641-0 | 643-0 | 638-0 | 637-0 | 05/05/06 |
| Jul '07 (SN07) | 643-0 | +3-0 | 645-0 | 647-0 | 643-0 | 640-0 | 05/05/06 |

*Figure 28.2.* How futures prices are reported on financial services websites.

## The Market Participants

Should you at some time decide to trade in futures contracts, either for speculation or in connection with a risk management strategy, your orders to buy or sell will be communicated from the brokerage office you use to the appropriate trading pit or electronic trading platform for execution. If you are a buyer, your order will seek a seller at the lowest available price. If you are a seller, your order will seek a buyer at the highest available price. Market fluctuation is a process of finding fair prices for both buyers and sellers.

In either case, the person who takes the opposite side of your trade may be or may represent someone who is a commercial hedger or perhaps someone who is a public speculator. Or, quite possibly, the other party may be an independent trader. In becoming acquainted with futures markets, you should have at least a general understanding of who these various market participants are, what they are doing and why.

## Hedgers

The details of hedging can be somewhat complex but the principle is simple. Hedgers are individuals and firms that make purchases and sales in the futures market for the purpose of establishing a known price level—weeks or months in advance—for something they later intend to buy or sell in the cash market (such as at a grain elevator or in the bond market). In this way they attempt to protect themselves against the risk of an unfavorable price change in the interim.

Consider this example: A jewelry manufacturer will need to buy additional gold from his supplier in six months. Between now and then, however, he fears the price of gold may increase. That could be a problem because he has already published his catalog for the year ahead.

To lock in the price level at which gold is presently being quoted for delivery in six months, he buys a futures contract at a price of $550 an ounce. If, six months later, the cash market price of gold has risen, he will have to pay his supplier that increased amount to acquire gold. However, the extra cost may be offset by a corresponding profit when the futures contract bought at $550 is sold for $570. In effect, the hedge provided insurance against an increase in the price of gold. It locked in a net cost, regardless of what happened to the cash market price of gold. Had the price of gold declined instead of risen, he would have incurred a loss on his futures position, but this would have been offset by the lower cost of acquiring gold in the cash market.

The number and variety of hedging possibilities are practically limitless. A cattle feeder can hedge against a decline in livestock prices and a meat packer or supermarket chain can hedge against an increase in livestock prices. Borrowers can hedge against higher interest rates, and lenders against lower interest rates. In addition, investors can hedge against a decline in stock prices.

Whatever the hedging strategy, the common denominator is that hedgers willingly give up the opportunity to benefit from favorable price changes in order to achieve protection against unfavorable price changes.

## Speculators

Were you to speculate in futures contracts, the person taking the opposite side of your trade on any given occasion could be a hedger or it might well be a speculator—someone whose opinion about the probable direction of prices may differ from your own.

The arithmetic of speculation in futures contracts—including the opportunities it offers and the risks it involves—will be discussed in detail later on. For now, just know that speculators are individuals and firms who seek to profit from anticipated increases or decreases in futures prices. In so doing, they help provide the risk capital needed to facilitate hedging.

Someone who expects a futures price to increase would purchase futures contracts in the hope of later being able to sell them at a higher price. This is known as "going long." Conversely, someone who expects a futures price to decline would sell futures contracts in the hope of later being able to buy back identical and offsetting contracts at a lower price. The practice of selling futures contracts in anticipation of lower prices is known as "going short." One of the unique features of futures trading is that one can initiate a transaction with a sale as well as with a purchase.

## The Process of Price Discovery

Futures prices increase and decrease largely because of the myriad factors that influence buyers' and sellers' judgments about what a particular product will be worth at a given time in the future (anywhere from less than a month to more than two years).

As new supply and demand developments occur and as new and more current information becomes available, these judgments are reassessed, and the price of a particular futures contract may be bid upward or downward. The process of reassessment (price discovery) is continuous.

Thus, in January, the price of a July futures contract would reflect the consensus of buyers' and sellers' opinions at that time as to what the value of a commodity or item will be when the contract expires in July. On any given day, with the arrival of new or more accurate information, the price of the July futures contract might increase or decrease in response to changing expectations. As the term indicates, futures markets "discover"—or reflect—cash market prices. They do not set them.

Competitive price discovery is a major economic function—and, indeed, a major economic benefit—of futures trading. In summary, futures prices are an ever changing barometer of supply and demand and, in a dynamic market, the only certainty is that prices will change.

### *Minimum Price Changes*

Exchanges establish the minimum amount that the price can fluctuate upward or downward. This is known as the "tick." For example, each tick for grain is .0025¢ per bushel. On a 5,000 bushel futures contract, that's $12.50. On a gold futures contract, the tick is 10¢ per ounce, so one tick on a 100 ounce contract is $10. You'll want to familiarize yourself with the minimum price fluctuation—the tick size—for whatever futures contracts you plan to trade. You'll also need to know how a price change of any given amount will affect the value of the contract.

### Daily Price Limits

Exchanges establish daily price limits for trading in some futures contracts. The limits are stated in terms of the previous day's closing price plus and minus so many cents or dollars per trading unit. Once a futures price has increased by its daily limit, there can be no trading at any higher price until the next trading session. Conversely, once a futures price has declined by its daily limit, there can be no trading at any lower price until the next session. Thus, if the daily limit for a particular grain is currently 10¢ a bushel and the previous day's settlement was $3.00, there cannot be trading during the current day at any price below 2.90 or above 3.10. The price is allowed to increase or decrease by the limit amount each day.

For come contracts, daily price limits are eliminated during the month in which the contract expires. Because prices can become particularly volatile during the expiration month (also called the "delivery" or "spot" month), persons lacking experience in futures trading may wish to liquidate their positions prior to that time. At the very least, they should trade cautiously, and with an understanding of the risks which may be involved.

Daily price limits set by the exchanges are subject to change. They can, for example, be increased or decreased on successive days. Because of daily price limits, there may be occasions when it is not possible to liquidate an existing futures position at will. In this event, possible alternative strategies should be discussed with a broker.

### Position Limits

Although the average trader is unlikely to ever approach them, exchanges and the Commodity Futures Trading Commission (CFTC) establish limits on the maximum speculative position that any one person can have at one time in any one futures contract. The purpose is to prevent one buyer or seller from being able to exert undue influence on the price in either the establishment or liquidation of positions. Position limits are stated in number of contracts or total units of the commodity.

The easiest way to obtain the types of information just discussed is to ask your broker or other advisor to provide you with a copy of the contract specifications for the specific futures contracts you are thinking about trading. You can also obtain the information from the exchange where the contract is traded.

### Daily Close

At the end of a day's trading, the exchange's clearing organization matches each clearing firm's purchases made that day with corresponding sales and tallies each clearing firm's gains or losses based on that session's price changes—a massive undertaking considering that several million futures contracts are bought and sold on an average day. Each firm, in turn, calculates the gains and losses for each of its customers having futures contracts.

Gains and losses on futures contracts are not only calculated on a daily basis, they are credited and deducted by the clearing firm on a daily basis. For example, if a speculator were to have a $300 profit as a result of the day's price changes, that amount would be immediately credited to his brokerage account and, unless required for other purposes, could be withdrawn. On the other hand, if the day's price changes had resulted in a $300 loss, his account would be immediately debited for that amount.

The process just described is known as a daily cash settlement and is an important feature of futures trading. As will be seen when we discuss margin requirements, it is also the reason a customer who incurs a loss on a futures position may be called on to deposit additional funds to his account.

## The Arithmetic of Futures Trading

### Leverage

To say that gains and losses in futures trading are the result of price changes is an accurate explanation but by no means a complete explanation. Perhaps more so than in any other form of speculation or investment, gains and losses in futures trading are highly leveraged. An understanding of leverage—and of how it can work to your advantage or disadvantage—is crucial to an understanding of futures trading.

The leverage of futures trading stems from the fact that only a relatively small amount of money (known as initial margin) is required to buy or sell a futures contract. On a particular day, a margin deposit of only $1,000 might enable you to buy or sell a futures contract covering $25,000 worth of soybeans. Or for $20,000, you might be able to purchase a futures contract covering common stocks worth $200,000. The smaller the margin in relation to the value of the futures contract, the greater the leverage will be.

If you speculate in futures contracts and the price moves in the direction you anticipated, high leverage can produce large profits in relation to your initial margin. Conversely, if prices move in the opposite direction, high leverage can produce large losses in relation to your initial margin.

Leverage is a two-edged sword. For example, assume that in anticipation of rising stock prices you buy one June S&P 500 E-mini stock index futures contract at a time when the June index is trading at 1400. And assume your initial margin requirement is $4,000. Since the value of the futures contract is 50 times the index, each one point change in the index represents a $50 gain or loss.

Thus, an increase in the index from 1400 to 1420 would produce a $1,000 profit (20 x $50) and a decrease from 1400 to 1380 would be a $1,000 loss on your $4,000 margin deposit. That's a 25 percent gain or loss as the result of less than a two percent change in the stock index.

Said another way, while buying (or selling) a futures contract provides exactly the same dollars and cents profit potential as owning (or selling short) the actual commodities or items covered by the contract, low margin requirements sharply increase the percentage profit or loss potential.

Futures trading, therefore, requires not only the necessary financial resources but also the necessary emotional temperament. For example, it can be one thing to have the value of your portfolio of common stocks decline from $200,000 to $190,000 (a five percent loss) but quite another, at least emotionally, to deposit $20,000 as margin and end up losing half of it as the result of only a five percent decline.

It is essential for anyone considering trading in futures contracts—whether it's sugar or stock indexes, pork bellies or petroleum—to clearly understand the concept of leverage as well as the amount of gain or loss that will result from any given change in the futures price of the particular futures contract you would be trading. If you cannot afford the risk, or even if you are uncomfortable with the risk, the only sound advice is don't trade. Futures trading is not for everyone.

### Margins

As is apparent from the preceding discussion, the arithmetic of leverage is the arithmetic of margins. An understanding of margins—and of the several different kinds of margin—is essential to an understanding of futures trading.

If your previous investment experience has mainly involved common stocks, you know that the term margin—as used in connection with securities—has to do with the cash down payment and money borrowed from a broker to purchase stocks. But used in connection with futures trading, margin has an altogether different meaning and serves an altogether different purpose.

Rather than providing a down payment, the margin required to buy or sell a futures contract is solely a deposit of good faith money that can be drawn on by your brokerage firm to cover losses that you may incur in the course of futures trading. It is much like money held in an escrow account.

Minimum margin requirements for a particular futures contract at a particular time are set by the exchange on which the contract is traded. They are typically about five percent of the current value of the futures contract.

Exchanges continuously monitor market conditions and risks and, as necessary, raise or reduce their margin requirements. Individual brokerage firms may require higher margin amounts from their customers than the exchange-set minimums.

There are two margin-related terms you should know: initial margin and maintenance margin.

Initial margin (sometimes called original margin) is the sum of money that the customer must deposit with the brokerage firm for each futures contract to be bought or sold. On any day that profits accrue on your open positions, the profits will be added to the balance in your margin account. On any day losses accrue, the losses will be deducted from the balance in your margin account.

If and when the funds remaining available in your margin account are reduced by losses to below a certain level—known as the maintenance margin requirement—your broker will require that you deposit additional funds to bring the account back to the level of the initial margin. You may also be asked for additional margin if the exchange or your brokerage firm raises its margin requirements. Requests for additional margin are known as margin calls.

Assume, for example, that the initial margin needed to buy or sell a particular futures contract is $2,000 and that the maintenance margin requirement is $1,500. Should losses on open positions reduce the funds remaining in your trading account to $1,400 (an amount less than the maintenance requirement), you will receive a margin call for the $600 needed to restore your account to $2,000.

Before trading in futures contracts, be sure you understand the brokerage firm's margin agreement and know how and when the firm expects margin calls to be met. Some firms may require only that you mail a personal check. Others may insist you wire transfer funds from your bank or provide same-day or next-day delivery of a certified or cashier's check. If margin calls are not met in the prescribed time and form, the firm can protect itself by liquidating your open positions at the available market price (possibly resulting in a loss for which you would be liable).

## Basic Trading Strategies

Even if you should decide to participate in futures trading in a way that doesn't involve having to make day-to-day trading decisions (such as a managed account or commodity pool), it is nonetheless useful to understand the dollars and cents of how futures trading gains and losses are realized. If you intend to trade your own account, such an understanding is essential.

Dozens of different strategies and variations of strategies are employed by futures traders in pursuit of speculative profits. Here is a brief description and illustration of several basic strategies.

### *Buying (Going Long) to Profit from an Expected Price Increase*

Someone expecting the price of a particular commodity or item to increase over a given period of time can seek to profit by buying futures contracts. If correct in forecasting the direction and timing of the price change, the futures contract can later be sold for the higher price, thereby yielding a profit. (For simplicity, examples do not take into account commissions and other transaction costs. These costs are important, however, and you should be sure you fully understand them.) If the price declines rather than increases, the trade will result in a loss. Because of leverage, the gain or loss may be greater than the initial margin deposit.

For example, assume it's now January, the July soybean futures contract is presently quoted at $6.00 a bushel, and over the coming months you expect the price to increase. You decide to deposit the required initial margin of $1,000 and buy one July soybean futures contract. Further assume that by April the July soybean futures price has risen to $6.40, and you decide to take your profit by selling. Since each contract is for 5,000 bushels, your 40-cent a bushel profit would be 5,000 bushels x 40¢ or $2,000 less transaction costs.

**Table 28.1.** Going Long: An Example

| If the price rises: | | Price Per Bushel | Value of 5,000 Bushel Contract |
|---|---|---|---|
| January | Buy 1 July soybean futures contract | $6.00 | $30,000 |
| April | Sell 1 July soybean futures contract | $6.40 | $32,000 |
| | **GAIN** | **$ .40** | **$ 2,000** |
| **If the price falls:** | | | |
| January | Buy 1 July soybean futures contract | $6.00 | $30,000 |
| April | Sell 1 July soybean futures contract | $5.60 | $28,000 |
| | **LOSS** | **$ .40** | **$ 2,000** |

*For simplicity, examples do not take into account commissions and other transaction costs. These costs are important, however, and you should be sure you fully understand them.

Suppose, however, that rather than rising to $6.40, the July soybean futures price had declined to $5.60 and that, in order to avoid the possibility of further loss, you elect to sell the contract at that price. On 5,000 bushels your 40-cent a bushel loss would thus come to $2,000 plus transaction costs.

Note that the loss in this example exceeded your $1,000 initial deposit. Your broker would then call upon you, as needed, for additional funds to cover the loss. Had you not offset the position and the soybean contract was open in your account, your broker would ask you to deposit more margin funds into your account to cover the projected losses marked to the settlement price.

## *Selling (Going Short) to Profit from an Expected Price Decrease*

The only way going short to profit from an expected price decrease differs from going long to profit from an expected price increase is the sequence of the trades. Instead of first buying a futures contract, you first sell a futures contract. If, as expected, the price declines, a profit can be realized by later purchasing an offsetting futures contract at the lower price. The gain per unit will be the amount by which the purchase price is below the earlier selling price.

For example, assume that in January your research or other available information indicates a probable decrease in cattle prices over the next several months. In the hope of profiting, you deposit an initial margin of $700 and sell one April live cattle futures contract at a price of, say, 85¢ a pound. Each contract is for 40,000 pounds, meaning each 1¢ a pound change in price will increase or decrease the value of the futures contract by $400. If, by March, the price has declined to 80¢ a pound, an offsetting futures contract can be purchased at 5¢ a pound below the original selling price. On the 40,000 pound contract, that's a gain of 5¢ x 40,000 pounds or $2,000 less transaction costs.

**Table 28.2.** Going Short: An Example

| | | Price Per Pound | Value of 40,000 Pound Contract |
|---|---|---|---|
| **If the price falls** | | | |
| January | Sell 1 April live cattle futures contract | 85¢ | $34,000 |
| March | Buy 1 April live cattle futures contract | 80¢ | $32,000 |
| | **GAIN** | **5¢** | **$ 2,000** |
| **If the price rises** | | | |
| January | Sell 1 April live cattle futures contract | 85¢ | $34,000 |
| March | Buy 1 April live cattle futures contract | 90¢ | $36,000 |
| | **LOSS** | **5¢** | **$ 2,000** |

For simplicity, examples do not take into account commissions and other transaction costs. These costs are important, however, and you should be sure you fully understand them.

Assume you were wrong. Instead of decreasing, the April live cattle futures price increases to 90¢ a pound by the time in March when you eventually liquidate your short futures position through an offsetting purchase. The outcome would be as shown in Table 28.2.

In this example, the loss of 5¢ a pound on the future transaction resulted in a total loss of the $2,000 plus transaction costs.

## Spreads

While most speculative futures transactions involve a simple purchase of futures contracts to profit from an expected price increase—or an equally simple sale to profit from an expected price decrease—numerous other possible strategies exist. Spreads are one example.

A spread, at least in its simplest form, involves buying one futures contract and selling another futures contract. The purpose is to profit from an expected change in the relationship between the purchase price of one and the selling price of the other.

As an illustration, assume it's now November, that the March Chicago Board of Trade (CBOT) mini wheat futures price is presently $3.50 a bushel, and the May CBOT mini wheat futures price is presently $3.55 a bushel, a difference of 5¢. Your analysis of market conditions indicates that, over the next few months, the price difference

**Table 28.3.** Spread: An Example

|  |  |  | Spread |
|---|---|---|---|
| November | Sell March Mini Wheat @ 3.50 bu. | Buy March Mini Wheat @ 3.55 bu. | 5¢ |
| February | Buy March Mini Wheat @ 3.60 bu. | Sell March Mini Wheat @ 3.75 bu. | 15¢ |
|  | **$.10 LOSS** | **$.20 GAIN** |  |

Net gain = 10¢ per bushel
Gain on 1,000 bushel contract = $100

For simplicity, examples do not take into account commissions and other transaction costs. These costs are important, however, and you should be sure you fully understand them.0104 between the two contracts will widen to become greater than 5¢. To profit if you are right, you could sell the March futures contract (the lower priced contract) and buy the May futures contract (the higher priced contract).

Assume time and events prove you right and that, by February, the March futures price has risen to $3.60 and May futures price is $3.75, a difference of 15¢. By liquidating both contracts at this time, you can realize a net gain of 10¢ a bushel. Since each contract is 1,000 bushels, the total gain is $100.

Had the spread (the price difference) narrowed by 10¢ a bushel rather than widened by 10¢ a bushel, the transactions just illustrated would have resulted in a loss of $100.

Because of the potential of one leg of the spread to hedge against price loss in the other leg and because gains and losses occur only as the result of a change in the price difference—rather than as a result of a change in the overall level of futures prices—spreads are often considered more conservative and less risky than having an outright long or short futures position. In general, this may be the case.

It should be recognized, though, that the loss from a spread can be as great as—or even greater than—that which might be incurred in having an outright futures position. An adverse widening or narrowing of the spread during a particular time period may exceed the change in the overall level of futures prices, and it is possible to experience losses on both of the futures contracts involved (that is, on both legs of the spread).

Virtually unlimited numbers and types of spread possibilities exist, as do many other, even more complex futures trading strategies. These, however, are beyond the scope of an introductory text and should be considered only by someone who fully understands the risk/reward arithmetic involved.

### *Stop Orders*

A stop order is an order placed with your broker to buy or sell a particular futures contract if and when the price reaches a specified level. Stop orders are often used by futures traders in an effort to limit the amount they might lose if the futures price moves against their position.

For example, were you to purchase a crude oil futures contract at $61 a barrel and wished to limit your loss to $1 a barrel, you might place a stop order to sell an offsetting contract if the price should fall to $60 a barrel. If and when the market reaches whatever price you specify, a stop order becomes an order to execute the desired trade.

There can be no guarantee, however, that it will be possible under all market conditions to execute the order at the price specified. In an active, volatile market, the market price may be declining (or rising) so rapidly that there is no opportunity to liquidate your position at the stop price you have designated. It is important to understand each exchange's rules and regulations as to the type of orders permitted and the nuances of each.

In the event that prices have risen or fallen in a market that utilizes a maximum daily limit, and there is presently no trading in the contract (known as a "lock limit" market), it may not be possible to execute your order at any price. In addition, although it happens infrequently, it is possible that markets may be lock limit for more than one day, resulting in substantial losses to futures traders who may find it impossible to liquidate losing futures positions.

Subject to the kinds of limitations just discussed, stop orders can nonetheless provide a useful tool for the futures trader who seeks to limit his losses.

In addition to providing a way to limit losses, stop orders can also be employed to protect profits.

For instance, if you have bought crude oil futures at $61 a barrel and the price is now at $64 a barrel, you might wish to place a stop order to sell if and when the price declines to $63. This (again subject to the described limitations of stop orders) could protect $2 of your existing $3 profit while still allowing your position to benefit from any continued increase in price.

# Part Three

# Taking Action

Chapter 29

# *What You Should Know about Financial Planning*

You may have come across the term "financial planning" recently and wondered what it means. You may have decided to start your own financial plan but you're not sure how. Or you may feel it's time you went to a financial planner for some professional advice. Whatever your situation, the following information can help you decide what's right for you. This chapter explains financial planning and its benefits. It describes what you should expect and highlights the importance of your role in the financial planning process. The answers to some common questions about financial planning are also provided.

## *What Is Financial Planning?*

Financial planning is the process of meeting your life goals through the proper management of your finances. Life goals can include buying a home, saving for your child's education, or planning for retirement. The financial planning process as described by the Certified Financial Planner Board of Standards Inc. (CFP Board), consists of six steps that help you take a "big picture" look at where you are financially. Using these six steps, you can work out where you are now, what you may need in the future, and what you must do to reach your goals. The process involves gathering relevant financial information, setting life goals, examining your current financial status and coming up with a strategy or plan for how you can meet your goals given your current situation and future plans. For more details on the financial planning process, see the section titled "The Financial Planning Process consists of the Following Six Steps."

## The Benefits of Financial Planning

Financial planning provides direction and meaning to your financial decisions. It allows you to understand how each financial decision you make affects other areas of your finances. For example, buying a particular investment product might help you pay off your mortgage faster or it might delay your retirement significantly. By viewing each financial decision as part of a whole, you can consider its short and long-term effects on your life goals. You can also adapt more easily to life changes and feel more secure that your goals are on track.

## Can You Do Your Own Financial Planning?

Some personal finance software packages, magazines, or self-help books can help you do your own financial planning. However, you may decide to seek help from a professional financial planner if the following situations describe you:

- You need expertise you don't possess in certain areas of your finances (For example, a planner can help you evaluate the level of risk in your investment portfolio or adjust your retirement plan due to changing family circumstances.)

- You want to get a professional opinion about the financial plan you developed for yourself

- You don't feel you have the time to spare to do your own financial planning

- You have an immediate need or unexpected life event such as a birth, inheritance, or major illness

- You feel that a professional adviser could help you improve on how you are currently managing your finances

- You know that you need to improve your current financial situation but don't know where to start

## What Is a Financial Planner?

A financial planner is someone who uses the financial planning process to help you figure out how to meet your life goals. The planner can take a "big picture" view of your financial situation and make financial planning recommendations that are right for you. The planner can look at all of your needs including budgeting and saving, taxes, investments, insurance, and retirement planning. Or, the planner may work with you on a single financial issue but within the context of your overall situation. This big picture approach to your financial goals may set the planner apart from other financial advisers, who may have been trained to focus on a particular area of your financial life.

## Financial Advisers Who May Work with You

In addition to providing you with general financial planning services, many financial planners are also registered as investment advisers or hold insurance or securities licenses that allow them to buy or sell products. Other planners may have you use more specialized financial advisers to help you implement their recommendations. With the right education and experience, each of the following advisers could take you through the financial planning process. Ethical financial planners will refer you to one of these professionals for services that they cannot provide and disclose any referral fees they may receive in the process. Similarly, these advisers should refer you to a planner if they cannot meet your financial planning needs.

**Accountant:** Accountants provide you with advice on tax matters and help you prepare and submit your tax returns to the Internal Revenue Service. All accountants who practice as Certified Public Accountants (CPAs) must be licensed by the state(s) in which they practice.

**Estate planner:** Estate planners provide you with advice on estate taxes or other estate planning issues and put together a strategy to manage your assets at the time of your death. While attorneys, accountants, financial planners, insurance agents, or trust bankers may all provide estate planning services, you should seek an attorney to prepare legal documents such as wills, trusts, and powers of attorney. Many estate planners hold the Accredited Estate Planner (AEP) designation.

269

**Financial planner:** Financial planners are described above under the heading "What Is a Financial Planner." In addition, many financial planners have earned the Certified Financial Planner™ certification, or the Chartered Financial Consultant (ChFC) or Personal Financial Specialist (CPA/PFS) designations. Financial planners can take you through the financial planning process.

**Insurance agent:** Insurance agents are licensed by the state(s) in which they practice to sell life, health, property, and casualty or other insurance products. Many insurance agents hold the Chartered Life Underwriter (CLU) designation. Financial planners may identify and advise you on your insurance needs, but can only sell you insurance products if they are also licensed as insurance agents.

**Investment adviser:** Anybody who is paid to provide securities advice must register as an investment adviser with the Securities and Exchange Commission or relevant state securities agencies, depending on the amount of money he or she manages. Because financial planners often advise people on securities-based investments, many are registered as investment advisers. Investment advisers cannot sell securities products without a securities license. For that, you must use a licensed securities representative such as a stockbroker.

**Stockbroker:** Also called registered representatives, stockbrokers are licensed by the state(s) in which they practice to buy and sell securities products such as stocks, bonds, and mutual funds. They generally earn commissions on all of their transactions. Stockbrokers must be registered with a company that is a member of the National Association of Securities Dealers (NASD) and pass NASD-administered securities exams.

## Be Sure You're Getting Financial Planning Advice

The government does not regulate financial planners as financial planners; instead, it regulates planners by the services they provide. For example, a planner who also provides securities transactions or advice is regulated as a stockbroker or investment adviser. As a result, the term "financial planner" may be used inaccurately by some financial advisers. To add to the confusion, many of the financial advisers previously described can also offer financial planning services. To be sure that you are getting financial planning advice, ask if the adviser follows the six steps described below.

## *The Financial Planning Process Consists of the Following Six Steps*

### *1. Establishing and Defining the Client-Planner Relationship*

The financial planner should clearly explain or document the services to be provided to you and define both his and your responsibilities. The planner should explain fully how he will be paid and by whom. You and the planner should agree on how long the professional relationship should last and on how decisions will be made.

### *2. Gathering Client Data, Including Goals*

The financial planner should ask for information about your financial situation. You and the planner should mutually define your personal and financial goals, understand your time frame for results, and discuss, if relevant, how you feel about risk. The financial planner should gather all the necessary documents before giving you the advice you need.

### *3. Analyzing and Evaluating Your Financial Status*

The financial planner should analyze your information to assess your current situation and determine what you must do to meet your goals. Depending on what services you have asked for, this could include analyzing your assets, liabilities and cash flow, current insurance coverage, investments, or tax strategies.

### *4. Developing and Presenting Financial Planning Recommendations and/or Alternatives*

The financial planner should offer financial planning recommendations that address your goals, based on the information you provide. The planner should go over the recommendations with you to help you understand them so that you can make informed decisions. The planner should also listen to your concerns and revise the recommendations as appropriate.

### *5. Implementing the Financial Planning Recommendations*

You and the planner should agree on how the recommendations will be carried out. The planner may carry out the recommendations or serve as your "coach," coordinating the whole process with you and other professionals such as attorneys or stockbrokers.

271

### *6. Monitoring the Financial Planning Recommendations*

You and the planner should agree on who will monitor your progress towards your goals. If the planner is in charge of the process, he or she should report to you periodically to review your situation and adjust the recommendations, if needed, as your life changes.

## *How to Make Financial Planning Work for You*

You are the focus of the financial planning process. As such, the results you get from working with a financial planner are as much your responsibility as they are those of the planner. To achieve the best results from your financial planning engagement, you will need to be prepared to avoid some of the common mistakes by considering the following advice:

**Set measurable financial goals:** Set specific targets of what you want to achieve and when you want to achieve results. For example, instead of saying you want to be "comfortable" when you retire or that you want your children to attend "good" schools, you need to quantify what "comfortable" and "good" mean so that you'll know when you've reached your goals.

**Understand the effect of each financial decision:** Each financial decision you make can affect several other areas of your life. For example, an investment decision may have tax consequences that are harmful to your estate plans. Or a decision about your child's education may affect when and how you meet your retirement goals. Remember that all of your financial decisions are interrelated.

**Re-evaluate your financial situation periodically:** Financial planning is a dynamic process. Your financial goals may change over the years due to changes in your lifestyle or circumstances, such as an inheritance, marriage, birth, house purchase, or change of job status. Revisit and revise your financial plan as time goes by to reflect these changes so that you stay on track with your long-term goals.

**Start planning as soon as you can:** Don't delay your financial planning. People who save or invest small amounts of money early, and often, tend to do better than those who wait until later in life. Similarly, by developing good financial planning habits such as saving, budgeting, investing, and regularly reviewing your finances early in life, you will be better prepared to meet life changes and handle emergencies.

**Be realistic in your expectations:** Financial planning is a common sense approach to managing your finances to reach your life goals. It cannot change your situation overnight; it is a life-long process. Remember that events beyond your control—such as inflation or changes in the stock market or interest rates—will affect your financial planning results.

**Realize that you are in charge:** If you're working with a financial planner, be sure you understand the financial planning process and what the planner should be doing. Provide the planner with all of the relevant information on your financial situation. Ask questions about the recommendations offered to you and play an active role in decision-making.

## Common Questions about Financial Planning

### Who can use the term "financial planner"?

The government does not regulate financial planners as financial planners; instead, it regulates planners as stock brokers, insurance agents, or investment advisers, depending on the services they provide. As a result anybody can "hang out a shingle" and call himself or herself a financial planner. CFP Board's free brochure, "10 Questions to Ask When Choosing a Financial Planner," can help you look for someone who is qualified to offer financial planning advice. The brochure contains questions to ask during an initial interview with a planner to help you determine if he or she is right for you. (To obtain a copy of this brochure, call 888-237-6275 or visit the CFP Board website at http://www.CFP.net.)

### Why should I choose a financial planner over another type of financial adviser?

A financial planner should focus on your needs first before recommending a course of action. Most planners have been trained to take a broad look at your financial situation, while accountants, investment advisers, stockbrokers, or insurance agents may focus on a particular area of your financial life. Always ask a financial adviser what qualifies him or her to offer financial planning services.

### What is the best age to start financial planning?

While it is true that the younger you start the more beneficial the process will be, financial planning is worthwhile at any age. Although younger people may have more decisions to make regarding their financial lives, changing laws and circumstances can lead middle-aged people and seniors to have to adjust their financial plans as well. Changes in tax law, for example, may require many people to revisit certain investments or estate plans, and adequate disability planning becomes more important as people age.

### *How are financial planners paid?*

There is currently no uniform method by which financial planners are paid. A planner can be paid by a salary paid by the company for which the planner works; by fees based on an hourly rate, a flat rate, or on a percentage of your assets and/or income; by commissions paid by a third party from the products sold to you to carry out the financial planning recommendations; or by a combination of fees and commissions whereby fees are charged for the amount of work done to develop financial planning recommendations and commissions are received from any products sold. Be sure to ask the planner how he or she is paid.

### *Do I have to pay a financial planner for the first interview? How much does a planner typically charge?*

Most financial planners will provide you with one free half-hour or hour meeting to talk about your reasons for wanting to work with them. During these initial interviews, the planners will also decide if they can help you and explain how they would work with you. Like other professionals, the rates financial planners charge depend on their experience, geographic location, level of services, and your needs. Interview more than one planner to get an idea of the going rate for financial planning services.

## *Learn about Financial Planning Online*

CFP Board's website (http://www.CFP.net/learn) is a comprehensive resource for financial planning, offering useful information for visitors at every stage of the financial planning learning curve. Interactive tools provide help for your personal situation, including changing jobs, managing debt, planning your retirement and more.

# Chapter 30

# *Tips for Checking Out Brokers and Investment Advisers*

### *Selecting Your Broker*

Before making a securities investment, you must decide which brokerage firm (also referred to as a broker/dealer) and sales representative (also referred to as a stockbroker, account executive, or registered representative) to use.

Federal or state securities laws require brokers, investment advisers, and their firms to be licensed or registered, and to make important information public. But it's up to you to find that information and use it to protect your investment dollars. The good news is that this information is easy to get, and one phone call or internet search may save you from sending your money to a con artist, a bad financial professional, or disreputable firm.

Before you invest or pay for any investment advice, make sure your brokers, investment advisers, and investment adviser representatives are licensed. Always check and see if they or their firms have had run-ins with regulators or other investors.

This is very important, because if you do business with an unlicensed securities broker or a firm that later goes out of business, there

---

This chapter includes information from "Invest Wisely: Advice from Your Securities Industry Regulators," 11/2005; "Accounts: Opening a Brokerage Account," 7/2000; and "Protect Your Money: Check Out Brokers and Investment Advisers," 2/2007. All three documents were produced by the U.S. Securities and Exchange Commission (www.sec.gov).

may be no way for you to recover your money—even if an arbitrator or court rules in your favor.

## *Brokers and Brokerage Firms*

The Central Registration Depository (or "CRD") is a computerized database that contains information about most brokers, their representatives, and the firms they work for. For instance, you can find out if brokers are properly licensed in your state and if they have had run-ins with regulators or received serious complaints from investors. You'll also find information about the brokers' educational backgrounds and where they've worked before their current jobs.

You can ask either your state securities regulator or the National Association of Securities Dealers (NASD) to provide you with information from the CRD. Your state securities regulator may provide more information from the CRD than NASD, especially when it comes to investor complaints, so you may want to check with them first. You'll find contact information for your state securities regulator on the website of the North American Securities Administrators Association (http://www.nasaa.org). To contact NASD, either visit NASD's BrokerCheck website (available through a link at http://www.nasd.com) or call NASD's toll-free BrokerCheck hotline at 800-289-9999.

## *Investment Advisers*

People or firms that get paid to give advice about investing in securities generally must register with either the U.S. Securities and Exchange Commission (SEC) or the state securities agency where they have their principal place of business. Investment advisers who manage $25 million or more in client assets generally must register with the SEC. If they manage less than $25 million, they generally must register with the state securities agency in the state where they have their principal place of business.

Some investment advisers employ investment adviser representatives, the people who actually work with clients. In most cases, these people must be licensed or registered with your state securities regulator to do business with you. So be sure to check them out with your state securities regulator.

To find out about investment advisers and whether they are properly registered, read their registration forms, called the "Form ADV." The Form ADV has two parts. Part 1 has information about the adviser's business and whether they've had problems with regulators or clients. Part 2 outlines the adviser's services, fees, and strategies.

Before you hire an investment adviser, always ask for and carefully read both parts of the ADV.

You can view an adviser's most recent Form ADV online by visiting the Investment Adviser Public Disclosure (IAPD) website (http://www.advisorinfo.sec.gov). At present, the IAPD database contains Forms ADV only for investment adviser firms that register electronically using the Investment Adviser Registration Depository. In the future, the database will expand to encompass all registered investment advisers—individuals as well as firms—in every state.

You can also get copies of Form ADV for individual advisers and firms from the investment adviser, your state securities regulator, or the SEC, depending on the size of the adviser. You'll find contact information for your state securities regulator on the website of the North American Securities Administrators Association (http://www.nasaa.org). If the investment adviser is registered with the SEC, you can get the Form ADV at a cost of 24 cents per page (plus postage; call in advance for current pricing information) from the SEC.

Office of Public Reference
Room 1580
100 F Street, NE
Washington, DC 20549-0102
Phone: 202-551-8090
Fax: 202-777-1027
E-mail: publicinfo@sec.gov

Because some investment advisers and their representatives are also brokers, you may want to check both the CRD and Form ADV.

Once you've checked out the registration and record of your financial professional or firm, there's more to do. For example, if you plan to do business with a brokerage firm, you should find out whether the brokerage firm and its clearing firm are members of the Securities Investor Protection Corporation (SIPC). SIPC provides limited customer protection if a brokerage firm becomes insolvent—although it does not insure against losses attributable to a decline in the market value of your securities. If you've placed your cash or securities in the hands of a non-SIPC member, you may not be eligible for SIPC coverage if the firm goes out of business.

Here are a few questions to get you started:

- What experience do you have, especially with people in my circumstances?

- Where did you go to school? What is your recent employment history?

- What licenses do you hold? Are you registered with the SEC, a state, or NASD?

- Are the firm, the clearing firm, and any other related companies that will do business with me members of SIPC?

- What products and services do you offer?

- Can you only recommend a limited number of products or services to me? If so, why?

- How are you paid for your services? What is your usual hourly rate, flat fee, or commission?

- Have you ever been disciplined by any government regulator for unethical or improper conduct or been sued by a client who was not happy with the work you did?

- For registered investment advisers, will you send me a copy of both parts of your Form ADV?

Remember, part of making the right investment decision is finding the brokerage firm and the sales representative that best meet your personal financial needs. Do not rush. Do the necessary background investigation on both the firm and the sales representative. Resist salespeople who urge you to immediately open an account with them.

## Opening a Brokerage Account

When you open a brokerage account, you must sign a new account agreement. You should carefully review all the information in this agreement because it determines your legal rights regarding your account.

Do not sign the new account agreement unless you thoroughly understand it and agree with the terms and conditions it imposes on you. Do not rely on statements about your account that are not in this agreement.

Ask for a copy of any account documentation prepared for you by your broker.

The broker should ask you about your investment goals and personal financial situation, including your income, net worth, and investment experience, and how much risk you are willing to take on. Be honest. The broker relies on this information to determine which investments will best meet your investment goals and tolerance for risk. If a broker tries to sell you an investment before asking you these questions, that's a very bad sign. It signals that the broker has a greater interest in earning a commission than recommending an investment to you that meets your needs.

When opening a new account, the brokerage firm may ask you to sign a legally binding contract to use the arbitration process to settle any future dispute between you and the firm or your sales representative. Signing this agreement means that you give up the right to sue your sales representative and firm in court.

You may have your securities registered either in your name or in the name of your brokerage firm. Ask your sales representative about the relative advantages and disadvantages of each arrangement.

The new account agreement requires that you make three critical decisions:

### 1. Who will make the final decisions about what you buy and sell in your account?

You will have the final say on investment decisions unless you give "discretionary authority" to your broker. Discretionary authority allows your broker to invest your money without consulting you about the price, the type of security, the amount, and when to buy or sell. Do not give discretionary authority to your broker without seriously considering the risks involved in turning control over your money to another person.

### 2. How will you pay for your investments?

Most investors maintain a "cash" account that requires payment in full for each security purchase. But if you open a "margin" account, you can buy securities by borrowing money from your broker for a portion of the purchase price.

Be wary of buying stocks on margin. Make sure you understand how a margin account works, and what happens in the worst case scenario before you agree to buy on margin. Unlike other loans, like for a car or a home, that allow you to pay back a fixed amount every month, when you buy stocks on margin you can be faced with paying back the entire margin loan all at once if the price of the stock drops suddenly and dramatically. The firm has the authority to immediately sell any security in your account, without notice to you, to cover any shortfall resulting from a decline in the value of your securities. You may owe a substantial amount of money even after your securities are sold. The margin account agreement generally provides that the securities in your margin account may be lent out by the brokerage firm at any time without notice or compensation to you.

### 3. How much risk should you assume?

In a new account agreement, you must specify your overall investment objective in terms of risk. Categories of risk may have labels such as "income," "growth," or "aggressive growth." Be certain that you fully understand the distinctions among these terms, and be certain that the risk level you choose accurately reflects your investment goals. Be sure that the investment products recommended to you reflect the category of risk you have selected.

## The Investment Decision

Never invest in a product that you don't fully understand. Consult information sources such as business and financial publications.

Ask your sales representative for the prospectus, offering circular, or most recent annual report—and the "Options Disclosure Document" if you are investing in options. Read them. If you have questions, talk with your sales representative before investing.

You also may want to check with another brokerage firm, an accountant, or a trusted business adviser to get a second opinion about a particular investment you are considering.

Keep good records of all information you receive, copies of forms you sign, and conversations you have with your sales representative.

Nobody invests to lose money. However, investments always entail some degree of risk. Be aware of these points:

1. The higher the expected rate of return, the greater the risk; depending on market developments, you could lose some or all of your initial investment, or a greater amount.

2. Some investments cannot easily be sold or converted to cash. Check to see if there is any penalty or charge if you must sell an investment quickly or before its maturity date.

3. Investments in securities issued by a company with little or no operating history or published information may involve greater risk.

4. Securities investments, including mutual funds, are NOT federally insured against a loss in market value.

5. Securities you own may be subject to tender offers, mergers, reorganizations, or third party actions that can affect the value of your ownership interest. Pay careful attention to public announcements and information sent to you about such transactions. They involve complex investment decisions. Be sure you fully understand the terms of any offer to exchange or sell your shares before you act. In some cases, such as partial or two-tier tender offers, failure to act can have detrimental effects on your investment.

6. The past success of a particular investment is no guarantee of future performance.

## Protect Yourself

A high pressure sales pitch can mean trouble. Be suspicious of anyone who tells you, "Invest quickly or you will miss out on a once in a lifetime opportunity."

Remember:

- Never send money to purchase an investment based simply on a telephone sales pitch.

- Never make a check out to a sales representative.

- Never send checks to an address different from the business address of the brokerage firm or a designated address listed in the prospectus.

If your sales representative asks you to do any of these things, contact the branch manager or compliance officer of the brokerage firm.

Never allow your transaction confirmations and account statements to be delivered or mailed to your sales representative as a substitute for receiving them yourself. These documents are your official record of the date, time, amount, and price of each security purchased or sold. Verify that the information in these statements is correct.

Certain activities may indicate problems in the handling of your account and, possibly, violations of state and federal securities laws.

Be alert for these signs of trouble:

1. Recommendations from a sales representative based on "inside" or "confidential information," an "upcoming favorable research report," a "prospective merger or acquisition," or the announcement of a "dynamic new product."

2.  Representations of spectacular profit, such as, "Your money will double in six months." Remember, if it sounds too good to be true, it probably is!

3.  "Guarantees" that you will not lose money on a particular securities transaction, or agreements by a sales representative to share in any losses in your account.

4.  An excessive number of transactions in your account. Such activity generates additional commissions for your sales representative, but may provide no better investment opportunities for you.

5.  A recommendation from your sales representative that you make a dramatic change in your investment strategy, such as moving from low risk investments to speculative securities, or concentrating your investments exclusively in a single product.

6.  Switching your investment in a mutual fund to a different fund with the same or similar investment objectives. Unless there is a legitimate investment purpose, a switch recommended by your sales representative may simply be an attempt to generate additional commissions for the sales representative.

7.  Pressure to trade the account in a manner that is inconsistent with your investment goals and the risk you want or can afford to take.

8.  Assurances from your sales representative that an error in your account is due solely to computer or clerical error. Insist that the branch manager or compliance officer promptly send you a written explanation. Verify that the problem has been corrected on your next account statement.

## *If You Have a Problem*

If you have a problem with your sales representative or your account, promptly talk to the sales representative's manager or the firm's compliance officer. Confirm your complaint to the firm in writing. Keep written records of all conversations. Ask for written explanations.

If the problem is not resolved to your satisfaction, contact the appropriate regulators. Investor complaint information assists these regulators in identifying violations of the securities laws and prosecuting violators. However, none of these organizations is authorized to provide legal representation to individual investors or to get your money back for you.

Obtain information on using arbitration to resolve your dispute by contacting the NASD, New York Stock Exchange, American Stock Exchange, Municipal Securities Rulemaking Board, Boston Stock Exchange, Chicago Board Options Exchange, Chicago Stock Exchange, Pacific Stock Exchange, or Philadelphia Stock Exchange. Each of these organizations operates a forum to resolve disputes between brokerage firms and their customers. It may be desirable to consult an attorney knowledgeable about securities laws. Your local bar association can assist you in locating a securities attorney.

# Chapter 31

# *Investing Basics*

Wise investing requires knowledge of key financial concepts and an understanding of your personal investment profile and how these work together to impact investing decisions. This chapter will:

- Discuss the difference between saving and investing;

- Illustrate the risk/rate-of-return tradeoff;

- Explain the importance of the time-value of money and asset allocation;

- Challenge you to think about your personal risk tolerance; and

- Help you to recognize that your tax bracket, financial goals, and time horizon are key factors in defining an appropriate investment plan and asset mix for you and your family.

## The Difference between Saving and Investing

Even though the words "saving" and "investing" are often used interchangeably, there are differences between the two.

Saving provides funds for emergencies and for making specific purchases in the relatively near future (usually three years or less).

"Investing Basics," by Joan E. Witter, MS, © 2006 Rutgers Cooperative Research and Extension. Reprinted with permission. For more information visit http://www.investing.rutgers.edu.

Safety of the principal and liquidity of the funds (ease of converting to cash) are important aspects of savings dollars. Because of these characteristics, savings dollars generally yield a low rate of return and do not maintain purchasing power.

Investing, on the other hand, focuses on increasing net worth and achieving long-term financial goals. Investing involves risk (of loss of principal) and is to be considered only after you have adequate savings.

**Table 31.1.** Savings vs. Investment Dollars

| *Savings $$* | *Investment $$* |
|---|---|
| Safe | Involve risk |
| Easily accessible | Volatile in short time periods |
| Low return | Offer potential appreciation |
| Used for short-term goals | For mid- and long-term goals |

## Investment Return

Total return is the profit (or loss) on an investment. It is a combination of current income (cash received from interest, dividends, etc.) and capital gains or losses (the change in value of the investment between the time you bought and sold it). The published rate of return for a selected investment is usually expressed as a percentage of the current price on an annual basis. However, the real rate of return is the rate of return earned after inflation, which is further reduced by income taxes and transaction costs.

Historically, stocks have had the highest average annual investment return of all types of investments, especially over long time periods of ten years or more. The average annual rates of return for major investment asset classes from 1925–2004, according to the Chicago investment research firm, Ibbotson Associates, were as follows:

- 10.4% large company stocks
- 12.7% small company stocks
- 5.4% government bonds
- 3.7% Treasury Bills
- 3.0% inflation

**Table 31.2.** Illustration of "Total Return" and "Rate of Return"

| Current Income | + Capital Gain (or loss) | = Total RETURN |
| --- | --- | --- |
| Example: $2 | + $1 | = $3 |

| Annual return | divided by current price of security | = Rate Of RETURN |
| --- | --- | --- |
| Example: $3 | divided by $24 (per share) | = .125 or 12.5% |

## Risk

ALL investments involve some risk because the future value of an investment is never certain. Risk, simply stated, is the possibility that the actual return on an investment will vary from the expected return or that the initial principal will decline in value. Risk implies the possibility of loss on your investment.

Factors which affect the risk level of an investment include the following:

- Inflation
- Business failure
- Changes in the economy
- Interest rate changes

Generally speaking, risk and rate of return are directly related. As the risk level of an investment increases, the potential return usually increases as well. As investors incur a greater risk of loss of principal the also achieve the potential for higher returns. Here's a list of investments rated from highest risk to lowest risk:

- High Risk
  - Futures contracts and collectibles
- Medium Risk (highest risks within this category listed first)
  - Aggressive growth: junk bonds, stocks, mutual funds
  - Real estate
  - High quality corporate: stocks and bonds, mutual funds
- Low Risk (highest risks within this category listed first)

- Life insurance (investment component); government securities (Treasury Bills and notes, bonds, mutual funds)

- Insured savings accounts; savings bonds; money market funds; certificates of deposit

## Diversification

You can do several things to offset the impact of some types of risk. Diversifying your investment portfolio by selecting a variety of securities is one frequently used strategy. Done properly, diversification can reduce about 70% of the total risk of investing. Think about it. If you put all of your money in one place, your return will depend solely on the performance of that one investment. Alternatively, if you invest in several assets, your return will depend on an average of your various investment returns. Here are three basic ways to diversify your investments:

- By choosing securities from a variety of asset classes, for example, a mix of stock, bonds, cash and real estate

- By choosing a variety of securities or funds within one asset class, for example, stocks from large, medium, small, and international companies in different industries

- By choosing a variety of maturity dates for fixed-income (bond) investments

By diversifying, you won't lose as much as if you invested in just one security right before its market value goes down. However, if the market goes straight up from the time you started, you won't make as much in a diversified portfolio either. However, historically, most people are concerned about protection from dramatic losses.

## Dollar-Cost Averaging

Another technique to help soften the impact of fluctuations in the investment market is dollar-cost averaging. You invest a set amount of money on a regular basis over a long period of time—regardless of the price per share of the investment. In doing so, you purchase more shares when the price per share is down and fewer shares when the market is high. As a result, you will acquire most of the shares at a below-average cost per share.

Look at the dollar-cost averaging illustration in Table 31.3 below. One hundred dollars is invested each month. Due to fluctuations in the market, the number of shares purchased with the $100 each month varies, because the shares vary in price from $5 to $10. You can see that, when the share price is down, you acquire more shares as in months 2, 3, and 4. You benefit when/if the price per share goes up.

**Table 31.3.** Dollar-Cost Averaging Illustration

|         | Regular Investment | Share Price | Shares Acquired |
|---------|---------|-------------|---------|
| Month 1 | $100 | $10.00 | 10.0 |
| Month 2 | 100 | 7.50 | 13.3 |
| Month 3 | 100 | 5.00 | 20.0 |
| Month 4 | 100 | 7.50 | 13.3 |
| Month 5 | 100 | 10.00 | 10.0 |
| **TOTAL** | **$500** | | **66.6** |

Your Average Share Cost: $500 divided by 66.6 = $7.50

As most investors know, market timing—always buying low and selling high—is very hard to accomplish. Dollar-cost averaging takes much of the emotion and guesswork out of investing. Profits will accelerate when investment market prices rise. At the same time, losses will be limited during times of declining prices. For most people, dollar-cost averaging is not so much a way of making extra money as a way to limit risk.

## The Time-Value of Money

Now that you understand the concepts of risk and return, let's turn to an element that is at the heart and soul of building wealth and financial security—time.

Here is how time can work for you:

1. The longer you invest, the more money you will accumulate.

2. The more money you invest, the more it will accumulate because of the magic of compound interest.

Compounding works like this: The interest earned on your investments is reinvested or left on deposit. At the next calculation, interest is earned on the original principal plus the reinvested interest.

Earning interest on accumulated interest over time generates more and more money.

Compounding also applies to dividends and capital gains on investments when they are reinvested. The illustration given in Table 31.4 and the questions below can give you a first-hand opportunity to calculate the impact of time on the value of your investment accumulation. Please complete the exercise before moving ahead to the next section

**Table 31.4.** How Time Affects the Value of Money

| | | Investor A | | Investor B | |
|---|---|---|---|---|---|
| Age | Years | Contributions | Year End Value | Contributions | Year End Value |
| 25 | 1 | $ 2,000 | $2,188 | $ 0 | $ 0 |
| 26 | 2 | 2,000 | 4,580 | 0 | 0 |
| 27 | 3 | 2,000 | 7,198 | 0 | 0 |
| 28 | 4 | 2,000 | 10,061 | 0 | 0 |
| 29 | 5 | 2,000 | 13,192 | 0 | 0 |
| 30 | 6 | 2,000 | 16,617 | 0 | 0 |
| 31 | 7 | 2,000 | 20,363 | 0 | 0 |
| 32 | 8 | 2,000 | 24,461 | 0 | 0 |
| 33 | 9 | 2,000 | 28,944 | 0 | 0 |
| 34 | 10 | 2,000 | 33,846 | 0 | 0 |
| 35 | 11 | 0 | 37,021 | 2,000 | 2,188 |
| 36 | 12 | 0 | 40,494 | 2,000 | 4,580 |
| 37 | 13 | 0 | 44,293 | 2,000 | 7,198 |
| 38 | 14 | 0 | 48,448 | 2,000 | 10,061 |
| 39 | 15 | 0 | 52,992 | 2,000 | 13,192 |
| 40 | 16 | 0 | 57,963 | 2,000 | 16,617 |
| 41 | 17 | 0 | 63,401 | 2,000 | 20,363 |
| 42 | 18 | 0 | 69,348 | 2,000 | 24,461 |
| 43 | 19 | 0 | 75,854 | 2,000 | 28,944 |
| 44 | 20 | 0 | 82,969 | 2,000 | 33,846 |
| 45 | 21 | 0 | 90,752 | 2,000 | 39,209 |
| 46 | 22 | 0 | 99,265 | 2,000 | 45,075 |
| 47 | 23 | 0 | 108,577 | 2,000 | 51,490 |

## *How Time Affects the Value of Money*

Investor A invests $2,000 a year for 10 years, beginning at age 25. Investor B waits 10 years, then invests $2,000 a year for 31 years. Compare the total contributions and the total value at retirement of the two investments. This example (see Table 31.4) assumes a 9 percent fixed rate of return, compounded monthly. All interest is left in the account to allow interest to be earned on interest.

*Table 31.4. continued*

| | | Investor A | | Investor B | |
|---|---|---|---|---|---|
| Age | Years | Contributions | Year End Value | Contributions | Year End Value |
| 48 | 24 | 0 | 118,763 | 2,000 | 58,508 |
| 49 | 25 | 0 | 129,903 | 2,000 | 66,184 |
| 50 | 26 | 0 | 142,089 | 2,000 | 74,580 |
| 51 | 27 | 0 | 155,418 | 2,000 | 83,764 |
| 52 | 28 | 0 | 169,997 | 2,000 | 93,809 |
| 53 | 29 | 0 | 185,944 | 2,000 | 104,797 |
| 54 | 30 | 0 | 203,387 | 2,000 | 116,815 |
| 55 | 31 | 0 | 222,466 | 2,000 | 129,961 |
| 56 | 32 | 0 | 243,335 | 2,000 | 144,340 |
| 57 | 33 | 0 | 266,162 | 2,000 | 160,068 |
| 58 | 34 | 0 | 291,129 | 2,000 | 177,271 |
| 59 | 35 | 0 | 318,439 | 2,000 | 196,088 |
| 60 | 36 | 0 | 348,311 | 2,000 | 216,670 |
| 61 | 37 | 0 | 380,985 | 2,000 | 239,182 |
| 62 | 38 | 0 | 416,724 | 2,000 | 263,807 |
| 63 | 39 | 0 | 455,816 | 2,000 | 290,741 |
| 64 | 40 | 0 | 498,574 | 2,000 | 320,202 |
| 65 | 41 | 0 | 545,344 | 2,000 | 352,427 |
| Value at Retirement | | | $545,344 | | $352,427 |
| Less Total Contributions | | | ($20,000) | | ($62,000) |
| Net Earnings | | | $525,344 | | $290,427 |

Source: National Institute for Consumer Education, 1998

Using the data for investors A and B shown in Table 34.1, answer the following questions.

1. At $2,000 a year, how much did Investor A invest in the ten years between the ages of 25 and 35?

2. What is the value of Investor A's investment when the Investor is 35?

3. At $2,000 a year, how much did Investor B invest over the 31 years, from age 35 through 65?

4. What is the value at retirement of Investor A's investment?

5. What is the value at retirement of Investor B's investment?

6. What are Investor A's net earnings?

7. What are Investor B's net earnings?

8. What advice would you give to your children about investing for their retirement?

The answers to questions 1–7 can be found at the end of this chapter.

Note that Investor A, who invested much less than Investor B, has a much higher nest egg at retirement age, because of a 10-year head start. As you can see from this example, compound interest is especially magical when money is steadily invested and left to grow over a long period.

## Asset Allocation

In the final analysis, your overall investment return will be closely associated with the asset categories and allocations that you select. An investor's group of investments, frequently called an investment portfolio, can be divided in numerous ways among stocks, bonds, and cash management options. You might choose a 20/40/40 portfolio—20% stocks, 40% bonds, and 40% cash options. Or a 75/20/5 ratio—75% stocks, 20% bonds, and 5% cash.

Several factors will impact the exact rate of return that you receive on your investment portfolio. Studies show that the most important one, asset allocation, will account for about 90% of your return. The selection of individual securities and market timing will account for the remaining 10% or so.

The critical question, of course, is: "What is the ideal asset allocation for you?" Here are several factors to consider as you make this decision.

## *Your Investment Goals*

Goals are specific things (for example, buy a car) that people want to do with their money. As people move through various life stages, their needs and financial goals change. Your selection of investments should relate closely to your financial goals; each goal will define the amount and liquidity of the money needed as well as the number of years available for the investment to grow.

## *Your Risk Tolerance*

Risk tolerance is a person's emotional and financial capacity to ride out the ups and downs of the investment market without panicking when the value of investments goes down. Risk tolerances vary widely. Some are associated with personality factors, while others are based on changing needs dictated by your stage in the life cycle. If you won't sleep well at night when the principal value of your investment goes down, you should select saving and investment options with lower risk. On the other hand, it's important to realize that investments which guarantee the safety of principal will not grow your money quickly and may not maintain purchasing power in times of inflation or over a long time span. In reality it's necessary to take some risk just to maintain purchasing power. The question is: "What kind of risks are you willing to take?"

## *Your Time Horizon*

As discussed earlier, time is a very important resource to investors. For example, young investors with a long time horizon may choose investments that exhibit wide price swings, knowing that time is available for fluctuations to average out. Families investing for a specific mid-life goal (for example, funding a child's education or purchasing a home) may choose a more moderate course which has opportunity for growth, but provides more safety for the principal. Individuals nearing retirement and those with the need to depend on investment income to cover daily expenses, may wish to select investments that lock in gains and provide a guaranteed income stream.

## *Your Tax Situation*

The return on any investment is influenced by your federal, state, and local tax situation. Investment earnings may be:

- **Taxable:** Taxes paid yearly on interest, dividends and annual capital gain distributions from investments.

- **Tax-deferred:** Taxes on earnings are deferred until withdrawal. Tax-deferred earnings include contributions and returns associated with IRAs, 401(k)s, and other retirement saving plans.

- **Tax-exempt:** Earnings are wholly or partly free from taxes. Roth IRAs and most municipal bonds are common examples. (Tax-exempt status may be different at the state and federal levels.)

Before selecting an investment, learn its tax consequences for you. Remember, what counts is not what you make on an investment, but what you get to keep both now and in the long run.

### *Time and Skill to Manage Your Portfolio*

Some investments require little or no time commitment or special knowledge. Others, such as rental property, or a portfolio of high-risk individual stocks may require constant monitoring and management. How much time are you willing and able to spend?

In a nutshell, the asset allocation which you select must be customized to your situation, needs, and temperament.

## Summary

In this chapter we have discussed basic financial concepts that you need to understand before becoming involved in an investing program. You've learned about the difference between saving and investing, the predictable trade-off between risk and return, the importance of time to an investment program, and about asset allocation. In addition, you considered various aspects of your personal situation and their possible impact on your asset allocation decisions.

The steps below suggest important actions for you to take to establish a solid foundation for future investing activity. Once completed, you will be ready to begin developing a personal investment plan.

### *Action Steps*

- Review your current financial holdings and determine if they are in saving or investment vehicles.

- Determine the rate of return for your current financial holdings.

- Establish short-, medium-, and long-term financial goals for you and your family. Estimate the length of time between now and when you want to achieve each goal.

- Identify your characteristics and needs as an investor.

- Set aside time each week to read a family financial magazine.

- Assess your interest, skill, and time to make decisions about your investment plan and portfolio.

- Proceed on your own or seek assistance.

## Answers to Questions about How Time Affects Money

1. $20,000
2. $37,021
3. $62,000
4. $545,344
5. $352,427
6. $525,344
7. $290,427

## References

Garman, E.T. & Forgue, R.E. (2006). *Personal finance. 8th Edition.* Boston: Houghton Mifflin Company.

Quinn, J. B. (1997). *Making the most of your money.* New York: Simon & Schuster.

*2005 Yearbook* (2004). Chicago: Ibbotson & Associates.

*Consumer approach to investing* (1998). National Institute for Consumer Education. Ypsilanti, MI.

## Author Profile

Joan Witter worked on the Cooperative Extension staff at Michigan State University for over 20 years. She received both B.S. and M.A. degrees from Michigan State University and is currently Program Leader Emeritus, Extension Family Resource Management Programs.

# Chapter 32

# *Finding Money to Invest*

Many Americans don't invest because they have little or no savings that can be transferred to investment products. Studies estimate that as many as 70% of Americans live from "paycheck to paycheck," courting financial disaster if their income is suddenly reduced or stopped. Generally, Americans are not saving for a "rainy" day; they are consuming it all today. The individual saving rate in the United States fell to a negative number (-0.5) in 2005, the first time since the Great Depression of the 1930s. This means that Americans were spending more than they earned.

## *Are You Satisfied with the Amount You Save?*

This chapter is designed to help you "find" money to fund your investment plans. We will suggest tools for success, but you have to supply the desire, self-discipline, wise decisions, and good planning to be successful.

Review your financial status by answering these questions:

- Do I have three to six months income in an emergency fund?

- Do I save regularly?

- Do I know how much I need to save to achieve future goals?

"Finding Money to Invest," by Joyce H. Christenbury, M.Ed., © 2006 Rutgers Cooperative Research and Extension. Reprinted with permission. For more information visit http://www.investing.rutgers.edu.

- Do I save to purchase big-ticket items instead of buying on credit?
- When I use credit, do I save to make as large a down payment as possible?
- Do I save at least 10% of my personal disposable income?
- Do I know how much I need to save for retirement?

The more times you answer "yes" to these questions, the more likely you are a prudent saver. A "no" can help you identify areas where you could do better. Once you have a sound savings program in place, you are ready to invest surplus funds. Unfortunately, many people feel their savings are not sufficient, and they see no way to meet their immediate needs and have extra funds to invest.

Through this chapter, you will explore strategies that will help you:

- Identify ways to increase your savings
- Fund your savings program
- Accumulate funds to begin your investment program.

## Strategies for Saving Money to Invest

**Establish a regular savings program:** The first strategy is to set up a regular savings program if you do not already have one. Saving means putting money aside from present earnings to provide for a known or unexpected need in the future. It is an integral part of family and personal financial planning. Having a specific goal provides motivation to save. You probably will not get very far saving for the sake of saving.

**Needs versus wants:** Individuals and families save to satisfy their needs and wants. Needs are items that are necessary for survival such as food, shelter, clothing, and medical care. Wants are all the other things we think we need, but could do without. If we spend our money to satisfy wants before we meet our needs, we will probably experience financial difficulties. The pressure to acquire present wants is often greater than the willingness to provide for future needs or even future wants.

Generally speaking, four major financial needs require planning for in the near and distant future:

- Emergencies from the normal course of living such as car repairs or replacing a major appliance

- Loss of income as a result of death, divorce, disability, or unemployment

- Other family goals such as education for your children or a special vacation

- Retirement

Once goals have been set, a major thought in most people's minds is "How am I going to reach this goal? There is no way I can save that much money!" However, most people find that, if they really put their minds to it and they have set realistic goals, they can save the necessary money.

As we noted earlier, a regular savings program is critical to a family's immediate well-being as well as their long-term security. To adequately fund a savings program and begin an investment program, you must identify a specific amount to save from each paycheck and honor that commitment. Regular savings in small amounts is generally more effective than setting aside larger sums at sporadic intervals. As your salary increases, increase the amount you commit to savings.

**Pay yourself first:** Another important concept for your savings program is to "pay yourself first." Make your "savings bill" a part of your spending plan, just like rent or mortgage payments, utility bills, clothing, car payments and upkeep, child care, or any other bill that you normally incur. When you pay your other bills, pay your savings bill by depositing the money into a savings account or other financial instrument. One painless way to accomplish this is payroll deduction if it is available. Your employer deposits your savings directly from your paycheck into a credit union, bank account, or a money market fund for a higher interest rate. If you never see the money, you won't miss it or be tempted to use it for something else before it reaches your savings account. Note how quickly small amounts of money can grow with time (Refer to Table 32.1).

The table can be used to find out how long it will take to reach your financial goals. It shows the growth of monthly $10 deposits invested at various interest rates. Put aside $10 a month for five years at 10%, for example, and you'll have $781—the figure at the intersection of the year five and 10% interest columns. If you can invest $50 each month, you will have five times $781, or $3,905.

**Table 32.1.** How $10.00 a Month Will Grow*

| Year | 3% | 4% | 5% | 6% | 7% | 8% | 9% | 10% | 11% | 12% | 13% | 14% | 15% |
|---|---|---|---|---|---|---|---|---|---|---|---|---|---|
| 1 | $122 | $122 | $123 | $124 | $125 | $125 | $126 | $127 | $127 | $128 | $129 | $130 | $130 |
| 2 | 247 | 249 | 253 | 256 | 258 | 261 | 264 | 267 | 270 | 272 | 275 | 278 | 281 |
| 3 | 376 | 382 | 389 | 359 | 402 | 408 | 415 | 421 | 428 | 435 | 442 | 449 | 457 |
| 4 | 509 | 520 | 532 | 544 | 555 | 567 | 580 | 592 | 605 | 618 | 632 | 646 | 660 |
| 5 | 646 | 665 | 683 | 701 | 720 | 740 | 760 | 781 | 802 | 825 | 848 | 872 | 897 |
| 6 | 788 | 812 | 841 | 868 | 897 | 926 | 957 | 989 | 1,023 | 1,058 | 1,094 | 1,132 | 1,171 |
| 7 | 933 | 968 | 1,008 | 1,046 | 1,086 | 1,129 | 1,173 | 1,220 | 1,268 | 1,320 | 1,374 | 1,430 | 1,490 |
| 8 | 1,083 | 1,129 | 1,182 | 1,234 | 1,289 | 1,348 | 1,409 | 1,474 | 1,543 | 1,615 | 1,692 | 1,773 | 1,859 |
| 9 | 1,238 | 1,297 | 1,366 | 1,435 | 1,507 | 1,585 | 1,667 | 1,755 | 1,849 | 1,948 | 2,054 | 2,168 | 2,288 |
| 10 | 1,397 | 1,472 | 1,559 | 1,647 | 1,741 | 1,842 | 1,850 | 2,066 | 2,190 | 2,323 | 2,467 | 2,621 | 2,787 |
| 15 | 2,270 | 2,461 | 2,684 | 2,923 | 3,188 | 3,483 | 3,812 | 4,279 | 4,589 | 5,046 | 5,557 | 6,129 | 6,769 |
| 20 | 3,283 | 3,668 | 4,128 | 4,644 | 5,240 | 5,929 | 6,729 | 7,657 | 8,736 | 9,991 | 11,455 | 13,163 | 15,160 |
| 25 | 4,460 | 5,141 | 5,980 | 6,965 | 8,148 | 9,574 | 11,295 | 13,379 | 15,906 | 18,976 | 22,714 | 27,273 | 32,841 |
| 30 | 5,827 | 6,940 | 8,357 | 10,095 | 12,271 | 15,003 | 18,445 | 22,793 | 28,302 | 35,299 | 44,206 | 55,571 | 70,098 |

*Adapted from: *How To Save $1,000 Or More A Year* by Denise M. Matejic, Rutgers Cooperative Extension; Garman, E.T. and Forgue, R.E. (2006). *Personal Finance.* Houghton Mifflin, Co.; and *Kiplinger's Retirement Report* February 1994.

**Save bonus money:** Saving "bonus" money is also an easy strategy. Bonus money is money earned or received that was not expected, such as tax refunds, gift money, overtime pay, rebates, and refunds. Saving this money over time will boost your saving dollars and provide a larger balance on which to earn interest for the future. (Note: if you consistently receive a large tax refund, you may want to adjust your withholding. A tax refund means that the government has had your money interest-free during the year; you were losing the use of the money to fund your financial goals.)

**Save coupon money:** Another strategy to boost your savings is to save coupon money. Many people use coupons to reduce their grocery and personal care bills, but few think of actually saving the money they saved! To make this strategy a reality, put aside the amount you "saved" by using coupons at the grocery store or drugstore. The amount saved is probably printed on each receipt. Put the "savings" (the money you did not spend) in a special "coupon saving jar." Every month or so add this cash to your savings account. Saving just $2 a week for 52 weeks gives you a savings total of $104 which could be your "seed" money to open an investment account. However, remember that you aren't saving if you buy something that you don't need or that costs more than a comparable product even with the coupon.

**Continue installment loan repayments:** Most of us have one or more installment loans that we are repaying. Once you pay off an installment loan (assuming other loans are not overdue), continue to make "payments" to your savings account. For example, when you pay off your car loan, continue writing a check for the same amount, but make the check payable to your savings account. You were able to get along without this money for the duration of the car loan, so continue to live at the same level and save the "car payment." This is a good way to save for the down payment on your next car when the old car needs to be replaced. It also adds a substantial amount of money to your savings account on a regular basis. This same strategy can be used when other household expenses end (for example, childcare).

**Collect loose change:** Another painless strategy is to collect loose change. At the end of each day, empty out your pockets and wallet and put the change in a special container. Every other week or once a month, deposit the change in your savings account. Don't cheat on yourself by "stealing" change that has been collected. Take it all to the bank. Some people even go so far as to keep all their change. They only pay for cash purchases with bills and save all their coins. Develop a plan that works for you and stick to it.

**Save lunch money:** Saving lunch money is another way you and your family can save money. Get up ten minutes earlier and make your own lunch. Save the money you would have spent on lunch. If all family members do this, the family can realize a nice sum that they can add to their savings. Working together to reach a family goal, such as a new TV or a summer vacation, can be an excellent family activity.

**Shop for sale prices:** Another strategy that can work for all family members on a wide variety of purchases is to save the money you "save" when you buy items on sale. When you buy an item on sale, save the difference between the sale price you paid and the "full" price you would have paid if the item had not been on sale. Put this money in a safe place and on a regular basis deposit it into your savings or investment account. Using this strategy can add large amounts to your savings program. The key is that you actually save this difference and apply it to your savings or investment program.

**Plan a "Nothing Week":** Once in a while, have a "Nothing Week," an entire week when you and your family agree not to spend any more money than is absolutely necessary. You would not go to the movies, out to eat, bowling, etc. Plan to do special activities, but save the money instead of spending it. Add this money to your savings program. Another similar strategy is to use a crash budget approach. A crash budget works like a crash diet—you try to cut out all unnecessary spending and save as much as possible in a given period of time, say two weeks or a month. Add all the savings to your savings or investment program.

If the crash budget sounds unbearable, consider a "Cut-Back Week." During this week, do what the family would normally do, but think of ways to make it less expensive and save the difference. For example, rent a movie instead of going to the theater, make long-distance phone calls on the weekend when the rates are lower, write a letter or send an e-mail instead of calling, drink mix-your-own lemonade instead of soft drinks, etc.

**Avoid paying credit charges:** A critical savings strategy to consider is avoiding the use of credit. Unless credit purchases are paid off in full each month, interest consumes dollars that could be spent funding your saving and investing goals. Suppose that you have a balance of $1,000 on a credit card that carries a 19.8% interest rate and a full grace period. If you make no more charges against the account and only pay the minimum payment of 3% per month, you will pay approximately $165 in interest over one year. If you continue making only minimum monthly payments for the rest of the $1,000 with no additional charges, you will take eight years and three months to pay it off, and you will have paid $843 in interest.

Carefully evaluate all spending decisions, especially those being paid with credit. Make every spending decision on the basis of how it will satisfy your goals. Eliminate spending for items that have little or no value relative to your goals. Also be aware of your needs and wants as you make purchases.

## Breaking Habits Can Yield Dollars to Invest

Some of the items we buy are needs, items that are necessary for survival. Other purchases are wants, all the things we think we need, but could do without. Buying items to satisfy our wants can become a habit; before we know it, we are spending lots of money on these items. Find money to improve your financial situation by identifying some of your money habits. Then break those habits or at least reduce the number of times you enjoy the habit each day, week, or month. Review Table 32.2 for specific examples.

Going further, if your family drinks iced tea instead of a 2-liter soda for the evening meal, you can probably save at least $5 a week or $260 ($5x52=$260) a year. By drinking tap water instead of other beverages, you can save $7 a week or $364 ($7x52=$364) a year.

**Table 32.2.** Looking For Money

| | | | |
|---|---|---|---|
| Cable TV | | $40/month= | $480/year |
| Video rentals | 3@ $3/weekend= | $36/month= | $432/year |
| Movie tickets | 2@ $7/visit= | $14/month= | $168/year |
| Treats at movie | 2@ $5/visit= | $10/month= | $120/year |
| Dry cleaning | 4 garments @$7/mo= | $28/month= | $336/year |
| Car wash | $5/week= | $20/month= | $240/year |

Let's look at those who feed the soda machines at work. By bringing soda from home ($.30 each) instead of feeding the machine ($.75 each), a person who drinks two sodas per day could save $234 over the course of a year ($.75-$.30 = $.45 x 2/day = $.90 x 5 days/week = $4.50 x 52 weeks = $234). Changing or adjusting a few habits can result in big savings for you and your family. To see how easy this can be, use the following steps to help you identify and change habits.

## Steps to Breaking Money Habits

- Step 1. Identify the habit, determine frequency, and calculate total cost
- Step 2. Make a decision to change
- Step 3. Act immediately
- Step 4. Share your plan
- Step 5. Stick with your plan to change
- Step 6. Celebrate your success

By following these six easy steps, you can gain better control of your financial resources and increase the money available for investing. Put this six-step plan to work for you and your family.

### Step 1. Identify the Habit, Determine Frequency, and Calculate Total Cost

Using worksheet shown in Table 32.3, "So Where's The Money?" think of some habits you might be able to adjust. Select from the products or services listed or add your own choices to the list. Then determine how often you purchase the product or service. Next, calculate the total cost of enjoying the product or service for one year. Armed with this information, you are ready to advance to Step 2 in your quest to break habits and collect funds for investing.

Calculate your total monthly and yearly costs. Are you happy with where your money is going? If you aren't, now is the time to learn about ways to break habits and begin a savings program for you and your family.

### Step 2. Make a Decision to Change

The second step to breaking habits involves looking for alternatives and choosing a different way of spending your money. This action step

**Table 32.3.** So Where's the Money?

### How often do you do the following?

| Product or Service | How Often Used | Monthly Cost x 12 | =Yearly Cost |
|---|---|---|---|
| | | **Cost** | |
| Hair Care (example) | 4 Times/Month | $100.00 x 12 | = $1200.00 |
| Nail Care | | | |
| Dry Cleaning | | | |
| Eating Out | | | |
| Cell Phones/Pagers | | | |
| Vending Machines | | | |
| Snacks | | | |
| Music CDs/Movie DVDs | | | |
| Cigarettes/Alcohol | | | |
| Brand Name Clothes/Shoes | | | |
| Video/DVD Rentals | | | |
| Cable/Satellite Television | | | |
| Movie Tickets/Snacks | | | |
| Pay-Per-View Television | | | |
| Bingo/Video Poker/Lottery | | | |
| Video/DVD Purchases | | | |
| | | | |
| | | | |

demands that you take control of the situation. One way to do this is to review your money habits and where you spend money, then identify how you can make changes. For example, have you ever stopped to consider how much you and other family members are spending for hair and nail care? If you spend $15.00 per week each month for hair care, that's $60.00 per month or $720.00 per year. Add a nail care bill of $15.00 per month or $180.00 per year. That is a lot of money.

What can you do? It is important for you and other family members to look good and feel good about yourselves. You can take control and make changes that will help you capture some of the money going to these expenditures and redirect its use toward other family goals and still be well-groomed. "How can I do that?" you ask. Learn how to do these tasks yourself, or barter with a friend or neighbor who has these skills. You do something for them that they can't do, and they do your hair and nails. Every once in awhile, you might treat yourself or other family members to a special makeover. Otherwise, save the money you would be spending on hair and nail care, and put this money toward your family goals.

Once you get into the swing of breaking habits, you and your family can come up with ideas on how to change and adjust spending. Ask yourself:

- Am I getting the best buys?

- Am I spending more than I need to?

- How could I change my spending?

Be specific and honest as you review expenditures. Come up with creative ways to save money, and share these ideas with others. Here is an example from the clothing area to get you started.

- First, do inventories of each person's clothing: evaluate items— which are still useable, need replacing, or need to be added?

- Once you know what needs to be purchased, check out sales at different stores and look for the best buys.

- Avoid buying designer clothing, as it is usually very expensive. Ask yourself and family members if it is worth the extra cost. Consider what else you could buy if you bought items that cost less and had money left.

- Check out second-hand outlets, flea markets, thrift stores, and manufacturers' outlet stores.

- Be a knowledgeable shopper; don't think that the outlet stores are always cheaper than other stores.

- Know the prices of what you plan to buy and comparison shop for the best deal.

- Make simple repairs.

- Swap clothing with family and friends.

- Develop a positive attitude about recycled clothing and share that attitude with your children.

- Well-maintained clothing from relatives and friends can greatly enhance a wardrobe.

- When shopping for clothes, read all care labels very carefully. Only buy washable items. Dry cleaning can become quite expensive over the life of a garment.

By adopting these strategies, you will see your clothing budget shrink. Add the money you no longer spend on clothing to your investment plan. With these budget reduction ideas for clothing in mind, brainstorm ways to save money in other budget categories with family, friends, neighbors, and co-workers. Develop money saving lists for:

- Using utilities;
- Buying home furnishings;
- Purchasing health and beauty aids;
- Shopping in the grocery store;
- Buying a car (new and/or used);
- Selecting telephone and cable television features;
- Buying toys and other gift items;
- Selecting insurance coverage;
- Financing large ticket items and other purchases.

Some habits are very hard to break even when they are dangerous to our health and physical well being as well as financial well-being. Examples that quickly come to mind are smoking, overeating, drinking alcohol, and gambling. These activities can be life threatening and/or result in financial ruin. If you smoke a pack of cigarettes a day, what is the cost for a year? A pack-a-day habit adds up fast:

- $6.00/pack/day = $42.00/week = a whopping $2,184.00/year

Remember, if you believe in yourself, you can kick any habit. Once you get into the swing of breaking habits, you and your family can come up with numerous ideas on how to change and adjust spending. Perhaps together the family could turn the task of saving into a friendly competition for the "Saver of the Year Award." The winner would be the person who saved the most dollars or the largest percentage of their income in a given period of time. By making the decision to change, you are ready to advance to Step 3 in breaking habits and finding money to invest.

### Step 3. Act Immediately

Now that you have all these great ideas to keep more of your money, how will you keep yourself motivated? Writing down your new desired behavior is one strategy. By recording the change, you are committing yourself to a new behavior. It is necessary to start your new behavior immediately. For best results, begin within 24 hours after making the decision to change or adjust spending. The sooner you begin a new behavior, the sooner the new behavior will become a habit. Step 4 will further assist you in adopting new behaviors.

### Step 4. Share Your Plan

To further establish a new behavior, share your plan with others. Tell family, friends, and co-workers about your plan. By giving others the opportunity to support you, you boost your determination to succeed. If your behavior change involves the entire family, all family members must work together for the family to succeed. Refer back to the worksheet in Table 32.3, "So Where's The Money?" Go over the chart with the entire family. Together, decide ways the family can break habits and develop a savings plan. Now is also a good time to make a family "piggy bank." The "bank" can be an empty jar or a small box. Once the family decides on their family financial goal, they can put a picture identifying the goal on the "bank."

Examples of goals include paying off a bill, buying something for the house, visiting family in another state, or accumulating money for school shoes. The "bank" needs to be kept where all can see it and all can help by adding money. After accumulating a sum of money, the family might want to open a savings account at a local bank or credit union. Once this account has grown to cover emergencies, additional savings may then be invested so the family will realize a larger return on their money.

Even with the best of intentions, sometimes staying focused on your savings plan is hard. The next step of the action plan will help you move forward.

### Step 5. Stick with Your Plan to Change

Step 5 is a critical step toward breaking habits and increasing family savings. You and family members must always look for new ways to reduce spending and increase savings. It is important to reinforce the fact that you can change your attitudes and break habits. Stay focused on your goal. It takes about 30 days for a new behavior to become a habit. Here are some specific activities for you and your family that will help you gain control of your finances, but still have fun as a family. By engaging in activities such as these, we are changing our attitudes and choosing activities that are more "money friendly." Changing attitudes and lifelong habits will serve you well immediately and over a lifetime and set an example for your children by instilling the value of saving.

- **Plan a family outing:** Choose activities that are free or inexpensive, such as attending a free concert in the park, visiting a museum, borrowing videos from the library, or attending story hour at the library.

- **Plan a family night:** Have a special treat, ask family members to share a talent, remind family members how much you appreciate everyone working together to cut back spending. Together, count the money that the family has saved, talk about the goal toward which the family is saving, and how soon you think you will reach the goal.

- **Have a "make your own pizza" night:** Instead of going out for pizza, put the difference of the cost of food prepared at home and the cost of eating out in the family "bank."

- **Pack lunches instead of eating out.**

- **Look for food specials at fast food restaurants:** Bring home the food as a surprise instead of taking the kids out. Not only is this a money saver but a time saver and stress reducer (no arguments over where to go and what to eat).

- **Video rental might be less costly than going to the movies:** Swapping weeks to rent videos with neighbors might be less costly than going each weekend yourself. Borrow videos from the public library.

Yes, you can do it—you can change your attitude. You can break habits and save for things that are really important to you and your family. You just have to stick with your plan. If you are successful, you will reach Step 6 of our action plan.

### *Step 6. Celebrate Your Success*

The last step to breaking habits is to celebrate your success. Once you have reached your initial goals, let others know of your success. Enjoy the fruits of your savings. Then continue with your new behaviors that are now habits. You have the tools necessary to be successful. Remember to trim all unnecessary expenses and keep your needs and wants in perspective. Watch the pennies you save grow into dollars which can be used to fund your saving and investment programs.

## Be a Comparison Shopper

Comparison shopping is the customer's best, but least used, technique when spending regardless of the type of expenditure. Comparing prices and products can save as much as 50% off a price you might have paid without making the comparison. Comparison shopping makes good sense. It is important to remember that an over-spender isn't just someone who spends more than he earns. An over-spender is also anyone who pays too much for things, especially when items or services purchased are conveniently available for less.

Internet shoppers can find comparison shopping resources at "shopping bot" (short for robot) websites such as http://www.mysimon.com and http://www.bestbuys.com. The benefits of comparison shopping are more than the money saved. Comparison shopping puts you in control of your finances. It helps you learn more about the products and services you are interested in buying. As a more informed consumer, you are able to make better spending decisions. Additionally, each success will reinforce your resolve to comparison shop again. By making wise consumer decisions and getting a good value for less, shoppers are able to save and/or invest the money saved.

## Untapped Strategies: Potential Money Sources to Fund Your Investment Program

Do you know that sometimes you can collect dollars instead of pennies by becoming a more knowledgeable consumer? By using the strategies that follow, you may be able to add large sums of money to your family's savings and investment program. Throughout the country, billions of dollars remain in accounts that have been abandoned or forgotten. These accounts include checking and saving accounts, pension benefits, and insurance benefits. How could anyone possibly forget about something of value? Well, maybe.... You neglected to retrieve a security deposit after moving out of an apartment. Perhaps dividends on a stock or mutual fund have been going to the wrong address. Maybe you switched banks and failed to close out all your old accounts. Or you changed jobs frequently and previous employers don't know where to send pension benefits. Perhaps you are entitled to benefits of a life insurance policy or cash left by a relative who has died. In any event, you might be entitled to unclaimed property held by your state or the Pension Benefit Guaranty Corporation. Or you might be the beneficiary of a long-lost insurance policy. Fortunately, receiving your just rewards is not extremely difficult if you know how to proceed.

To locate missing bank accounts and other unclaimed cash, contact your state's unclaimed property office or visit the website http://www.missingmoney.com. In most states, owners can recover their cash whenever they learn about it, no matter how long it has been in the state fund. About half of the states pay interest on money left in interest-bearing accounts. Instead of waiting for a state to find you, which is unlikely, you can contact the state's unclaimed property office.

When you write or call about abandoned property, give your name (maiden or former names, if necessary), Social Security number, current address, and all previous addresses while you lived in the state. If you are applying for property that was held in someone else's name, provide his or her Social Security number and former addresses. States normally take two to three weeks to write back saying whether there is property waiting for you. If you are due a windfall, they will send you an abandoned-property claim form to complete.

Return the completed form with proof that the cash belongs to you. If it's in your name, you will need to supply only a current ID, such as a copy of your driver's license, and any document that links you to the money (for example, a pay stub, savings passbook, or utility bill). For property that belonged to you when you lived at an earlier address, you must provide proof that you lived there. A copy of a tax return will do. Expect to get your check in about two months.

From time to time, you may see advertisements of asset finders, people who offer to find lost property for you. Beware of such ads. If you decide to hire such a firm, pay no more than 10% of the assets recovered and check out the firm with the Better Business Bureau. According to one state property fund director, "If you ever get a card or letter from a company offering to find your money, take that as a tip that the firm knows you have money waiting. So call or write to the state fund yourself. Then you'll get all the money you're due."

According to the Pension Benefit Guaranty Corporation (PBGC), more than 7,000 people in the United States are owed uncollected pension benefits. The PBGC, a federal agency, has launched a nationwide search on the internet to find workers who are owed benefits and who could not be located when pension plans closed. To check if your name is on the list of hard-to-find beneficiaries, log onto the Pension Search Directory at http://pbgc.gov/search. The directory identifies about 1,000 companies mainly in the transportation, machinery, retail trade, apparel, and financial services industries. If you do not have a computer, check for availability at a public library or libraries at high schools, community colleges, or universities. If you are not able to access a computer and you feel you are owed benefits, write to the Pension Benefit Guaranty Corporation, Missing Participant Program, 1200 K Street, NW, Suite 930, Washington, DC 20005. Include the participant's or beneficiary's name, address, daytime telephone number, Social Security number, date of birth, and the name and location of the employer.

Another place to look for lost cash is the Internal Revenue Service. Yes, the IRS has more than $68 million in unclaimed tax-refund checks that were returned because of an incorrect address or other delivery problems. The average check amount is $690. If you think you are owed a tax refund, but have not received it, call the IRS at 800-829-1040.

The last place where you might look for ready cash is lost insurance policies, yours or those of relatives where you might be the beneficiary. If you think there is a lost policy in your family, send a stamped, self-addressed business envelope to the Missing Policy Service, American Council of Life Insurance, 1001 Pennsylvania Avenue, NW, Washington, DC 20004-2599. The Council will send you a tracer form to complete and return. The Council will then circulate copies to about 100 large life insurance companies. The service is free and takes from three to six months.

## Strategies to Stretch Your Money

Whether you save pennies to make dollars, break habits and bank the savings, or find that you are the beneficiary of a long-lost life insurance policy, you are the one who has to manage your funds to best meet your individual and/or family goals. Remember that saving money does not make one a tightwad. On the contrary, saving money often

312

allows you to have more of what is important to you and your family. As you continue on your path to saving money, you may find that the following ideas will serve you well as road marks on your journey.

**Adopt the two-week rule:** If you think you really want something, wait two weeks to get it. The purpose of this habit is to make you an impulse saver, not an impulse spender. The two-week rule does not mean losing out on a once-in-a-lifetime opportunity. How many items, such as expensive clothing, a new piece of furniture, a boat or recreational vehicle, or a new car, would not be there in two weeks? If you wait two weeks to buy big-ticket items, two good things can happen. You may find the same item less expensive somewhere else. Or you may discover that you really did not want the item once the initial excitement wore off.

**Avoid unnecessary waste:** Another principle to practice is keeping items that are still good. You can avoid waste, which translates into savings or more money for other activities. You don't have to keep using items that need to be replaced, but do continue using those that still have value. The money that you would use for premature replacements can fund your savings and investment programs or purchase other goods and services for you and your family.

In a similar vein, don't waste goods and services. Don't leave the television on when nobody is watching it or operate the air conditioner when nobody is going to be in the house for hours. Don't throw away a tube of toothpaste that is good for a few more brushes. These actions are related to the conservation of resources, not money; but in the end you save money, too.

Another related principle is to develop a positive philosophy regarding care and maintenance of goods. By taking proper care of products, using them in the intended manner, and maintaining them according to manufacturer's instructions, you can greatly extend the useful life of an item. Instead of buying a new item, use the well-cared-for item and invest the money you would have spent. Let it be earning interest for you and contributing to your long-term financial security.

**Become a coupon clipper:** Would you think it was crazy to take a few dollar bills out of your wallet each week and throw them into the garbage can? That is exactly what you are doing by not using coupons for items that you normally buy or taking advantage of dozens of money-saving opportunities each day. If you spent five minutes a week cutting out coupons for your grocery shopping and saved at least

$6.00 a week, that is the same as getting paid $72.00 an hour after taxes. In a year, you would save a minimum of $300.00. You would need to deposit $5,000.00 and get a 6% yield tax-free to make that much money. Remember, pennies do make dollars.

**Treat yourself:** And finally, practice treating yourself. Having saved money by not buying things you don't need allows you to spend money for the things you want and that make your life enjoyable. Learn to truly enjoy the fruits of your labor.

## Summary

If you are able to provide the desire and self-discipline, you will be able to "find" the money necessary to fund your saving and investment programs. Improving your financial health through increased savings is not a matter of luck, rather it reflects planning, defined goals, wise decisions, and a desire for personal success. The various savings strategies included in this chapter offer you the groundwork needed to initiate a saving and investment program for you and your family.

## Action Steps

- Establish an emergency fund containing an amount equal to three to six months of your income.

- Determine amount of money needed to fund your high-cost goals (house, education, retirement, etc.).

- Develop a plan to insure that you save the money needed to fund your goals.

- Set up a regular savings program, if you do not already have one.

- Identify two strategies you could implement to help you accumulate funds to invest.

- Identify a money-consuming habit you have that you would be willing to change.

- Calculate the amount of money you can realize in one year by changing this habit.

- Change your behavior, save the appropriate amount of money, and invest it.

- Track your investment and watch it grow.

## References

Bruce, L. Negative personal savings rate: What does it mean? <www.bankrate.com/brm/news/sav/20060308a1.asp>.

Consumer Literacy Consortium. (1998, April). 66 ways to save money. Consumer Federation of America.

Chatzky, J.S. (1998, May 29-31). Save your change—it could grow to thousands of dollars. *USA Weekend*, 11.

Cruz, H. (1996, April 15). Saving money does not make one a tightwad. *The Greenville News*, D1.

Detweiler, Gerri. (1993). *The ultimate credit handbook*. New York: Penguin Group.

Folsom, David. (1997, September 15). Finding money made easy. *Bottom Line Personal*, 8.

Kiplinger Washington Editors, Inc. (1998, September). $13 million in missing pensions. *Kiplinger's Retirement Report* 5 (9), 6.

NCFE. (1997). Do without a little now...gain a lot more later on. *The NCFE Motivator Newsletter*, 3.

O'Neill, B. (1997). Public policy: Creating an environment for increased U.S. savings, U.S. savings rates: An overview. *AAFCS Family Economics and Resource Management Biennial*, 1-4.

Razzi, E. (1998, September). 33 ways to save at home. *Kiplinger's Personal Finance Magazine*, 111-116.

Sheets, K. and Spears, G. (1996, May). 101 ways to keep more cash. *Kiplinger's Personal Finance Magazine*, 32-39.

## Author Profile

Joyce H. Christenbury, M.Ed., CFCS, is a Professor Emerita of Family and Youth Development Department with the Clemson University Cooperative Extension Service. As an Extension family resource management specialist, she provided leadership in the area of family resource management with an emphasis on helping individuals and families develop skills needed to cope with today's complex marketplace. Professor Christenbury received her undergraduate degree in Home Economics Education from Winthrop University, Rock Hill, SC and her masters from the University of North Carolina at

Greensboro in housing, management, and equipment. Prior to joining the Clemson faculty in 1973, Christenbury taught in the College of Home Economics at the University of Delaware in Newark, Delaware.

# Chapter 33

# Asset Allocation, Diversification, and Rebalancing

## Asset Allocation

Asset allocation involves dividing an investment portfolio among different asset categories, such as stocks, bonds, and cash. The process of determining which mix of assets to hold in your portfolio is a very personal one. The asset allocation that works best for you at any given point in your life will depend largely on your time horizon and your ability to tolerate risk.

- **Time horizon:** Your time horizon is the expected number of months, years, or decades you will be investing to achieve a particular financial goal. An investor with a longer time horizon may feel more comfortable taking on a riskier, or more volatile, investment because he or she can wait out slow economic cycles and the inevitable ups and downs of our markets. By contrast, an investor saving up for a teenager's college education would likely take on less risk because he or she has a shorter time horizon.

- **Risk tolerance:** Risk tolerance is your ability and willingness to lose some or all of your original investment in exchange for greater potential returns. An aggressive investor, or one with a high-risk tolerance, is more likely to risk losing money in order to get better results. A conservative investor, or one with a

From "Beginners' Guide to Asset Allocation, Diversification, and Rebalancing," U.S. Securities and Exchange Commission (www.sec.gov), September 2005.

low-risk tolerance, tends to favor investments that will preserve his or her original investment.

## Risk Versus Reward

When it comes to investing, risk and reward are inextricably en-
twined. All investments involve some degree of risk. If you intend to
purchases securities—such as stocks, bonds, or mutual funds—it's
important that you understand before you invest that you could lose
some or all of your money.

The reward for taking on risk is the potential for a greater investment return. If you have a financial goal with a long time horizon,
you are likely to make more money by carefully investing in asset
categories with greater risk, like stocks or bonds, rather than restricting your investments to assets with less risk, like cash equivalents.
On the other hand, investing solely in cash investments may be appropriate for short-term financial goals.

## Investment Choices

While the U.S. Securities and Exchange Commission (SEC) cannot recommend any particular investment product, you should know
that a vast array of investment products exists—including stocks and
stock mutual funds, corporate and municipal bonds, bond mutual
funds, lifecycle funds, exchange-traded funds, money market funds,
and U.S. Treasury securities. For many financial goals, investing in a
mix of stocks, bonds, and cash can be a good strategy.

- **Stocks:** Stocks have historically had the greatest risk and
  highest returns among the three major asset categories. As an
  asset category, stocks are a portfolio's "heavy hitter," offering the
  greatest potential for growth. Stocks hit home runs, but also strike
  out. The volatility of stocks makes them a very risky investment
  in the short term. Large company stocks as a group, for example,
  have lost money on average about one out of every three years.
  And sometimes the losses have been quite dramatic. But investors that have been willing to ride out the volatile returns of
  stocks over long periods of time generally have been rewarded
  with strong positive returns.

- **Bonds:** Bonds are generally less volatile than stocks but offer
  more modest returns. As a result, an investor approaching a financial goal might increase his or her bond holdings relative to

318

his or her stock holdings because the reduced risk of holding more bonds would be attractive to the investor despite their lower potential for growth. You should keep in mind that certain categories of bonds offer high returns similar to stocks. But these bonds, known as high-yield or junk bonds, also carry higher risk.

- **Cash:** Cash and cash equivalents—such as savings deposits, certificates of deposit, treasury bills, money market deposit accounts, and money market funds—are the safest investments, but offer the lowest return of the three major asset categories. The chances of losing money on an investment in this asset category are generally extremely low. The federal government guarantees many investments in cash equivalents. Investment losses in non-guaranteed cash equivalents do occur, but infrequently. The principal concern for investors investing in cash equivalents is inflation risk. This is the risk that inflation will outpace and erode investment returns over time.

Stocks, bonds, and cash are the asset categories you would likely choose from when investing in a retirement savings program or a college savings plan. But other asset categories—including real estate, precious metals and other commodities, and private equity—also exist, and some investors may include these asset categories within a portfolio. Investments in these asset categories typically have category-specific risks. Before you make any investment, you should understand the risks of the investment and make sure the risks are appropriate for you.

## Why Asset Allocation Is So Important

By including asset categories with investment returns that move up and down under different market conditions within a portfolio, an investor can protect against significant losses. Historically, the returns of the three major asset categories have not moved up and down at the same time. Market conditions that cause one asset category to do well often cause another asset category to have average or poor returns. By investing in more than one asset category, you'll reduce the risk that you'll lose money and your portfolio's overall investment returns will have a smoother ride. If one asset category's investment return falls, you'll be in a position to counteract your losses in that asset category with better investment returns in another asset category.

In addition, asset allocation is important because it has major impact on whether you will meet your financial goal. If you don't include enough risk in your portfolio, your investments may not earn a large enough return to meet your goal. For example, if you are saving for a long-term goal, such as retirement or college, most financial experts agree that you will likely need to include at least some stock or stock mutual funds in your portfolio. On the other hand, if you include too much risk in your portfolio, the money for your goal may not be there when you need it. A portfolio heavily weighted in stock or stock mutual funds, for instance, would be inappropriate for a short-term goal, such as saving for a family's summer vacation.

## How to Get Started

Determining the appropriate asset allocation model for a financial goal is a complicated task. Basically, you're trying to pick a mix of assets that has the highest probability of meeting your goal at a level of risk you can live with. As you get closer to meeting your goal, you'll need to be able to adjust the mix of assets.

If you understand your time horizon and risk tolerance—and have some investing experience—you may feel comfortable creating your own asset allocation model. "How to" books on investing often discuss general "rules of thumb," and various online resources can help you with your decision. In the end, you'll be making a very personal choice. There is no single asset allocation model that is right for every financial goal. You'll need to use the one that is right for you.

Some financial experts believe that determining your asset allocation is the most important decision that you'll make with respect to your investments—that it's even more important than the individual investments you buy. With that in mind, you may want to consider asking a financial professional to help you determine your initial asset allocation and suggest adjustments for the future. But before you hire anyone to help you with these enormously important decisions, be sure to do a thorough check of his or her credentials and disciplinary history.

## Diversification

A diversified portfolio should be diversified at two levels: between asset categories and within asset categories. So in addition to allocating your investments among stocks, bonds, cash equivalents, and possibly other asset categories, you'll also need to spread out your investments within each asset category. The key is to identify investments in segments of each asset category that may perform differently under different market conditions.

One of way of diversifying your investments within an asset category is to identify and invest in a wide range of companies and industry sectors. But the stock portion of your investment portfolio won't be diversified, for example, if you only invest in only four or five individual stocks. You'll need at least a dozen carefully selected individual stocks to be truly diversified.

Because achieving diversification can be so challenging, some investors may find it easier to diversify within each asset category through the ownership of mutual funds rather than through individual investments from each asset category. A mutual fund is a company that pools money from many investors and invests the money in stocks, bonds, and other financial instruments. Mutual funds make it easy for investors to own a small portion of many investments. A total stock market index fund, for example, owns stock in thousands of companies.

Be aware, however, that a mutual fund investment doesn't necessarily provide instant diversification, especially if the fund focuses on only one particular industry sector. If you invest in narrowly focused mutual funds, you may need to invest in more than one mutual fund to get the diversification you seek. Within asset categories, that may mean considering, for instance, large company stock funds as well as some small company and international stock funds. Between asset categories, that may mean considering stock funds, bond funds, and money market funds. Of course, as you add more investments to your portfolio, you'll likely pay additional fees and expenses, which will, in turn, lower your investment returns. So you'll need to consider these costs when deciding the best way to diversify your portfolio.

## Lifecycle Funds

To accommodate investors who prefer to use one investment to save for a particular investment goal, such as retirement, some mutual fund companies have begun offering a product known as a "lifecycle fund." A lifecycle fund is a diversified mutual fund that automatically shifts towards a more conservative mix of investments as it approaches a particular year in the future, known as its "target date." A lifecycle fund investor picks a fund with the right target date based on his or her particular investment goal. The managers of the fund then make all decisions about asset allocation, diversification, and rebalancing. It's easy to identify a lifecycle fund because its name will likely refer to its target date. For example, you might see lifecycle funds with names like "Portfolio 2015," "Retirement Fund 2030," or "Target 2045."

## Changing Your Asset Allocation

As you get closer to your investment goal, you'll likely need to change your asset allocation. For example, most people investing for retirement hold less stock and more bonds and cash equivalents as they get closer to retirement age. You may also need to change your asset allocation if there is a change in your risk tolerance, financial situation, or the financial goal itself.

But savvy investors typically do not change their asset allocation based on the relative performance of asset categories—for example, increasing the proportion of stocks in one's portfolio when the stock market is hot. Instead, that's when they "rebalance" their portfolios.

## Rebalancing

Rebalancing is bringing your portfolio back to your original asset allocation mix. This is necessary because over time some of your investments may become out of alignment with your investment goals. You'll find that some of your investments will grow faster than others. By rebalancing, you'll ensure that your portfolio does not over-emphasize one or more asset categories, and you'll return your portfolio to a comfortable level of risk.

For example, let's say you determined that stock investments should represent 60% of your portfolio. But after a recent stock market increase, stock investments represent 80% of your portfolio. You'll need to rebalance.

When you rebalance, you'll also need to review the investments within each asset allocation category. If any of these investments are out of alignment with your investment goals, you'll need to make changes to bring them back to their original allocation within the asset category.

There are basically three different ways you can rebalance your portfolio:

1. You can sell off investments from over-weighted asset categories and use the proceeds to purchase investments for under-weighted asset categories.

2. You can purchase new investments for under-weighted asset categories.

3.  If you are making continuous contributions to the portfolio, you can alter your contributions so that more investments go to under-weighted asset categories until your portfolio is back into balance.

Before you rebalance your portfolio, you should consider whether the method of rebalancing you decide to use will trigger transaction fees or tax consequences. Your financial professional or tax adviser can help you identify ways that you can minimize these potential costs.

## When to Consider Rebalancing

You can rebalance your portfolio based either on the calendar or on your investments. Many financial experts recommend that investors rebalance their portfolios on a regular time interval, such as every six or twelve months. The advantage of this method is that the calendar is a reminder of when you should consider rebalancing.

Others recommend rebalancing only when the relative weight of an asset class increases or decreases more than a certain percentage that you've identified in advance. The advantage of this method is that your investments tell you when to rebalance. In either case, rebalancing tends to work best when done on a relatively infrequent basis.

## Where to Find More Information

You can find out more about your risk tolerance by completing free online questionnaires available on numerous websites maintained by investment publications, mutual fund companies, and other financial professionals. Some of the websites will even estimate asset allocations based on responses to the questionnaires. While the suggested asset allocations may be a useful starting point for determining an appropriate allocation for a particular goal, investors should keep in mind that the results may be biased towards financial products or services sold by companies or individuals maintaining the websites.

Once you've started investing, you'll typically have access to online resources that can help you manage your portfolio. The websites of many mutual fund companies, for example, give customers the ability to run a "portfolio analysis" of their investments. The results of a portfolio analysis can help you analyze your asset allocation, determine whether your investments are diversified, and decide whether you need to rebalance your portfolio.

# Chapter 34

# *Keys to Being a Smarter Investor*

Like many investors, you're probably torn between greed and fear... On the one hand, you want to generate as high a return as possible from your investments in order to pay for a comfortable retirement, fund the high cost of college education, start a small business, pass money on to your heirs, or finance a myriad of other major life expenses. At the same time, you may fear the investment markets. Perhaps you've been burned by market declines, bad investment advice, or taking on too much risk by grabbing for high returns. Or maybe investments and investing appear so complicated you're afraid to venture beyond the basic savings accounts you know.

This information, produced by the Financial Planning Association (FPA), the membership association for the financial planning community, offers 20 key steps to rein in that greed and ease your fears through the wise management of your investments. The chapter is not designed to make you a great stock picker or predict the next market boom or decline. Rather, it shows you how to apply time-tested investing principles and techniques so that despite the inevitable ups and downs of the markets, you can realistically achieve your family's financial goals.

The information presented here is also valuable whether you intend to manage your investments yourself or work closely with a financial planner or other investment advisor.

---

"20 Keys to Being a Smarter Investor," http://www.fpanet.org/public/tools/investing_brochure.cfm. Reprinted with permission from the Financial Planning Association®. © 2004.

325

**1. Understand the difference between saving and investing:** Saving is for smaller, near-term goals, such as the next family vacation, a car, or a financial emergency. Keep cash in a savings account, money market, or short-term certificate of deposit where you would have little or no risk of losing principal and can have immediate access to your funds.

Investing is for larger, longer-term goals—at least five years away—such as retirement or college. Investing carries risk such as loss of principal or not earning as much as anticipated. But wise investing also provides a greater opportunity for earning a significantly higher rate of return over the long run than you can earn through savings.

**2. Put the rest of your financial house in order first:** Before investing, consider tackling several other household financial issues. Create a budget, or spending plan, in order to free up money for regular investing. Pay off expensive credit cards or other high-interest consumer debt that eat up valuable investment dollars. Build a cash emergency fund and buy the right kinds and amount of insurance to protect against a financial setback—otherwise, you may be forced to raid your investment accounts for cash at a time when the market is down or with costly tax consequences.

**3. Clarify your goals:** Smart investing means investing with a specific purpose—those life goals such as retirement or passing money on to heirs. Investing with purpose makes it easier to stick to your investment plan and to invest income you might otherwise spend. Goals should be realistic, with a specific amount to accumulate by a reasonable target date. "Retirement" isn't a goal. What kind of retirement you want and when you want to retire are. Write down your goals and discuss them with your family.

**4. Don't just grab for the highest return:** One of the most misunderstood aspects of investing is the belief that investing is all about seeking the highest possible returns. This misperception is why so many investors got into trouble during the booming stock market of the late 1990s when they disdained "average" returns and began chasing the riskiest of stocks. Their purpose was simply to "make as much money as possible in the shortest time." This example illustrates why investment goals are important. With reasonable, specific goals, you can make informed, realistic investment decisions designed to accomplish your financial goals without taking unnecessary risk. Making decisions based on these investment goals is what steers you on an even course between the rocky shores of greed and fear.

**5. Understand your own tolerance for risk:** In addition to understanding the risks of each type of asset and investment vehicle, you need to understand how much risk you're willing to take and which types of risk worry you the most. Risk tolerance is partly a function of your investment goals, how much time you have to invest, other financial resources you have, and, frankly, your "fear factor." Investments that keep you awake at night, regardless of how "good" they might be for your needs, are not the right investments for you.

Accurately gauging your tolerance for risk can be tricky, however. It's easy to feel confident when the market is up and conservative when it is down. A CFP® (Certified Financial Planner) professional can help you assess where you truly stand.

Questions you and your planner might ask include:

- Are you more concerned about losing principal or losing purchasing power?

- How much principal are you willing to lose?

- How worried were you about your investments during the recent market decline?

- Which of your current investments keep you awake at night?

- Do you track your investments daily (a possible indication of unease)?

**6. Educate yourself about investments and investing:** Even if you work with a financial planner or other investment advisers, you need to have a solid understanding of how different types of investments work, their potential returns, their risks, and how you can assemble them in a cohesive portfolio that's right for your needs and goals.

Pay particular attention to investment risk. All investments carry some degree of risk. While stocks in general tend to perform well over long periods of time, for example, their short-term risk can be high, as many investors painfully learned during the market decline of 2000–2002. Risk is not limited to stocks, either. You can lose money in real estate, corporate bonds, gold, and commodities.

Even so-called "safe" investments carry some risk. U.S. Treasury bonds, for example, are federally guaranteed against loss of principal as long as you hold them until they mature. Because they are subject to interest-rate risks like any other type of bond, however, it's possible to lose money if you sell them before maturity.

Don't understand interest-rate risk? If you don't understand how a particular investment works, or the risks that come with it, don't invest in it. Instead, invest a little in education first. Ask your financial planner or investment adviser for resources to help you make the best decisions.

**7. Hold realistic market expectations:** One of the downfalls for many investors during the booming market of the late 1990s was their belief that high double-digit returns were normal for stocks. But historical investment returns reveal otherwise.

According to Ibbotson Associates, large-company stocks, such as those found on the Dow and the S&P 500, returned an annual average of 10.7 percent from 1926 through 2001. During the same period, small-company stocks returned 12.5 percent and long-term government bonds averaged 5.3 percent.

But these are only averages over many years. In any given year, you will probably not earn the annual "average" return. You'll earn either more or less than the average. Knowing the historical average returns can keep these fluctuations in perspective.

**8. Follow a detailed written plan:** Formally, this is called an investment policy statement. It's a road map to keep you on course through good times and bad, to eliminate investment ideas that don't fit your circumstances, and to provide a way to monitor the actual performance of your investments. This plan is, of course, subject to changes over the course of your investing lifetime.

The plan outlines such things as:

- Investment goals and time horizons
- Minimum average annual return needed to achieve those goals
- Current income needs from the portfolio (if any)
- Types of investments you will and won't include
- What investment vehicles you'll use, such as individual securities, mutual funds, separately managed accounts, or taxable and tax-favored accounts
- How assets are to be allocated within the total portfolio
- Rebalancing procedures
- Potential tax consequences
- Estimated risk level of the portfolio

**9. Allocate investments according to goals and needs:** How will you divvy up your investment dollars among various asset categories such as large-company and small-company stocks, international equities, government and corporate bonds, cash, real estate, and other assets?

The answer depends on several factors. Key among them are your investment goals and your timeline for achieving them. The sooner you'll need the funds, usually the more conservative your investments should be.

Also, what other financial resources are available to you? If Social Security and a good pension will generate most of your income needs in retirement, you may feel comfortable with a more aggressive approach to your investment portfolio. You may opt for a more conservative approach, however, if your investment portfolio will be a primary source of retirement income.

**10. Diversify your investments:** Too often, individual portfolios invest heavily in a single type of asset, often to the near exclusion of other types. A popular choice in recent years has been large-company U.S. stocks, also called "large-caps." These stocks outperformed other major asset categories in 1989 and from 1995 to 1998. Yet, in all other years between 1965 and 2004, large-caps were outperformed by small company stocks, international stocks, intermediate bonds, or investment real estate.

Because it's almost impossible to identify in advance which asset classes will lead the way during any given time, it's wisest to spread dollars among several investment classes. Research has shown that this diversification reduces risk while at the same time maintaining or even improving portfolio performance.

Investors also may want to diversify within broad categories. Among stocks, for example, they might divide their money between value and growth stocks, or between large-cap and small-cap. They may also want to include a variety of industries or sectors like technology, consumer goods, and healthcare.

**11. Don't overload on company stock:** As many employees at Enron and other large bankrupt companies learned the hard way, loading up your 401(k) with your employer's stock can be disastrous. Both your job and your retirement security are riding on the fortunes of a single employer and a single industry.

Financial planners typically recommend limiting company stock to no more than 10 or 20 percent of the account's value. But this can be difficult to do if the employer will only match your plan contributions with company stock while restricting how soon you might sell the stock and diversify through other investment options offered.

Consequently, you may need to try to diversify your overall portfolio through other types of assets you hold outside your 401(k) plan.

**12. Don't chase "hot" performance:** Today's hot investments are often tomorrow's cold turkeys. The most recent glaring example of this was tech stocks, represented by the NASDAQ (National Association of Securities Dealers Automated Quotations) stock index. The NASDAQ returned a record-smashing 85.6 percent in 1999, but fell nearly 40 percent the following year, and lost another 21 percent the next year.

The major problem with chasing the current hottest investments is that by the time most investors discover that an asset category or specific investment is "hot," the investment often has already realized much or most of its run-up in value. Consequently, investors often get in at about the time the investment is ready to fall.

Calculations by DALBAR, a consulting firm, show that stock investors who frequently trade in and out of mutual funds earned a meager 3.51 percent annually between 1984 and 2003—dramatically below the 12.98 percent annual average earned by the S&P 500 stock index over the same period.

**13. Don't ignore "cool" performance:** The opposite of chasing hot investments is ignoring those suffering through tough times. Real estate investment trusts, for example, did poorly in 1998 and 1999, but boomed in 2000 and 2001 when stocks faltered. Government bonds lost money in 1994, but returned nearly 14.5 percent the next year.

A time-tested way to avoid the problems of ignoring cool performance and chasing hot performance is to stay diversified and stick with the asset allocations spelled out in your investment plan.

**14. Stay in the market:** Nervous investors often sit on the sidelines during down markets until they're "convinced" the market is rebounding. But by the time they get up enough nerve to get back in, they've likely missed much of the rebounding market's gains, which commonly occur in the early stages of recovery.

SEI Investments studied 12 bear markets since World War II. Investors who either stayed in the market through its bottom, or were fortunate to enter at the bottom, saw the S&P 500 gain an average of 32.5 percent (not counting dividends) during the first year of recovery. Investors who missed even just the first week of recovery saw their gains that first year slide to 24.3 percent. Those who waited three months before getting back in gained only 14.8 percent.

**15. Start investing early:** Remember the famous image of Archimedes moving the world on the end of a long lever? Investing over time provides that same kind of leverage. The longer you invest money (the longer the lever), the more it "works" for you by growing faster and faster.

For example, invest $10,000 at an eight percent annual return inside a tax-deferred account such as an IRA and you end up with $21,589 after ten years. Keep the money in for 20 years and it grows to $46,610. Keep it in for 30 years and the same $10,000 initial investment balloons to $100,627.

**16. Invest regularly and automatically:** Greed and fear often tempt investors to try to "time" the market by judging when to be in during up markets and out during down markets. But even professional investors can't consistently time the market.

That's why CFP® professionals strongly recommend investing on a regular basis regardless of what the market is doing. This keeps your eyes on the long-term goals and not on the interim volatility. Funding investment accounts through automatic withdrawals from your paycheck makes this a lot easier.

**17. Pay attention to investment expenses:** During booming markets, investors often don't pay much attention to investment expenses. But the market decline of 2000–2002 and the recent mutual fund scandals have made investors more aware of overhead, trading costs, and other investment expenses. You can't control the market but you can control your expenses. Investing with an eye toward lowering investment costs can significantly improve your returns over many years.

**18. Don't let taxes dictate:** Investing with an eye on tax-saving strategies can save money. But many investment advisers believe that tax-saving strategies should not override the underlying economics of a particular investment. For example, investors sometimes are reluctant to sell a profitable asset, even though it might make economic sense to do so, because they hate paying the capital gains taxes—only to see the investment stumble in a down market, costing them far more in lost value than if they had sold it and paid the taxes in the first place.

**19. Rebalance your portfolio:** The asset mix that you originally assigned to your portfolio will probably become unbalanced over time as different types of assets perform differently. A portfolio allocated to 65 percent stocks, 25 percent bonds and 10 percent cash might shift to a 75/20/5 mix during a booming stock market.

You'll want to return these allocations to their original mix after the boom—otherwise, your portfolio has become riskier because it's more heavily weighted to stocks than before. You can adjust by either selling off some stocks and reinvesting in the other categories, or perhaps diverting new money into the under-weighted categories.

How often to rebalance your portfolio depends on several factors including your income needs, age, and life events. Many experts recommend rebalancing at least once a year, depending on individual circumstances.

**Monitor and revise your investment plan:** As with any financial plan, you should revisit your investment plan at least once a year.

First, you'll want to see if you're sticking with the guidelines outlined in your investment policy statement. Second, you may want to make changes if the financial circumstances in your life or your tolerance for risk have changed. For example, you may want to adjust investment mixes as you near or enter retirement. A marriage, divorce, death in the family, birth of a child, or a new job also may warrant a different asset allocation. Third, you may also want to make changes if a particular investment is underperforming its competition or is not generating the income you need.

## You're Not Alone

Investing can be overwhelming, but there is plenty of help out there. Your CFP® professional can provide investing expertise, objectivity, advice on how your investment plan fits in with your overall financial needs, and even day-to-day management of your investments.

Whether you turn over the management of your investments to a professional or do it all yourself, you are ultimately responsible for the results. This is your money and these are your life goals. The more you learn about investing and the more care you take to develop a sound investment plan, the less likely it is you'll be caught between those nasty twins—greed and fear.

Chapter 35

# How You Can Avoid the Biggest Investor Mistakes

Understanding how different investments work is the first step toward profitable investing. The second is making sure you—and your mutual fund manager—always maintain the correct wealth-building mindset. That is particularly important now, when many experts expect single-digit stock returns over the next decade or so.

To become the best possible investor you can, it is imperative to avoid the big mistakes. Behavioral finance researchers investigate how human beings study and act on investment information and their findings can benefit investors.

Those who invest directly in stocks are particularly prone to making devastating mistakes, perhaps even experiencing Enron-style setbacks.

But mutual fund investors are not insulated against these mistakes. In fact, a fund manager can compound any mistakes made by fund owners—after all, professionals are human. Thus, it should come as no surprise that behavioral finance research makes a strong case for buying and holding low-cost, broadly diversified index funds.

## The Biggest Fund Mistakes

The four biggest behavioral mistakes investors make with mutual funds are:

"Fund Investors' Biggest Mistakes and How You Can Avoid Them," by Albert Fredman, *AAII Journal*, May 2002. © 2002 American Association of Individual Investors. All Rights reserved. Reprinted with permission.

- Being overconfident in your ability to predict future investment performance of markets and fund managers;

- Hanging on to a mediocre mutual fund in the hope of eventually getting "even;"

- Being too myopic about the inevitable short-term losses accompanying stock ownership; and

- Being oblivious to the corrosive impact of compounding costs on long-term returns.

A closer look at these mistakes and the impact they will have on your performance can help you identify your own susceptibility to error.

## *Overconfidence*

People typically are overconfident. For instance, research indicates that people overestimate their abilities as drivers. In addition, it's common for a person to think of himself as being above-average. And gender matters: Men tend to exhibit more overconfidence than women.

Overconfidence also applies to investing acumen. Individuals feel confident of their abilities to pick sectors, superstar fund managers, or to properly time the market. Fund managers themselves often are overconfident of their skill to pick winning stocks and sectors, and to time the market.

A moderate amount of overconfidence is beneficial in many areas of life. People who have confidence tend to be happier and work harder. They also can better cope with life's uncertainties.

Unfortunately, being overconfident about investments is dangerous because the stock market is highly effective at deflating overblown egos. Most people don't realize how difficult it is to beat, let alone match, the S&P 500's long-term average return of about 11% annually.

Overconfidence often leads to overtrading. Investors' fund trading proclivities are evident from the tens of millions of exchange-traded fund shares changing hands daily. A person might be buying and selling actively managed mutual funds in an effort to find the next Peter Lynch. The widely popular discount brokerage trading arenas allow impulsive individuals to jump from one fund family to the next with a quick phone call or a few mouse clicks. The overconfident investor may also make big bets by concentrating on a favorite fund or even margining a position.

Overconfidence tends to ebb and flow with the stock market cycle. Overall, individuals were far more overconfident during the roaring bull market in the late 1990s than they are today.

A bull market is conducive to overconfidence because people attribute their investment successes to superior skill. Pride can boost confidence when the individual has had a string of successes. In reality, luck probably played a bigger role than skill. The so-called "conviction" stage of the market cycle occurred when stock prices approached their zenith in late 1999 and early 2000. Since then, the level of confidence and the trading activity of individual investors have both fallen sharply.

But even if you hold onto the same stock fund for years, your investment results could be disappointing if your manager is too overconfident. Many managers exhibit overconfidence, as evidenced by their rapid-fire trading and consequent high portfolio turnover rates, which often exceeds 100%. In fact, evidence indicates that fund managers who have done exceptionally well during a particular year will trade more actively the following year. Thus, having success leads to more overconfidence and higher portfolio turnover.

A major problem with high turnover is that it translates into high transaction costs. These costs are not reflected in a fund's expense ratio, which may already be high. Rather, the transaction costs accompanying high turnover diminish a fund's total returns. This problem is much more serious at a time when pre-cost investment returns are low. For taxable account holders, high turnover also leads to larger taxable distributions and a higher tax bite, assuming a fund is profitable on average.

## Clinging to Losers

Everyone hates to lose. Many individuals will not part with a losing investment until they get "even," which is usually considered to be their original purchase price. Locking in a loss really injures self esteem. A loss appears larger to most people than a gain of equal absolute value. In fact, research indicates that individuals find the pain of a $10,000 loss to be about twice the magnitude of the pride associated with a $10,000 gain. Thus, people try to avoid the psychologically painful feeling of regret.

Being averse to loss certainly makes sense, but individuals do not always analyze it rationally. Ironically, losers often increase their risk in an attempt to eliminate a loss. Like gamblers, would-be investors often increase their bets when their luck sours to avoid finishing in the red. An impulsive individual might hastily double a position in a volatile sector fund that has recently plummeted 50% to "average down" its cost. But a recent low price can easily drift lower.

Professionals also are affected by loss aversion. Mutual fund managers may take greater risks to overcome a high expense ratio or a losing streak.

The get-even syndrome can be very detrimental to an investor's financial well-being. If an investment slips into the red, individuals hold on steadfastly, hoping for a rebound. Individuals may avoid selling a fund that has gone down in order to avoid the regret of having made a bad investment. By selling, the loss is finalized; by not selling some hope of a rebound remains. But don't be too patient with a loser.

Let's say you want to double your money in eight years. A moderate, 9.05% yearly return will do the job, assuming a reasonably favorable market climate. However, the more years you stick with a dud, the harder it is to "catch-up" to your initial target. A 25% slide in the value of your investment over a five-year horizon means you must garner 38.67% yearly over the remaining three years if your goal is to double your money in eight years. Even a zero-return investment hurts plenty if held too long. With a 0% return during the first five years, you must earn 25.99% per year during the remaining three years to double your money in eight years! Like the gambler struggling to recoup losses, investors often take on excessive risk as they scramble to catch up after selling a loser.

With investor psychology, a few "magic" words may work wonders. By using a positive frame of reference, an investor may be much more willing to part with a loser. Instead of thinking "by selling this dog I'd have to realize a huge, humiliating loss," simply think "I'm going to 'transfer my assets' to a more productive use." This frame can be particularly useful if you're trying to convince someone else to abandon a loser.

## Grabbing Gains

On the flip side, abundant research indicates that people are too quick to take their gains. They don't let their profits run far enough because they want to lock them in while they have a chance, fearing that their gains will revert to losses. Pride and regret play a role in their thinking.

For instance, suppose an investor sees a promising stock fund that he wants in his portfolio, but to invest in this fund he must sell another.

The typical pride-seeking investor would sell a fund that's in the black rather than one that's in the red. By selling a fund showing a profit—even though it may be small—our investor experiences the feeling of pride. Regret is avoided (or postponed) by not selling the loser. With a taxable account, however, it makes better sense to sell the loser and realize a tax loss rather than pay taxes on a gain. In any event, losers often continue to under-perform, particularly if they are saddled with high costs.

When a rebound occurs in a fund that was in the red, many investors exit too quickly—with little or no gain in hand. By cashing out, investors are eliminating any chance for making decent returns on their stock funds, which could conceivably reward them for the extended period of pain.

## Being Too Myopic

"Myopic loss aversion" is another term for investor shortsightedness, and it usually afflicts people with long time horizons. Shortsighted investors with long-term horizons tend to be too conservative with their asset allocations. This is common among people saving for retirement.

It's a truism of equity investing that the route to long-term gains is punctuated with periods of short-term losses. Markets are extremely volatile, upsetting compulsive worriers. People who worry excessively may sell a good stock fund at the first sign of trouble.

An individual who suffers from myopic loss aversion may quickly sell out when the market averages plunge by 5% or 10% in a week or so. The person fears losing it all! The fact is that prices often rebound within a matter of days or weeks.

Suppose a 30-something individual is saving for retirement. Each year's investment in equities can be viewed as an isolated gamble. Some people may hold less than their optimal equity allocation because they overemphasize the potential from losses in a single month, quarter, or other brief period. Conversely, if investors focus on the potential outcome over several decades, they are more likely to hold the correct amount of equities. Unlike casino gambling, the expected long-run payoff for equity investing is positive, provided the individual maintains a sensibly diversified portfolio and can remain invested for many years.

Time diversification, or the law of averages, works well for the long-term investor. This assumes that the individual is not saddled with perennial losers—always weed out the clunkers, as explained above.

337

One rule of thumb for a moderately risk-tolerant individual is to allocate "110 minus your age" to equities. Thus, a 40 year old might have 70% allocated to a mix of equity-oriented mutual funds. Investors with short time horizons might best be served with a very modest (if any) stake in equities.

## Ignoring Costs Over Time

People, particularly those who are not financially savvy, often treat small numbers as unimportant. Their bias toward big numbers may cause them to focus on those funds that generated the highest returns during the past year.

These same people will also ignore what may seem to be minor differences in small numbers, such as expense ratios. The reported net return earned on a fund equals its gross return minus its costs. Expense ratios of mutual funds range from less than 0.20% for low cost index funds to more than 2%.

Assume a $10,000 initial investment and a 10% return. An actively managed large-cap domestic equity fund with a 1.25% expense ratio consumes $895 (or 5.55%) of the $16,105 future gross wealth in five years. In contrast, over 40 years, the fund's $166,062 in costs devours 36.69% of the $452,593 gross wealth. (Stated differently, only 63.31% of the gross return remains.)

The expense drag is far less with a broad-based domestic equity index fund. With a 0.20% expense ratio, the latter would cost an investor $31,775 in 40 years, a modest 7.02% of the future index value. Thus, the fund earns 92.98% of the return of the zero-cost index. Even lower expense ratios can be found on the lowest-cost index funds and the broad-based exchange-traded funds.

The expense ratio is not the only cost mutual fund investors face. More funds—even some index funds—are imposing front-end loads these days. Furthermore, as discussed earlier, high portfolio turnover ratios in turn lead to high transaction costs.

In addition to brokerage commissions—which typically are modest— mutual fund performance is impacted by the following more significant kinds of indirect trading costs:

**Bid-asked spread:** A stock held by a fund might be quoted at 25 bid and 25.50 asked. The difference between bid and asked prices affects investors when they buy at the asked and sell at the bid. This often occurs.

**Price-impact cost:** Buying a stock tends to bid up its price while selling tends to push it down. The larger the transaction, the higher the price-impact cost. Because mutual funds often trade stocks in large blocks, their price-impact costs can be high.

**Opportunity cost:** Mutual funds are often not able to complete a trade rapidly. It may take days or weeks to acquire or dispose of a block of stock in a particular company. In the meantime, the price can move against the fund manager, adversely impacting the results.

While difficult to quantify, trading costs of a large-cap domestic equity fund might consume 75 to 90 basis points of gross value yearly. Conversely, trading costs are minuscule with a broad-based domestic equity index fund.

The examples discussed before referred only to expense ratios. The impact of trading costs can be added in. An actively managed domestic equity fund could easily have expenses plus transaction costs that equal 2% yearly, causing it to consume a staggering 52% of future gross wealth in 40 years! Stated differently, that fund returns less than half of the market's return in 40 years. This is most devastating to younger investors with multi-decade time horizons.

## Behavioral Lessons

Studying the common mistakes of mutual fund investors reveals several important behavioral lessons.

### Behavioral Lesson #1: Don't try to beat the market.

Optimism can have an adverse effect on investment decisions when people set unrealistic expectations. Overconfident investors feel that their winners were due to skill and, thus, that they can continue to win. However, luck often plays the bigger part, and anyone's good fortune can turn on a dime.

Overconfidence can lead to substantial losses when investors overestimate their ability to identify market-beating investments. Individuals and fund managers who try too hard to beat the stock market often find that the market will beat them. That's because trying to beat the market can lead to overtrading and inadequate diversification.

The secret in making big money over long periods of time lies not in making the big gain; rather, it is to avoid the big setbacks.

## *Behavioral Lesson #2: Accept the fact that stock markets will fluctuate.*

A shortsighted investor might view the stock market as akin to a gambling casino, overemphasizing the potential for (and harm caused by) near-term losses. These are the kinds of investors who might put all (or most) of their long-term assets in a money market fund to avoid losing principal.

Unfortunately, these people don't realize that inflation's long-term impact on wealth can be far more devastating than simply having to ride with the short-term ups and downs.

If you focus on the potential outcome over several decades, you are more likely to hold the correct amount of equities.

## *Behavioral Lesson #3: Build a well-balanced portfolio.*

Keeping your asset-class balance is essential for being an emotionally successful investor. Elementary portfolio diversification is still the best way to guard against the risk of irreparable financial harm and its accompanying emotional consequences.

Build a well-designed portfolio based on factors such as your age, time horizon, earnings, net worth, and risk tolerance.

Those who jump in and out of investments frequently don't have a well-thought-out portfolio. Being overweight in a volatile fund or stock can cause an undue amount of emotional stress, which in turn can trigger indiscriminate selling.

A well-balanced portfolio is definitely easier on one's emotional state.

## *Behavioral Lesson #4: Use low-cost, tax-efficient index funds.*

Over time, small differences among expense ratios can add up to big costs. Compounding high expense ratios with rapid-fire portfolio turnover is the recipe for poor performance, particularly in a taxable account.

Succinctly stated: High Costs + Taxes = Mediocrity

The way to escape the corrosive impact of high costs is to use broad-based index funds for your portfolio core—or your entire equity allocation. Favor index funds that target the S&P 500, Wilshire 5000, or Russell 3000.

Exchange-traded funds provide a low-cost option for disciplined investors following a buy-and-hold program.

Costs will weigh even heavier going forward as equity returns are likely to be far lower during the next 10 to 15 years than experienced during the unprecedented bull market years.

### *Behavioral Lesson #5: Know when to sell (and when to stay put).*

It's often said that the sell decision is more difficult than the buy decision.

A disciplined program for selling is needed to avoid the financially debilitating mistakes of clinging to losers, selling winners too soon, overtrading, and panic-driven selling during a market tumble. A pattern of unfocused selling year-after-year typically leads to disastrous investment results.

The first step to intelligent selling is to build a well-balanced portfolio. However, everyone experiences disappointments.

Don't let the prospect of regret prevent you from selling a loser that could impede the performance of your portfolio. Humility can pay in this case.

Chapter 36

# *How to Get and Understand Financial Statements, Corporate Reports, and Other Information For Investors*

## *Getting Info about Companies*

### *Corporate Reports*

Corporate reports are a treasure trove of information for investors: they tell you whether a company is making money or losing money and why. You'll find this information in the company's quarterly reports on Form 10-Q, annual reports (with audited financial statements) on Form 10-K, and periodic reports of significant events on Form 8-K.

It's usually easy to find information about large companies from the companies themselves, newspapers, brokerage firms, and the U.S. Securities and Exchange Commission (SEC). By contrast, it can be extremely difficult to find information about small companies. Generally, smaller companies only have to file reports with the SEC if they have $10 million or more in assets and 500 or more shareholders, or list their securities on an exchange or NASDAQ.

To invest wisely and avoid investment scams, research each investment opportunity thoroughly and ask questions.

---

This chapter includes information from the following publications of the U.S. Securities and Exchange Commission (www.sec.gov): "Getting Info about Companies," 4/2005; "Information about Some Companies Not Available from the SEC," 2/2006; "Beginners' Guide to Financial Statement," 7/2004; "Information Available to Investment Company Shareholders," 4/2005; and "Mutual Fund Prospectus, Tips for Reading One," 2/2003.

You can get corporate reports from the following sources:

- **The SEC:** You can find out whether a company files reports by using the SEC's database known as EDGAR (Electronic Data Gathering, Analysis, and Retrieval; available online at http://www.sec.gov/edgar.shtml). For companies that do not file on EDGAR, you can contact the SEC through their website (http://www.sec.gov), by e-mail at publicinfo@sec.gov, or by calling 202-551-8090.

- **The company:** Ask the company if it is registered with the SEC and files reports with us. That information may be listed on its website.

- **Other government regulators:** Banks do not have to file reports with the SEC, but file with banking regulators. Visit the websites at the Federal Reserve System's National Information Center of Banking Information (http://www.ffiec.gov/nicpubweb/nicweb/NicHome.aspx), the Office of the Comptroller of the Currency (http://www.occ.treas.gov), or the Federal Deposit Insurance Corporation (http://www.fdic.gov).

### *Other Types of Information*

To find out whether a company has been cleared to sell its securities in a particular state and whether it is in good standing, you can contact the following:

- **Your state securities regulator:** Contact the North American Securities Administrators Association to get the name and phone number of your state securities regulator to see if the company has been cleared to sell securities in your state.

- **The Secretary of State where the company is incorporated:** You can find out whether the company is a corporation in good standing and has filed annual reports with the state through the secretary of state where the company is incorporated.

You can find general financial information about companies from reference books and commercial databases. The SEC cannot recommend or endorse any particular research firm, its personnel, or its products. But there are a number of resources you may consult:

- Bloomberg News Service and Lexis/Nexis provide news stories about a company. Dun & Bradstreet, Moody's, Hoover's Profiles, and Standard & Poor's Corporate Profiles provide financial data about companies. These and other sources are available in many libraries or law and business school libraries.

## Information about Some Companies Not Available from the SEC

Investors are sometimes surprised to learn the SEC does not have information about all public companies. This happens when a company's securities offering is exempt from the SEC registration requirements, and the company doesn't have to file reports with the SEC. Just because there is an absence of information does not necessarily mean that a company has violated the federal securities laws. But be aware that when reliable information is scarce, fraudsters can more easily spread false information about the company.

### Registration Requirements

Many companies that sell their securities to the public must register those securities under the Securities Act of 1933. These companies must give investors a prospectus describing the company and important facts about the offering. But some company's securities offerings may meet an exemption from the registration requirements. Some of the more common exemptions companies use are:

- intrastate offerings;
- regulation A and D offerings;
- private offerings; and
- sales of securities through employee benefit plans.

### Reporting Requirements

If a company registers its securities under the Securities Act, the company must then file periodic reports with the SEC under the Securities Exchange Act of 1934. The obligation to file reports continues at least through the end of the fiscal year in which the registration statement became effective. After that, the company is required to continue reporting unless it satisfies the following "thresholds," in which case the company's filing obligations are suspended if the company has fewer than:

- 300 shareholders of the class of securities offered; or

345

- 500 shareholders of the class of securities offered and less than $10 million in total assets for each of its last three fiscal years.

Even if a company doesn't have to register its securities for an offering, it still may have to file reports with the SEC if the company lists its securities on an exchange or the NASDAQ Stock Market or has 500 or more shareholders and $10 million or more in assets.

## Beginners' Guide to Financial Statements

### Financial Statements

Financial statements show you where a company's money came from, where it went, and where it is now.

There are four main financial statements. They are: balance sheets, income statements, cash flow statements, and statements of shareholders' equity. Balance sheets show what a company owns and what it owes at a fixed point in time. Income statements show how much money a company made and spent over a period of time. Cash flow statements show the exchange of money between a company and the outside world also over a period of time. The fourth financial statement, called a "statement of shareholders' equity," shows changes in the interests of the company's shareholders over time.

### Balance Sheets

A balance sheet provides detailed information about a company's assets, liabilities and shareholders' equity.

Assets are things that a company owns that have value. This typically means they can either be sold or used by the company to make products or provide services that can be sold. Assets include physical property, such as plants, trucks, equipment and inventory. It also includes things that can't be touched but nevertheless exist and have value, such as trademarks and patents. And cash itself is an asset. So are investments a company makes.

Liabilities are amounts of money that a company owes to others. This can include all kinds of obligations, like money borrowed from a bank to launch a new product, rent for use of a building, money owed to suppliers for materials, payroll a company owes to its employees, environmental cleanup costs, or taxes owed to the government. Liabilities also include obligations to provide goods or services to customers in the future.

Shareholders' equity is sometimes called capital or net worth. It's the money that would be left if a company sold all of its assets and paid off all of its liabilities. This leftover money belongs to the shareholders, or the owners, of the company.

The following formula summarizes what a balance sheet shows: Assets = Liabilities + Shareholders' Equity. A company's assets have to equal, or "balance," the sum of its liabilities and shareholders' equity.

A company's balance sheet is set up like the basic accounting equation shown. On the left side of the balance sheet, companies list their assets. On the right side, they list their liabilities and shareholders' equity. Sometimes balance sheets show assets at the top, followed by liabilities, with shareholders' equity at the bottom.

Assets are generally listed based on how quickly they will be converted into cash. Current assets are things a company expects to convert to cash within one year. A good example is inventory. Most companies expect to sell their inventory for cash within one year. Noncurrent assets are things a company does not expect to convert to cash within one year or that would take longer than one year to sell. Noncurrent assets include fixed assets. Fixed assets are those assets used to operate the business but that are not available for sale, such as trucks, office furniture, and other property.

Liabilities are generally listed based on their due dates. Liabilities are said to be either current or long-term. Current liabilities are obligations a company expects to pay off within the year. Long-term liabilities are obligations due more than one year away.

Shareholders' equity is the amount owners invested in the company's stock plus or minus the company's earnings or losses since inception. Sometimes companies distribute earnings, instead of retaining them. These distributions are called dividends.

A balance sheet shows a snapshot of a company's assets, liabilities and shareholders' equity at the end of the reporting period. It does not show the flows into and out of the accounts during the period.

## Income Statements

An income statement is a report that shows how much revenue a company earned over a specific time period (usually for a year or some portion of a year). An income statement also shows the costs and expenses associated with earning that revenue. The literal "bottom line" of the statement usually shows the company's net earnings or losses. This tells you how much the company earned or lost over the period.

Income statements also report earnings per share (or "EPS"). This calculation tells you how much money shareholders would receive if the company decided to distribute all of the net earnings for the period. (Companies almost never distribute all of their earnings. Usually they reinvest them in the business.)

To understand how income statements are set up, think of them as a set of stairs. You start at the top with the total amount of sales made during the accounting period. Then you go down, one step at a time. At each step, you make a deduction for certain costs or other operating expenses associated with earning the revenue. At the bottom of the stairs, after deducting all of the expenses, you learn how much the company actually earned or lost during the accounting period. People often call this "the bottom line."

At the top of the income statement is the total amount of money brought in from sales of products or services. This top line is often referred to as gross revenues or sales. It's called "gross" because expenses have not been deducted from it yet. So the number is "gross" or unrefined.

The next line is money the company doesn't expect to collect on certain sales. This could be due, for example, to sales discounts or merchandise returns.

When you subtract the returns and allowances from the gross revenues, you arrive at the company's net revenues. It's called "net" because, if you can imagine a net, these revenues are left in the net after the deductions for returns and allowances have come out.

Moving down from the net revenue line, there are several lines that represent various kinds of operating expenses. Although these lines can be reported in various orders, the next line after net revenues typically shows the costs of the sales. This number tells you the amount of money the company spent to produce the goods or services it sold during the accounting period.

The next line subtracts the costs of sales from the net revenues to arrive at a subtotal called "gross profit" or sometimes "gross margin." It's considered "gross" because there are certain expenses that haven't been deducted from it yet.

The next section deals with operating expenses. These are expenses that go toward supporting a company's operations for a given period—for example, salaries of administrative personnel and costs of researching new products. Marketing expenses are another example. Operating expenses are different from "costs of sales," which were deducted above, because operating expenses cannot be linked directly to the production of the products or services being sold.

Depreciation is also deducted from gross profit. Depreciation takes into account the wear and tear on some assets, such as machinery, tools and furniture, which are used over the long term. Companies spread the cost of these assets over the periods they are used. This process of spreading these costs is called depreciation or amortization. The "charge" for using these assets during the period is a fraction of the original cost of the assets.

After all operating expenses are deducted from gross profit, you arrive at operating profit before interest and income tax expenses. This is often called "income from operations."

Next companies must account for interest income and interest expense. Interest income is the money companies make from keeping their cash in interest-bearing savings accounts, money market funds and the like. On the other hand, interest expense is the money companies paid in interest for money they borrow. Some income statements show interest income and interest expense separately. Some income statements combine the two numbers. The interest income and expense are then added or subtracted from the operating profits to arrive at operating profit before income tax.

Finally, income tax is deducted and you arrive at the bottom line: net profit or net losses. (Net profit is also called net income or net earnings.) This tells you how much the company actually earned or lost during the accounting period. Did the company make a profit or did it lose money?

### Earnings Per Share or EPS

Most income statements include a calculation of earnings per share or EPS. This calculation tells you how much money shareholders would receive for each share of stock they own if the company distributed all of its net income for the period.

To calculate EPS, you take the total net income and divide it by the number of outstanding shares of the company.

### Cash Flow Statements

Cash flow statements report a company's inflows and outflows of cash. This is important because a company needs to have enough cash on hand to pay its expenses and purchase assets. While an income statement can tell you whether a company made a profit, a cash flow statement can tell you whether the company generated cash.

A cash flow statement shows changes over time rather than absolute dollar amounts at a point in time. It uses and reorders the information from a company's balance sheet and income statement.

The bottom line of the cash flow statement shows the net increase or decrease in cash for the period. Generally, cash flow statements are divided into three main parts. Each part reviews the cash flow from one of three types of activities: operating activities; investing activities; and financing activities.

**Operating activities:** The first part of a cash flow statement analyzes a company's cash flow from net income or losses. For most companies, this section of the cash flow statement reconciles the net income (as shown on the income statement) to the actual cash the company received from or used in its operating activities. To do this, it deducts from net income any non-cash items (such as depreciation expenses) and any cash that was used or provided by other operating assets and liabilities.

**Investing activities:** The second part of a cash flow statement shows the cash flow from all investing activities, which generally include purchases or sales of long-term assets, such as property, plant and equipment, as well as investment securities. If a company buys a piece of machinery, the cash flow statement would reflect this activity as a cash outflow from investing activities because it used cash. If the company decided to sell off some investments from an investment portfolio, the proceeds from the sales would show up as a cash inflow from investing activities because it provided cash.

**Financing activities:** The third part of a cash flow statement shows the cash flow from all financing activities. Typical sources of cash flow include cash raised by selling stocks and bonds or borrowing from banks. Likewise, paying back a bank loan would show up as a use of cash flow.

### *Read the Footnotes*

The footnotes to financial statements are packed with information. Here are some of the highlights:

- **Significant accounting policies and practices:** Companies are required to disclose the accounting policies that are most important to the portrayal of the company's financial condition and results. These often require management's most difficult, subjective or complex judgments.

- **Income taxes:** The footnotes provide detailed information about the company's current and deferred income taxes. The information is broken down by level—federal, state, local and/or foreign, and the main items that affect the company's effective tax rate are described.

- **Pension plans and other retirement programs:** The footnotes discuss the company's pension plans and other retirement or post-employment benefit programs. The notes contain specific information about the assets and costs of these programs, and indicate whether and by how much the plans are over- or under-funded.

- **Stock options:** The notes also contain information about stock options granted to officers and employees, including the method of accounting for stock-based compensation and the effect of the method on reported results.

## Read the MD&A

You can find a narrative explanation of a company's financial performance in a section of the quarterly or annual report titled, "Management's Discussion and Analysis of Financial Condition and Results of Operations." MD&A is management's opportunity to provide investors with its view of the financial performance and condition of the company. It's management's opportunity to tell investors what the financial statements show and do not show, as well as important trends and risks that have shaped the past or are reasonably likely to shape the company's future.

The SEC's rules governing MD&A require disclosure about trends, events or uncertainties known to management that would have a material impact on reported financial information. The purpose of MD&A is to provide investors with information that the company's management believes to be necessary to an understanding of its financial condition, changes in financial condition and results of operations. It is intended to help investors to see the company through the eyes of management. It is also intended to provide context for the financial statements and information about the company's earnings and cash flows.

## *Financial Statement Ratios and Calculations*

Listed below are just some of the many ratios that investors calculate from information on financial statements and then use to evaluate a company. As a general rule, desirable ratios vary by industry.

- Debt-to-equity ratio compares a company's total debt to shareholders' equity. Both of these numbers can be found on a company's balance sheet. To calculate debt-to-equity ratio, you divide a company's total liabilities by its shareholder equity, or Debt-to-Equity Ratio = Total Liabilities / Shareholders' Equity. If a company has a debt-to-equity ratio of 2 to 1, it means that the company has two dollars of debt to every one dollar shareholders invest in the company. In other words, the company is taking on debt at twice the rate that its owners are investing in the company.

- Inventory turnover ratio compares a company's cost of sales on its income statement with its average inventory balance for the period. To calculate the average inventory balance for the period, look at the inventory numbers listed on the balance sheet. Take the balance listed for the period of the report and add it to the balance listed for the previous comparable period, and then divide by two. (Remember that balance sheets are snapshots in time. So the inventory balance for the previous period is the beginning balance for the current period, and the inventory balance for the current period is the ending balance.) To calculate the inventory turnover ratio, you divide a company's cost of sales (just below the net revenues on the income statement) by the average inventory for the period, or Inventory Turnover Ratio = Cost of Sales / Average Inventory for the Period.

  If a company has an inventory turnover ratio of 2 to 1, it means that the company's inventory turned over twice in the reporting period.

- Operating margin compares a company's operating income to net revenues. Both of these numbers can be found on a company's income statement. To calculate operating margin, you divide a company's income from operations (before interest and income tax expenses) by its net revenues, or Operating Margin = Income from Operations / Net Revenues.

Operating margin is usually expressed as a percentage. It shows, for each dollar of sales, what percentage was profit.

- P/E ratio compares a company's common stock price with its earnings per share. To calculate a company's P/E ratio, you divide a company's stock price by its earnings per share, or P/E Ratio = Price per share / Earnings per share.

  If a company's stock is selling at $20 per share and the company is earning $2 per share, then the company's P/E Ratio is 10 to 1. The company's stock is selling at 10 times its earnings.

- Working capital is the money leftover if a company paid its current liabilities (that is, its debts due within one-year of the date of the balance sheet) from its current assets. Working Capital = Current Assets—Current Liabilities.

## Information Available to Investment Company Shareholders

Before you invest in any traditional investment company—such as a mutual fund, closed-end fund, or unit investment trust (UIT)—you should read the fund's prospectus and any other available information from the fund. Below you'll find descriptions of the different types of information that investment companies provide to investors.

### Prospectus

An investment company prospectus contains important information about its fees and expenses, investment objectives, investment strategies, risks, performance, pricing, and more. A UIT's prospectus (but not a mutual fund's or closed-end fund's prospectus) will also typically list the securities that the UIT holds.

When an investor purchases shares of a mutual fund or a UIT, the fund or UIT must provide the investor with a prospectus. Similarly, when an investor purchases shares of a closed-end fund during the fund's public offering, the fund must provide the investor with a prospectus. When an investor purchases shares of a closed-end fund on the secondary market, however, the investor will not necessarily receive a prospectus. This is because the investor is purchasing his or her shares from another investor rather than from the fund itself.

## *Profile*

Some mutual funds (but not closed-end funds or UITs) also furnish investors with a "profile," which summarizes key information contained in the fund's prospectus, such as the fund's investment objectives, principal investment strategies, principal risks, performance, fees and expenses, identity of the fund's investment adviser, investment requirements, and other information.

## *Statement of Additional Information (SAI)*

Mutual funds and closed-end funds (but not UITs) also are required to have statements of additional information (SAIs). Although funds are not required to provide investors with the SAI, they must give investors the SAI upon request and without charge.

The SAI conveys information about the fund that is not necessarily needed by investors to make an informed investment decision, but that some investors find useful. The SAI affords the fund an opportunity to expand discussions of the matters described in the prospectus. The SAI generally includes the fund's financial statements and information (or additional information) about: the history of the fund; some fund policies (such as on borrowing and concentration policies); officers, directors, and persons who control the fund; investment advisory, and other services; brokerage commissions; tax matters; and performance such as yield and average annual total return information (for mutual funds only).

## *Shareholder Reports*

A mutual fund and a closed-end fund also must provide shareholders with annual and semi-annual reports, 60 days after the end of the fund's fiscal year and 60 days after the fund's fiscal mid-year. These reports contain a variety of updated financial information, a list of the fund's portfolio securities, and other information. The information in the shareholder reports will be current as of the date of the particular report (that is, the last day of the fund's fiscal year for the annual report, and the last day of the fund's fiscal mid-year for the semi-annual report).

## *How to Obtain These Documents*

Investors can obtain all of these documents by: calling or writing to the investment company (all investment companies have toll-free telephone numbers); from the investment company's website; contacting a broker that sells the investment company's shares; accessing the SEC's EDGAR database; or contacting the SEC's Office of Public Reference at 202-551-8090 (phone), 202-942-9001 (fax), or publicinfo@sec.gov (e-mail).

## Mutual Fund Prospectus, Tips for Reading One

When you purchase shares of a mutual fund, the fund must provide you with a prospectus. But you can—and should—request and read a fund's prospectus before you invest. The prospectus is the fund's primary selling document and contains valuable information, such as the fund's investment objectives or goals, principal strategies for achieving those goals, principal risks of investing in the fund, fees and expenses, and past performance. The prospectus also identifies the fund's managers and advisers and describes its organization and how to purchase and redeem shares.

While they may seem daunting at first, mutual fund prospectuses contain a treasure trove of valuable information. The SEC requires funds to include specific categories of information in their prospectuses and to present key data (such as fees and past performance) in a standard format so that investors can more easily compare different funds.

Here's some of what you'll find in mutual fund prospectuses:

- **Date of issue:** The date of the prospectus should appear on the front cover. Mutual funds must update their prospectuses at least once a year, so always check to make sure you're looking at the most recent version.

- **Risk/return bar chart and table:** Near the front of the prospectus, right after the fund's narrative description of its investment objectives or goals, strategies, and risks, you'll find a bar chart showing the fund's annual total returns for each of the last 10 years (or for the life of the fund if it is less than 10 years old). All funds that have had annual returns for at least one calendar year must include this chart. Except in limited circumstances, funds also must include a table that sets forth returns—both before and after taxes—for the past 1-, 5-, and 10-year periods. The table will also include the returns of an appropriate broad-based index for comparison purposes. Table 36.1. provides an example of what the table will look like. Note: Be sure to read any footnotes or accompanying explanations to make sure that you fully understand the data the fund provides in the bar chart and table. Also, bear in mind that the bar chart and table for a multiple-class fund (that offers more than one class of fund shares in the prospectus) will typically show performance data and returns for only one class.

**Table 36.1.** Sample return table

|  | 1-year | 5-year (or life of fund) | 10-year (or life of fund) |
|---|---|---|---|
| Return before taxes | \_\_\_% | \_\_\_% | \_\_\_% |
| Return after taxes on distributions | \_\_\_% | \_\_\_% | \_\_\_% |
| Return after taxes on distributions and sale of fund shares | \_\_\_% | \_\_\_% | \_\_\_% |
| Index (reflects no deductions for [fees, expenses, or expenses]) | \_\_\_% | \_\_\_% | \_\_\_% |

- **Fee table:** Following the performance bar chart and annual returns table, you'll find a table that describes the fund's fees and expenses. These include the shareholder fees and annual fund operating expenses described in greater detail in our publication on Mutual Fund Fees and Expenses. The fee table includes an example that will help you compare costs among different funds by showing you the costs associated with investing a hypothetical $10,000 over a 1-, 3-, 5-, and 10-year period.

- **Financial highlights:** This section, which generally appears towards the back of the prospectus, contains audited data concerning the fund's financial performance for each of the past 5 years. Here you'll find net asset values (for both the beginning and end of each period), total returns, and various ratios, including the ratio of expenses to average net assets, the ratio of net income to average net assets, and the portfolio turnover rate.

# Chapter 37

# *How You Can Learn More about Foreign Companies and Markets*

There are different ways you can invest internationally: through mutual funds, American Depositary Receipts, U.S.–traded foreign stocks, or direct investments in foreign markets. This chapter explains the basic facts about international investing and how you can learn more about foreign companies and markets. Although this information covers foreign stocks, much of it also applies to foreign bonds.

As investors have learned, the market value of investments can change suddenly. This is true in the U.S. securities markets, but the changes may be even more dramatic in markets outside the United States. The world's economies are becoming more interrelated, and dramatic changes in stock value in one market can spread quickly to other markets.

Keep in mind that even if you only invest in stocks of U.S. companies you already may have some international exposure in your investment portfolio. Many of the factors that affect foreign companies also affect the foreign business operations of U.S. companies. The fear that economic problems around the globe will hurt the operations of U.S. companies can cause dramatic changes in U.S. stock prices.

Sudden changes in market value are only one important consideration in international investing. Changes in foreign currency exchange rates will affect all international investments, and there are other

---

Excerpted from "International Investing: Get the Facts," U.S. Securities and Exchange Commission (www.sec.gov), January 2007. The complete text of this document is available online at http://www.sec.gov/pdf/ininvest.pdf.

special risks you should consider before deciding whether to invest. The degree of risk may vary, depending on the type of investment and the market. For example, international mutual funds may be less risky than direct investments in foreign markets, and investing in developed economies may avoid some of the risks of investing in emerging markets.

### Why have Americans been investing in foreign markets in increasing numbers?

Two of the chief reasons why people invest internationally are diversification and growth.

- **Diversification:** Spreading your investment risk among foreign companies and markets that are different than the U.S. economy.

- **Growth:** Taking advantage of the potential for growth in some foreign economies, particularly in emerging markets.

Of course, you have to balance these considerations against the possibility of higher costs, sudden changes in value, and the special risks of international investing.

### What are the special risks in international investing?

Although you take risks when you invest in any stock, international investing has some special risks:

**Changes in currency exchange rates:** When the exchange rate between the foreign currency of an international investment and the U.S. dollar changes, it can increase or reduce your investment return. How does this work? Foreign companies trade and pay dividends in the currency of their local market. When you receive dividends or sell your international investment, you will need to convert the cash you receive into U.S. dollars. During a period when the foreign currency is strong compared to the U.S. dollar, this strength increases your returns because your foreign earnings translate into more dollars. If the foreign currency weakens compared to the U.S. dollar, this weakness your returns because your earnings translate into fewer dollars. In addition to exchange rates, you should be aware that some countries may impose foreign currency controls that restrict or delay you from moving currency out of a country.

**Dramatic changes in market value:** Foreign markets, like all markets, can experience dramatic changes in market value. One way to reduce the impact of these price changes is to invest for the long term and try to ride out sharp upswings and downturns in the market. Individual investors frequently lose money when they try to "time" the market in the United States and are even less likely to succeed in a foreign market. When you "time" the market you have to make two astute decisions—deciding when to get out before prices fall and when to get back in before prices rise again.

**Political, economic, and social events:** It is difficult for investors to understand all the political, economic, and social factors that influence foreign markets. These factors provide diversification, but they also contribute to the risk of international investing.

**Lack of liquidity:** Foreign markets may have lower trading volumes and fewer listed companies. They may only be open a few hours a day. Some countries restrict the amount or type of stocks that foreign investors may purchase. You may have to pay premium prices to buy a foreign security and have difficulty finding a buyer when you want to sell.

**Less information:** Many foreign companies do not provide investors with the same type of information as U.S. public companies. It may be difficult to locate up-to-date information, and the information the company publishes may not be in English.

**Reliance on foreign legal remedies:** If you have a problem with your investment, you may not be able to sue the company in the United States. Even if you sue successfully in a U.S. court, you may not be able to collect on a U.S. judgment against a foreign company. You may have to rely on whatever legal remedies are available in the company's home country.

**Different market operations:** Foreign markets often operate differently from the major U.S. trading markets. For example, there may be different periods for clearance and settlement of securities transactions. Some foreign markets may not report stock trades as quickly as U.S. markets. Rules providing for the safekeeping of shares held by custodian banks or depositories may not be as well developed in some foreign markets, with the risk that your shares may not be protected if the custodian has credit problems or fails.

## What are the costs of international investments?

International investing can be more expensive than investing in U.S. companies. In smaller markets, you may have to pay a premium to purchase shares of popular companies. In some countries there may be unexpected taxes, such as withholding taxes on dividends. Transaction costs such as fees, broker's commissions, and taxes often are higher than in U.S. markets. Mutual funds that invest abroad often have higher fees and expenses than funds that invest in U.S. stocks, in part because of the extra expense of trading in foreign markets.

## What are the different ways to invest internationally?

**Mutual funds:** One way to invest internationally is through mutual funds. There are different kinds of funds that invest in foreign stocks.

- **Global funds:** Invest primarily in foreign companies, but may also invest in U.S. companies.

- **International funds:** Generally limit their investments to companies outside the United States.

- **Regional or country funds:** Invest principally in companies located in a particular geographic region (such as Europe or Latin America) or in a single country. Some funds invest only in emerging markets, while others concentrate on more developed markets.

- **International index funds:** Try to track the results of a particular foreign market index. Index funds differ from actively managed funds, whose managers pick stocks based on research about the companies.

International investing through mutual funds can reduce some of the risks mentioned earlier. Mutual funds provide more diversification than most investors could achieve on their own. The fund manager also should be familiar with international investing and have the resources to research foreign companies. The fund will handle currency conversions and pay any foreign taxes, and is likely to understand the different operations of foreign markets. Like other international investments, mutual funds that invest internationally probably will have higher costs than funds that invest only in U.S. stocks.

**American Depositary Receipts:** The stocks of most foreign companies that trade in the U.S. markets are traded as American Depositary Receipts (ADRs) issued by U.S. depositary banks. Each ADR represents one or more shares of a foreign stock or a fraction of a share. If you own an ADR you have the right to obtain the foreign stock it represents, but U.S. investors usually find it more convenient to own the ADR. The price of an ADR corresponds to the price of the foreign stock in its home market, adjusted for the ratio of ADRs to foreign company shares.

Owning ADRs has some advantages compared to owning foreign shares directly:

- When you buy and sell ADRs, you are trading in the U.S. market. Your trade will clear and settle in U.S. dollars.

- The depositary bank will convert any dividends or other cash payments into U.S. dollars before sending them to you.

- The depositary bank may arrange to vote your shares for you as you instruct.

On the other hand, there are some disadvantages:

- It may take a long time for you to receive information from the company because it must pass through an extra pair of hands. You may receive information about shareholder meetings only a few days before the meeting, well past the time when you could vote your shares.

- Depositary banks charge fees for their services and will deduct these fees from the dividends and other distributions on your shares. The depositary bank also will incur expenses, such as for converting foreign currency into U.S. dollars, and usually will pass those expenses on to you.

**U.S.–Traded Foreign Stocks:** Although most foreign stocks trade in the U.S. markets as ADRs, some foreign stocks trade here in the same form as in their local market. For example, Canadian stocks trade in the same form in the United States as they do in the Canadian markets, rather than as ADRs.

**Stocks Trading on Foreign Markets:** If you want to buy or sell stock in a company that only trades on a foreign stock market, your broker may be able to process your order for you. These foreign companies do not file reports with the U.S. Securities and Exchange (SEC), however, so you will need to do additional research to get the information you need to make an investment decision. Always make sure any broker you deal with is registered with the SEC. It's against the law for unregistered foreign brokers to call you and solicit your investment.

### What information is available on ADRs and U.S.–traded stocks?

There are different trading markets in the United States, and the information available about an ADR or foreign stock will depend on where it trades. For companies that trade on the following markets, information is available from the SEC:

- New York Stock Exchange
- American Stock Exchange
- The NASDAQ Stock Market
- Regional stock exchanges
- The OTC Bulletin Board

For stocks and ADRs trading on these markets, foreign companies file annual reports with the SEC, as well as other information available in their home countries. Annual reports contain financial statements audited by independent accountants using U. S. audit standards. The financial statements either will be prepared using U.S. accounting principles or will show what the key results would have been under U.S. accounting principles. This makes it easier to compare a company's financial position to similar U.S. companies. The shares of hundreds of foreign companies trade in these markets, usually as ADRs.

**Over-the-counter (OTC) market:** These companies generally have not registered with the SEC, and they publish information based solely on foreign requirements, including different accounting and auditing policies. The OTC market is much less liquid than other U.S. securities markets, so it may be difficult to execute trades at favorable prices. Most foreign companies trading in the OTC market have not registered with the SEC. These companies may not let U.S. shareholders participate in offerings of new shares, such as "rights" offers to existing shareholders, because that would require SEC registration.

### What should I do if I want to invest?

International investments are like any other investment. You should learn as much as you can about a company before you invest. Try to learn about the political, economic, and social conditions in the company's home country, so you will understand better the factors that affect the company's financial results and stock price. If you invest internationally through mutual funds, make sure you know the countries where the fund invests and understand the kinds of investments it makes.

Here are some sources of additional information:

**SEC reports:** More than 1,100 foreign companies file reports with the SEC. The SEC doesn't require foreign companies to file electronically, so their reports usually are not available through the SEC's website. You can get paper copies from the Public Reference Branch by calling 202-942-8090 or by writing them at Securities and Exchange Commission, 450 Fifth Street, N.W., Washington, DC 20549. There is a copying fee for this service.

**Mutual fund firms:** You can get the prospectus for a particular mutual fund directly from the mutual fund firm. Many firms also have websites that provide helpful information about international investing.

**The company:** Foreign companies often prepare annual reports, and some companies also publish an English language version of their annual report. Ask your broker for copies of the company's reports or check to see if they are available from the SEC. Some foreign companies post their annual reports and other financial information on their websites.

**Broker-dealers:** Your broker may have research reports on particular foreign companies, individual countries, or geographic regions. Ask whether updated reports are available on a regular basis. Your broker also may be able to get copies of SEC reports and other information for you.

**Publications:** Many financial publications and international business newspapers provide extensive news coverage of foreign companies and markets.

**Electronic information:** Information about foreign companies may be available on the internet. You should be wary, however, of "hot tips," overblown statements, and information posted on the internet

363

from unfamiliar sources. You can find information about how to protect yourself from investment fraud over the internet by visiting the "Investor Assistance and Complaints" section of the SEC website (http://www.sec.gov).

## *How can I avoid international stock scams?*

Whether it's foreign currency trading, "prime European bank" securities, or fictitious coconut plantations in Costa Rica, you should be skeptical about exotic-sounding international investment "opportunities" offering returns that sound too good to be true. They usually are. In the past, con artists have used the names of well-known European banks or the International Chamber of Commerce—without their knowledge or permission—to convince unsophisticated investors to part with their money.

Some promoters based in the United States try to make their investment schemes sound more enticing by giving them an international flavor. Other promoters actually operate from outside the United States and use the internet to reach potential investors around the globe.

Remember that when you invest abroad and something goes wrong, it's more difficult to find out what happened and locate your money. As with any investment opportunity that promises quick profits or a high rate of return, you should stop, ask questions, and investigate before you invest.

Tracking down information on international investments requires some extra effort, but it will make you a more informed investor. One of the most important things to remember is to read and understand the information before you invest.

If you have more questions or if you have a problem with your international investment, contact the SEC. The website is http://www.sec.gov, and the e-mail address is help@sec.gov. You can also request educational brochures by calling toll-free 800-SEC-0330.

You also can contact the SEC at this office:

### *Office of Investor Education and Assistance*
U.S. Securities and Exchange Commission
450 Fifth Street, NW
Washington, DC 20549
Toll-Free: 800-SEC-0330
Phone: 202-942-7040
Website: http:www.sec.gov
E-mail: help@sec.gov

# Chapter 38

# *Understanding Market Indices*

If you open the financial pages of many newspapers, you will find a number of major market indices listed. Each of the indices tracks the performance of a specific "basket" of stocks considered to represent a particular market or sector of the U.S. stock market or the economy. For example, the Dow Jones Industrial Average (DJIA) is an index of 30 "blue chip" U.S. stocks of industrial companies (excluding transportation and utility companies). The S&P 500 Composite Stock Price Index is an index of 500 stocks from major industries of the U.S. economy. There are indices for almost every conceivable sector of the economy and stock market. Many investors are familiar with these indices through index funds and exchange-traded funds whose investment objectives are to track the performance of a particular index.

The following are general descriptions of some major market indices. You can also find them described on their sponsors' websites and in the available information of the funds that track them (for example, the prospectus for an S&P 500 Index fund will describe the S&P 500 Composite Price Index). These indices have been selected at random and many other indices exist that are not described here. Finally, please note that the SEC does not regulate the content of these indices.

---

"Market Indices," U.S. Securities and Exchange Commission (www.sec.gov), 11/2000.

## *Dow Jones Industrial Average (DJIA)*

The Dow Jones Industrial Average is an index of 30 "blue chip" stocks of U.S. "industrial" companies. The Index includes substantial industrial companies with a history of successful growth and wide investor interest. The Index includes a wide range of companies—from financial services companies, to computer companies, to retail companies—but does not include any transportation or utility companies, which are included in separate indices. The stocks included in the DJIA are not changed often. Unlike many other indices, the DJIA is not a "weighted" index (that is, the Index does not take market capitalization into account).

## *NYSE Composite Index*

The NYSE Composite Index tracks the price movements of all common stocks listed on the New York Stock Exchange. The Index is "capitalization-weighted" (that is, each stock's weight in the Index is proportionate to the stock's market capitalization).

## *S&P 500 Composite Stock Price Index*

The S&P 500 Composite Stock Price Index is a capitalization-weighted index of 500 stocks intended to be a representative sample of leading companies in leading industries within the U.S. economy. Stocks in the Index are chosen for market size (large-cap), liquidity, and industry group representation.

## *Wilshire 5000 Total Market Index*

The Wilshire 5000 Total Market Index measures the performance of all U.S. headquartered equity securities with readily available price data. The Index is a capitalization-weighted Index. The Index includes all of the stocks contained in the S&P 500 Composite Stock Price Index. The Index is intended to measure the entire U.S. stock market.

## *Russell 2000® Index*

The Russell 2000® Index is a capitalization-weighted index designed to measure the performance of a market consisting of the 2,000 smallest publicly traded U.S. companies (in terms of market capitalization) that are included in the Russell 3000® Index.

## *NASDAQ-100 Index*

The NASDAQ-100 Index is a "modified capitalization-weighted" index designed to track the performance of a market consisting of the 100 largest and most actively traded non-financial domestic and international securities listed on The NASDAQ Stock Market, based on market capitalization. To be included in the Index, a stock must have a minimum average daily trading volume of 100,000 shares. Generally, companies on the Index also must have traded on NASDAQ, or been listed on another major exchange, for at least two years.

You can also find short descriptions of these and many other market indices on the NASDAQ website (http://www.nasdaq.com).

# Chapter 39

# *Understanding Closing Prices*

Many investors use closing prices reported in the newspapers to monitor their holdings. But not all closing prices are the same, and the differences may be important to you.

"Closing price" generally refers to the last price at which a stock trades during a regular trading session. For many market centers, including the New York Stock Exchange, the American Stock Exchange, and the NASDAQ Stock Market, regular trading sessions run from 9:30 A.M. to 4:00 P.M. Eastern Time.

But a number of market centers offer after-hours trading. Some financial publications and market data vendors use the last trade in these after-hours markets as the closing price for the day. Others, however, publish the 4:00 P.M. price as the closing price and display prices for after-hours trading separately.

This discrepancy in the way the media and others report closing prices can cause confusion—especially when a single, low-volume after-hours trade occurs at a price that's substantially different from the 4:00 P.M. closing price. For example, an investor might read on a company's website that its stock closed at one price but then see a much different price on the consolidated tape flashing across the bottom of her or his television screen. Or, the next day, the investor might hear that the stock opened "up" when, in fact, it opened "down" compared with the price at the 4:00 P.M. close.

---

"Closing Price," U.S. Securities and Exchange Commission (www.sec.gov), 8/2004.

369

To help clear up this confusion, the central distributor of transaction prices for exchange-traded securities—the Consolidated Tape Association (CTA)—implemented a system designed to make closing prices uniform. Under this system, the regular session closing price for stocks will be the 4:00 P.M. price. Sometimes orders come in before 4:00 P.M., but they can't be filled until after 4:00 P.M. Therefore, the CTA produces a 4:15 P.M. Market Summary for vendors and the media that includes regular session trades that are reported before 4:15 P.M. but should be included in regular session 4:00 P.M. prices. Any trades that take place during after-hours trading sessions will be "tagged" with the letter "T" on the consolidated tape and will not affect the regular session closing price (or the regular session high and low prices). The NASDAQ Stock Market, which operates a similar system for trades in its securities, uses similar conventions.

Because the closing price for the same stock may continue to be reported differently among various media and market data vendors, investors should try to understand what the reported price is based on. For example:

- Does the newspaper or vendor indicate that the closing price is based on the regular trading session price established on the security's primary market, such as the New York Stock Exchange, the American Stock Exchange, or the NASDAQ Stock Market?

- Does the closing price reflect the last trade reported over the consolidated tape as of the close of the regular trading session at 4:00 P.M. Eastern Time?

- Does the closing price reflect the last trade reported over the consolidated tape in after-hours trading?

Investors may be able to find this information if their newspaper or vendor system describes how the closing price is being reported.

# Chapter 40

# *Analyzing Analyst Recommendations*

Research analysts study publicly traded companies and make recommendations on the securities of those companies. Most specialize in a particular industry or sector of the economy. They exert considerable influence in today's marketplace. Analysts' recommendations or reports can influence the price of a company's stock—especially when the recommendations are widely disseminated through television appearances or through other electronic and print media. The mere mention of a company by a popular analyst can temporarily cause its stock to rise or fall—even when nothing about the company's prospects or fundamentals has recently changed.

Analysts often use a variety of terms—buy, strong buy, near-term or long-term accumulate, near-term or long-term over-perform or under-perform, neutral, hold—to describe their recommendations. But the meanings of these terms can differ from firm to firm. Rather than make assumptions, investors should carefully read the definitions of all ratings used in each research report. They should also consider the firm's disclosures regarding what percentage of all ratings fall into either "buy," "hold/neutral," and "sell" categories.

While analysts provide an important source of information in today's markets, investors should understand the potential conflicts of interest analysts might face. For example, some analysts work for firms that underwrite or own the securities of the companies the

---

"Analyzing Analyst Recommendations," U.S. Securities and Exchange Commission (www.sec.gov), 4/2005.

analysts cover. Analysts themselves sometimes own stocks in the companies they cover—either directly or indirectly, such as through employee stock-purchase pools in which they and their colleagues participate.

As a general matter, investors should not rely solely on an analyst's recommendation when deciding whether to buy, hold, or sell a stock. Instead, they should also do their own research—such as reading the prospectus for new companies or for public companies, the quarterly and annual reports filed with the U.S. Securities and Exchange Commission (SEC)—to confirm whether a particular investment is appropriate for them in light of their individual financial circumstances. This alert discusses the potential conflicts of interest analysts face, describes the New York Stock Exchange (NYSE) and NASD (National Association of Securities Dealers) rules concerning analyst recommendations, and provides tips for researching investments.

## Who Analysts Are and Who They Work for

Analysts historically have served an important role, promoting the efficiency of our markets by ferreting out facts and offering valuable insights on companies and industry trends. Analysts generally fall into one of three categories:

- Sell-side analysts typically work for full-service broker-dealers and make recommendations on the securities they cover. Many of the more popular sell-side analysts work for prominent brokerage firms that also provide investment banking services for corporate clients—including companies whose securities the analysts cover.

- Buy-side analysts typically work for institutional money managers—such as mutual funds, hedge funds, or investment advisers—that purchase securities for their own accounts. They counsel their employers on which securities to buy, hold, or sell and stand to make money when they make good calls.

- Independent analysts typically aren't associated with firms that underwrite the securities they cover. They often sell their research reports on a subscription or other basis. Some firms that have discontinued their investment banking operations now market themselves as more independent than multi-service firms, emphasizing their lack of conflicts of interest.

## Potential Conflicts of Interest

Many analysts work in a world with built-in conflicts of interest and competing pressures. On the one hand, sell-side firms want their individual investor clients to be successful over time because satisfied long-term investors are a key to a firm's long-term reputation and success. A well-respected investment research team is an important service to customers.

At the same time, however, several factors can create pressure on an analyst's independence and objectivity. The existence of these factors does not necessarily mean that the research analyst is biased. But investors should take them into account before making an investment decision. Some of these factors include:

**Investment banking relationships:** When companies issue new securities, they hire investment bankers for advice on structuring the deal and for help with the actual offering. Underwriting a company's securities offerings and providing other investment banking services can bring in more money for firms than revenues from brokerage operations or research reports. Here's what an investment banking relationship may mean:

1. **The analyst's firm may be underwriting the offering:** If so, the firm has a substantial interest—both financial and with respect to its reputation—in assuring that the offering is successful. Analysts are often an integral part of the investment banking team for initial public offerings—assisting with "due diligence" research into the company, participating in investor road shows, and helping to shape the deal. Upbeat research reports and positive recommendations published after the offering is completed may "support" new stock issued by a firm's investment banking clients.

2. **Client companies prefer favorable research reports:** Unfavorable analyst reports may hurt the firm's efforts to nurture a lucrative, long-term investment banking relationship. An unfavorable report might alienate the firm's client or a potential client and could cause a company to look elsewhere for future investment banking services.

3. **Positive reports attract new clients:** Firms must compete with one another for investment banking business. Favorable analyst coverage of a company may induce that company to

hire the firm to underwrite a securities offering. A company might be unlikely to hire an underwriter to sell its stock if the firm's analyst has a negative view of the stock.

**Brokerage commissions:** Brokerage firms usually don't charge for their research reports. But a positive-sounding analyst report can help firms make money indirectly by generating more purchases and sales of covered securities—which, in turn, result in additional brokerage commission.

**Analyst compensation:** Brokerage firms' compensation arrangements can put pressure on analysts to issue positive research reports and recommendations. For example, some firms link compensation and bonuses—directly or indirectly—to the number of investment banking deals the analyst lands or to the profitability of the firm's investment banking division.

**Ownership interests in the company:** An analyst, other employees, and the firm itself may own significant positions in the companies an analyst covers. Analysts may also participate in employee stock-purchase pools that invest in companies they cover. And in a growing trend called "venture investing," an analyst's firm or colleagues may acquire a stake in a start-up by obtaining discounted, pre-IPO (initial public offering) shares. These practices allow an analyst, the firm he or she works for, or both, to profit, directly or indirectly, from owning securities in companies the analyst covers.

## *Disclosure and Recent Rule Changes*

The rules of the NYSE and NASD require analysts in some circumstances to disclose certain conflicts of interest when recommending the purchase or sale of a specific security. On May 10, 2002, the SEC (Securities and Exchange Commission) approved proposed changes to these rules, strengthening the disclosures that analysts and firms must make. The NYSE and NASD decided upon an implementation schedule of between 60 and 180 calendar days for the new rules in order to provide reasonable time periods for firms to develop and implement policies, procedures and systems to comply with the new requirements. These rules implement key structural reforms aimed at increasing analysts' independence and further managing conflicts of interest. They also require increased disclosure of conflicts in research reports and public appearances. Key provisions of the rules include the following:

**No promises of favorable research:** NYSE and NASD rules now prohibit analysts from offering a favorable research rating or specific price target to induce investment banking business from companies. The rule changes also impose "quiet periods" that bar a firm that is acting as manager or co-manager of a securities offering from issuing a report on a company within 40 days after an initial public offering or within 10 days after a secondary offering for an inactively traded company.

- *Significance of the change:* Promising research coverage to a company will not be as attractive if the research may not be issued within the initial days following the offering.

**Limitations on relationships and communications:** The rule changes prohibit research analysts from being supervised by the investment banking department. In addition, investment banking personnel are prohibited from discussing research reports with analysts prior to distribution, unless staff from the firm's legal/compliance department monitor those communications. Analysts are also prohibited from sharing draft research reports with the target companies, other than to check facts after approval from the firm's legal/compliance department.

- *Significance of the change:* These provisions help protect research analysts from influences that could impair their objectivity and independence.

**Analyst compensation:** The rule changes bar securities firms from tying an analyst's compensation to specific investment banking transactions. Furthermore, if an analyst's compensation is based on the firm's general investment banking revenues, that fact must be disclosed in the firm's research reports.

- *Significance of the change:* Prohibiting compensation from specific investment banking transactions significantly curtails a potentially major influence on research analysts' objectivity.

**Firm compensation:** The rule changes require a securities firm to disclose in a research report if it managed or co-managed a public offering of equity securities for the company or if it received any compensation for investment banking services from the company in the past 12 months. A firm also must disclose if it expects to receive or intends to seek compensation for investment banking services from the company during the next three months.

- *Significance of the change:* Requiring securities firms to disclose compensation from investment banking clients can alert investors to potential biases in their recommendations.

**Restrictions on personal trading by analysts:** The rule changes bar analysts and members of their households from investing in a company's securities prior to its initial public offering if the company is in the business sector that the analyst covers. In addition, the rule changes require "blackout periods" that prohibit analysts from trading securities of the companies they follow for 30 days before and five days after they issue a research report about the company, and also prohibits analysts from trading against their most recent recommendations—subject to exceptions for unanticipated significant changes in the personal financial circumstances of the beneficial owner of a research analyst account.

- *Significance of the change:* Prohibiting analysts from trading around the time they issue research reports should reduce conflicts arising from personal financial interests.

**Disclosures of financial interests in covered companies:** The rule changes require analysts to disclose if they own shares of recommended companies. Firms are also required to disclose if they own 1% or more of a company's equity securities as of the previous month end.

- *Significance of the change:* Requiring analysts and securities firms to disclose financial interests can alert investors to potential biases in their recommendations.

**Disclosures in research reports regarding the firm's ratings:** The rule changes require firms to clearly explain in research reports the meaning of all ratings terms they use, and this terminology must be consistent with its plain meaning. Additionally, firms must provide the percentage of all the ratings that they have assigned to buy, hold, and sell categories, and the percentage of investment banking clients in each category. Firms are also required to provide a graph or chart that plots the historical price movements of the security and indicates those points at which the firm initiated and changed ratings and price targets for the company.

- *Significance of the change:* These disclosures will assist investors in deciding what value to place on a securities firm's ratings and provide them with better information to assess its research.

**Disclosures during public appearances by analysts:** The rule changes require disclosures from analysts during public appearances, such as television or radio interviews. Guest analysts will have disclose if they or their firm have a position in the stock; if the company is an investment banking client of the firm; if the analyst or a member of the analyst's household is an officer, director, or advisory board member of the recommended issuer; and other material conflicts.

- *Significance of the change:* This disclosure will inform investors who learn of analyst opinions and ratings through the media— rather than in written research reports—of analyst and firm conflicts.

## What Conflicts May Mean to You

The fact that an analyst—or the analyst's firm—may have a conflict of interest does not mean that his or her recommendation is flawed or unwise. But it's a fact you should know and consider in assessing whether the recommendation is wise for you.

It's up to you to educate yourself to make sure that any investments you choose match your goals and tolerance for risk. Remember that analysts generally do not function as your financial adviser when they make recommendations—they're not providing individually tailored investment advice, and they're not taking your personal circumstances into consideration.

## Uncovering Conflicts

In addition to paying close attention to the disclosures that firms and analysts make, here are some steps you can take to assess whether and to what extent analyst conflicts may exist:

**Identify the underwriter:** Before you buy, confirm whether the analyst's firm underwrote a recommended company's stock by looking at the prospectus, which is part of the registration statement for the offering. Note that firms are required to disclose in research reports whether they managed or co-managed a public offering. You'll find a list of the lead or managing underwriters on the front cover of both the preliminary and final copies of the prospectus. By convention, the name of the lead underwriter—the firm that stands to make the most money on the deal—will appear first, and any co-managers will generally be listed second in alphabetical order. Other firms participating in the deal will be listed only in the "Underwriting" or "Plan of Distribution" sections of the final supplement to the prospectus. You can search for registration statements using the SEC's EDGAR [Electronic Data Gathering, Analysis, and Retrieval] database at www.sec.gov/edgar.shtml. The final supplement to the prospectus will appear in EDGAR as a "424" filing.

**Research ownership interests:** A company's registration statement and its annual report on Form 10-K will tell you who the beneficial owners of more than five percent of a class of equity securities are. Research reports on a company must disclose whether the securities firm issuing the report (or any of its affiliates) beneficially owns one percent or more of any class of common equity securities of the subject company. The issuer's registration statement will also tell you about private sales of the company's securities during the past three years. In addition to the disclosure requirements in the new rules, you may be able to ascertain ownership by checking the following SEC forms:

- **Schedules 13D and 13G:** Any person who acquires a beneficial ownership of more than five percent must file a Schedule 13D. Schedule 13G is a much abbreviated version of Schedule 13D that is only available for use by a limited category of "persons," such as banks, broker-dealers, or insurance companies.

- **Forms 3, 4, and 5:** Officers, directors, and beneficial owners of more than 10 percent must report their holdings—and any changes in their holdings—to the SEC on Forms 3, 4, and 5.

- **Form 144:** If an analyst or a firm holds "restricted" securities from the company—meaning those acquired in an unregistered, private sale from the issuer or its affiliates—then investors can find out whether the analyst or the firm recently sold the stock by researching their Form 144 filings.

As of November 4, 2002, all statements of beneficial ownership on Schedules 13D and 13G (including those relating to the securities of foreign private issuers) must be submitted electronically using the SEC's EDGAR system. While the SEC does not require that Forms 3, 4, 5, or 144 be sent electronically, some filers choose to do so. If you can't find a form on EDGAR, please contact the SEC's Office of Public Reference by telephone at 202-551-8090 or by e-mail at publicinfo@sec.gov. Or check the "Quotes" section of the NASDAQ Stock Market's website at http://quotes.nasdaq.com.

## Unlock the Mystery of "Lock-ups"

If the analyst's firm acquired ownership interests through venture investing, the shares generally will be subject to a "lock-up" agreement during and after the issuer's initial public offering. Lock-up agreements prohibit company insiders—including employees, their friends and family, and venture capitalists—from selling their shares for a set period of time without the underwriter's permission. While the underwriter can choose to end a lock-up period early—whether because of market conditions, the performance of the offering, or other factors—lock-ups generally last for 180 days after the offering's registration statement becomes effective.

After the lock-up period ends, the firm may be able to sell the stock. If you're considering investing in a company that has recently conducted an initial public offering, you'll want to check whether a lock-up agreement is in effect and when it expires or if the underwriter waived any lock-up restrictions. This is important information because a company's stock price may be affected by the prospect of lock-up shares being sold into the market when the lock-up ends. It is also a data point you can consider when assessing research reports issued just before a lock-up period expires—which are sometimes known as "booster shot" reports.

To find out whether a company has a lock-up agreement, check the "Underwriting" or "Plan of Distribution" sections of the prospectus. That's where companies must disclose that information. You can contact the company's shareholder relations department to ask for its prospectus, or use the SEC's EDGAR database if the company has filed its prospectus electronically. For companies that do not file on EDGAR, you can contact the SEC's Office of Public Reference by telephone at 202-551-8090 or by e-mail at publicinfo@sec.gov. There are also commercial websites you can use for free that track when companies' lock-up agreements expire. The SEC does not endorse these websites and makes no representation about any of the information or services contained on these websites.

## How You Can Protect Yourself

We advise all investors to do their homework before investing. If you purchase a security solely because an analyst said the company was one of his or her "top picks," you may be doing yourself a disservice. Especially if the company is one you've never heard of, take time to investigate:

- When assessing a firm's research report of a company, be sure to read all of the disclosures about the firm and analysts' conflicts of interest and the types of research recommendations that the firm has made.

- Research the company's financial reports using the SEC's EDGAR database at http://www.sec.gov/edgar.shtml, or call the company for copies. If you can't analyze them on your own, ask a trusted professional for help.

- Find out if a lock-up period is about to expire or whether the underwriter waived it. While that may not necessarily affect your decision to buy, it may put an analyst recommendation in perspective.

- Confirm whether the analyst's firm underwrote one of the company's recent stock offerings—especially its IPO.

- Learn as much as you can about the company by reading independent news reports, commercial databases, and reference books. Your local library may have these and other resources.

- Talk to your broker or financial adviser and ask questions about the company and its prospects. But bear in mind that if your broker's firm issued a positive report on a company, your broker will be hard-pressed to contradict it. Be sure to ask your broker whether a particular investment is suitable for you in light of your financial circumstances.

Above all, always remember that even the soundest recommendation from the most trust-worthy analyst may not be a good choice for you. That's one reason we caution investors never to rely solely on an analyst's recommendation when buying or selling a stock. Before you act, ask yourself whether the decision fits with your goals, your time horizon, and your tolerance for risk. Know what you're buying—or selling—and why.

# Chapter 41

# *Trade Execution: What Every Investor Should Know*

## *Understanding Trade Execution*

When you place an order to buy or sell stock, you might not think about where or how your broker will execute the trade. But where and how your order is executed can impact the overall costs of the transaction, including the price you pay for the stock. Here's what you should know about trade execution:

### *Trade Execution Isn't Instantaneous*

Many investors who trade through online brokerage accounts assume they have a direct connection to the securities markets. But they don't. When you push that enter key, your order is sent over the internet to your broker—who in turn decides which market to send it to for execution. A similar process occurs when you call your broker to place a trade.

While trade execution is usually seamless and quick, it does take time. And prices can change quickly, especially in fast-moving markets. Because price quotes are only for a specific number of shares, investors may not always receive the price they saw on their screen or the price their broker quoted over the phone. By the time your order

This chapter begins with "Trade Execution: What Every Investor Should Know," 6/2004, and continues with "Trade Execution: Rules Your Brokerage Firm Must Follow," 9/2004, U.S. Securities and Exchange Commission (www.sec.gov).

reaches the market, the price of the stock could be slightly—or very—different.

No U.S. Securities and Exchange Commission (SEC) regulations require a trade to be executed within a set period of time. But if firms advertise their speed of execution, they must not exaggerate or fail to tell investors about the possibility of significant delays.

### *Your Broker Has Options for Executing Your Trade*

Just as you have a choice of brokers, your broker generally has a choice of markets to execute your trade:

- For a stock that is listed on an exchange, such as the New York Stock Exchange (NYSE), your broker may direct the order to that exchange, to another exchange (such as a regional exchange), or to a firm called a "third market maker." A "third market maker" is a firm that stands ready to buy or sell a stock listed on an exchange at publicly quoted prices. As a way to attract orders from brokers, some regional exchanges or third market makers will pay your broker for routing your order to that exchange or market maker—perhaps a penny or more per share for your order. This is called "payment for order flow."

- For a stock that trades in an over-the-counter (OTC) market, such as the NASDAQ, your broker may send the order to a "NASDAQ market maker" in the stock. Many NASDAQ market makers also pay brokers for order flow.

- Your broker may route your order—especially a "limit order"—to an electronic communications network (ECN) that automatically matches buy and sell orders at specified prices. A "limit order" is an order to buy or sell a stock at a specific price.

- Your broker may decide to send your order to another division of your broker's firm to be filled out of the firm's own inventory. This is called "internalization." In this way, your broker's firm may make money on the "spread"—which is the difference between the purchase price and the sale price.

### *Your Broker Has a Duty of "Best Execution"*

Many firms use automated systems to handle the orders they receive from their customers. In deciding how to execute orders, your broker has a duty to seek the best execution that is reasonably available for its customers' orders. That means your broker must evaluate the orders it receives from all customers in the aggregate and periodically assess which competing markets, market makers, or ECNs offer the most favorable terms of execution.

The opportunity for "price improvement"—which is the opportunity, but not the guarantee, for an order to be executed at a better price than what is currently quoted publicly—is an important factor a broker should consider in executing its customers' orders. Other factors include the speed and the likelihood of execution.

Here's an example of how price improvement can work: Let's say you enter a market order to sell 500 shares of a stock. The current quote is $20. Your broker may be able to send your order to a market or a market maker where your order would have the possibility of getting a price better than $20. If your order is executed at $20.05, you would receive $10,025.00 for the sale of your stock—$25.00 more than if your broker had only been able to get the current quote for you.

Of course, the additional time it takes some markets to execute orders may result in your getting a worse price than the current quote—especially in a fast-moving market. So, your broker is required to consider whether there is a trade-off between providing its customers' orders with the possibility—but not the guarantee—of better prices and the extra time it may take to do so.

## *You Have Options for Directing Trades*

If for any reason you want to direct your trade to a particular exchange, market maker, or ECN, you may be able to call your broker and ask him or her to do this. But some brokers may charge for that service. Some brokers offer active traders the ability to direct orders in NASDAQ stocks to the market maker or ECN of their choice.

SEC rules aimed at improving public disclosure of order execution and routing practices require all market centers that trade national market system securities to make monthly, electronic disclosures of basic information concerning their quality of executions on a stock-by-stock basis, including how market orders of various sizes are executed relative to the public quotes. These reports must also disclose information about effective spreads—the spreads actually paid by investors whose orders are routed to a particular market center. In addition, market centers must disclose the extent to which they provide executions at prices better than the public quotes to investors using limit orders.

These rules also require brokers that route orders on behalf of customers to disclose, on a quarterly basis, the identity of the market centers to which they route a significant percentage of their orders. In addition, brokers must respond to the requests of customers interested in learning where their individual orders were routed for execution during the previous six months.

With this information readily available, you can learn where and how your firm executes its customers' orders and what steps it takes to assure best execution. Ask your broker about the firm's policies on payment for order flow, internalization, or other routing practices—or look for that information in your new account agreement. You can also write to your broker to find out the nature and source of any payment for order flow it may have received for a particular order.

If you're comparing firms, ask each how often it gets price improvement on customers' orders. And then consider that information in deciding with which firm you will do business.

## Rules Your Brokerage Firm Must Follow

Broker-dealers that are exchange specialists or NASDAQ market makers have special functions in the securities markets because they trade for their own accounts while also handling orders for customers. These special functions require them to comply with specific SEC rules—Rules 11Ac1-1 and 11Ac1-4 under the Securities Exchange Act of 1934—regarding the publishing of quotes and handling customer orders.

These rules, which include the "Quote Rule" and the "Limit Order Display Rule," aim to increase the information that is publicly available concerning the prices at which investors may buy and sell exchange-listed and NASDAQ Market System securities.

### Quote Rule

The Quote Rule requires specialists and market makers to provide quotation information. The quote information the specialist or market maker publishes must be the best prices at which he is willing to trade (the lowest price the dealer will accept from a customer to sell the securities and the highest price the dealer will pay a customer to purchase the securities).

A specialist or market maker may still trade at better prices in certain private trading systems, called electronic communications networks, or ECNs, without publishing an improved quote. This is true only when the ECN itself publishes the improved prices and makes those prices available to the investing public. The Quote Rule ensures that the public has access to the best prices at which specialists and market makers are willing to trade—even if those prices are in private trading systems.

### *Limit Order Display Rule*

Limit orders are orders to buy or sell securities at a specified price. The Limit Order Display Rule requires that specialists and market makers publicly display certain limit orders they receive from customers. If the limit order is for a price that is better than the specialist's or market maker's quote, the specialist or market maker must publicly display it. The rule benefits investors because the publication of trading interest at prices that improve specialists' and market makers' quotes present investors with improved pricing opportunities.

# Chapter 42

# *Holding Your Securities*

## *Holding Your Securities: Get the Facts*

As an individual investor, you have up to three choices when it comes to holding your securities:

- **Physical certificate:** The security is registered in your name on the issuer's books, and you receive an actual, hard copy stock or bond certificate representing your ownership of the security.

- **"Street name" registration:** The security is registered in the name of your brokerage firm on the issuer's books, and your brokerage firm holds the security for you in "book-entry" form. "Book-entry" simply means that you do not receive a certificate. Instead, your broker keeps a record in its books that you own that particular security.

- **"Direct" registration:** The security is registered in your name on the issuer's books, and either the company or its transfer agent holds the security for you in book-entry form. The "Direct Registration System" (also known as "DRS") allows investors to transfer securities held this way.

---

This chapter includes the following publications of the U.S. Securities and Exchange Commission (www.sec.gov): "Holding Your Securities: Get the Facts," 3/2003; "Stock Certificates, Proving Ownership," 9/2004; "Stock Certificates, Lost, Stolen," 10/2004; and "Stock and Bond Certificates, Old," 8/2004.

This chapter explains these choices in greater detail, by laying out the advantages and disadvantages of each and by answering frequently asked questions. Depending on the type of security and where you purchase it, you may or may not have all these choices about how your securities are held. For example, not all companies offer direct registration, and some no longer issue physical certificates. You should ask your broker or the company what options you have.

### Physical Certificate

When you buy a security, whether through your broker or from the company itself, you can ask to have the actual stock or bond certificates sent to you. You may have to pay a nominal fee for the added expense of issuing a paper certificate. It's important that you safeguard your certificates until you sell or transfer your securities. It can be difficult to prove that you once owned a certificate that has been lost, stolen, or destroyed. Your broker—or the company or its transfer agent—will generally charge a fee to replace a lost or stolen stock certificate.

The advantages of holding a physical certificate include the following:

- The company knows how to reach you and will send all company reports and other information to you directly.

- You may find it easier to pledge your securities as collateral for a loan if you hold the certificates yourself in physical certificate form.

There are some disadvantages, including the following:

- When you want to sell your stock, you will have to send the certificate to your broker or the company's transfer agent to execute the sale. This may make it harder for you to sell quickly.

- If you lose your certificate, you may be charged a fee for a replacement certificate.

- If you move, you will have to contact the company with your change of address so that you do not miss any important mailings.

### Street Name Registration

You may have your security registered in street name and held in your account at your broker-dealer. Many brokerage firms will automatically put your securities into street name unless you give them specific instructions to the contrary. Under street name registration, your firm will keep records showing you as the real or "beneficial" owner, but you will not be listed directly on the issuer's books. Instead, your brokerage firm (or some other nominee) will appear as the owner on the issuer's books.

While you will not receive a certificate, your firm will send to you, at least four times a year, an account statement that lists all your securities at the broker-dealer. Your broker-dealer will also credit your account with your dividend and interest payments and will provide you with consolidated tax information. Your broker-dealer will send you issuer mailings such as annual reports and proxies.

The advantages of letting your brokerage firm hold your securities in "street name" include the following:

- Because your securities are already with your broker, you can place limit orders that direct your broker to sell a security at a specific price.

- Your brokerage firm is responsible for safeguarding your securities certificates so you don't have to worry about your securities certificates being lost or stolen.

- Your brokerage firm may keep you informed of important developments, such as tender offers or when bonds are called.

- It is easier to set up a margin account.

The disadvantages include these:

- You may experience a slight delay in receiving your dividend and interest payments from your brokerage firm. For example, some firms only pass along these payments to investors on a weekly, bi-weekly, or monthly basis.

- Since your name is not on the books of the company, the company will not mail important corporate communications directly to you.

## Direct Registration

If a company offers direct registration for its securities, you can choose to be registered directly on the books of the company regardless of whether you bought your securities through your broker or directly from the company or its transfer agent through a direct investment

389

plan. Direct registration allows you to have your security registered in your name on the books of the issuer without the need for a physical certificate to serve as evidence of your ownership. While you will not receive a certificate, you will receive a statement of ownership and periodic account statements, dividends, annual reports, proxies, and other mailings directly from the issuer.

The advantages of direct registration include the following:

- Since you are "registered" on the books of the company as the shareholder, you will receive annual and other reports, dividends, proxies, and other communications directly from the company.

- If you want to sell your securities through your broker, you can instruct your broker to electronically move your securities via DRS from the books of the company and then to sell your securities. Your broker should be able to do this quickly without the need for you filling out complicated and time-consuming forms.

- You do not have to worry about safekeeping or losing certificates, or having them stolen.

The disadvantages include the following:

- If you choose to buy or sell registered securities through a company's direct investment plan, you usually will not be able to buy or sell at a specific market price or at a specific time. Instead, the company will purchase or sell shares for the plan at established times—for example, on a daily, weekly, or monthly basis—and at an average market price.

While it is solely your decision how to hold your securities, you should carefully review each of the alternative forms of security registration and should consult with your financial advisor or broker-dealer to determine which form is best for you.

## Frequently Asked Questions about Holding Securities

### What is the Direct Registration System?

The Direct Registration System, or DRS, is a system that enables an investor to electronically move his or her security position held in direct registration book-entry form back and forth between the issuer and the investor's broker-dealer.

### *After I make my decision on how I want to hold my security, what do I do?*

You should check with the issuer or your broker-dealer to find out if the issuer offers direct registration. If you are purchasing a security, tell your broker-dealer you want to hold your securities in direct registration. If you currently hold a certificate, you can mail or take your certificate either to the issuer or to your broker-dealer with instructions to change to direct registration. If you currently hold your security in street name registration, you can instruct your broker-dealer or the issuer to move your security position to the issuer for direct registration. In any situation, you will receive a statement of ownership from the issuer acknowledging your DRS book-entry position once the change has been made.

If you want a certificate or if you want to use street name registration, tell your broker-dealer your choice at the time of purchase. If you elect a certificate, one will be sent to you. If you choose street name registration, your broker-dealer will send you a confirmation and periodic account statements acknowledging your ownership. If you currently hold a certificate, you can deliver the certificate to your broker-dealer with instructions to change your registration to street name registration. If you currently hold in street name registration, you can tell your broker-dealer to obtain a certificate for you.

### *What do I have to do to sell my security?*

To sell a security held in direct registration, you can:

- instruct the issuer to sell your security (many issuers have programs in place to accommodate sale requests); or

- instruct your broker-dealer or the issuer to electronically move your security to your broker-dealer for your broker-dealer to sell; or

- request a physical certificate and deliver it to your broker-dealer to sell.

To sell a security held in street name registration, you can:

- instruct your broker-dealer to sell your security; or

- request a physical certificate and deliver it to another broker-dealer to sell; or

391

- instruct your broker-dealer or the issuer to electronically move your security to the issuer for the issuer to sell (many issuers have programs in place to accommodate sale requests) or to electronically move to another broker-dealer to sell.

To sell a security for which you hold a physical certificate, you can:

- deliver the certificate to your broker-dealer with your instructions to sell; or

- deliver the certificate to the issuer with your instructions (a) to change the registration to DRS and move the position to your broker-dealer to sell if your security is eligible for direct registration or (b) for the issuer to sell if the issuer has a program in place to accommodate sale requests.

When selling a security through the issuer, the issuer will sell your security under the terms and conditions in place for that issue. For example, some sell orders will be executed on the day the issuer receives them, and some orders are aggregated for frequent, but not daily, execution. (Note: you should ask the issuer if it offers a selling service and what the terms and conditions are.) Proceeds from the sale will be mailed to you three business days after the date of sale.

When selling through your broker-dealer, your instructions will be acted on immediately and in accordance with the guidelines it provides to you. Proceeds from the sale will be made available to you or credited to your account three business days after the date of sale.

### *Can I place a limit order? Market order? Stop order?*

Only a broker-dealer can execute a limit, market, or stop order. As a result, you can place any of these types of orders only if you use a broker-dealer to execute a transaction for securities held in direct registration, street-name, or in certificate form.

### *What about my relationship with my broker-dealer if I use direct registration?*

You can maintain your relationship with your broker-dealer regardless of your choice of registration.

When you purchase a security to hold in direct registration, you can tell either your broker-dealer or the issuer to include pertinent broker-dealer information in the issuer's records.

If you do not have your broker-dealer information included in the issuer's records at the time of purchase and later want to or if you want to change the broker-dealer information in the issuer's records, you may do so. You should contact either your broker-dealer or the issuer to obtain information on the procedures and the documents required for such actions.

### *If I hold certificates and there is a stock distribution, will I get a certificate for my additional shares?*

If the issue is eligible for direct registration, you will probably receive a statement of ownership instead of an additional certificate.

### *What are the fees associated with direct registration? With street name registration? With a certificate?*

There are no fees charged by an issuer for direct registration. However, because broker-dealers offer differing services and plans, you should contact your broker-dealer to learn what, if any, fees it charges.

### *If I opt for direct registration, what happens if I lose my statement of ownership?*

If you ever need a duplicate statement of ownership, you should contact the issuer. The issuer will mail you a new statement of ownership.

### *How are my securities protected if I choose street name ownership?*

Nearly all broker-dealers are members of Securities Investor Protection Corporation (SIPC). As a result your securities and money held at your broker-dealer are protected up to $500,000 with a $100,000 limit for cash. Many broker-dealers also carry insurance in excess of SIPC's coverage. However, SIPC does not protect you against losses caused by a decline in the market value of your securities.

## *Stock Certificates, Proving Ownership*

If you are trying to establish whether you or a family member own securities or not, here are some steps you can take.

Establishing your ownership is easier if you can remember which firm arranged for your purchase of the security and whether the security was held in your name or in the firm's name. Depending on how you came to own the security, take these steps:

**Brokerage firm:** If you bought the security through a brokerage firm, contact the firm and ask if they have a record of your ownership. The firm would have purchased the stock for your account either in your name or the firm's name. Either way, the brokerage firm may have a record of the purchase. But keep in mind, brokerage firms are required to keep these records for only six years.

**Transfer agent:** If the brokerage firm cannot find any record of your account, you should contact the transfer agent who handles the company's securities. Transfer agents keep records of securities owners who hold certificates.

You can find the name and address of a company's transfer agent in the company's annual report. Many companies file their annual reports with the U.S. Securities and Exchange Commission (SEC). Check the SEC's Electronic Data Gathering, Analysis, and Retrieval (EDGAR) database to see if the company filed its annual report with the SEC. If no annual report is on file, call the company for the transfer agent's name and address. Some companies also maintain investor relations offices that can be contacted by telephone and may be able to provide useful investor information.

**Company:** If the stock was purchased directly from the company issuing the securities, then the company should have a record of the purchase. The company should also be able to tell you whether it issued physical certificates (on paper) or whether the sale was simply recorded in its computers, called book entry.

If the company is not actively traded and you cannot locate it, you can contact its state of incorporation for information. A state's office of the secretary of state or corporate division usually maintains state corporate records.

**States:** If these efforts prove futile, you may have to try another approach. Your securities or your securities account may have been turned over to the state for safekeeping according to the state's laws on escheatment. Under these laws, broker-dealers, transfer agents, and financial institutions are required to turn over securities and other unclaimed property to the state of the owner's last known address after they have lost contact with the owner for a period of time.

Each state has an office that handles unclaimed property, either for safekeeping or disposal. You can search the records of each state's inventory of unclaimed property by clicking the National Association of Unclaimed Property Administrators website (http://www.unclaimed.org). Check the unclaimed property listings in each state where you had dealings with a broker or transfer agent. That may help you determine whether that state is holding your securities or account.

## Stock Certificates, Lost, Stolen

Brokerage firms, banks, transfer agents, and corporations have procedures in place to help investors replace lost or stolen certificates.

If your securities certificate is lost, accidentally destroyed, or stolen, you should immediately contact the transfer agent and request that a "stop transfer" be placed against the missing securities. Your broker may be able to assist you with this process.

The "stop transfer" helps to prevent someone from transferring ownership from your name to another's. The transfer agent or broker-dealer will report the certificates missing to the SEC's lost and stolen securities program.

If you are expecting a certificate through the mail, and it doesn't arrive, you should immediately contact the organization that arranged the transaction—typically your brokerage firm. While many companies choose to use registered or certified mail to deliver securities certificates to individuals, some prefer regular mail so as not to call attention to the potential value of the item.

### *Replacing Securities Certificates*

You can get a new certificate to replace the missing one. However, before issuing a new certificate, corporations usually require the following:

- The owner must state all the facts surrounding the loss in an affidavit;

- The owner must buy an indemnity bond to protect the corporation and the transfer agent against the possibility that the lost certificate may be presented later by an innocent purchaser. The bond usually costs between one or two percent of the current market value of your missing certificates; and

- The owner must request a new certificate before an innocent purchaser acquires it.

395

If you later find the missing certificate, you should notify whomever you called to place the "stop transfer" so that the lost or stolen securities report may be removed. Otherwise, you may have difficulty selling the securities.

The SEC recommends that you keep a copy of both sides of your certificates in a place separate from the certificates themselves. If a certificate is lost or stolen and then transferred on the books of the transfer agent to another owner, it may be impossible for you to establish that you owned it because the transfer agent will no longer have a record of your name. But if you have a record of the certificate numbers, the transfer agent should be able to reconstruct when it was transferred and to whom.

Securities certificates are valuable and should be safeguarded. To avoid the cost and burden of safeguarding certificates, some investors opt for letting their brokerage firm or another company hold their securities for them. And increasingly, certificates for many securities are not even available: with these book entry securities, your ownership is reflected on the books of a company.

The actual transfer of securities is governed by state law, rather than the federal securities laws. The SEC seldom has any jurisdiction over these issues.

## Old Stock and Bond Certificates

An old stock or bond certificate may still be valuable even if it no longer trades under the name printed on the certificate. The company may have merged with another company or simply changed its name. You can use the resources described below to find out if an old stock or bond certificate has value. Even if you learn that a certificate has no value, you may find that the certificate itself has value as a collectable.

These resources may be found on the internet, at public libraries, stock exchanges, or stockbrokers' offices. But please note that the SEC cannot recommend or endorse any of these entities, their personnel, or their products or services.

**Scripophily.com:** The company is named after the hobby of collecting old stock and bond certificates. For a fee, Scripophily.com researches whether your stock or bond certificate has any value. The company also is a large buyer and seller of collectable certificates, with a list and images of more than 4,500 different companies.

**Financial Stock Guide Service:** Published by Financial Information, Inc. since 1927, this comprehensive guide is a good starting point for all research on old stock certificates. This listing, updated annually, contains a directory of actively traded stocks and obsolete securities. You can have the Custom Research department of Financial Information research your certificate by calling 800-367-3441.

**Robert D. Fisher Manual of Valuable and Worthless Securities:** Published by R.M. Smythe & Co., Inc., this is a multi-volume resource that is particularly helpful guide if you are trying to trace the value of very old stock certificates. R.M. Smythe will research your certificate for a fee.

**Moody's Industrial Manual and Moody's OTC Industrial Manual:** Published by Mergent Company, these manuals give brief summaries of companies' histories, backgrounds, mergers and acquisitions, subsidiaries, principal plants, and properties. This guide is updated annually. You can learn how to obtain a subscription to the manuals by going online or calling 800-342-5647.

**National Stock Summary:** Published by the Pink Sheets LLC, this monthly publication summarizes all over-the-counter and inactive listed stock offerings. It also includes the recent prices of such securities, as they have appeared either in the national daily quotation services or in the leading daily newspapers and financial periodicals. The Pink Sheets will research your certificate for a fee.

# Chapter 43

# *Direct Investment Plans (DRIPs)*

Many companies allow you to buy or sell shares directly through a direct stock plan (DSP). You can also have the cash dividends you receive from the company automatically reinvested into more shares through a dividend reinvestment plan (DRIP).

Here are descriptions of the two different types of plans:

- **Direct stock plans:** Some companies allow you to purchase or sell stock directly through them without your having to use or pay commissions to a broker. But you may have to pay a fee for using the plan's services. Some companies require that you already own stock in the company or are employed by the company before you may participate in their direct stock plans. You may be able to buy stock by investing a specific dollar amount rather than having to pay for an entire share. In that case, you could have your checking account debited on a regular basis to make investments in the plan. Some plans require a minimum amount of investment or require you to maintain specific minimums in your account.

  DSPs usually will not allow you to buy or sell your securities at a specific market price or at a specific time. Rather, the company will purchase or sell shares for the plan at established times— for example, on a daily, weekly, or monthly basis—and at an

---

"Direct Investment Plans: Buying Stock Directly from the Company," U.S. Securities and Exchange Company (www.sec.gov), 3/2002.

average market price. You can find when the company will buy and sell shares and how it determines the price by reading the company's disclosure documents. Depending on the plan, you may be able to have your shares transferred to your broker to have them sold, but the plan may charge you a fee to do so.

- **Dividend reinvestment plans:** Dividend reinvestment plans let you take advantage of the power of compounding. Instead of receiving cash dividends from the company, you may purchase more of a company's stock by having the dividends reinvested. You must sign an agreement with the company for this to be done. If you have a brokerage account or mutual fund, your firm may also have a dividend reinvestment plan. You should check with your firm or the company to see whether you will be charged for this service.

The features and services offered in DSPs vary depending on the kind of plan and the company offering the plan. Before setting up a plan, read the company's disclosure information to learn how its particular plan works. The plan will tell you how to enroll, the number of shares needed to open an account, any fees or charges that apply, the minimum or maximum you can buy or sell, the dates when you can invest, and how to withdraw, transfer, or sell your shares. Many large companies have internet sites that can provide you with information about their plans or tell you who to contact for more information.

# Chapter 44

# *Periodic Payment Plans Can Be an Expensive Way to Invest*

Are you considering investing in a periodic payment plan? This chapter explains this kind of investment, describes the costs involved with these plans, and highlights the questions every investor should ask before investing.

### *What is a periodic payment plan?*

A "periodic payment plan" is the legal name for an investment that might also be referred to as a "contractual plan" or "systematic investment plan." Periodic payment plans allow investors to accumulate shares of a mutual fund indirectly by contributing a fixed, often small amount of money on a regular basis. Many of these plans are sold to military personnel. Periodic payment plans, however, do not provide any special benefits to military personnel, nor are military personnel required to participate in the plans.

### *How do periodic payment plans work?*

A plan typically requires monthly investments over a period of 10, 15, or 25 years. Most plans allow an investor to start a plan for a modest sum of money, such as $50 per month. An investor in a periodic payment plan does not directly own shares of a mutual fund. Instead, he or she owns an interest in the plan trust. The plan trust

---

"Periodic Payment Plans," U.S. Securities and Exchange Commission (www.sec.gov), 6/2005.

invests the investor's regular payments, after deducting applicable fees, in shares of a mutual fund. An investor in a plan has a beneficial interest in those shares.

### *Is it more expensive to invest in a periodic payment plan than directly in a mutual fund?*

It can be, especially if you don't participate in the plan for the entire length of time specified in the contract. Periodic payment plans are subject to a special sales charge, usually called a "creation and sales charge." The sales charge also may be referred to as a "front-end load." The plan's sponsor generally receives the sales charge as compensation for creating the plan and for selling expenses and commissions with respect to the plan. By law, this sales charge may equal up to 50% of any of the plan's first twelve monthly payments, and most plans impose the maximum sales charge. Unless you are able to make a large investment or otherwise take advantage of discounts for larger sized investments, you may find that the fees and expenses of a periodic payment plan cost more than those you would have paid to invest directly in a mutual fund.

Under a typical $50 per month plan, the sales charge reduces the amount of your investment by $25 for each of the first twelve monthly payments. After the first twelve monthly payments, some plans impose a reduced sales charge, but many plans do not impose any sales charge on the remaining payments under the term of the plan. But if you increase your monthly payment by changing your plan's "face amount," or total value of scheduled payments, you will likely pay a greater amount in total sales charges. This is because a plan will typically adjust the sales charges you pay to reflect the higher monthly payment. Regardless of the sales charges you pay, you will most likely have to pay continuing annual fees.

If you invest in a periodic payment plan, you may also pay service fees to the plan's custodian, whose primary responsibility is safekeeping plan assets and maintaining plan records. Under some plans, investors are required to pay the custodian a small monthly fee for processing each plan payment, often called a "custodian fee." Other fees charged by plan custodians may include annual account fees, completed plan fees, termination fees, inactive account fees, and similar charges. In addition to the sales charge and any service fees, an investor in a periodic payment plan will indirectly pay the operating expenses of the mutual fund shares held by the plan trust, which may include management fees, 12b-1 fees (covering distribution expenses and sometimes shareholder service expenses), and other expenses.

402

You can read about the fees and expenses of a periodic payment plan in the plan's prospectus. You should be sure you understand a plan's fees and expenses because they lower investment returns.

### *What is the difference between a periodic payment plan and an automatic investment program?*

The difference largely boils down to cost. Most investors making regular investments in mutual funds do not participate in periodic payment plans. Instead, these investors buy shares of mutual funds directly from the funds through services known as automatic investment programs, asset builders, or account builders. These services allow investors to purchase shares on a regular basis, including, for example, by electronically transferring money from a designated bank account or paycheck. Most mutual funds do not charge a fee for setting up or terminating these automated transfer services. Investors participating in these automated transfer services may be able to avoid or reduce minimum investment requirements.

Like periodic payment plans, automatic investment programs and similar services allow investors to take advantage of an investment strategy known as dollar-cost averaging. By making regular investments with the same amount of money each time, investors buy more of an investment when its price is low and less of the investment when its price is high.

### *Do other investment options offer features similar to those provided by periodic payment plans?*

Before investing in a periodic payment plan, investors should consider other investment options that may offer similar features with greater flexibility or at a lower cost, or both. Purchasing shares of mutual funds directly through automatic investment plans or similar services is one option. Investors may also consider purchasing shares of mutual funds with no or low minimum investment requirements. In addition, some investors may be eligible to invest in broadly diversified mutual funds through their employer's retirement plan. The financial sections of popular websites and other financial portals available on the internet can help you search, sort, and compare mutual funds by various criteria, such as fund type, initial investment minimum, expense ratio, and whether you will incur a sales charge. By reviewing other investment options, you can help determine whether a periodic payment plan is your best investment opportunity.

### *What are the consequences of missing payments in a periodic payment plan?*

You'll likely pay a higher percentage of your total investment in sales charges, and if you miss payments for an extended period of time, your plan may be terminated. After you complete your first 12 monthly payments, the total sales charges you pay for investing in a periodic payment plan as a percentage of your total investments decreases with each payment you make. This is because you'll pay a major portion, if not all, of your sales charges in the first 12 payments. When you miss payments or terminate your plan, you'll pay a higher percentage of your total investment in sales charges than if you completed every payment for the entire term of the plan. In addition, if you stop making payments for an extended period of time, the sponsor or custodian may terminate your plan. A sponsor or custodian typically has a right to terminate your plan if you fail to make payments for a period of 6 or 12 months. You may also incur an inactive account fee if you miss payments for an extended period of time.

### *What are some of the principal risks of investing in a periodic payment plan?*

Understanding the risks of an investment can help you determine whether the investment is right for you. Some of the principal risks of participating in a periodic payment plan are the following:

- You will almost certainly lose money if you withdraw your investments or terminate your plan during the first few years of the plan, unless you are eligible for a full refund. This is because most plans require you to pay a sales charge of up to 50% of your first twelve monthly investments. You would need extraordinary investment returns to recoup those fees and begin to realize a profit.

- Your plan does not reduce the risk of owning shares of a mutual fund. A periodic payment plan usually invests in a mutual fund whose portfolio consists primarily of common stock. Investments in common stock can experience wide price swings, both up and down. If you need to terminate your plan when the value of the plan's shares is less than your cost, you will lose money.

## _Can I get a refund if I cancel my plan?_

If you recently invested in a periodic payment plan, you should know that you have certain rights if you decide to cancel your plan:

- **45-day cancellation and refund right:** After you receive notice of your cancellation rights, you have a right to cancel your plan within 45 days. You will receive a notice regarding your cancellation rights within 60 days after your first investment in the plan. If you elect to cancel your plan within the 45-day period, you will receive a cash payment equal to the current value of your account plus a refund of any sales charge or fees that you paid under the plan.

- **18-month cancellation and refund right:** Under most plans, you may also cancel your plan within 18 months of your first investment in the plan. If you elect to cancel your plan within the 18-month period, you will receive a cash payment equal to the current value of your account plus a partial refund of any sales charge you paid under the plan. This partial refund will equal the amount by which the total amount of any sales charge you paid exceeds 15% of your total investments in the plan. You should receive written notice of your 18-month cancellation right if you miss three or more payments within the first 15 months of your plan. Unless you have already received a notice, you'll receive written notice of the cancellation right if you miss any payment in the three months prior to the expiration of the 18-month cancellation right.

## _What questions should I ask before I invest in a periodic payment plan?_

Knowing the answers to these questions may help you decide whether investing in a periodic payment plan is right for you.

- Have I paid off my credit card and other high interest debt? It is often best to pay yourself first by paying off high-cost credit card debt before beginning any investment program.

- Am I confident that I will be able to continue to make payments for the term of the plan? Periodic payment plans are long-term investment vehicles, and you will almost certainly lose money if you withdraw your investments or terminate your plan during the first few years of the plan, unless you are eligible for a full refund.

- What fees are charged by the plan? Under what circumstances does the plan waive or reduce certain fees?

- What are the plan's investment objectives? What are the risks of investing in the plan? Am I comfortable with these investment objectives and risks?

- What other investment options are available to me? Is there a lower cost, more flexible mutual fund available with the same investment objectives? Am I eligible to invest in a broadly diversified mutual fund through my retirement plan at work?

- When can the sponsor change the mutual fund in which the plan invests?

- When can the sponsor or custodian cancel my plan? Can I make a partial withdrawal without terminating the plan?

- Can I continue making monthly investments after completing the scheduled investments under the plan? What fees apply to these additional investments?

- What are my statutory rights to a refund if I cancel my plan?

### *Where can I find more information?*

Investors can learn more about a periodic payment plan by reading all of the plan's available information, including its prospectus. The prospectus is the plan's selling document and contains valuable information about the plan and underlying mutual fund investment, such as investment strategies, principal risks, fees and expenses, and past performance. If you know the exact name of a plan, you can obtain a copy of a plan's prospectus by searching the Mutual Fund Prospectuses section of the SEC's EDGAR [Electronic Data Gathering, Analysis, and Retrieval] database and downloading the prospectus for free. To access EDGAR, visit http://www.sec.gov/edgar.shtml. A broker selling the plan can also provide you with a copy of the plan's prospectus.

Investors should understand how mutual funds work, what factors to consider, and how they can avoid common problems, before they invest in a periodic payment plan or any mutual fund.

### *Who should I contact if I have a problem?*

If you encounter a problem with a periodic payment plan, you can send your complaint to the SEC using their online complaint form at www.sec.gov/complaint.shtml. You can also reach them by regular mail at:

Securities and Exchange Commission
Office of Investor Education and Assistance
100 F Street, N.E.
Washington, DC 20549-0213

# Chapter 45

# *Margin: Borrowing Money to Pay for Stocks*

"Margin" is borrowing money from your broker to buy a stock and using your investment as collateral. Investors generally use margin to increase their purchasing power so that they can own more stock without fully paying for it. But margin exposes investors to the potential for higher losses. Here's what you need to know about margin.

## *Understand How Margin Works*

Let's say you buy a stock for $50 and the price of the stock rises to $75. If you bought the stock in a cash account and paid for it in full, you'll earn a 50 percent return on your investment. But if you bought the stock on margin—paying $25 in cash and borrowing $25 from your broker—you'll earn a 100 percent return on the money you invested. Of course, you'll still owe your firm $25 plus interest.

The downside to using margin is that if the stock price decreases, substantial losses can mount quickly. For example, let's say the stock you bought for $50 falls to $25. If you fully paid for the stock, you'll lose 50 percent of your money. But if you bought on margin, you'll lose 100 percent, and you still must come up with the interest you owe on the loan.

In volatile markets, investors who put up an initial margin payment for a stock may, from time to time, be required to provide additional cash if the price of the stock falls. Some investors have been

"Margin: Borrowing Money to Pay for Stocks," U.S. Securities and Exchange Commission (www.sec.gov), 8/2005.

shocked to find out that the brokerage firm has the right to sell their securities that were bought on margin—without any notification and potentially at a substantial loss to the investor. If your broker sells your stock after the price has plummeted, then you've lost out on the chance to recoup your losses if the market bounces back.

## Recognize the Risks

Margin accounts can be very risky and they are not suitable for everyone. Before opening a margin account, you should fully understand that:

- You can lose more money than you have invested;

- You may have to deposit additional cash or securities in your account on short notice to cover market losses;

- You may be forced to sell some or all of your securities when falling stock prices reduce the value of your securities; and

- Your brokerage firm may sell some or all of your securities without consulting you to pay off the loan it made to you.

You can protect yourself by knowing how a margin account works and what happens if the price of the stock purchased on margin declines. Know that your firm charges you interest for borrowing money and how that will affect the total return on your investments. Be sure to ask your broker whether it makes sense for you to trade on margin in light of your financial resources, investment objectives, and tolerance for risk.

## Read Your Margin Agreement

To open a margin account, your broker is required to obtain your signature. The agreement may be part of your account opening agreement or may be a separate agreement. The margin agreement states that you must abide by the rules of the Federal Reserve Board, the New York Stock Exchange, the National Association of Securities Dealers, Inc., and the firm where you have set up your margin account. Be sure to carefully review the agreement before you sign it.

As with most loans, the margin agreement explains the terms and conditions of the margin account. The agreement describes how the interest on the loan is calculated, how you are responsible for repaying the loan, and how the securities you purchase serve as collateral for the loan. Carefully review the agreement to determine what notice, if any, your firm must give you before selling your securities to collect the money you have borrowed.

## Know the Margin Rules

The Federal Reserve Board and many self-regulatory organizations (SROs), such as the NYSE (New York Stock Exchange) and NASD (National Association of Securities Dealers), have rules that govern margin trading. Brokerage firms can establish their own requirements as long as they are at least as restrictive as the Federal Reserve Board and SRO rules. Here are some of the key rules you should know:

### Before You Trade—Minimum Margin

Before trading on margin, the NYSE and NASD, for example, require you to deposit with your brokerage firm a minimum of $2,000 or 100 percent of the purchase price, whichever is less. This is known as the "minimum margin." Some firms may require you to deposit more than $2,000.

### Amount You Can Borrow—Initial Margin

According to Regulation T of the Federal Reserve Board, you may borrow up to 50 percent of the purchase price of securities that can be purchased on margin. This is known as the "initial margin." Some firms require you to deposit more than 50 percent of the purchase price. Also be aware that not all securities can be purchased on margin.

### Amount You Need after You Trade—Maintenance Margin

After you buy stock on margin, the NYSE and NASD require you to keep a minimum amount of equity in your margin account. The equity in your account is the value of your securities less how much you owe to your brokerage firm. The rules require you to have at least 25 percent of the total market value of the securities in your margin account at all times. The 25 percent is called the "maintenance requirement." In fact, many brokerage firms have higher maintenance requirements, typically between 30 to 40 percent, and sometimes higher depending on the type of stock purchased.

Here's an example of how maintenance requirements work. Let's say you purchase $16,000 worth of securities by borrowing $8,000 from your firm and paying $8,000 in cash or securities. If the market value of the securities drops to $12,000, the equity in your account will fall to $4,000 ($12,000 − $8,000 = $4,000). If your firm has a 25 percent maintenance requirement, you must have $3,000 in equity in your account (25 percent of $12,000 = $3,000). In this case, you do have enough equity because the $4,000 in equity in your account is greater than the $3,000 maintenance requirement.

But if your firm has a maintenance requirement of 40 percent, you would not have enough equity. The firm would require you to have $4,800 in equity (40 percent of $12,000 = $4,800). Your $4,000 in equity is less than the firm's $4,800 maintenance requirement. As a result, the firm may issue you a "margin call," since the equity in your account has fallen $800 below the firm's maintenance requirement.

## Understand Margin Calls—You Can Lose Your Money Fast and with No Notice

If your account falls below the firm's maintenance requirement, your firm generally will make a margin call to ask you to deposit more cash or securities into your account. If you are unable to meet the margin call, your firm will sell your securities to increase the equity in your account up to or above the firm's maintenance requirement.

Always remember that your broker may not be required to make a margin call or otherwise tell you that your account has fallen below the firm's maintenance requirement. Your broker may be able to sell your securities at any time without consulting you first. Under most margin agreements, even if your firm offers to give you time to increase the equity in your account, it can sell your securities without waiting for you to meet the margin call.

## Ask Yourself These Key Questions

- Do you know that margin accounts involve a great deal more risk than cash accounts where you fully pay for the securities you purchase? Are you aware you may lose more than the amount of money you initially invested when buying on margin? Can you afford to lose more money than the amount you have invested?

- Did you take the time to read the margin agreement? Did you ask your broker questions about how a margin account works and whether it's appropriate for you to trade on margin? Did your broker explain the terms and conditions of the margin agreement?

- Are you aware of the costs you will be charged on money you borrow from your firm and how these costs affect your overall return?

- Are you aware that your brokerage firm can sell your securities without notice to you when you don't have sufficient equity in your margin account?

# Chapter 46

# *Market Volatility Procedures and Trading Suspensions*

## *Circuit Breakers and Other Market Volatility Procedures*

The major stock and commodities exchanges have instituted procedures to limit mass or panic selling in times of serious market declines and volatility. These mechanisms are known as "circuit breakers," the "Collar Rule," and price limits. Circuit breakers establish whether trading will be halted temporarily or stopped entirely. The Collar Rule and price limits affect the way trading in the securities and futures markets takes place. Here's a description of each one:

**Circuit breakers:** The securities and futures markets have circuit breakers that provide for brief, coordinated, cross-market trading halts during a severe market decline as measured by a single day decrease in the Dow Jones Industrial Average (DJIA). There are three circuit breaker thresholds—10%, 20%, and 30%—set by the markets at point levels that are calculated at the beginning of each quarter. The formulas for these thresholds are set forth in the New York Stock Exchange (NYSE) Rule 80B.

For example, on July 1, 2000, the average value for the DJIA for the preceding month (June 2000) was used to calculate point levels

This chapter includes "Circuit Breakers and Other Market Volatility Procedures," 7/2005; "Trading Halts and Delays," 4/2001; "Trading Suspensions: When the SEC Suspends Trading in a Stock," 7/2005. All three documents are publications of the U.S. Securities and Exchange Commission (www.sec.gov).

(rounded to the nearest 50 points). This resulted in the Level One (10%) circuit breaker set at 1,050 points, Level Two (20%) circuit breaker set at 2,100 points, and the Level Three (30%) circuit breaker set at 3,150 points.

**Collar Rule:** Under NYSE Rule 80A, if the DJIA moves up or down two percent (2%) from the previous closing value, program trading orders to buy or sell the Standard & Poor's 500 stocks as part of index arbitrage strategies must be entered with directions to have the order executions effected in a manner that stabilizes share prices. The collar restrictions are lifted if the DJIA returns to or within one percent (1%) of its previous closing value.

The 2% collar rule threshold is set by the NYSE at a point level that is calculated at the beginning of each quarter. For example, on July 1, 2000, the average value for the DJIA for the preceding month (June 2000) was used to calculate a point level (rounded to the nearest 10 points). This resulted in the 2% collar rule threshold being set at 210 points.

**Price limits:** The futures exchanges set the price limits that aim to lessen sharp price swings in contracts, such as stock index futures. A price limit does not stop trading in the futures, but prohibits trading at prices below the pre-set limit during a price decline. Intra-day price limits are removed at pre-set times during the trading session, such as ten minutes after the thresholds are reached or at 3:30 P.M. (all times are Eastern), whichever is earlier. Daily price limits remain in effect for the entire trading session. Specific price limits are set by the exchanges for each stock index futures contract. There are no price limits for U.S. stock index options, equity options, or stocks.

## Trading Halts and Delays

Securities exchanges, such as the New York Stock Exchange (NYSE) and American Stock Exchange (Amex), as well as the NASDAQ (National Association of Securities Dealers Automated Quotations) Stock Market, have the authority to halt and delay trading in a security. A trading halt—which typically lasts less than an hour but can be longer—is called during the trading day to allow a company to announce important news or where there is a significant order imbalance between buyers and sellers in a security. A trading delay (or "delayed opening") is called if either of these situations occurs at the beginning of the trading day.

There are two types of trading halts and delays—regulatory and nonregulatory. The most common regulatory halt and delay happen when a company has pending news that may affect the security's price (a "news pending" halt or delay). By halting or delaying trading, market participants can have time to assess the impact of the news. Another type of regulatory halt happens when a market halts trading in a security when there is uncertainty over whether the security continues to meet the market's listing standards. When a regulatory halt or delay is imposed by a security's primary market, the other U.S. markets that also trade the security honor this halt.

Nonregulatory halts or delays occur on exchanges, such as the NYSE and Amex (but not on NASDAQ), when there is a significant imbalance in the pending buy and sell orders in a security. When an imbalance occurs, trading is stopped to alert market participants to the situation and to allow the exchange specialists to disseminate information to investors concerning a price range where trading may begin again on this exchange. A nonregulatory trading halt or delay on one exchange does not preclude other markets from trading this security.

The U.S. Securities and Exchange Commission (SEC) does not halt or delay trading in a security for news pending or order imbalances, but it can suspend trading for up to ten days and, if appropriate, take action to revoke a security's registration.

## Trading Suspensions! When the SEC Suspends Trading in a Stock

The federal securities laws allow the SEC to suspend trading in any stock for up to ten trading days. This section answers some of the typical questions the SEC receives from investors about trading suspensions.

### When can the SEC suspend a stock from trading?

When it serves the public interest and will protect investors, the SEC may suspend trading. For instance, the SEC may act when public information about a company is not current, accurate, or adequate. The SEC has acted when serious questions arose about a company's assets, operations, or other financial information.

### Why couldn't the SEC forewarn me that it was about to suspend trading before I bought the security in the first place?

The SEC cannot announce that it's working on a suspension. This work is conducted in confidentially to maintain our effectiveness and to guard against the destruction of evidence if our work becomes widely known. Confidentiality also protects a company and its shareholders if the SEC ultimately decides not to issue a trading suspension. Mindful of the seriousness of suspensions, the SEC moves as quickly as possible when it considers a trading suspension.

### *What happens when the ten-day suspension period ends? Will the SEC issue a statement about the status of the company after the suspension has ended?*

No. The SEC will not comment publicly on the status of a company when the ten-day suspension ends because the company may still have serious legal problems. For instance, the SEC may continue to investigate a company to determine whether it has defrauded investors. The public will not know if the SEC is continuing its investigation until the SEC publicly announces an enforcement action against the company.

### *Will trading automatically resume after ten days?*

It depends on the market where the stock trades. Different rules apply in different markets.

For stocks that trade in the OTC or the over-the-counter market, trading does not automatically resume when a suspension ends. (The OTC market includes the Bulletin Board and the Pink Sheets.) Before trading can resume for OTC stocks, SEC regulations require a broker-dealer to review information about a company before publishing a quote. If a broker-dealer does not have confidence that a company's financial statements are current and accurate, especially in light of the questions raised by the SEC, then a broker-dealer may not publish a quote for the company's stock.

In contrast to OTC stocks, stocks that trade on an exchange or NASDAQ resume trading as soon as an SEC suspension ends.

### *If the suspended stock resumes trading, why is it trading at a much lower price?*

The trading suspension may raise serious questions and cast doubts about the company in the minds of investors. While some investors may be willing to buy the company's stock, they will do so only at significantly lower prices.

## Why would the SEC take such action when it knows it will hurt current shareholders?

Because a suspension often causes a dramatic decline in the price of the security, the SEC suspends trading only when it believes the public may be making investment decisions based on false or misleading information. Suspensions give notice to current and potential investors that we have serious concerns about a company. A suspension may prevent potential investors from being victimized by a fraud.

## How can I find out if the stock will trade again after a suspension?

You can contact the broker-dealer who sold you the stock or a broker-dealer who quoted the stock before the suspension. Ask the broker-dealer if it intends to resume publishing a quote in the company's stock.

## If there is no market to sell my security, what can I do with my shares?

If there is no market to trade the shares, they may be worthless. You may want to contact your financial or tax adviser to determine how to treat such a loss on your tax return.

## What can I do if the company acted wrongfully and I have lost money?

To get your money back, you will need to consider taking legal action on your own. The SEC cannot act as your lawyer. You must continue to pursue all of your legal remedies.

To learn how to file an arbitration action against a broker-dealer, you can contact the Director of Arbitration at the National Association of Securities Dealers (online at http://www.nasdadr.com) or the New York Stock Exchange (online at http://www.nyse.com/regulation). NASD and the NYSE also offer mediation as an option before going to arbitration.

## Where can I get information about trading suspensions?

You can find a list of companies whose stocks have been suspended by the SEC since October 1995 on the SEC's website (http://www.sec.gov).

# Chapter 47

# *After-Hours Trading: Understanding the Risks*

The New York Stock Exchange and the NASDAQ Stock Market— the highest volume market centers in the U.S. today—have traditionally been open for business from 9:30 A.M. to 4:00 P.M. Eastern Time. Although trading outside that window—or "after-hours" trading—has occurred for some time, it used to be limited mostly limited to high net worth investors and institutional investors.

But that changed by the end of the last century. Some smaller exchanges now offer extended hours. And, with the rise of Electronic Communications Networks, or ECNs, everyday individual investors can gain access to the after-hours markets. Before you decide to trade after-hours, you need to educate yourself about the differences between regular and extended trading hours, especially the risks. You should consult your broker and read any disclosure documents on this option. Check your broker's website for available information on trading after-hours. As with trading during regular hours, the services offered by brokers during extended hours vary. You should therefore shop around to find the firm that best suits your trading needs.

While after-hours trading presents investing opportunities, there are also the following risks for those who want to participate:

- **Inability to see or act upon quotes:** Some firms only allow investors to view quotes from the one trading system the firm

---

"After-Hours Trading: Understanding the Risks," U.S. Securities and Exchange Commission (www.sec.gov), 3/2005.

uses for after-hours trading. Check with your broker to see whether your firm's system will permit you to access other quotes on other ECNs. But remember that just because you can get quotes on another ECN does not necessary mean you will be able to trade based on those quotes. You need to ask your firm if it will route your order for execution to the other ECN. If you are limited to the quotes within one system, you may not be able to complete a trade, even with a willing investor, at a different trading system.

- **Lack of liquidity:** Liquidity refers to your ability to convert stock into cash. That ability depends on the existence of buyers and sellers and how easy it is to complete a trade. During regular trading hours, buyers and sellers of most stocks can trade readily with one another. During after-hours, there may be less trading volume for some stocks, making it more difficult to execute some of your trades. Some stocks may not trade at all during extended hours.

- **Larger quote spreads:** Less trading activity could also mean wider spreads between the bid and ask prices. As a result, you may find it more difficult to get your order executed or to get as favorable a price as you could have during regular market hours.

- **Price volatility:** For stocks with limited trading activity, you may find greater price fluctuations than you would have seen during regular trading hours. News stories announced after-hours may have greater impacts on stock prices.

- **Uncertain prices:** The prices of some stocks traded during the after-hours session may not reflect the prices of those stocks during regular hours, either at the end of the regular trading session or upon the opening of regular trading the next business day.

- **Bias toward limit orders:** Many electronic trading systems currently accept only limit orders, where you must enter a price at which you would like your order executed. A limit order ensures you will not pay more than the price you entered or sell for less. If the market moves away from your price, your order will not be executed. Check with your broker to see whether orders not executed during the after-hours trading session will be canceled or whether they will be automatically entered when regular trading hours begin. Similarly, find out if an order you placed during regular hours will carry over to after-hours trading.

- **Competition with professional traders:** Many of the after-hours traders are professionals with large institutions, such as mutual funds, who may have access to more information than individual investors.

- **Computer delays:** As with online trading, you may encounter during after-hours delays or failures in getting your order executed, including orders to cancel or change your trades. For some after-hours trades, your order will be routed from your brokerage firm to an electronic trading system. If a computer problem exists at your firm, this may prevent or delay your order from reaching the system. If you encounter significant delays, you should call your broker to determine the extent of the problem and what you can to get your order executed.

# Chapter 48

# Day Trading:
# Your Dollars at Risk

Day traders rapidly buy and sell stocks throughout the day in the hope that their stocks will continue climbing or falling in value for the seconds to minutes they own the stock, allowing them to lock in quick profits. Day traders usually buy on borrowed money, hoping that they will reap higher profits through leverage, but running the risk of higher losses too.

While day trading is neither illegal nor is it unethical, it can be highly risky. Most individual investors do not have the wealth, the time, or the temperament to make money and to sustain the devastating losses that day trading can bring.

Here are some of the facts that every investor should know about day trading:

**Be prepared to suffer severe financial losses:** Day traders typically suffer severe financial losses in their first months of trading, and many never graduate to profit-making status. Given these outcomes, it's clear: day traders should only risk money they can afford to lose. They should never use money they will need for daily living expenses, retirement, take out a second mortgage, or use their student loan money for day trading.

**Day traders do not "invest":** Day traders sit in front of computer screens and look for a stock that is either moving up or down in value.

"Day Trading: Your Dollars at Risk," U.S. Securities and Exchange Commission (www.sec.gov), 4/2005.

They want to ride the momentum of the stock and get out of the stock before it changes course. They do not know for certain how the stock will move, they are hoping that it will move in one direction, either up or down in value. True day traders do not own any stocks overnight because of the extreme risk that prices will change radically from one day to the next, leading to large losses.

**Day trading is an extremely stressful and expensive full-time job:** Day traders must watch the market continuously during the day at their computer terminals. It's extremely difficult and demands great concentration to watch dozens of ticker quotes and price fluctuations to spot market trends. Day traders also have high expenses, paying their firms large amounts in commissions, for training, and for computers. Any day trader should know up front how much they need to make to cover expenses and break even.

**Day traders depend heavily on borrowing money or buying stocks on margin:** Borrowing money to trade in stocks is always a risky business. Day trading strategies demand using the leverage of borrowed money to make profits. This is why many day traders lose all their money and may end up in debt as well. Day traders should understand how margin works, how much time they'll have to meet a margin call, and the potential for getting in over their heads.

**Don't believe claims of easy profits:** Don't believe advertising claims that promise quick and sure profits from day trading. Before you start trading with a firm, make sure you know how many clients have lost money and how many have made profits. If the firm does not know, or will not tell you, think twice about the risks you take in the face of ignorance.

**Watch out for "hot tips" and "expert advice" from newsletters and websites catering to day traders:** Some websites have sought to profit from day traders by offering them hot tips and stock picks for a fee. Once again, don't believe any claims that trumpet the easy profits of day trading. Check out these sources thoroughly and ask them if they have been paid to make their recommendations.

**Remember that "educational" seminars, classes, and books about day trading may not be objective:** Find out whether a seminar speaker, an instructor teaching a class, or an author of a publication about day trading stands to profit if you start day trading.

**Check out day trading firms with your state securities regulator:** Like all broker-dealers, day trading firms must register with the SEC (Securities and Exchange Commission) and the states in which they do business. Confirm registration by calling your state securities regulator and at the same time ask if the firm has a record of problems with regulators or their customers. You can find the telephone number for your state securities regulator in the government section of your phone book or by calling the North American Securities Administrators Association (NASAA) at 202-737-0900. NASAA also provides this information on its website at http://www.nasaa.org/QuickLinks/ContactYourRegulator.cfm.

# Chapter 49

# *When Does "Investing" Become a Gambling Problem?*

Some investors may be at risk for problem gambling in the financial markets.

When people gamble excessively, and their behavior negatively affects other areas of their lives, gambling becomes a problem. Problem gambling may occur in the traditional recreational forms of gambling, such as sports betting, casinos, or the lottery. It can also be a problem in any financial transaction, including the financial markets, when money is risked in an attempt to gain more money.

All investments include risk of some kind. Investors should always know the risk that they are taking and choose investments to match their risk tolerance. The problem gambler can find gambling opportunities in all market areas, including simple stock purchases.

Most investors identify specific, long-term goals, such as college tuition for their children, or economic security in retirement and choose investment products that match their goals.

A small percentage of "investors" are risking large sums of money in market transactions. Their goal is to make a lot of money quickly and to experience the excitement of the action. These gamblers "play" the markets as they would play casino games. Further, those who have a gambling problem in the markets seek the same experiences as those who have a gambling problem in recreational forms of gambling.

---

Some problem gamblers in the markets have never engaged in recreational gambling, while others have gambled problematically at some time in one or more recreational forms of gambling.

When the problem becomes severe, the behaviors reach the level of a psychiatric disorder, pathological gambling (also referred to as compulsive or addictive gambling). This disorder is characterized by obsessive thoughts of gambling and out-of-control gambling, resulting in serious negative consequences in most areas of functioning.

When does investing become problem gambling? If you think that you or someone you care about may have a gambling problem in the financial markets, respond to the following self-scoring set of statements which identify the major characteristics of a gambling problem in the markets.

## Financial Markets Gambling Questionnaire

Note: All questions refer to either past or present thinking or behaviors.

1. I have been preoccupied with seeking daily information about the status of my investments or trades or have been preoccupied with thoughts of past and future investments or trades. Yes/No

2. A major reason I have invested or traded is to escape or avoid worries, pressures, anxiety, depression or other unpleasant mood. Yes/No

3. I have experienced extreme highs when I win and extreme lows when I lose in the market. Yes/No

4. I have felt uncomfortable when any cash accumulated in my brokerage account and have needed to quickly find a way to keep it in action. Yes/No

5. I have been restless or irritable when unable to be active in the markets, such as, when short of money, away on vacation or when trying to cut back on trades. Yes/No

6. I have needed to increase the amount invested or traded to maintain the high or excitement of being in action. Yes/No

7. My investments or trades have become increasingly speculative or risky over time. Yes/No

8. I have had more money at risk in the markets than I could afford to lose. Yes/No

9. I have often engaged in high volume investing or trading, for example, to try and outguess the direction of the market. Yes/No

10. My investments or trades have been highly leveraged. Yes/No

11. I have not opened brokerage statements to avoid having to think about my losses. Yes/No

12. I have borrowed money from family, friends, credit cards or other sources to invest or trade. Yes/No

13. I have borrowed money to invest or trade and have not paid it back. Yes/No

14. I have had to have someone else provide money to relieve a crisis caused by my investing or trading. Yes/No

15. I have lied to people to try and hide that I was investing or trading or to hide how much money was involved. Yes/No

16. When losses have piled up, I continued the same investments and trades or increased the amount, believing my strategy was due to work or hoping my luck would change and I would regain the losses. Yes/No

17. I have wanted to stop investing or trading but did not think I could or I have been unsuccessful when I have tried to control, cut back or stop investing or trading. Yes/No

18. I have risked losing or lost important work, family, or other commitments due to the amount of time and money taken up by my trading or investing. Yes/No

19. I have committed an illegal act to get money to continue to invest or trade or to pay back a loan taken to fund my investment activity. Yes/No

20. I have wondered whether I was gambling excessively in the markets. Yes/No

### Scoring Key

Score one point for every Yes answer:

**0:** No gambling problem
**1 or 2:** Possible future problem
**3 or 4:** Mild current problem
**5 or 6:** Moderate current problem
**7 or more:** Severe current problem

**Note:** The scores in this screen are only suggestive and do not provide a diagnosis of a gambling problem. This assessment can only be made by a qualified mental health or addiction professional.

You should seek a mental health consultation if you are concerned about your answers to these statements or you believe the statements apply to someone you care about.

## Information about Problem Gambling

Gamblers and their families and friends may get more information about pathological gambling, and about professional and self-help treatment resources in the 50 states and Puerto Rico by calling:

**National Council on Problem Gambling**
Helpline: 800-522-4700
Office: 202-547-9204

The text in this chapter was produced by:

**Connecticut Council on Problem Gambling**
47 Clapboard Hill Road
Guilford, CT 06437
Helpline: 800-346-6238 (CT)
Office: 203-453-0138
Website: http://www.ccpg.org

## Information about Investing

You can obtain more educational information for investors, including such publications as "Invest Wisely" or "Ask Questions about Your Investment," from:

**U.S. Securities and Exchange Commission (SEC)**
Office of Investor Education and Assistance
Mail Stop 11-2, 450 Fifth Street, NW
Washington, DC 20549
Toll-Free: 800-SEC-0330
Website: http://www.sec.gov

# Part Four

# Avoiding Fraud and Unscrupulous Practices

# Chapter 50

# *How to Avoid Investment Fraud*

## *How to Avoid Fraud*

Your net worth might make you a target for scams. Scam artists don't care how you have come across your money. They don't care whether you worked hard all your life to earn your money, or whether you hit the lottery the first time you played. It is your money they want. The only thing that may stand between a fraudster and your money is your preparedness when you are approached.

### *What can I do to avoid being scammed?*

Ask questions and check out the answers. Fraudsters rely on the sad truth that many people simply don't bother to investigate before they invest. It's not enough to ask a promoter for more information or for references—fraudsters have no incentive to set you straight. Savvy investors take the time to do their own independent research.

Research the company before you invest. You'll want to fully understand the company's business and its products or services before investing. Before buying any stock, check out the company's financial statements on the U.S. Securities and Exchange Commission (SEC) website (http://www.sec.gov), or contact your state securities regulator.

---

This chapter includes the following publications of the U.S. Securities and Exchange Commission (www.sec.gov): "How to Avoid Fraud," April 2005; and "Fake Seals and Phony Numbers: How Fraudsters Try to Look Legit," January 2005.

All but the smallest public companies have to file financial statements with us. If the company doesn't file with the SEC, you'll have to do a great deal of work on your own to make sure the company is legitimate and the investment appropriate for you. That's because the lack of reliable, readily available information about company finances can open the door to fraud. Remember that unsolicited e-mails, message board postings, and company news releases should never be used as the sole basis for your investment decisions.

Know the salesperson. Spend some time checking out the person touting the investment before you invest—even if you already know the person socially. Always find out whether the securities salespeople who contact you are licensed to sell securities in your state and whether they or their firms have had run-ins with regulators or other investors. You can check out the disciplinary history of brokers and advisers quickly—and for free—using the SEC's and the National Association of Securities Dealers (NASD)'s online databases. Your state securities regulator may have additional information.

Be wary of unsolicited offers. Be especially careful if you receive an unsolicited fax or e-mail about a company—or see it praised on an internet bulletin board—but can find no current financial information about the company from other independent sources. Many fraudsters use e-mail, faxes, and internet postings to tout thinly traded stocks, in the hopes of creating a buying frenzy that will push the share price up so that they can sell their shares. Once they dump their stock and quit promoting the company, the share price quickly falls. And be extra wary if someone you don't know and trust recommends foreign or "off-shore" investments. When you send your money abroad, and something goes wrong, it's more difficult to find out what happened and to locate your money.

Here are some red flags warnings of fraud:

- **If it sounds too good to be true, it is:** Compare promised yields with current returns on well-known stock indexes. Any investment opportunity that claims you'll get substantially more could be highly risky. And that means you might lose money.

- **"Guaranteed returns" aren't:** Every investment carries some degree of risk, and the level of risk typically correlates with the return you can expect to receive. Low risk generally means low yields, and high yields typically involve high risk. If your money is perfectly safe, you'll most likely get a low return. High returns represent potential rewards for folks who are willing and financially able to take big risks. Most fraudsters spend a lot of time trying to convince investors that extremely high returns are "guaranteed" or "can't miss." Don't believe it.

- **Beauty isn't everything:** Don't be fooled by a pretty website—they are remarkably easy to create.

- **Pressure to send money "right now":** Scam artists often tell their victims that this is a once-in-a-lifetime offer, and it will be gone tomorrow. But resist the pressure to invest quickly, and take the time you need to investigate before sending money. If it is that good an opportunity, it will wait.

Con artists are experts at gaining your confidence. So be certain to treat all unsolicited investment opportunities with extreme caution. Whether you hear about the opportunity through an e-mail, phone call, or a fax, be certain to check out both the person and firm making the offer and the investment they are pushing.

Remember—an educated investor is the best defense against fraud! For more information on how to invest wisely and avoid fraud, please visit the Investor Information section of the SEC's website (www.sec.gov).

## Fake Seals and Phony Numbers: How Fraudsters Try to Look Legit

It's a hard, cold fact: fraudsters lie. That's how they attempt to make money. They lie when they promise you "guaranteed" high returns with little or no risk. And they lie when they forget to mention that the company or product they're touting doesn't exist.

Some fraudsters tell straightforward lies, fabricating facts, or making bogus claims. That's why the SEC encourages investors to do their own independent research and to remember that wonderful, timeless adage: "If it sounds too good to be true, it probably is." Other fraudsters salt their stories with grains of truth to give their schemes an air of legitimacy. For many years, the SEC and securities regulators around the globe have been encouraging investors to investigate before they invest—to ask tough questions about their investments and the people who sell them. Taking their cue from us, some fraudsters now pretend to do the same.

One ruse fraudsters use involves assurances that an investment has been registered with the appropriate agency. The fraudsters will purport to give you the agency's telephone number and invite you to verify for yourself the "authenticity" of their claims. But even if the agency does exist, the contact information almost certainly will be false. Instead of speaking with an actual government official, you'll reach the fraudsters or their colleagues—who will give the company, the promoter, or the transaction high marks.

Another trick involves the misuse of a regulator's seal. The fraudsters copy the official seal or logo from the regulator's website—or create a bogus seal for a fictitious entity—and then use that seal on documents or webpages to make the deal look legitimate. You should be aware that the SEC—like other state and federal regulators in the U.S. and around the world—does not allow private entities to use its seal. Moreover, the SEC does not "approve" or "endorse" any particular securities, issuers, products, services, professional credentials, firms, or individuals.

Here's how you can protect yourself against these and other deceptive tactics:

- **Deal only with real regulators:** It's not hard to figure out who the real regulators are and how you can contact them. You'll find a list of international securities regulators on the website of the International Organization of Securities Commissions (http://www.iosco.org) and a directory of state and provincial regulators in Canada, Mexico, and the U.S. on the website of the North American Securities Administrators Association (http://www.nasaa.org). If someone encourages you to verify information about a deal with an entity that doesn't appear on these lists—such as the "Federal Regulatory and Compliance Department," the "Securities and Registration Compliance" agency, or the "U.S. Securities Registration Bureau"—you're probably dealing with fraudsters. You'll find legitimate contact information for the SEC in the Contact Us section of the SEC website (http://www.sec.gov). If you're ever unsure whether you're dealing with someone from the real SEC, get in touch with the SEC yourself and ask. You can do this by going directly to the SEC website (do not use links you might have received in an e-mail) or by calling them toll-free at 800-SEC-0330.

- **Be skeptical of government "approval":** The SEC does not evaluate the merits of any securities offering, nor do they determine whether a particular security is a "good" investment. Instead, the SEC's staff reviews registration statements for securities offerings and declares those statements "effective" if the companies appear to have satisfied our disclosure rules. In general, all securities offered in the U.S. must be registered with the SEC or must qualify for an exemption from the registration requirements. You can check to see whether a company has registered its securities with the SEC and download its disclosure documents using the EDGAR [Electronic Data Gathering, Analysis, and Retrieval] database of company filings.

- **Look past fancy seals and impressive letterheads:** Most people who use computers know how easy it can be to copy and paste images. As a result, today's technology allows fraudsters to create impressive, legitimate-looking websites and stationery at little to no cost. Don't be taken in by a glossy brochure, a glitzy website, or the presence of a regulator's official seal on a webpage or document. Again, the SEC does not authorize private companies to use our seal—even as a legitimate link to their website. If you see the SEC seal on a company's website or materials, think twice.

- **Check out the broker and the firm:** Always verify whether any broker offering to buy or sell securities is properly licensed to do business in your state, province, or country. If the person claims to work with a U.S. brokerage firm, call NASD's Public Disclosure Program hotline at 800-289-9999 or visit NASD's website to check out the background of both the individual broker and the firm. Be sure to confirm whether the firm actually exists and is current in its registration, and ask whether the broker or the firm has a history of complaints. You can often get even more information from your state securities regulator.

- **Be wary of "advance fee" or "recovery room" schemes:** An increasing number of investment-related frauds target investors worldwide who purchase "microcap" stocks, the low-priced and thinly traded stocks issued by the smallest of U.S. companies. If the stock price falls or the company goes out of business, the fraudsters swoop in, falsely claiming that they can help investors recover their losses—for a substantial fee disguised as some type of tax, deposit, or refundable insurance bond. As soon as an unwary investor pays the "advance fees," the fraudsters disappear—leaving the investor with even higher losses.

If you want to invest wisely and steer clear of frauds, you must get the facts. Never, ever, make an investment based solely on a promoter's promises or what you see on the internet—especially if the investment involves a small, thinly-traded company that isn't well known. And don't even think about investing on your own in small companies that don't file regular reports with the SEC, unless you are willing to investigate each company thoroughly and to check the truth of every statement about the company.

# Chapter 51

# *Outrageous Advertising: Beware*

Note: Mark Hulbert, the author of this information, is the editor of the *Hulbert Financial Digest*, a newsletter that ranks the performance of investment advisory newsletters.

I am continually mystified by individuals' gullibility in the face of exaggerated investment performance claims. Investors who are nobody's fool when it comes to outrageous advertisements in other areas of their lives suddenly become naïve when confronted with equally outrageous investment performance claims. It doesn't make sense.

For example, most of you wouldn't give the time of day to a used car salesman who told you that an old car had only been driven to church on Sundays. Yet many of you not only gave the time of day, but actually paid good money—to refer to a successful ad campaign of several years ago—to an investment newsletter that claimed that in 13 years' time it had turned $10,000 into more than $40 million.

In order to boost your immunity to such claims, I'm devoting this space to a review of some advertising that, in my opinion, strains credulity. In the process I will identify certain warning signs that you should be on the lookout for when reading an investment ad.

If you're convinced that your immunity to outrageous claims already is strong, and therefore you don't need any help from me, then all power to you. But remember that, at least in my experience, some of the most gullible investors are those who believe they are not.

Let me stress that not all advertising for investment newsletters is false or misleading. Some ads are admirable in telling the truth, the whole truth, and nothing but the truth. But until and unless all ads live up to that standard, you need to be on your guard.

## *Maximum Returns*

One of the most important lessons to learn concerns the highest return you can realistically expect to earn over long periods. I believe that this practical maximum is around 20% to 25% annualized, and even that is achievable by only a select few.

An illustration of the use to which you can put this lesson comes from an e-mail I received concerning a newsletter that is not currently tracked by the *Hulbert Financial Digest* (*HFD*). It claimed to have produced an 847% annualized return over the past three years. Since the *HFD* has not calculated a track record for this service, I have no basis for ascertaining the veracity of this claim. But even if it were true, I nevertheless would not place high odds on this service being able to sustain this pace into the future.

There are several different perspectives that help us appreciate why such a practical maximum exists. One is that returns much higher than 20% to 25% annualized are economically impossible over long periods. Consider how large your portfolio would grow to if it were able to achieve an 847% annualized return. Even if it began with as little as $1,000, within 10 years it would be worth more than the combined gross domestic products of all nations.

Another perspective is provided by the highest long-term returns that have been produced historically. Take Warren Buffett, for instance, who is widely credited with being the most successful investor alive today. Since the mid-1960s, the book value of his company, Berkshire Hathaway, has grown at an annualized pace of around 23%. While that return is more than enough to turn both Buffett and his shareholders into extremely wealthy individuals, it's a far cry from the exaggerated performances that too often are advertised.

The next time you receive an advertisement for performance as good or better than Buffett's, ask yourself how often such individuals come along and how likely it is that he or she would be selling advice to you.

It is possible, but I wouldn't bet on it.

This investment lesson doesn't mean that rates greater than 25% annualized are unattainable over short time periods. It simply means that those high short-term rates are unsustainable. Another way of putting this is that regression to the mean is a powerful force.

## Choosing Time Periods

A related trick that advertisers play is to truthfully report performance that nevertheless is not current. Since even broken clocks are right twice a day, advertisers have no difficulty finding some period in which their clients looked like geniuses.

This trick usually is a last resort, however, to be used when nothing else is available. After all, if a newsletter's long-term record is good, then its advertiser undoubtedly will point this out, including providing specific dates and performance numbers. If an advertisement doesn't provide such specificity, it is at least a warning sign to tread carefully.

Consider an advertising brochure I received for a newsletter editor. According to the ad, the advisor "was recently rated as the #1 market timer by... the *Hulbert Financial Digest*." Though the brochure did not specify the recent period over which the advisor was so highly ranked, it did say that the *HFD* has "given him other awards covering periods of five years, which puts him in a different league from advisors who shine in the #1 slot for a single fleeting year."

This was news to me. The advisor's system was nowhere near to being ranked in first position for recent performance. How far back must we go to find a period over which he ranked first? To the end of 1994, at which point it was in first place for performance over the trailing year. Even so, at that time his rank over longer periods was well down the list.

The president of the company that publishes the newsletter explained that the source of the blunder was an individual who simply lifted language from an old and out-of-date advertisement. Evidently, prior to going to press, no one had bothered to determine whether the claim was still true.

## The Whole Truth

Another trick that investment advisers often play is to create many different portfolios. This increases the odds that at least one portfolio will perform well. But that does not mean that the adviser is a good bet for future performance.

I'm reminded of this lesson by an advertisement for a new newsletter. I had not tracked this new service, but did track several other newsletters published by the same advisor, and the picture painted by their track records is far less impressive. Needless to say, the advertisement for the new newsletter does not mention the track records of each of these other newsletters.

The lesson to learn: Because advertisers can be counted on to put their clients' best feet forward, don't expect them to give you the full, unvarnished truth. If their clients are tracked by independent monitoring services such as the *Hulbert Financial Digest*, look to those services to get a fuller picture. If they are not tracked, get the advisers to answer—in writing—questions such as: What was their worst-performing account over various periods such as the last year, five years, and 10 years? How many clients left their money management in a loss position? Money managers are not required to answer such questions. But by the same token, you are not required to utilize the services of those who refuse.

## *Figures Don't Lie*

Another advertising sleight-of-hand is to confuse arithmetic averages with geometric ones. The former does not take in account the effect of compounding, and thus overstates the real returns.

To illustrate, assume that 10 years ago you invested $10,000 in a 5% savings account and that you reinvested the interest annually. Your account now would be worth $16,289, for a 10-year gain of 52.89%. If you used an arithmetic average to calculate your annual gain, you would report that you gained 5.29% per year (52.89 divided by 10) instead of the 5% you earned every year (which is the geometric average of 52.89% over 10 years).

The difference between these two returns may seem modest in this case, but it becomes huge when focusing on the higher returns of the equity market over the past two decades.

## *Backtesting*

Another thing to be on your guard against is backtesting. Statisticians refer to the practice as data snooping or data mining. Regardless of what it is called, the track records produced by the practice are far less reliable than track records produced in real time.

Data mining has become an increasingly prevalent practice in recent years, due to the advent of powerful personal computers and readily accessible historical databases. With thousands of investors mining these databases, more and more spurious patterns are being "discovered." That is why so many strategies with an apparently great track record seem to stop working the moment you start following them.

My favorite example of this comes from Codexa Corp.'s CEO, David Leinweber. To illustrate the perils of data mining, several years ago he searched through all the data on a United Nations CD-ROM to find the indicator most correlated with the S&P 500. His discovery: butter production in Bangladesh.

One of the best defenses against data mining is to test strategies over a different time frame than that used to discover its existence. A strategy might look good over the last decade, but how did it perform in previous decades, for example?

Advertisers are quite ingenious in how they describe the backtesting done by their clients. For example, a newsletter advertisement I received a few years ago bragged about the impressive performance that emerged from the "system testing" of his client's strategy. It sounds better than "backtesting" or "data snooping," but in reality it is the same thing.

## Too Good to Be True

You've heard it countless times, and it seems trite to repeat it once again. But it remains very good advice nonetheless: If an advertisement makes an investment strategy appear too good to be true, it probably is.

Chapter 52

# Precious Metals and Other Commodities: Beware of Unrealistic Promises

Consumers should be alert to companies that sell investments in precious metals and other commodities based on sales pitches claiming that customers can make a lot of money, with little risk, by purchasing metal through a financing agreement. Sometimes these companies offer opportunities to speculate on the price movement of precious metals, or other commodities such as heating oil, without actually taking delivery of the commodity.

The United States Commodity Futures Trading Commission (CFTC) is the federal agency that regulates the trading of commodity futures and options contracts in the United States and takes action against firms suspected of illegally or fraudulently selling commodity futures and options. Over the past several years, the CFTC has taken enforcement action against wrongdoers who lured customers to purchase purported interests in precious metals without taking delivery, through various misrepresentations including claims that they would earn large profits with little risk.

Certain companies advertise on radio, television or internet websites, or make telephone "cold calls," to promote the purchase of precious metals such as gold, silver, and platinum. In the CFTC's experience, the advertisements, infomercials, and telephone solicitations often promise quick riches—such as the ability to double or

"Beware of Promises of Easy Profits from Buying Precious Metals and Other Commodities," Commodity Futures Trading Commission (www.cftc.gov), February 2006.

triple the customer's initial investment in just two or three months—all with low risk. Companies making such statements typically ask that customers pay only a small percentage of the total purchase price, and also claim that they (or another company) will purchase and store the metal. These companies also pretend to arrange financing for the customer's metal purchase so the customer can obtain a larger profit by controlling a larger amount of metal with their relatively small down payment. Companies often discourage customers from taking delivery of the metal. These companies often charge a commission for the purchase transaction, a loan origination fee, an interest charge on the remaining balance (which accrues over time), and fees relating to storage and shipping of the metal they pretend to purchase for the customer. Sometimes, not all of these fees are disclosed up front.

## What's Wrong with Such Sales Pitches?

The CFTC's experience has been that companies making such pitches often:

- lie about or overstate their ability to predict prices or the direction of the metals markets;

- minimize the degree of investment risk involved in metals investments;

- fraudulently fail to disclose how much the price of metal must go up for the customer to break even (let alone profit), since hefty finance and storage fees and commissions are deducted from the customer's account before any profits accrue;

- falsely claim to be purchasing and storing the metal, when they do not actually do so. Indeed, companies often discourage customers from taking delivery of the metal;

- charge phony "storage" fees for metal, when no metal is actually purchased or stored;

- charge phony "interest" fees that diminish a customer's account equity to the point where the customer has to deposit additional funds with the company or have his account closed out at a total loss. The interest fees are phony because no metal has been purchased, as promised, and the financing arrangement therefore is fictitious;

- fail to point out that, because you are buying on "margin" or with leverage, you will have to send the company additional funds (or sell a portion of your "metal position") if the price of the precious metals moves unfavorably.

## Warning Signs of Commodity "Come-Ons"

If you are solicited by a company to purchase commodities, watch for the warning signs listed below:

- Avoid any company that predicts or guarantees large profits with little or no financial risk.

- Be wary of high-pressure tactics to convince you to send or transfer cash immediately to the firm, through overnight delivery companies, the internet, by mail, or otherwise.

- Be skeptical about unsolicited phone calls about investments from offshore salespersons or companies with which you are unfamiliar.

- Prior to purchasing, contact the CFTC (www.cftc.gov/cftc/cftchome.htm) or other authorities, including your state's securities commissioner (http://www.nasaa.org), Attorney General's consumer protection bureau (www.naag.org/index2.html), the Better Business Bureau (www.bbb.com), and the National Futures Association (www.nfa.futures.org).

- Be sure you get all information about the company and verify that data, if possible. If you can, check the company's materials with someone whose financial advice you trust.

- Learn all possible information about fees and commissions charged, and the basis for each of these charges.

- If in doubt, don't invest. If you can't get solid information about the company, the salesperson, and the investment, you may not want to risk your money.

## Use Extra Care when Dealing with Foreign Companies

- Sometimes companies that solicit customer investments in precious metals (or their purported storage facilities) are located outside the United States, even if they do not reveal that fact to you while soliciting your investment. United States government agencies generally have little or no regulatory authority over entities operating outside the United States. If you transfer funds to foreign firms, or place funds with United States firms that are later transferred to offshore companies, it may be difficult or impossible for you to recover your money. Storing metal offshore, particularly in countries with secrecy laws, might make it difficult for you to verify your investment.

- Ask where all companies that would handle your funds are located, where any telephone call you receive originates, where your funds will be deposited and kept, and where the metal will be stored. If possible, telephone the company.

## *For More Information and Contacts*

- Have you checked whether the company and salesperson are registered with the CFTC or are members of the National Futures Association (NFA)? You can do this easily by calling the NFA (800-621-3570 or 800-676-4NFA) or by checking the NFA's registration and membership information on its website at http://www.nfa.futures.org/basicnet. While registration may not be required, you might want to confirm the status and disciplinary record of a particular company or salesperson.

- Have you checked with the NFA to determine whether the company or salesperson has been disciplined by commodity regulators?

- For other consumer advisories concerning possible fraudulent activity in the commodity futures and options industry, see the following Consumer Alerts: www.cftc.gov/cftc/cftccustomer.htm.

- The CFTC's website also offers general information about trading in the commodity futures and options markets. For example, the CFTC offers brochures on-line, such as "Futures and Options What You Should Know Before You Trade" (www.cftc.gov/opa/brochures/opafutures.htm) and "Glossary: The Language of the Futures Industry" (www.cftc.gov/opa/glossary/opaglossary_a.htm). To obtain this and other information, go to the CFTC site map (www.cftc.gov/cftc/cftcmap.htm).

Questions concerning this advisory may be addressed to the CFTC's Office of Public Affairs at 202-418-5080, or write to:

Commodity Futures Trading Commission
Office of Public Affairs
Three Lafayette Centre
1155 21st Street, N.W.
Washington, DC 20581

# Chapter 53

# *Mini-Tender Offers: Proceed with Caution*

Most investors welcome tender offers because they frequently provide a rare opportunity to sell securities at a premium above market price. But investors should know that not all tender offers are alike.

"Mini-tender" offers—tender offers for less than five percent of a company's stock—have been increasingly used to catch investors off guard. Many investors who hear about mini-tender offers surrender their securities without investigating the offer, assuming that the price offered includes the premium usually present in larger, traditional tender offers. But they later learn that they cannot withdraw from the offer and may end up selling their securities at below-market prices.

If you've been asked to tender your securities, find out first whether the offer is a mini-tender offer. And remember that mini-tender offers typically do not provide the same disclosure and procedural protections that larger, traditional tender offers provide. For example, when a bidder—the person or group of people behind the offer—makes a tender offer for more than five percent of the company's shares, all of the U.S. Securities and Exchange Commission (SEC)'s tender offer rules apply. These rules require bidders to:

- Disclose important information about themselves;
- Disclose the terms of the offer;

"Mini-Tender Offers: Tips for Investors," U.S. Securities and Exchange Commission (www.sec.gov), January 2006.

- File their offering documents with the SEC; and

- Provide the target company and any competing bidders with information about the tender offer.

The rules also give investors important protections, including the right to:

- Change their minds and withdraw from the transaction while the offer remains open;

- Have their shares accepted on a "pro rata" basis (if the offer is for less than all of the company's outstanding shares and investors tender too many shares); and

- Be treated equally by the bidder.

But none of the rules listed above applies to mini-tender offers.

Instead, the only rules that encompass mini-tender offers—Section 14(e) of the Securities Exchange Act and Regulation 14E—provide that bidders must:

- Not engage in fraud or deceptive practices;

- Hold open tender offers for minimum time periods; and

- Make prompt payment to investors after the offer closes.

Regulation 14E also requires the target company to state its position about the offer by recommending that investors accept or reject the offer. The company may also state that it remains neutral or takes no position. But because bidders in mini-tender offers don't have to notify the target, the target may not even know about the offer.

Investors need to scrutinize mini-tender offers carefully. Some bidders make mini-tender offers at below-market prices, hoping that they will catch investors off guard if the investors do not compare the offer price to the current market price. Others make mini-tender offers at a premium—betting that the market price will rise before the offer closes and then extending the offer until it does or improperly canceling if it doesn't.

With most mini-tender offers, investors typically feel pressured to tender their shares quickly without having solid information about the offer or the people behind it. And they've been shocked to learn that they generally cannot withdraw from mini-tender offers.

Here are the steps you should take if you are asked to sell your stock, bonds, limited partnership interests, or other securities through a mini-tender offer:

- Find out whether the offer is a mini-tender offer. Most bidders won't use the term "mini-tender offer" to describe their offer to buy your shares. Instead, they may call it a "Solicitation to Purchase Shares of XYZ Corporation." Ask the bidder—or your broker—what percentage of the company the bidder seeks to purchase. If the answer is less than five percent, you're dealing with a mini-tender offer, and you should proceed with caution.

- Get a copy of the offering document. And be sure to read the disclosure carefully. Do not make an investment decision until you see the disclosure about the offer.

- Determine whether the bidder has adequate financing. Some bidders make mini-tender offers because they can do so at virtually no cost. These individuals often do not have the financing necessary to purchase the shares in the offer. Before you surrender your securities in a mini-tender offer, ask tough questions—and demand answers—about the bidder's ability to pay once the offer closes.

- Identify the current market price for your securities. For stock, you can easily get price information in many newspapers, on-line, or from your broker or investment adviser. For bonds and limited partnerships, you may need to talk with your broker or investment adviser because these prices may be hard to find. For limited partnerships, contact the general partner to get a list of firms that buy and sell the limited partnership, or ask your broker or investment adviser.

- Find out the "final" tender offer price after all deductions are taken. In some tender offers, you may get a lower price because deductions are taken from the tender offer price for dividend payments. Also, some bidders in mini-tender offers fail to disclose clearly that certain fees or expenses may also be deducted from the offer price.

- Ask when you'll be paid for the shares you tender. Bidders in mini-tender offers sometimes fail to provide prompt payment, sometimes delaying for weeks or months. Before you tender your shares, be sure to find out when the bidder will pay you for your shares.

- Consult with your broker or other financial adviser. Make sure you understand the terms of the tender offer before tendering your shares. Ask for any additional written information that may be available.

- If you want to sell your shares, determine where you can get your best price. Check all your alternatives for selling your securities. For instance, compare how much you will receive if you sell through your broker versus the tender offer.

- Remember that once you agree to a mini-tender offer, you are probably locked in. If the tender offer is for less than five percent of the company's stock, exercise extreme caution. Unlike other tender offers, you generally cannot change your mind after you have tendered your shares in a mini-tender offer, even if the offer hasn't yet closed. In addition, the bidder can extend the tender offer without giving you the right to withdraw your shares. And in the meantime, you've lost control over the securities you tendered.

If you've run into trouble with a mini-tender offer, act promptly. By law, you only have a limited time to take legal action.

Contact the SEC's Office of Investor Education and Assistance for help. You can send your complaints using their online complaint form. Or you can reach them as follows:

U.S. Securities and Exchange Commission
Office of Investor Education and Assistance
450 5th Street, NW
Washington, DC 20549-0213
Fax: (202) 772-9295
http://www.sec.gov

# Chapter 54

# *Mutual Company Conversions: Abuse Potential*

Many banks and insurance companies in the U.S. are organized as "mutual companies." A mutual company is one that is owned—and sometimes governed—by its members instead of being owned by public or private shareholders. In the case of a mutual savings bank or a mutual savings association, the members are the financial institution's depositors. In the case of a mutual insurance company, the members are the insurance company's policyholders.

Over the past two decades, a number of mutual companies have converted to a stock form of ownership—either to raise money, to expand operations, to enhance employee benefit options, or for some combination of these or other reasons. A host of federal and state banking laws govern "mutual-to-stock" conversions of banks and savings associations, including the rights—and responsibilities—of depositors. Similarly, state insurance laws govern insurance company conversions.

This alert briefly describes how mutual-to-stock conversions work in the context of banks and savings associations and provides tips for investors who participate in these transactions.

While some of the concepts described in this alert apply generally to insurance company conversions, insurance regulation rests exclusively in the hands of the state governments. Always read the prospectus for any conversion carefully, and contact your state insurance regulator if you have questions or concerns regarding an insurance company conversion.

---

"Mutual-to-Stock Conversions: Tips for Investors," U.S. Securities and Exchange Commission (www.sec.gov), June 2005.

## *How Bank and Savings Association Mutual-to-Stock Conversions Work*

When a bank or savings association converts from mutual to stock form, the financial institution (or its holding company) generally issues stock in an initial public offering (or "IPO"). Historically, individual investors have had a difficult time purchasing shares in IPOs—largely because of the way those deals are structured and sold. With a bank or savings association mutual-to-stock conversion, however, eligible depositors have a unique opportunity to participate and purchase shares because federal and state banking regulations require that the bank or savings association give depositors first priority to purchase the stock over all other interested investors. These priority subscription rights allow depositors to purchase up to a set amount of shares at the "subscription price," which is the value the company assigns to its shares before the shares trade publicly. Stock offered as a result of a conversion sometimes generates significant investor interest because of the potential for the stock price to increase. If the IPO is over-subscribed—that is, if depositors and others who have been given priority under federal and state banking regulations collectively sign up to purchase more shares than the converting bank or savings association plans to offer—then the general public will not have a chance to take part in the IPO.

To ensure that only depositors benefit from their priority stock subscription rights, federal and state banking regulations prohibit depositors from transferring ownership of their subscription rights— or of the stock itself—prior to completion of the conversion. These restrictions on depositors—and any additional restrictions that the financial institution imposes—will always appear in the prospectus for the conversion. In addition, converting banks and savings associations typically require depositors to sign a "subscription agreement" or "stock order form" that contains written certification (signed under penalty of perjury) that the depositor is purchasing the conversion stock for his or her "own account" and that he or she has "no agreement or understanding regarding the sale or transfer of" any shares he or she receives.

But, as several enforcement actions taken by the U.S. Securities and Exchange Commission (SEC) in this area confirm, opportunists (or "fraudsters") periodically attempt to circumvent these laws and participate illegally in mutual bank or savings association conversions. Links to these enforcement actions are included at the end of this alert.

## How Fraudsters Take Advantage

The rare ability for ordinary individuals to get in on the ground floor of an IPO makes mutual-to-stock conversions ripe for abuse. Although there are many variations of this type of scheme, in the typical case, the fraudster will identify and approach a depositor who has non-transferable subscription rights, offering to "loan" the depositor the money required to purchase the maximum number of shares. Converting financial institutions typically require depositors to pay up front and in full for the shares they request at the time they submit their subscription agreements or stock order forms. Those sums can easily be tens or hundreds of thousands of dollars—amounts that many depositors cannot afford on their own.

In exchange for funding the purchase, the fraudster typically will require the depositor to either transfer the conversion stock to an account that the fraudster controls or sell the stock and give the fraudster a majority of the profits. The fraudster will further persuade the depositor to keep secret their arrangement and to submit subscription documents or stock order forms that falsely (or misleadingly) represent to the bank or savings association that the depositor is the true purchaser of the stock, has not transferred his or her subscription rights to any person or entity, and has entered into no agreement regarding the sale or transfer of the stock. After the conversion occurs, the fraudster typically will determine when to sell the stock (but sometimes lets the depositor decide when to sell) and will split any profits with the depositor. In most cases, the fraudster gets well over half the profits, and frequently the fraudster gets over 75% of the profits.

Mutual depositors who enter into agreements with such fraudsters should be aware that these fraudsters may be violating not only state and federal banking laws, but also the anti-fraud provisions of the federal securities laws and various federal criminal laws. Moreover, mutual depositors should be aware that, by entering into such agreements, they may be violating these laws themselves and may be subject to civil enforcement actions or criminal prosecution.

## What Investors Need to Know

Key concepts for investors to bear in mind when considering whether to participate in a mutual bank conversion include the following:

- **Know the rules:** By law, depositors cannot sell or transfer their priority subscription rights, or the stock itself, prior to the completion of a financial institution's conversion. Moreover, depositors cannot enter into agreements or arrangements to sell or transfer either their subscription rights or the underlying conversion stock.

- **Read the prospectus and stock order forms carefully:** These documents may contain broader, more explicit restrictions than the threshold set by applicable state and federal banking laws. Typically, prospectuses prohibit any agreements regarding the sale or transfer of the stock. Financial institutions have the right to reject any stock order forms that do not comply with either the letter of the law or the wording of the prospectus.

- **"Neither a borrower nor a lender be":** Shakespeare's words ring especially true in the context of mutual bank conversions. If someone offers to lend you money so that you can participate—or participate more fully—in the conversion, be extremely wary. Be even more wary if the source of the money is someone you do not know. The loan agreement may make you unable to certify truthfully that you are the true holder of the subscription rights and the true purchaser of the stock and that you have no agreements regarding the sale or transfer of the stock.

- **Watch out for opportunists:** The opportunist may tell you that he or she is a lawyer—or a consultant or a professional investor or some similarly impressive tale—who has experience with similar mutual bank conversion transactions. The opportunist may even approach you through one of your friends or family members. But if the people proposing a deal stand to profit from it, take their words and promises with a grain (or perhaps a pound) of salt. Fraudsters rarely act in the "best interests" of anyone but themselves.

- **Be wary of guarantees:** Some fraudsters will go to extreme lengths to assure you that the arrangement you're entering into is perfectly legitimate. They might tell you that they've done scores of these transactions and that this is simply how they work. Or they might downplay the warnings or restrictions in the prospectus or order form, telling you that "everyone" enters into such agreements or that the deal they're offering is legitimate. They may also tell you that you have no risk in the transaction. The cold, hard truth is that fraudsters lie.

- **Get the facts from the source:** If you have any questions about a mutual conversion transaction, ask the bank or savings association for more information. If you have any doubts about a transaction proposed to you by someone else, ask the bank or savings association whether the proposed arrangement is proper. You may be able to find helpful resources on the institution's website or by visiting a branch office.

The bottom line for investors is always to remember that if an opportunity sounds too good to be true, it probably is too good to be true.

## *Complaints or Problems?*

If you have any doubts or concerns relating to a mutual bank conversion transaction, be sure to contact your state banking regulator (a list of state banking authorities is available online at http://consumeraction.gov/banking.shtml) or the federal banking regulator that oversees the bank or savings association (a list of federal banking regulators can be found in Chapter 68—A Directory of Investor Protection Services Agencies).

If you are eligible to purchase stock in a mutual bank or savings association conversion, and someone proposes some sort of "mutually beneficial arrangement" involving your subscription rights or the stock itself, please file a detailed complaint with the SEC using their online Complaint Center (http://www.sec.gov/complaint.shtml). Be sure to include the name of the bank or savings association and provide any contact information for each individual involved. You should also send your information to the appropriate state and federal banking authorities.

# Chapter 55

# *Junk Faxes*

The U.S. Securities and Exchange Commission (SEC) frequently hears from frustrated citizens who've been inundated with "junk faxes"—unsolicited advertisements that clog up the memory, tie up the line, and eat up the paper on home or office fax machines. Some of these missives tout diet fads, office products, or vacation deals. Others purport to be "unbiased" investment newsletters that extol the virtues—and promote the stock—of some "hot" new company. Believe it or not, the SEC's Office of Investor Education and Assistance gets unwelcome junk faxes, too.

Here's what you should know about investment-related junk faxes, including the steps you can take to try and stop them:

- **Be skeptical and wary of unsolicited investment advice:** Paid promoters are generally behind the investment-related "junk" faxes you may receive. Some companies—especially smaller, "microcap" companies—pay people to write newsletters to "tout" or recommend their stocks. While this isn't illegal, the federal securities laws require the newsletters to disclose who paid them, the amount, and the type of payment. Compliance with this disclosure requirement, however, does not by itself indicate that the information disclosed is truthful. The Commission has charged individuals for disclosing false and misleading information concerning the origin of the fax, who paid for it, or the type of payment.

"Junk Faxes: How to Handle Those 'Blasted' Faxes," U.S. Securities and Exchange Commission (www.sec.gov), February 2006.

461

- **Don't believe any claim of "SEC Endorsement":** The SEC does not endorse or approve any investment product or service. If an investment-related junk fax suggests otherwise—either by invoking the SEC's name, providing the URL for the SEC website, or using the SEC seal—then you should exercise extreme caution.

- **The SEC does not have a "do not fax" list:** Junk faxes often contain a "disclaimer" or disclosure at the bottom of the page. Unfortunately, some junk faxes refer to the SEC (and provide the web address or contact information) just before the fax removal instructions. This has misled many into believing that the SEC is somehow involved or can assist them in getting their fax numbers removed from the distribution list. But that's not the case.

## *If You Need Help*

The Federal Communications Commission (FCC) can help. The FCC (not the SEC) has jurisdiction over junk faxes, including investment-related faxes. The Telephone Consumer Protection Act of 1991 (TCPA) and FCC rules prohibit entities from sending junk faxes to homes and offices. If you receive an unsolicited fax (investment-related or otherwise), be sure to complain to the FCC as follows:

- Online: Use the FCC's online Consumer Complaint Form at www.fcc.gov/cgb/complaints.html

- Phone: Call the FCC's Consumer Center at:
  888-CALL-FCC (888-225-5322) (voice); or
  888-TELL-FCC (888-835-5322) TTY

You can also send a letter summarizing your complaint and attaching any faxes you've received to the following address:

### *Federal Communications Commission*
Consumer and Governmental Affairs Bureau
Consumer Inquiries and Complaints Division
445 12th Street, SW
Washington, DC 20554

Note: Include as much detail as possible in your complaint. And be aware that it may take time and multiple complaints to obtain relief from the plague of junk faxes.

# Chapter 56

# *Identity Theft*

## *How Identity Theft Occurs*

Despite your best efforts to manage the flow of your personal information or to keep it to yourself, skilled identity thieves may use a variety of methods to gain access to your data.

### *How Identity Thieves Get Your Personal Information*

- They get information from businesses or other institutions by: stealing records or information while they're on the job; bribing an employee who has access to these records; hacking these records; conning information out of employees.

- They may steal your mail, including bank and credit card statements, credit card offers, new checks, and tax information.

- They may rummage through your trash, the trash of businesses, or public trash dumps in a practice known as "dumpster diving."

- They may get your credit reports by abusing their employer's authorized access to them, or by posing as a landlord, employer, or someone else who may have a legal right to access your report.

---

This chapter begins with excerpts from "Take Charge: Fighting Back Against Identity Theft," Federal Trade Commission (FTC), 2005. It continues with "When the News Reports Say Your Personal Information May Be at Risk," *FDIC Consumer News*, Federal Deposit Insurance Corporation (FDIC), Summer 2005, and "Who to Call to Report a Possible ID Theft," *FDIC Consumer News,* FDIC, Fall 2004.

- They may steal your credit or debit card numbers by capturing the information in a data storage device in a practice known as "skimming." They may swipe your card for an actual purchase, or attach the device to an ATM machine where you may enter or swipe your card.

- They may steal your wallet or purse.

- They may complete a "change of address form" to divert your mail to another location.

- They may steal personal information they find in your home.

- They may steal personal information from you through e-mail or phone by posing as legitimate companies and claiming that you have a problem with your account. This practice is known as "phishing" online, or pretexting by phone.

### *How Identity Thieves Use Your Personal Information*

- They may call your credit card issuer to change the billing address on your credit card account. The impostor then runs up charges on your account. Because your bills are being sent to a different address, it may be some time before you realize there's a problem.

- They may open new credit card accounts in your name. When they use the credit cards and don't pay the bills, the delinquent accounts are reported on your credit report.

- They may establish phone or wireless service in your name.

- They may open a bank account in your name and write bad checks on that account.

- They may counterfeit checks or credit or debit cards, or authorize electronic transfers in your name, and drain your bank account.

- They may file for bankruptcy under your name to avoid paying debts they've incurred under your name, or to avoid eviction.

- They may buy a car by taking out an auto loan in your name.

- They may get identification such as a driver's license issued with their picture, in your name.

- They may get a job or file fraudulent tax returns in your name.

- They may give your name to the police during an arrest. If they don't show up for their court date, a warrant for arrest is issued in your name.

## *If Your Personal Information Has Been Lost or Stolen*

If you've lost personal information or identification, or if it has been stolen from you, taking certain steps quickly can minimize the potential for identity theft.

- **Financial accounts:** Close accounts, like credit cards and bank accounts, immediately. When you open new accounts, place passwords on them. Avoid using your mother's maiden name, your birth date, the last four digits of your Social Security number (SSN) or your phone number, or a series of consecutive numbers.

- **Social Security number:** Call the toll-free fraud number of any of the three nationwide consumer reporting companies and place an initial fraud alert on your credit reports. An alert can help stop someone from opening new credit accounts in your name.

- **Driver's license/other government-issued identification:** Contact the agency that issued the license or other identification document. Follow its procedures to cancel the document and to get a replacement. Ask the agency to flag your file so that no one else can get a license or any other identification document from them in your name.

Once you've taken these precautions, watch for signs that your information is being misused.

If your information has been misused, file a report about the theft with the police, and file a complaint with the Federal Trade Commission, as well. If another crime was committed for example, if your purse or wallet was stolen or your house or car was broken into report it to the police immediately.

## *Identity Theft Victims: Immediate Steps*

If you are a victim of identity theft, take the following four steps as soon as possible, and keep a record with the details of your conversations and copies of all correspondence.

### *1. Place a fraud alert on your credit reports, and review your credit reports.*

Fraud alerts can help prevent an identity thief from opening any more accounts in your name. Contact the toll-free fraud number of any of the three consumer reporting companies below to place a fraud alert on your credit report. You only need to contact one of the three companies to place an alert. The company you call is required to contact the other two, which will place an alert on their versions of your report, too.

- Equifax: 800-525-6285; www.equifax.com; P.O. Box 740241, Atlanta, GA 30374- 0241

- Experian: 888-EXPERIAN (397-3742); http://www.experian.com; P.O. Box 9532, Allen, TX 75013

- TransUnion: 800-680-7289; http://www.transunion.com; Fraud Victim Assistance Division, P.O. Box 6790, Fullerton, CA 92834-6790

Once you place the fraud alert in your file, you're entitled to order free copies of your credit reports, and, if you ask, only the last four digits of your SSN will appear on your credit reports. Once you get your credit reports, review them carefully. Look for inquiries from companies you haven't contacted, accounts you didn't open, and debts on your accounts that you can't explain. Check that information, like your SSN, address(es), name or initials, and employers are correct. If you find fraudulent or inaccurate information, get it removed. Continue to check your credit reports periodically, especially for the first year after you discover the identity theft, to make sure no new fraudulent activity has occurred.

There are two types of fraud alerts: an initial alert, and an extended alert.

An initial alert stays on your credit report for at least 90 days. You may ask that an initial fraud alert be placed on your credit report if you suspect you have been, or are about to be, a victim of identity theft. An initial alert is appropriate if your wallet has been stolen or if you've been taken in by a "phishing" scam. When you place an initial fraud alert on your credit report, you're entitled to one free credit report from each of the three nationwide consumer reporting companies.

An extended alert stays on your credit report for seven years. You can have an extended alert placed on your credit report if you've been a victim of identity theft and you provide the consumer reporting company with an "identity theft report." When you place an extended alert on your credit report, you're entitled to two free credit reports within twelve months from each of the three nationwide consumer reporting companies. In addition, the consumer reporting companies will remove your name from marketing lists for pre-screened credit offers for five years unless you ask them to put your name back on the list before then.

To place either of these alerts on your credit report, or to have them removed, you will be required to provide appropriate proof of your identity: that may include your SSN, name, address, and other personal information requested by the consumer reporting company.

When a business sees the alert on your credit report, they must verify your identity before issuing you credit. As part of this verification process, the business may try to contact you directly. This may cause some delays if you're trying to obtain credit. To compensate for possible delays, you may wish to include a cell phone number, where you can be reached easily, in your alert. Remember to keep all contact information in your alert current.

## 2. Close the accounts that you know, or believe, have been tampered with or opened fraudulently.

Call and speak with someone in the security or fraud department of each company. Follow up in writing, and include copies (not originals) of supporting documents. It's important to notify credit card companies and banks in writing. Send your letters by certified mail, return receipt requested, so you can document what the company received and when. Keep a file of your correspondence and enclosures.

When you open new accounts, use new personal identification numbers (PINs) and passwords. Avoid using easily available information like your mother's maiden name, your birth date, the last four digits of your SSN or your phone number, or a series of consecutive numbers.

If the identity thief has made charges or debits on your accounts, or on fraudulently opened accounts, ask the company for the forms to dispute those transactions:

- For charges and debits on existing accounts, ask the representative to send you the company's fraud dispute forms. If the company doesn't have special forms, send a letter to dispute the fraudulent charges or debits. In either case, write to the company at the address given for "billing inquiries," NOT the address for sending your payments.

- For new unauthorized accounts, ask if the company accepts the ID Theft Affidavit. If not, ask the representative to send you the company's fraud dispute forms. If the company already has reported these accounts or debts on your credit report, dispute this fraudulent information.

Once you have resolved your identity theft dispute with the company, ask for a letter stating that the company has closed the disputed accounts and has discharged the fraudulent debts. This letter is your best proof if errors relating to this account reappear on your credit report or you are contacted again about the fraudulent debt.

### 3. File a report with your local police or the police in the community where the identity theft took place.

Then, get a copy of the police report or at the very least, the number of the report. It can help you deal with creditors who need proof of the crime. If the police are reluctant to take your report, ask to file a "Miscellaneous Incidents" report, or try another jurisdiction, like your state police. You also can check with your state Attorney General's office to find out if state law requires the police to take reports for identity theft. Check the Blue Pages of your telephone directory for the phone number or check http://www.naag.org for a list of State Attorneys General.

### 4. File a complaint with the Federal Trade Commission.

By sharing your identity theft complaint with the FTC, you will provide important information that can help law enforcement officials across the nation track down identity thieves and stop them. The FTC can refer victims' complaints to other government agencies and companies for further action, as well as investigate companies for violations of laws the agency enforces. Information for contacting the FTC is given at the end of this chapter.

## The Identity Theft Report

An identity theft report may have two parts:

**Part One:** Part One is a copy of a report filed with a local, state, or federal law enforcement agency, like your local police department, your State Attorney General, the Federal Bureau of Investigation (FBI), the U.S. Secret Service, the FTC, and the U.S. Postal Inspection Service. There is no federal law requiring a federal agency to take a report about identity theft; however, some state laws require local police departments to take reports. When you file a report, provide as much information as you can about the crime, including anything you know about the dates of the identity theft, the fraudulent accounts opened and the alleged identity thief. (Note: Knowingly submitting false information could subject you to criminal prosecution for perjury.)

**Part Two:** Part Two of an identity theft report depends on the policies of the consumer reporting company and the information provider (the business that sent the information to the consumer reporting company). That is, they may ask you to provide information or documentation in addition to that included in the law enforcement report which is reasonably intended to verify your identity theft. They must make their request within 15 days of receiving your law enforcement report, or, if you already obtained an extended fraud alert on your credit report, the date you submit your request to the credit reporting company for information blocking. The consumer reporting company and information provider then have 15 more days to work with you to make sure your identity theft report contains everything they need. They are entitled to take five days to review any information you give them. For example, if you give them information 11 days after they request it, they do not have to make a final decision until 16 days after they asked you for that information. If you give them any information after the 15-day deadline, they can reject your identity theft report as incomplete; you will have to resubmit your identity theft report with the correct information.

You may find that most federal and state agencies, and some local police departments, offer only "automated" reports—a report that does not require a face-to-face meeting with a law enforcement officer. Automated reports may be submitted online, or by telephone or mail. If you have a choice, do not use an automated report. The reason? It's more difficult for the consumer reporting company or information provider to verify the information. Unless you are asking a consumer reporting company to place an extended fraud alert on your credit report, you probably will have to provide additional information or documentation when you use an automated report.

## When the News Reports Say Your Personal Information May Be at Risk

You've probably seen reports on the news or in the paper about major "security breaches" in which a retailer, credit card processing firm, or some other company revealed that confidential account information was "lost" or stolen. Chances are that you worried about your credit card numbers, Social Security number, or other personal data being in the possession of identity thieves who might commit fraud in your name. Here's what to know and do:

- New rules require a financial institution or its service provider to notify customers of security breaches. Starting April 1, 2005, the Federal Deposit Insurance Corporation (FDIC) and other federal banking regulators require that banks issue notices in the event of unauthorized access to sensitive data, including Social Security numbers, account numbers, passwords, and other information that could result in "substantial harm or inconvenience to any customer." "If you receive one of these notices, your financial institution will spell out the steps you should take to protect yourself," said Kathryn Weatherby, an FDIC bank technology supervision specialist. "Or, if the situation is serious enough, your bank may replace your credit card with a new one and close your old account."

- Keep a close watch on your credit card bills and bank statements. Look at your monthly statements as soon as they arrive and report a discrepancy or anything suspicious, such as a missing payment or an unauthorized withdrawal. While federal and state laws may limit your losses if you're a victim of fraud or theft, your protections may be stronger if you report the problem quickly and in writing. Also contact your institution if a statement doesn't arrive on time because that could be a sign that an ID thief has stolen your mail and/or account information to commit fraud in your name from another location.

- Exercise your new rights to review your credit record and report fraudulent activity. Your credit report, which is prepared by a credit bureau, summarizes your history of paying debts and other bills. Under the Fair and Accurate Credit Transactions Act (FACTA), as of September 1, 2005, residents in all 50 states and U.S. territories, can get one free credit report each year from each of the nation's three major credit bureaus. The new law took effect in western states last December and has been gradually moving east. Experts suggest spreading out your requests throughout the year—get one free report every four months instead of three at the same time—to maximize your protection. To get your free report, go to http://www.annualcreditreport.com or call toll-free 877-322-8228. Review your credit report for warning signs of actual or potential ID theft, such as mention of a credit card, loan, or lease you never signed up for.

- If you already are a victim of ID theft or you suspect you are a target, FACTA gives you new rights to place a fraud alert in your credit files at all three major credit bureaus by calling or writing any one of their fraud departments. "These fraud alerts will help prevent an impostor from obtaining new credit in your name because, at a minimum, the lender will be required to make a reasonable attempt to verify the applicant's identity," explained Weatherby.

## Who to Call to Report a Possible ID Theft

**The fraud department at any one of the three major credit bureaus:** Ask for a fraud alert to be placed in your file at all three companies. The alert tells lenders and other users of credit reports to be careful before opening or changing accounts in your name. Also followup with a letter. The special toll-free numbers for the fraud departments are: Equifax at 800-525-6285, Experian at (888) 397-3742 and TransUnion at 800 680-7289. Get addresses and other details at http://www.equifax.com, http://www.experian.com and http://www.transunion.com.

**Your bank, credit card company or any other financial institution that may need to know:** Ask to speak with someone in the security or fraud department, and follow up with a letter. If necessary, close old accounts and open new ones, and select new passwords and "PINs"(personal identification numbers).

**Your local police or the police where the identity theft occurred:** Fill out a police report that will detail what happened and get a copy for future reference.

**The Federal Trade Commission (FTC):** Call toll-free 877-IDTHEFT (438-4338). Fill out a complaint form online at the FTC's ID Theft website at www.consumer.gov/idtheft. Or, mail a letter to: Identity Theft Clearinghouse, Federal Trade Commission, 600 Pennsylvania Avenue, NW, Washington, DC 20580. An "ID Theft Affidavit" available on the FTC website also can be used to help you prove you are an innocent victim and help you keep debts you did not incur from appearing on your credit report.

# Chapter 57

# *Safeguarding Online Brokerage Accounts*

Let's hope this never happens to you: You have a few free minutes so you decide to go online to check your brokerage account information. Your account balance is much lower than you expect—and you know that, at least for today, neither the market nor any of your securities fell in value. You see that there were several wire transfers of money from your account to an outside checking account. But you never authorized those transactions—instead, an identity thief did, and that thief has now stolen your cash as well as your personal information.

Like many investors, you may enjoy some of the conveniences of an online brokerage account, like checking your brokerage account information at any time of day or night, buying and selling securities, or even transferring money between your brokerage account and another account. But if you don't take steps to protect your personal information when you go online, you could be telling your own story of identity theft.

## *How Online Identity Theft Can Happen*

Many identity thieves use malicious software programs to attack vulnerable computers of online users. These software programs can monitor your computer activity and send information back to the

"Online Brokerage Accounts: What You Can Do to Safeguard Your Money and Your Personal Information," U.S. Securities and Exchange Commission (www.sec.gov), November 2005.

thief's computer. Sometimes, these programs will log your key strokes, which allows identity thieves to easily obtain username and password information for any of your online accounts, including your brokerage account.

Other identity thieves "phish" for your personal information. "Phishing" involves the use of fraudulent e-mails and copy-cat websites to trick you into revealing valuable personal information—such as your account number, your social security number, and the username and password information you use when accessing your account. Sometimes fraudsters will use phishing scams to try to get you to download keystroke logging or other malicious software programs unsuspectingly.

But not all identity thieves have gone "high tech." Many still use less sophisticated ways of stealing your personal information, such as looking over your shoulder when you're typing sensitive information or searching through your trash for confidential account information.

## *How to Protect Yourself Online*

You'll need to protect yourself against identity thieves, whether hackers, phishers, or snoops, when you use your online brokerage account. Here are a few suggestions on ways to keep your personal information and money more secure when you go online:

- **Beef up your security:** Personal firewalls and security software packages (with anti-virus, anti-spam, and spyware detection features) are a must-have for those who engage in online financial transactions. Make sure your computer has the latest security patches, and make sure that you access your online brokerage account only on a secure webpage using encryption. The website address of a secure website connection starts with "https" instead of just "http" and has a key or closed padlock in the status bar (which typically appears in the lower right-hand corner of your screen). Even if a webpage starts with "https" and contains a key or closed padlock, it's still possible that it may not be secure. Some phishers, for example, make spoofed websites which appear to have padlocks. To double-check, click on the padlock icon on the status bar to see the security certificate for the site. Following the "Issued to" in the pop-up window you should see the name matching the site you think you're on. If the name differs, you are probably on a spoofed site.

- **Use a security token (if available):** Using a security token can make it even harder for an identity thief to access your online brokerage account. That's because these small number-generating devices offer a second layer of security—a one-time pass-code that typically changes every 30 or 60 seconds. These unpredictable pass-codes can frustrate identity thieves. While fraudsters can use keystroke logging programs to obtain regular username and password information, they can't use these programs to obtain the security token pass-code. Ask your brokerage firm if you can protect your online account with a security token or similar security device.

- **Be careful what you download:** When you download a program or file from an unknown source, you risk loading malicious software programs on your computer. Fraudsters often hide these programs within seemingly benign applications. Think twice before you click on a pop-up advertisement or download a "free" game or gadget.

- **Use your own computer:** It's generally safer to access your online brokerage account from your own computer than from other computers. If you use a computer other than your own, for example, you won't know if it contains viruses or spyware. If you do use another computer, be sure to delete all of the your "Temporary Internet Files" and clear all of your "History" after you log off your account.

- **Don't respond to e-mails requesting personal information:** Legitimate entities will not ask you to provide or verify sensitive information through a non-secure means, such as e-mail. If you have reason to believe that your financial institution actually does need personal information from you, pick up the phone and call the company yourself—using the number in your rolodex, not the one the e-mail provides. Even though a web address in an e-mail may look legitimate, fraudsters can mask the true destination. Rather than merely clicking on a link provided in an e-mail, type the web address into your browser yourself (or use a bookmark you previously created).

- **Be smart about your password:** The best passwords are ones that are difficult to guess. Try using a password that consists of a combination of numbers, letters (both upper case and lower case), punctuation, and special characters. You should change your password regularly and use a different password for each of your accounts. Don't share your password with others and never reply to "phishing" e-mails with your password or other sensitive information. You also shouldn't store your password on your computer. If you need to write down your password, store it in a secure, private place.

- **Use extra caution with wireless connections:** Wireless networks may not provide as much security as wired internet connections. In fact, many "hotspots"—wireless networks in public areas like airports, hotels and restaurants—reduce their security so it's easier for individuals to access and use these wireless networks. Unless you use a security token, you may decide that accessing your online brokerage account through a wireless connection isn't worth the security risk.

- **Log out completely:** Closing or minimizing your browser or typing in a new web address when you're done using your online account may not be enough to prevent others from gaining access to your account information. Instead, click on the "log out" button to terminate your online session. In addition, you shouldn't permit your browser to "remember" your username and password information. If this browser feature is active, anyone using your computer will have access to your brokerage account information.

## How to Know If Your Identity Has Been Stolen

Sometimes, it can be extraordinarily difficult to determine whether someone has stolen your identity. If you take the steps below, you may be able to find out whether you've been victim of identity theft and protect yourself from further harm:

- **Read your statements:** Don't toss aside your monthly account statements. Read them thoroughly as soon as they arrive to make sure that all transactions shown are ones that you actually made, and check to see whether all of the transactions that you thought you made appear as well. Be sure that your brokerage firm has current contact information for you, including your mailing address and e-mail address. If you see a mistake on your statement or don't receive a statement, contact your brokerage firm immediately.

- **Monitor your credit report:** Reviewing your credit report may alert you to unauthorized activity, and, therefore, can be an effective way to fight identity theft. You can obtain a free credit report every 12 months from three different credit bureaus by contacting the Annual Credit Report Request Service (http://www.annualcreditreport.com).

**Investor tip:** Read your brokerage account agreement carefully because many firms take the position that you are responsible for the security of your account information, such as your username, password, and account number. In addition, your brokerage account agreement may provide information about what specific steps you should take if you notice any unauthorized account activity.

## What to Do If You Run into Trouble

Always act quickly when you come face to face with a potential fraud, especially if you've lost money or believe your identity has been stolen.

- **Identity theft:** If you think that your personal information has been stolen, visit the Federal Trade Commission's Identity Theft Resource Center at www.consumer.gov/idtheft/index.html for information on how to file a complaint and control the damage.

- **Securities scams:** Before you do business with any investment-related firm or individual, do your own independent research to check out their background and confirm whether they are legitimate.

- **Phishy e-mails:** If a phishing scam rolls into your e-mail box, be sure to tell the company right away. You can also report the scam to the FBI's Internet Crime Complaint Center at http://www.ic3.gov. If the e-mail purports to come from a brokerage firm or mutual fund company, be sure to pass along that tip to the SEC's Enforcement Division by forwarding the e-mail to enforcement@sec.gov.

# Chapter 58

# *Internet Investment Scams*

## *Online Investment Opportunities: 'Net Profit or 'Net Gloss?*

When it comes to investment opportunities on the internet, keep a watchful eye. The web has many legitimate investment opportunities, but it also plays host to some unscrupulous players. Unfortunately for potential investors, sometimes it's tough to tell the difference.

Some fraudulent investment promoters fool visitors through websites that make their "investment company" look like a solid, top-rated Wall Street investment firm. Other fly-by-night companies can feature slick-looking websites that use graphics, audio, and even video clips. Still others pique your curiosity with messages on Usenet groups that promise big profits and direct you to call or e-mail for more information. When you respond, you'll hear enticements such as the following:

- Offers of a "ground floor opportunity" for you to realize a better return on the investment than any other you're involved in

- Guarantees of big profits in a short time

- Claims that minimize or mask the risk involved

- Lots of pressure to act now because the "market is moving"

This chapter includes "Online Investment Opportunities: 'Net Profit or 'Net Gloss?" Federal Trade Commission (www.ftc.gov), December 1998; and "Internet Fraud: How to Avoid Internet Investment Scams," U.S. Securities and Exchange Commission (www.sec.gov), April 2005.

Before you respond to any online investment opportunities, the Federal Trade Commission says to look for these signs of a company that may not be on the up-and-up:

- **"This investment is IRA approved":** Some online investment opportunities may claim that their investment has been "approved" for your IRA. Don't believe it. The IRS does not "approve" investments for IRAs.

- **"Our website will match you with investment opportunities":** "Matchmaker" websites offer to find investment opportunities that appeal to your unique interests. Ask questions. Get satisfactory answers. Do the operators of the website disclose their identities and affiliations, if any, with the investments they're touting? Do they insist on their fee before they allow you to view their list of offerings? Who are you dealing with? Get detailed information about the company, be wary of any up-front fees, and keep your bank account information to yourself.

- **"Offshore investments are tax-free and confidential":** When the company behind the website claims to be located offshore or offers an "offshore, tax-free" investment, get a second opinion from someone you trust—your attorney, financial advisor, or accountant—who is knowledgeable about the tax implications of "offshore" investments.

- **"Submit your financial information online":** Some websites may ask you to submit personal financial information online to determine whether you're an "accredited investor." In addition to your name and e-mail address, you may be asked for your income level, bank account information, Social Security Number and other personal information. Sometimes, this is a ploy to develop a "lead list" of potential investors. In any case, be very careful before you submit any personal information online. Before you do, visit the site's privacy policy. It should tell you what personal information the site collects and how the information is used.

## How to Avoid Internet Investment Scams

The internet serves as an excellent tool for investors, allowing them to easily and inexpensively research investment opportunities. But the internet is also an excellent tool for fraudsters. That's why you should always think twice before you invest your money in any opportunity you learn about through the internet.

This alert tells you how to spot different types of internet fraud, what the U.S. Securities and Exchange Commission (SEC) is doing to fight internet investment scams, and how to use the internet to invest wisely.

## *Navigating the Frontier: Where the Frauds Are*

The internet allows individuals or companies to communicate with a large audience without spending a lot of time, effort, or money. Anyone can reach tens of thousands of people by building an internet website, posting a message on an online bulletin board, entering a discussion in a live "chat" room, or sending mass e-mails. It's easy for fraudsters to make their messages look real and credible. But it's nearly impossible for investors to tell the difference between fact and fiction.

## *Online Investment Newsletters*

Hundreds of online investment newsletters have appeared on the internet in recent years. Many offer investors seemingly unbiased information free of charge about featured companies or recommending "stock picks of the month." While legitimate online newsletters can help investors gather valuable information, some online newsletters are tools for fraud.

Some companies pay the people who write online newsletters cash or securities to "tout" or recommend their stocks. While this isn't illegal, the federal securities laws require the newsletters to disclose who paid them, the amount, and the type of payment. But many fraudsters fail to do so. Instead, they'll lie about the payments they received, their independence, their so-called research, and their track records. Their newsletters masquerade as sources of unbiased information, when in fact they stand to profit handsomely if they convince investors to buy or sell particular stocks.

Some online newsletters falsely claim to independently research the stocks they profile. Others spread false information or promote worthless stocks. The most notorious sometimes "scalp" the stocks they hype, driving up the price of the stock with their baseless recommendations and then selling their own holdings at high prices and high profits. For more information about separating the good from the bad, you may want to read the SEC publication "Tips for Checking Out Newsletters," available online at http://www.sec.gov/investor/pubs/cyberfraud/newsletter.htm.

## *Bulletin Boards*

Online bulletin boards—whether newsgroups, usenet, or web-based bulletin boards—have become an increasingly popular forum for investors to share information. Bulletin boards typically feature "threads" made up of numerous messages on various investment opportunities.

While some messages may be true, many turn out to be bogus—or even scams. Fraudsters often pump up a company or pretend to reveal "inside" information about upcoming announcements, new products, or lucrative contracts.

Also, you never know for certain who you're dealing with—or whether they're credible—because many bulletin boards allow users to hide their identity behind multiple aliases. People claiming to be unbiased observers who've carefully researched the company may actually be company insiders, large shareholders, or paid promoters. A single person can easily create the illusion of widespread interest in a small, thinly-traded stock by posting a series of messages under various aliases.

## *E-mail Spams*

Because "spam"—junk e-mail—is so cheap and easy to create, fraudsters increasingly use it to find investors for bogus investment schemes or to spread false information about a company. Spam allows the unscrupulous to target many more potential investors than cold calling or mass mailing. Using a bulk e-mail program, spammers can send personalized messages to thousands and even millions of internet users at a time.

## *How to Use the Internet to Invest Wisely*

If you want to invest wisely and steer clear of frauds, you must get the facts. Never, ever, make an investment based solely on what you read in an online newsletter or bulletin board posting, especially if the investment involves a small, thinly-traded company that isn't well known. And don't even think about investing on your own in small companies that don't file regular reports with the SEC, unless you are willing to investigate each company thoroughly and to check the truth of every statement about the company. For instance, you'll need to:

- get financial statements from the company and be able to analyze them;

- verify the claims about new product developments or lucrative contracts;

- call every supplier or customer of the company and ask if they really do business with the company; and

- check out the people running the company and find out if they've ever made money for investors before.

Here's how you can use the internet to help you invest wisely:

**Start with the SEC's EDGAR Database:** EDGAR stands for Electronic Data Gathering, Analysis, and Retrieval. The federal securities laws require many public companies to register with the SEC and file annual reports containing audited financial statements. For example, the following companies must file reports with the SEC:

- All U.S. companies with more than 500 investors and $10 million in net assets; and

- All companies that list their securities on The NASDAQ Stock Market or a major national stock exchange such as the New York Stock Exchange.

Anyone can access and download these reports from the SEC's EDGAR database for free (http://www.sec.gov/edgar.shtml). Before you invest in a company, check to see whether it's registered with the SEC and read its reports.

But some companies don't have to register their securities or file reports on EDGAR. For example, companies raising less than $5 million in a 12-month period may be exempt from registering the transaction under a rule known as "Regulation A." Instead, these companies must file a hard copy of the "offering circular" with the SEC containing financial statements and other information. Also, smaller companies raising less than one million dollars don't have to register with the SEC, but they must file a "Form D." Form D is a brief notice which includes the names and addresses of owners and stock promoters, but little other information. If you can't find a company on EDGAR, call the SEC at 202-551-8090 to find out if the company filed an offering circular under Regulation A or a Form D. And be sure to request a copy.

The difference between investing in companies that register with the SEC and those that don't is like the difference between driving on a clear sunny day and driving at night without your headlights. You're asking for serious losses if you invest in small, thinly-traded companies that aren't widely known just by following the signs you read on internet bulletin boards or online newsletters.

**Contact your state securities regulators:** Don't stop with the SEC. You should always check with your state securities regulator, which you can find on the website of the North American Securities Administrators Association (http://www.nasaa.org), to see if they have more information about the company and the people behind it. They can check the Central Registration Depository (CRD) and tell you whether the broker touting the stock or the broker's firm has a disciplinary history. They can also tell you whether they've cleared the offering for sale in your state.

**Check with NASD:** To check the disciplinary history of the broker or firm that's touting the stock, use the National Association of Security Dealers (NASD)'s BrokerCheck website (http://www.nasdbrokercheck.com), or call NASD's BrokerCheck Program hotline at 800-289-9999.

## *Online Investment Fraud: New Medium, Same Old Scam*

The types of investment fraud seen online mirror the frauds perpetrated over the phone or through the mail. Remember that fraudsters can use a variety of internet tools to spread false information, including bulletin boards, online newsletters, spam, or chat (including Internet Relay Chat or Web Page Chat). They can also build a glitzy, sophisticated webpage. All of these tools cost very little money and can be found at the fingertips of fraudsters.

Consider all offers with skepticism. Investment frauds usually fit one of the following categories:

**The "pump and dump" scam:** It's common to see messages posted online that urge readers to buy a stock quickly or tell you to sell before the price goes down. Often the writers will claim to have "inside" information about an impending development or to use an "infallible" combination of economic and stock market data to pick stocks. In reality, they may be insiders or paid promoters who stand to gain by selling their shares after the stock price is pumped up by gullible investors. Once these fraudsters sell their shares and stop hyping the stock, the price typically falls and investors lose their money. Fraudsters frequently use this ploy with small, thinly-traded companies because it's easier to manipulate a stock when there's little or no information available about the company.

**The pyramid:** Be wary of messages that read: "How To Make Big Money From Your Home Computer!!!" One online promoter claimed that investors could "turn $5 into $60,000 in just three to six weeks." In reality, this program was nothing more than an electronic version of the classic "pyramid" scheme in which participants attempt to make money solely by recruiting new participants into the program.

**The "risk-free" fraud:** "Exciting, Low-Risk Investment Opportunities" to participate in exotic-sounding investments—such as wireless cable projects, prime bank securities, and eel farms—have been offered through the internet. But no investment is risk-free. And sometimes the investment products touted do not even exist—they're merely scams. Be wary of opportunities that promise spectacular profits or "guaranteed" returns. If the deal sounds too good to be true, then it probably is.

**Off-shore frauds:** At one time, off-shore schemes targeting U.S. investors cost a great deal of money and were difficult to carry out. Conflicting time zones, differing currencies, and the high costs of international telephone calls and overnight mailings made it difficult for fraudsters to prey on U.S. residents. But the internet has removed those obstacles. Be extra careful when considering any investment opportunity that comes from another country, because it's difficult for U.S. law enforcement agencies to investigate and prosecute foreign frauds.

### The SEC Is Tracking Fraud

The SEC actively investigates allegations of internet investment fraud and, in many cases, has taken quick action to stop scams. They've also coordinated with federal and state criminal authorities to put internet fraudsters in jail. Here's a sampling of recent cases in which the SEC took action to fight internet fraud:

- Francis A. Tribble and Sloane Fitzgerald, Inc. sent more than six million unsolicited e-mails, built bogus websites, and distributed an online newsletter over a ten-month period to promote two small, thinly traded "microcap" companies. Because they failed to tell investors that the companies they were touting had agreed to pay them in cash and securities, the SEC sued both Tribble and Sloane to stop them from violating the law again and imposed a $15,000 penalty on Tribble. Their massive spamming campaign triggered the largest number of complaints to the SEC's online Enforcement Complaint Center.

- Charles O. Huttoe and twelve other defendants secretly distributed to friends and family nearly 42 million shares of Systems of Excellence Inc., known by its ticker symbol "SEXI." Huttoe drove up the price of SEXI shares through false press releases claiming non-existent multi-million dollar sales, an acquisition that had not occurred, and revenue projections that had no basis in reality. He also bribed co-defendant SGA Goldstar to tout SEXI to subscribers of SGA Goldstar's online "Whisper Stocks" newsletter. The SEC obtained court orders freezing Huttoe's assets and those of various others who participated in the scheme or who received fraud proceeds. Six people, including Huttoe and Theodore R. Melcher, Jr., the author of the online newsletter, were also convicted of criminal violations. Both Huttoe and Melcher were sentenced to federal prison. The SEC has thus far recovered approximately $11 million in illegal profits from the various defendants.

- Matthew Bowin recruited investors for his company, Interactive Products and Services, in a direct public offering done entirely over the internet. He raised $190,000 from 150 investors. But instead of using the money to build the company, Bowin pocketed the proceeds and bought groceries and stereo equipment. The SEC sued Bowin in a civil case, and the Santa Cruz, CA District Attorney's Office prosecuted him criminally. He was convicted of 54 felony counts and sentenced to 10 years in jail.

- IVT Systems solicited investments to finance the construction of an ethanol plant in the Dominican Republic. The internet solicitations promised a return of 50% or more with no reasonable basis for the prediction. Their literature contained lies about contracts with well known companies and omitted other important information for investors. After the SEC filed a complaint, they agreed to stop breaking the law.

- Gene Block and Renate Haag were caught offering "prime bank" securities, a type of security that doesn't even exist. They collected over $3.5 million by promising to double investors' money in four months. The SEC has frozen their assets and stopped them from continuing their fraud.

- Daniel Odulo was stopped from soliciting investors for a proposed eel farm. Odulo promised investors a "whopping 20% return," claiming that the investment was "low risk." When he

486

was caught by the SEC, he consented to the court order stopping him from breaking the securities laws.

If you believe that you have been the victim of a securities-related fraud, through the internet or otherwise, or if you believe that any person or entity may have violated or is currently violating the federal securities laws, you can submit a complaint using the SEC's online complaint form (http://www.sec.gov/complaint.shtml) or e-mail them at enforcement@sec.gov.

# Chapter 59

# *Phishing Fraud*

"Phishing" involves the use of fraudulent e-mails and copy-cat websites to trick you into revealing valuable personal information—such as account numbers for banking, securities, mortgage, or credit accounts, your social security numbers, and the login IDs and passwords you use when accessing online financial services providers. The fraudsters who collect this information then use it to steal your money or your identity or both.

When fraudsters go on "phishing" expeditions, they lure their targets into a false sense of security by hijacking the familiar, trusted logos of established, legitimate companies. A typical phishing scam starts with a fraudster sending out millions of e-mails that appear to come from a high-profile financial services provider or a respected internet auction house.

The e-mail will usually ask you to provide valuable information about yourself or to "verify" information that you previously provided when you established your online account. To maximize the chances that a recipient will respond, the fraudster might employ any or all of the following tactics:

- **Names of real companies:** Rather than create from scratch a phony company, the fraudster might use a legitimate company's name and incorporate the look and feel of its website (including the color scheme and graphics) into the phishy e-mail.

---

"'Phishing' Fraud: How to Avoid Getting Fried by Phony Phishermen," U.S. Securities and Exchange Commission (www.sec.gov), September 2004.

- **"From" an actual employee:** The "from" line or the text of the message (or both) might contain the names of real people who actually work for the company. That way, if you contacted the company to confirm whether "Jane Doe" truly is "VP of Client Services," you'd get a positive response and feel assured.

- **URLs that "look right":** The e-mail might include a convenient link to a seemingly legitimate website where you can enter the information the fraudster wants to steal. But in reality the website will be a quickly cobbled copy-cat—a "spoofed" website that looks for all the world like the real thing. In some cases, the link might lead to select pages of a legitimate website—such as the real company's actual privacy policy or legal disclaimer.

- **Urgent messages:** Many fraudsters use fear to trigger a response, and phishers are no different. In common phishing scams, the e-mails warn that failure to respond will result in your no longer having access to your account. Other e-mails might claim that the company has detected suspicious activity in your account or that it is implementing new privacy software or identity theft solutions.

## How to Protect Yourself from Phishing

The best way you can protect yourself from phony phishers is to understand what legitimate financial service providers and respectable online auction houses will and will not do. Most importantly, legitimate entities will not ask you to provide or verify sensitive information through a non-secure means, such as e-mail.

Follow these five simple steps to protect yourself from phishers:

1. **Pick up the phone to verify:** Do not respond to any e-mails that request personal or financial information, especially ones that use pressure tactics or prey on fear. If you have reason to believe that a financial institution actually does need personal information from you, pick up the phone and call the company yourself—using the number in your rolodex, not the one the e-mail provides!

2. **Do your own typing:** Rather than merely clicking on the link provided in the e-mail, type the URL into your web browser yourself (or use a bookmark you previously created). Even though a URL in an e-mail may look like the real deal, fraudsters can mask the true destination.

3. **Beef up your security:** Personal firewalls and security software packages (with anti-virus, anti-spam, and spyware detection features) are a must-have for those who engage in online financial transactions. Make sure your computer has the latest security patches, and make sure that you conduct your financial transactions only on a secure webpage using encryption. You can tell if a page is secure in a couple of ways. Look for a closed padlock in the status bar, and see that the URL starts with "https" instead of just "http." Some phishers make spoofed websites which appear to have padlocks. To double-check, click on the padlock icon on the status bar to see the security certificate for the site. Following the "Issued to" in the pop-up window you should see the name matching the site you think you're on. If the name differs, you are probably on a spoofed site.

4. **Read your statements:** Don't toss aside your monthly account statements! Read them thoroughly as soon as they arrive to make sure that all transactions shown are ones that you actually made, and check to see whether all of the transactions that you thought you made appear as well. Be sure that the company has current contact information for you, including your mailing address and e-mail address.

5. **Spot the sharks:** Visit the website of the Anti-Phishing Working Group at http://www.antiphishing.org for a list of current phishing attacks and the latest news in the fight to prevent phishing. There you'll find more information about phishing and links to helpful resources.

## *What to Do If You Run into Trouble*

Always act quickly when you come face to face with a potential fraud, especially if you've lost money or believe your identity has been stolen.

- **Phishy e-mails:** If a phishing scam rolls into your e-mail box, be sure to tell the company right away. You can also report the scam to the FBI's Internet Crime Complaint Center http://www.ic3.gov. If the e-mail purports to come from a brokerage firm or mutual fund company, be sure to pass along that tip to the SEC's (Securities and Exchange Commission) Enforcement Division by forwarding the e-mail to enforcement@sec.gov.

491

- **Identity theft:** If you think that your personal information has been stolen, visit the Federal Trade Commission's Identity Theft Resource Center at http://www.consumer.gov/idtheft/index.html for information on how to file a complaint and control the damage.

- **Securities scams:** Before you do business with any investment-related firm or individual, do your own independent research to check out their background and confirm whether they are legitimate. Report investment-related scams to the SEC using the online Complaint Center (http://www.sec.gov/complaint.shtml).

# Chapter 60

# *"Wrong Numbers"*
# *and Stock Tips on Your*
# *Answering Machine*

You come home after a long, honest day's work, stroll by your message machine, and see the light blinking. Did a loved one call with good news? Is there a friend calling to find out what you're doing tomorrow? Some people are finding that they have instead received a "misdialed" call from a stranger, leaving a "hot" investment tip for a friend. The message is designed to sound as if the speaker didn't realize that he or she was leaving the hot tip on the wrong machine. Maybe the message sounds like this:

- "Hey Tracy, it's Debbie. I couldn't find your old number and Tammy says this is the new one. I hope it's the right one. Anyway, remember that hot stock exchange guy that I'm dating? He gave my father that stock tip on the company that went from under a buck to like three bucks in two weeks and you were mad I didn't call you? Well I'm calling you now! This new company is supposed to be like the next really hot clothing thing. And they're making some big news announcement this week. The stock symbol is... He says buy now. It's at like 50 cents and it's going up to like 5 or 6 bucks this week so get as much as you can. Call me on my cell, I'm still in Orlando. My Dad and I are buying a bunch tomorrow and I already called Kelly and Ron too. Anyway I miss you, give me a call. Bye."

---

"'Wrong Numbers' and Stock Tips on Your Answering Machine," U.S. Securities and Exchange Commission (www.sec.gov), January 2006.

If you get a message like this, it's not a wrong number at all. Instead, it is from someone who is being paid to leave these messages on a whole lot of answering machines. The people paying for this message to go out on hundreds or thousands of answering machines own some of this stock. They are hoping you can be tricked into buying some too, as they stand to gain by selling their shares if the stock price rises because gullible investors buy. Once these fraudsters sell their shares and stop hyping the stock, the price typically falls and investors lose their money. Fraudsters frequently use this ploy with small, thinly-traded companies because it's easier to manipulate a stock when there's little or no information available about the company.

These scams have also migrated to e-mail and faxes. Be extremely wary of an e-mail message that starts out like this:

> Hey you!
> PLEASE don't tell anyone about this e-mail, because if the SEC finds out, I could get in big trouble for passing on this information, maybe even go to jail.
> This is super important! I hope I have the right e-mail for you. Your messages keep bouncing back because your mailbox is full, and I seem to remember this is your other account. I tried calling but you're not home...arghh! OK here's the news...

And look out for a fax transmission that says, "Will you please put your cell phone on. I have been trying to get you for two hours. I have a stock for you that will triple in price just like the last stock I gave you did. I can't get you on either phone. Either call me, or call Linda to place the new trade. We need to buy now. P.S. You better be good to me this Christmas. No other Stock Broker has given you back to back wins. Thanks, your shining star Financial Planner."

It is never a good idea to put your hard-earned money into a stock on the basis of a hot tip from somebody you don't know. There are unscrupulous individuals out there who have a financial stake in trying to drive up the price of companies that you've likely never heard of. Many fraudsters rely on internet chat room sites or spammed investment newsletters to promote companies, but phony misdialed number and misdirected e-mail scams are being reported more and more to the U.S. Securities and Exchange Commission (SEC).

So what should you do if you get one of these messages? Before you delete the phone message, trash the e-mail, or rip up the fax, the SEC would appreciate hearing details about the stock being hyped.

Be sure to tell them the phone number from which the call came (if you're able), forward the e-mail (including the header information), or send a copy of the fax. This kind of information is invaluable as they seek to enforce the federal securities laws. You can use the SEC's on-line complaint form, at www.sec.gov/complaint.shtml, e-mail at enforcement@sec.gov, send a fax at 202-772-9295, or you can call them at 800-SEC-0330. The SEC welcomes your help in ferreting out fraud in securities sales.

After you send the SEC the information, they suggest you delete the phone message or e-mail. Then congratulate yourself for not falling victim to this kind of scam!

Here's a list of red flags in many frauds:

- **If it sounds too good to be true, it is:** Any investment opportunity that claims that there are huge guaranteed rewards, especially for acting quickly, are incredibly risky, and more likely to lead to losing some, most, or all of your money.

- **"Guaranteed returns" aren't:** Every investment carries some degree of risk, and the level of risk typically correlates with the return you can expect to receive. Low risk generally means low yields, and high yields typically involve high risk. If your money is perfectly safe, you'll most likely get a low return. High returns represent potential rewards for folks who are willing to take big risks. Most fraudsters spend a lot of time trying to convince investors that extremely high returns are "guaranteed" or "can't miss." Don't believe it.

- **Check out the company before you invest:** If you've never heard of a company, broker, or adviser, spend some time checking them out before you invest. Most public companies make electronic filings with the SEC. There are computerized databases to check out brokers and advisers. Your state securities regulator may have additional information. And by the way—if a supposedly upright firm only lists a P.O. box, you'll want to do a lot of work before sending your money!

- **If it is that good, it will wait:** Scam artists usually try to create a sense of urgency—implying that if you don't act now, you'll miss out on a fabulous opportunity. But savvy investors take time to do their homework before investing. If you're told something is a once-in-a-lifetime, too-good-to-be-true opportunity that "just can't miss," just say "no." Your wallet will thank you.

# Chapter 61

# *Pump and Dump Schemes*

One of the most common internet frauds involves the classic "pump and dump" scheme. Here's how it works: A company's website may feature a glowing press release about its financial health or some new product or innovation. Newsletters that purport to offer unbiased recommendations may suddenly tout the company as the latest "hot" stock. Messages in chat rooms and bulletin board postings may urge you to buy the stock quickly or to sell before the price goes down. Or you may even hear the company mentioned by a radio or TV analyst.

Unwitting investors then purchase the stock in droves, creating high demand, and pumping up the price. But when the fraudsters behind the scheme sell their shares at the peak and stop hyping the stock, the price plummets, and investors lose their money.

Fraudsters frequently use this ploy with small, thinly traded companies because it's easier to manipulate a stock when there's little or no information available about the company. To steer clear of potential scams, always investigate before you invest:

- **Consider the source:** When you see an offer on the internet, assume it is a scam, until you can prove through your own research that it is legitimate. And remember that the people touting the stock may well be insiders of the company or paid promoters who stand to profit handsomely if you trade.

---

"Pump&Dump.con: Tips for Avoiding Stock Scams on the Internet," U.S. Securities and Exchange Commission (www.sec.gov), January 2005.

- **Find out where the stock trades:** Many of the smallest and most thinly traded stocks cannot meet the listing requirements of the NASDAQ Stock Market or a national exchange, such as the New York Stock Exchange. Instead they trade in the "over-the-counter" market and are quoted on OTC systems, such as the OTC Bulletin Board or the Pink Sheets. Stocks that trade in the OTC market are generally among the most risky and most susceptible to manipulation.

- **Independently verify claims:** It's easy for a company or its promoters to make grandiose claims about new product developments, lucrative contracts, or the company's financial health. But before you invest, make sure you've independently verified those claims.

- **Research the opportunity:** Always ask for—and carefully read—the prospectus or current financial statements. Check the U.S. Securities and Exchange (SEC)'s EDGAR (Electronic Data Gathering, Analysis, and Retrieval) database, online at http://www.sec.gov/edgar.shtml, to see whether the investment is registered. Some smaller companies don't have to register their securities offerings with the SEC, so always check with your state securities regulator, too (visit http://www.nasaa.org).

- **Watch out for high-pressure pitches:** Beware of promoters who pressure you to buy before you have a chance to think about and fully investigate the so-called "opportunity." Don't fall for the line that you'll lose out on a "once-in-a-lifetime" chance to make big money if you don't act quickly.

- **Always be skeptical:** Whenever someone you don't know offers you a hot stock tip, ask yourself: Why me? Why is this stranger giving me this tip? How might he or she benefit if I trade?

# Chapter 62

# *Promissory Note Fraud*

A promissory note is a form of debt—similar to a loan or an IOU—that a company may issue to raise money. Typically, an investor agrees to loan money to the company for a set period of time. In exchange, the company promises to pay the investor a fixed return on his or her investment, typically principal plus annual interest.

While promissory notes can be legitimate investments, those that are marketed broadly to individual investors often turn out to be scams. The U.S. Securities and Exchange Commission (SEC) and state securities regulators across the nation have joined forces to combat the fraudulent sale of promissory notes to investors. But they can't stop every fraud.

That's why you should ask tough questions—and demand answers—before you consider investing in a promissory note. Be sure you understand how they work and what risks they pose. These tips will explain how promissory note fraud can occur and will help you to spot the scams.

## Anatomy of a Promissory Note Fraud

Fraudsters across the nation have recently begun to use promissory notes as vehicles to defraud investors out of hundreds of millions of dollars. Most promissory note scams follow predictable, fraudulent fact patterns:

---

"Broken Promises: Promissory Note Fraud," U.S. Securities and Exchange Commission (www.sec.gov), January 2006.

- The fraudsters—who may or may not be affiliated with the company—persuade independent life insurance agents to sell promissory notes, luring them with lucrative commissions of up to twenty or even thirty percent. These agents often do not have a license to sell securities. And in selling the notes, they frequently rely solely on the information the company gives them—which later proves to be false or misleading.

- Investors purchase the promissory notes, enticed by the promise of a high, fixed-rate return—up to fifteen or twenty percent—with a very low level of risk. The promissory notes may appear all the more attractive because the seller falsely claims that they're "guaranteed" or insured. And few investors ask tough questions about these investments because they know and trust the sellers, insurance agents with whom they've done business in the past.

- The fraudsters use a portion of the money they collect from investors to pay the sellers their commissions. But they typically abscond with the rest, squandering it on personal expenses or high-flying life styles.

- They may also use some of the proceeds to support an elaborate "Ponzi" scheme in which money coming in from the sale of new notes pays the interest on older notes. Some fraudsters try to avoid repaying investors' principal by convincing investors to "roll-over" their promissory notes upon maturity. These investors may, for at least a time, continue to receive interest payments—but they rarely get their principal back.

Promissory note scams often target the elderly, bilking them of their retirement savings at a time when they can least afford to lose it. But no one is immune. Fraudsters rarely discriminate when it comes to separating investors from their money. And most investors don't even realize their investment dollars are at risk until it's far too late.

## Tips to Avoid Promissory Note Scams

Here's how you can avoid the costly mistake of investing in a sham promissory note:

- Bear in mind that legitimate corporate promissory notes are not usually sold to the general public. Instead, they tend to be sold privately to sophisticated buyers who do their own "due diligence" or research on the company. If someone calls you up or knocks on your door trying to sell you a promissory note, chances are you're dealing with a scam.

- Find out whether the investment is registered with the SEC or your state securities regulator—or whether it's exempt from registration. Most legitimate promissory notes can easily be verified by checking the SEC's EDGAR (Electronic Data Gathering, Analysis, and Retrieval) database, available online at http://www.sec.gov/edgar.shtml, or by calling your state securities regulator, which you can find at the website of the North American Securities Administrators Association (http://www.nasaa.org). If the promissory note is not registered, you'll have to do your own thorough investigation to confirm whether the company has the ability to pay its debt.

- Be skeptical if the seller tells you that the promissory note is not a security. The types of promissory notes involved in promissory note scams usually are securities and must be registered with either the SEC or your state securities regulator—or they must meet an exemption.

- Make sure the seller is properly licensed. Insurance agents can't sell securities—including promissory notes—without a securities license. Call your state securities regulator, and ask whether the person or firm is licensed to sell securities in your state and whether they have a record of complaints or fraud. You can also get this information by calling the National Association of Security Dealers (NASD)'s public disclosure hotline at (800) 289-9999 or by visiting their website (http://www.nasd.com).

- Beware of promises of "risk free" returns. These claims are usually the bait con artists use to lure their victims. Always remember that if it sounds too good to be true, it probably is.

- Watch out for promissory notes that are supposedly "insured" or "guaranteed," especially if a foreign insurance company is involved. Be sure to call your state insurance commissioner to find out whether the foreign insurance company can legally do business in the United States. The National Association of Insurance Commissioners website at http://www.naic.org lists contact information for insurance commissioners in the United States.

- Compare the rate of return on the promissory note with current market rates for similar fixed-rate investments, long-term Treasury bonds, or Federal Deposit Insurance Corporation (FDIC)-insured certificates of deposit. If the seller promises an above-market rate on a short-term note, proceed with caution.

## What to Do If You Run into Trouble

If you believe you've invested in a promissory note scam, act promptly. By law, you only have a limited time to take legal action.

Contact the SEC's Office of Investor Education and Assistance. You can send them your complaint by using their online complaint form (http://www.sec.gov/complaint.shtml). Or you can reach them at this address:

U.S. Securities & Exchange Commission
Office of Investor Education and Assistance
450 5th Street, NW
Washington, DC 20549-0213
Fax: 202-772-9295

You should also contact your state securities regulator and, if an insurance agent sold you the promissory note, your state insurance commissioner.

# Chapter 63

# *Pyramid and Ponzi Schemes*

## *Pyramid Schemes*

In the classic "pyramid" scheme, participants attempt to make money solely by recruiting new participants into the program. The hallmark of these schemes is the promise of sky-high returns in a short period of time for doing nothing other than handing over your money and getting others to do the same.

The fraudsters behind a pyramid scheme may go to great lengths to make the program look like a legitimate multi-level marketing program. But despite their claims to have legitimate products or services to sell, these fraudsters simply use money coming in from new recruits to pay off early stage investors. But eventually the pyramid will collapse. At some point the schemes get too big, the promoter cannot raise enough money from new investors to pay earlier investors, and many people lose their money. Table 63.1 shows how pyramid schemes can become impossible to sustain.

This chapter includes the following publications from the U.S. Securities and Exchange Commission (www.sec.gov): "Pyramid Schemes," September 2004; "Ponzi Schemes," April 2001; "Affinity Fraud: How to Avoid Investment Scams That Target Groups," January 2005; and "Auto Surfing: What You Need to Know," February 2006. "The Bottom Line about Multilevel Marketing Plans," is from the Federal Trade Commission, October 2000.

**Table 63.1.** Pyramid schemes become impossible to sustain

| Level | Number of participants needed |
|-------|-------------------------------|
| 1 | 6 |
| 2 | 36 |
| 3 | 216 |
| 4 | 1,296 |
| 5 | 7,776 |
| 6 | 46,656 |
| 7 | 279,936 |
| 8 | 1,679,616 |
| 9 | 10,077,696 |
| 10 | 60,466,176 |
| 11 | 362,797,056* |
| 12 | 2,176,782,336 |
| 13 | 13,060,694,016** |

*This is more than the entire U.S. population.
**This is more than the entire world population.

## "Ponzi" Schemes

Ponzi schemes are a type of illegal pyramid scheme named for Charles Ponzi, who duped thousands of New England residents into investing in a postage stamp speculation scheme back in the 1920s. Ponzi thought he could take advantage of differences between U.S. and foreign currencies used to buy and sell international mail coupons. Ponzi told investors that he could provide a 40% return in just 90 days compared with 5% for bank savings accounts. Ponzi was deluged with funds from investors, taking in $1 million during one three-hour period—and this was 1921! Though a few early investors were paid off to make the scheme look legitimate, an investigation found that Ponzi had only purchased about $30 worth of the international mail coupons.

Decades later, the Ponzi scheme continues to work on the "rob-Peter-to-pay-Paul" principle, as money from new investors is used to pay off earlier investors until the whole scheme collapses.

## Affinity Fraud: How to Avoid Investment Scams That Target Groups

Affinity fraud refers to investment scams that prey upon members of identifiable groups, such as religious or ethnic communities, the elderly, or professional groups. The fraudsters who promote affinity scams frequently are—or pretend to be—members of the group. They often enlist respected community or religious leaders from within the group to spread the word about the scheme, by convincing those people that a fraudulent investment is legitimate and worthwhile. Many times, those leaders become unwitting victims of the fraudster's ruse.

These scams exploit the trust and friendship that exist in groups of people who have something in common. Because of the tight-knit structure of many groups, it can be difficult for regulators or law enforcement officials to detect an affinity scam. Victims often fail to notify authorities or pursue their legal remedies, and instead try to work things out within the group. This is particularly true where the fraudsters have used respected community or religious leaders to convince others to join the investment.

Many affinity scams involve "Ponzi" or pyramid schemes, where new investor money is used to make payments to earlier investors to give the false illusion that the investment is successful. This ploy is used to trick new investors to invest in the scheme and to lull existing investors into believing their investments are safe and secure. In reality, the fraudster almost always steals investor money for personal use. Both types of schemes depend on an unending supply of new investors—when the inevitable occurs, and the supply of investors dries up, the whole scheme collapses and investors discover that most or all of their money is gone.

### How to Avoid Affinity Fraud

Investing always involves some degree of risk. You can minimize your risk of investing unwisely by asking questions and getting the facts about any investment before you buy. To avoid affinity and other scams, you should:

- Check out everything—no matter how trustworthy the person seems who brings the investment opportunity to your attention. Never make an investment based solely on the recommendation of a member of an organization or religious or ethnic group to which you belong. Investigate the investment thoroughly and check the truth of every statement you are told about the investment. Be aware that the person telling you about the investment may have been fooled into believing that the investment is legitimate when it is not.

- Do not fall for investments that promise spectacular profits or "guaranteed" returns. If an investment seems too good to be true, then it probably is. Similarly, be extremely leery of any investment that is said to have no risks; very few investments are risk-free. The greater the potential return from an investment, the greater your risk of losing money. Promises of fast and high profits, with little or no risk, are classic warning signs of fraud.

- Be skeptical of any investment opportunity that is not in writing. Fraudsters often avoid putting things in writing, but legitimate investments are usually in writing. Avoid an investment if you are told they do "not have the time to reduce to writing" the particulars about the investment. You should also be suspicious if you are told to keep the investment opportunity confidential.

- Don't be pressured or rushed into buying an investment before you have a chance to think about—or investigate—the "opportunity." Just because someone you know made money, or claims to have made money, doesn't mean you will too. Be especially skeptical of investments that are pitched as "once-in-a-lifetime" opportunities, particularly when the promoter bases the recommendation on "inside" or confidential information.

- Fraudsters are increasingly using the internet to target particular groups through e-mail spams. If you receive an unsolicited e-mail from someone you don't know, containing a "can't miss" investment, your best move is to pass up the "opportunity" and forward the spam to us at enforcement@sec.gov.

### *Recent Affinity Fraud Schemes*

Affinity frauds can target any group of people who take pride in their shared characteristics, whether they are religious, ethnic, or professional. The SEC has investigated and taken quick action against affinity frauds targeting a wide spectrum of groups. Some of our cases include the following:

- Armenian-American community loses $19 million: The SEC's complaint alleges that this affinity fraud targeted Armenian-

Americans with little investment experience, for some of whom English was a second language.

- Criminal charges against South Florida man for $51.9 million fraud: African American victims of this investment scheme were guaranteed that their investments would generate a 30% risk-free and tax-free annual return.

- "Church Funding Project" costs faithful investors over $3 million: This nationwide scheme primarily targeted African-American churches and raised at least $3 million from over 1000 investing churches located throughout the United States. Believing they would receive large sums of money from the investments, many of the church victims committed to building projects, acquired new debt, spent building funds, and contracted with builders.

- Baptist investors lose over $3.5 million: The victims of this fraud were mainly African-American Baptists, many of whom were elderly and disabled, as well as a number of Baptist churches and religious organizations located in a number of states. The promoter (Randolph, who was a minister himself and who is currently in jail) promised returns ranging between 7 and 30%, but in reality was operating a Ponzi scheme. In addition to a jail sentence, Randolph was ordered to pay $1 million in the SEC's civil action.

- More than 1,000 Latin American investors lose over $325 million: The victims sought low risk investments. Instead, the promoter (who has been sentenced to 12 years in prison) misappropriated their funds and lied about how much money was in their accounts.

- 125 members of various Christian churches lose $7.4 million: The fraudsters allegedly sold members non-existent "prime bank" trading programs by using a sales pitch heavily laden with Biblical references and by enlisting members of the church communities to unwittingly spread the word about the bogus investment.

- $2.5 million stolen from 100 Texas senior citizens: The fraudsters obtained information about the assets and financial condition of the elderly victims who were encouraged to liquidate their safe retirement savings and to invest in securities with higher returns. In reality, the fraudsters never invested the money and stole the funds.

If you have lost money in an affinity fraud scheme or have information about one of these scams, you should contact:

- The SEC Complaint Center (visit http://www.sec.gov/complaint.shtml).

- Your state's securities administrator. You can find links and addresses for your state regulator by visiting the North American Securities Administrators Association's website (http://www.nasaa.org). That organization also has investor tips for avoiding affinity fraud.

## The Bottom Line about Multilevel Marketing Plans

Multilevel or "network" marketing plans are a way of selling goods or services through distributors. These plans typically promise that if you sign up as a distributor, you'll receive commissions—for your sales and those of the people you recruit to become distributors. These recruits sometimes are referred to as your "downline."

Some multilevel marketing plans are legitimate. However, others are illegal pyramid schemes. In pyramids, commissions are based on the number of distributors recruited. Most of the product sales are made to these distributors—not to consumers in general. The underlying goods and services, which vary from vitamins to car leases, serve only to make the schemes look legitimate.

Joining a pyramid is risky because the vast majority of participants lose money to pay for the rewards of a lucky few. Most people end up with nothing to show for their money except the expensive products or marketing materials they're pressured to buy.

If you're thinking about joining what appears to be a legitimate multilevel marketing plan, take time to learn about the plan. What's the company's track record? What products does it sell? Does it sell products to the public-at-large? Does it have the evidence to back up the claims it makes about its product? Is the product competitively priced? Is it likely to appeal to a large customer base? How much is the investment to join the plan? Is there a minimum monthly sales commitment to earn a commission? Will you be required to recruit new distributors to earn your commission?

Be skeptical if a distributor tells you that for the price of a "start-up kit" of inventory and sales literature—and sometimes a commitment to sell a specific amount of the product or service each month—you'll be on the road to riches. Often consumers spend a lot of money to "build their business" by participating in training programs, buying sales leads or purchasing the products themselves. Too often, these purchases are all they ever see for their investments.

### *Your Responsibilities*

If you decide to become a distributor, you are legally responsible for the claims you make about the company, its product and the business opportunities it offers. That applies even if you're repeating claims you read in a company brochure or advertising flyer. The Federal Trade Commission (FTC) advises you to verify the research behind any claims about a product's performance before repeating those claims to a potential customer.

In addition, if you solicit new distributors, you are responsible for the claims you make about a distributor's earnings potential. Be sure to represent the opportunity honestly and avoid making unrealistic promises. If those promises fall through, remember that you could be held liable.

### *Evaluating a Plan*

The FTC suggests that you use common sense when evaluating a multilevel marketing opportunity and consider these tips as you make your decision:

1.  Avoid any plan that includes commissions for recruiting additional distributors. It may be an illegal pyramid.

2.  Beware of plans that ask new distributors to purchase expensive products and marketing materials. These plans may be pyramids in disguise.

3.  Be cautious of plans that claim you will make money through continued growth of your downline, that is, the number of distributors you recruit.

4.  Beware of plans that claim to sell miracle products or promise enormous earnings. Ask the promoter to substantiate claims.

5.  Beware of shills—"decoy" references paid by a plan's promoter to lie about their earnings through the plan.

6.  Don't pay or sign any contracts in an "opportunity meeting" or any other pressure-filled situation. Insist on taking your time to think over your decision. Talk it over with a family member, friend, accountant, or lawyer.

7.  Do your homework! Check with your local Better Business Bureau and state Attorney General about any plan you're considering—especially when the claims about the product or your potential earnings seem too good to be true.

8.  Remember that no matter how good a product and how solid a multilevel marketing plan may be, you'll need to invest sweat equity as well as dollars for your investment to pay off.

## *"Auto-Surfing": What You Need to Know*

In the world of marketing, people often get compensated—with cash or free products and services—for doing fairly easy things, like sampling new ice-cream flavors, filling out surveys, or allowing a firm to monitor the television shows you watch or the websites you visit. While some "money for nothing" opportunities may be perfectly legitimate, others can turn out to be frauds.

"Auto-surfing" is a form of online advertising that purportedly generates advertising revenue for companies that want to increase traffic to their websites. The premise behind auto-surfing is that companies that advertise on the internet are willing to pay to increase traffic to their websites. These companies hire an auto-surf firm or "host," which in turn pays individual web surfers to view certain websites on an automatically rotating basis. The more sites the individual visits, the more money he or she stands to earn.

While auto-surfing may sound easy and appealing—and risk-free—there can be a hitch. Some auto-surf programs require their surfers to pay to participate, although perhaps not initially. When you first sign up to auto-surf, the firm might assign a limited number of sites for you to visit and pay you accordingly. Once you've made a modest amount of money, the firm might encourage—or even require—you to purchase a "membership" so that you can maximize your earnings. The program will promise high—often double or triple digit—returns on your investment in the program, often within days or weeks of joining.

The line you'll hear is that the more you click, the more you collect. But the reality is that any scheme that requires you to pay to participate—and promises handsome rewards in no time at all for little to no effort on your part—bears many of the hallmarks of a "Ponzi" or pyramid scheme. These schemes look deceptively legitimate because the fraudsters behind them typically use money coming in from new recruits to pay off early stage investors. But eventually the pyramid will collapse when it gets too big. It's simply not possible to "rob-Peter-to-pay-Paul" forever.

510

The SEC warns investors to be wary of any sort of "get rich scheme quick" scheme—and to be especially leery of opportunities that require you to pay to play. Before you pay a dime to make extra cash in your spare time, be sure to do a little due diligence:

- **If it sounds too good to be true, it probably is:** Compare promised yields with current returns on well-known stock indexes. Any investment opportunity that claims you'll get substantially more could be highly risky—and that means you might lose money.

- **Check out the company before you invest:** Contact the secretary of state where the company is incorporated to find out whether the company is a corporation in good standing. (You can get information about secretaries of state from the National Association of Secretaries of State; visit their website at http://www.nass.org.). Also call your state securities regulator to see whether the company, its officers, or the promoters of the opportunity have a history of complaints or fraud. (Information about your state securities regulator can be obtained from the North American Securities Administrators Association; http://www.nasaa.org.) If a supposedly upright business lists only a P.O. box, you'll want to do a lot of work before sending your money!

- **Steer clear of testimonials:** Watch out if the company's promotional materials, contain "testimonials" from supposedly satisfied customers, especially if all the "testimonials" are full of praise.

- **"Guaranteed returns" aren't:** Every investment carries some degree of risk, and the level of risk typically correlates with the return you can expect to receive. Low risk generally means low yields, and high yields typically involve high risk. If your money is perfectly safe, you'll most likely get a low return. High returns represent potential rewards for folks who are willing to take big risks. Most fraudsters spend a lot of time trying to convince investors that extremely high returns are "guaranteed" or "can't miss." Don't believe it.

511

# Chapter 64

# *Worthless Stock Swap Scams*

Con artists across the globe have stepped up their efforts to rip off investors, especially non-U.S. residents who have lost money in the U.S. securities markets. While it's natural to want to recoup one's losses as quickly and as fully as possible, the U.S. Securities and Exchange Commission (SEC) warns investors to be extremely skeptical of offers to exchange worthless or poorly performing stocks for blue chips or "hot" performers.

Worthless stock is typically just that—worthless. And anyone who promises a quick way to recover from a bad investment is probably just lying to you. We encourage you to thoroughly investigate any investment opportunity, as well as the person promoting it, before you part with your money. This is especially critical if you are a non-U.S. investor seeking to invest in U.S. stocks—or if you learn about the opportunity over the telephone from a broker you don't know. The "broker" may well be a con artist, and the deal may be a dud. Remember, if an offer sounds too good to be true, it probably isn't true.

This alert tells you how to spot potential "stock swap" scams, how to evaluate the offers you hear about, and where to turn for help.

## *What to Watch Out For*

Although fraudsters use a wide variety of techniques to carry out their "worthless stock swap" scams, most of these frauds boil down to

"Worthless Stock: How to Avoid Doubling Your Losses," U.S. Securities and Exchange Commission (www.sec.gov), October 2005.

a predictable formula: a persuasive pitch, which nearly always contains false assurances of legitimacy, followed by demands for money. Here are some "red flags" to avoid:

**Aggressive cold calls from "boiler-rooms":** Con artists posing as U.S. or United Kingdom brokers will first identify investors who have lost money investing in "microcap" stocks, the low-priced and thinly traded stocks issued by the smallest of U.S. companies. Operating from remote boiler-rooms, they then mount an aggressive cold calling or e-mailing campaign, focusing their pitch on loss recovery. They might offer to swap a poorly performing stock for an established, blue chip stock—or they will claim that their firm or an anonymous "client" wants to purchase the shares directly.

**Impressive websites serving as fronts for virtual offices:** To make their schemes appear convincing, fraudsters will invite you to visit "their" website—which will have pages of detailed information and perhaps a photo or biography of the broker. But all too often the site will be nothing more than a fraudulent copy of a legitimate firm's website—with changes made only to the name and contact information. The con artists will adopt fake yet familiar-sounding names and operate out of virtual offices, using phony addresses, remote mail drops, and redirected phone and facsimile numbers to carry out their scams.

**Self-provided references:** Knowing that regulators encourage investors to investigate before they invest, fraudsters often pretend to do the same. They will falsely assure you that the investment is properly registered with the appropriate agency and purport to give you the agency's telephone number so that you can verify that "fact." Sometimes they will give you the name of a real agency—other times they will fabricate one. But even if the agency does exist, the contact information invariably will be false. Instead of speaking with a government official, you'll reach the fraudsters or their colleagues—who will give the company, the promoter, or the transaction high marks.

**Claims of government "approval":** Another ruse fraudsters use to appear credible involves the misuse of federal agency seals, including the seals of the SEC and the Federal Trade Commission. They will copy the official seal from the regulator's website and use it to create fake letterhead for a fictitious letter of approval. But you should know that the SEC and FTC—like other state and federal regulators in the U.S. and around the world—do not "approve" or "endorse" any particular stock transactions or "loss recovery" programs.

**Advance payment requests:** Regardless of how the fraudsters pitch their offers to "help", there's always a catch. Before they will complete the deal, they first will ask for an upfront "security deposit" or "margin payment"—or claim that you must post an "insurance" or "performance bond." The minute you pay the advance fee, the fraudsters nearly always disappear—leaving you with new losses. If you seem willing to make further payments, the con artists may instead keep asking for more—falsely claiming that the market price of the security has changed or that the payments will cover additional fees, taxes, bonds for the courier service, or other similar expenses. Only when you finally run out of patience or money to chase your losses do the fraudsters disappear for good.

## How to Protect Yourself

Regulators often refer to worthless stock scams as "recovery room operations," "advance fee schemes," or "reload scams" because the perpetrators prey on individuals who lost money once and are willing to invest even more in the hope of recovering their losses. Here are several ways to arm yourself against these thieving opportunists:

**Look past fancy websites and letterheads:** Anyone who knows how to "cut and paste" can create impressive, legitimate-looking websites and stationery at little to no cost. Don't be taken in by a glossy brochure, a glitzy website, or the presence of a regulator's official seal on a webpage or document. The SEC does not authorize private companies to use their seal. If you see the SEC seal on a company's website or materials, think twice—and then think twice again.

**Be skeptical of government "approval":** Like most regulators around the world, the SEC does not evaluate the merits of any securities offering, nor do they determine whether a particular security is a "good" investment. Moreover, the SEC never endorse specific firms, individuals, products, or services.

**Deal only with real regulators:** Don't be fooled by those who tell you how and where to check out their credentials. Go straight to a real regulator for help. Here are the URLs you'll need to find your regulator:

- International Regulators: http://www.iosco.org/lists
- U.S. Regulators:
  - SEC: http://www.sec.gov

515

- National Association of Securities Dealers: http://www.nasd.com or http://www.nasdbrokercheck.com

- State Regulators: http://www.nasaa.org

**Caution:** If your contact provides any of these links electronically (in an e-mail or on a website), do not simply click on those links. Type the full URL into your web browser yourself. Even though the URL looks right, a fraudster's link can take you to a very different destination.

**Independently determine whether the offering is registered:** In general, all securities offered in the U.S. must be registered with the SEC or qualify for an exemption. You can see whether a company has registered its securities with the SEC and download its disclosure documents using the SEC EDGAR (Electronic Data Gathering, Analysis, and Retrieval) database (http://www.sec.gov/edgar.shtml).

**Check out the broker and the firm:** Always verify whether the broker and the firm are properly licensed to do business in your state, province, or country. If the person claims to work at a U.S. brokerage firm, use NASD's BrokerCheck website (http://www.nasdbrokercheck.com) or call NASD's Public Disclosure Program hotline at (800) 289-9999. If the person works elsewhere, contact the securities regulator for that country—and also for your home country, if more than one country is involved. You can find information about the appropriate securities regulators from the International Organisation of Securities Commissions, online at http://www.iosco.org/lists.

**Independently verify references:** Never rely solely on references given to you by a broker you've never worked with before. The "international organizations" or "satisfied clients" they suggest you contact may well be part of the scam.

**Be wary of unusual banking instructions:** Most reputable brokerage firms in the U.S. would not ask you to send your money to a non-U.S. bank—or to a U.S. bank for further credit to another bank or entity. In fact, a U.S. broker probably would not ever ask you to send payment to their bank at all.

## *Where to Turn for Help*

If the case appears to involve a U.S. broker, please send your complaint in writing to the SEC using their Online Complaint Center (http://www.sec.gov/complaint.shtml). Be sure to include as many details as possible, including the names, addresses, telephone or fax numbers, and e-mail addresses or websites of any person or firm, the dates of each contact, and information on any specific representations and wire instructions provided by the broker.

Because many investment scams occur entirely outside the U.S., the SEC may not have jurisdiction to investigate and prosecute wrongdoers—even if the fraud involves stock issued by a U.S. company. If you run into trouble, contact the securities regulator for your home country and also the country where the broker does business.

# Chapter 65

# *Foreign Currency Trading Frauds*

Have you been solicited to trade foreign currency contracts (also known as "forex")? If so, you need to know how to spot foreign currency trading frauds.

The United States Commodity Futures Trading Commission (CFTC), the federal agency that regulates commodity futures and options markets in the United States, warns consumers to take special care to protect themselves from the various kinds of frauds being perpetrated in today's financial markets, including those involving so-called "foreign currency trading."

A new federal law, the Commodity Futures Modernization Act of 2000, makes clear that the CFTC has the jurisdiction and authority to investigate and take legal action to close down a wide assortment of unregulated firms offering or selling foreign currency futures and options contracts to the general public. In addition, the CFTC has jurisdiction to investigate and prosecute foreign currency fraud occurring in its registered firms and their affiliates.

The CFTC has witnessed the increasing numbers and growing complexity of financial investment opportunities in recent years, including a sharp rise in foreign currency trading scams. While much foreign currency trading is legitimate, various forms of foreign currency trading have been touted in recent years to defraud members of the public.

---

"Beware of Foreign Currency Trading Frauds," Commodity Futures Trading Commission (www.cftc.gov), March 2006.

Currency trading scams often attract customers through advertisements in local newspapers, radio promotions or attractive internet sites. These advertisements may tout high-return, low-risk investment opportunities in foreign currency trading, or even highly paid currency-trading employment opportunities. The CFTC urges you to be skeptical when promoters of foreign currency trading claim that their services or account management will earn high profits with minimal risks, or that employment as a currency trader will make you wealthy quickly.

## Understanding Legitimate Foreign Currency Operations

Generally speaking, foreign currency futures and options contracts may be traded legally on an exchange or board of trade that has been approved by the CFTC.

Even where currency trading does not occur on a Commission-approved exchange or board of trade, the trading can be conducted legally where, generally speaking, one or both parties to the trading is (or is a regulated affiliate of) a bank, insurance company, registered securities broker-dealer, futures commission merchant or other financial institution, or is an individual or entity with a high net worth.

Where forex firms do not fall into the categories of regulated entities outlined above and engage in foreign currency futures and options transactions with or for retail customers who do not have high net worths, the CFTC has jurisdiction over those firms and their transactions.

### Warning Signs of Fraud

If you are solicited by a company that claims to trade foreign currencies and asks you to commit funds for those purposes, you should be very careful. Watch for the warning signs listed below, and take the following precautions before placing your funds with any currency trading company.

#### *Stay Away from Opportunities That Sound Too Good to Be True*

Get-rich-quick schemes, including those involving foreign currency trading, tend to be frauds.

Always remember that there is no such thing as a "free lunch." Be especially cautious if you have acquired a large sum of cash recently and are looking for a safe investment vehicle. In particular, retirees with access to their retirement funds may be attractive targets for fraudulent operators. Getting your money back once it is gone can be difficult or impossible.

## Avoid Any Company that Predicts or Guarantees Large Profits

Be extremely wary of companies that guarantee profits, or that tout extremely high performance. In many cases, those claims are false.

The following are examples of statements that either are or most likely are fraudulent:

- "Whether the market moves up or down, in the currency market you will make a profit."

- "Make $1000 per week, every week"

- "We are out-performing 90% of domestic investments."

- "The main advantage of the forex markets is that there is no bear market."

- "We guarantee you will make at least a 30–40% rate of return within two months."

## Stay Away from Companies That Promise Little or No Financial Risk

Be suspicious of companies that downplay risks or state that written risk disclosure statements are routine formalities imposed by the government.

The currency futures and options markets are volatile and contain substantial risks for unsophisticated customers. The currency futures and options markets are not the place to put any funds that you cannot afford to lose. For example, retirement funds should not be used for currency trading. You can lose most or all of those funds very quickly trading foreign currency futures or options contracts. Therefore, beware of companies that make the following types of statements:

- "With a $10,000 deposit, the maximum you can lose is $200 to $250 per day."

- "We promise to recover any losses you have."

- "Your investment is secure."

521

## *Don't Trade on Margin Unless You Understand What It Means*

Margin trading can make you responsible for losses that greatly exceed the dollar amount you deposited.

Many currency traders ask customers to give them money, which they sometimes refer to as "margin," often sums in the range of $1,000 to $5,000. However, those amounts, which are relatively small in the currency markets, actually control far larger dollar amounts of trading, a fact that often is poorly explained to customers.

Don't trade on margin unless you fully understand what you are doing and are prepared to accept losses that exceed the margin amounts you paid.

## *Question Firms That Claim to Trade in the "Interbank Market"*

Be wary of firms that claim that you can or should trade in the "interbank market," or that they will do so on your behalf.

Unregulated, fraudulent currency trading firms often tell retail customers that their funds are traded in the "interbank market," where good prices can be obtained. Firms that trade currencies in the interbank market, however, are most likely to be banks, investment banks, and large corporations, since the term "interbank market" refers simply to a loose network of currency transactions negotiated between financial institutions and other large companies.

## *Be Wary of Sending or Transferring Cash on the Internet, by Mail, or Otherwise*

Be especially alert to the dangers of trading on-line; it is very easy to transfer funds on-line, but often can be impossible to get a refund.

It costs an internet advertiser just pennies per day to reach a potential audience of millions of persons, and phony currency trading firms have seized upon the internet as an inexpensive and effective way of reaching a large pool of potential customers.

Many companies offering currency trading on-line are not located within the United States and may not display an address or any other information identifying their nationality on their website. Be aware that if you transfer funds to those foreign firms, it may be very difficult or impossible to recover your funds.

## *Currency Scams Often Target Members of Ethnic Minorities*

Some currency trading scams target potential customers in ethnic communities, particularly persons in the Russian, Chinese, and Indian immigrant communities, through advertisements in ethnic newspapers and television "infomercials."

Sometimes those advertisements offer so-called "job opportunities" for "account executives" to trade foreign currencies. Be aware that "account executives" that are hired might be expected to use their own money for currency trading, as well as to recruit their family and friends to do likewise. What appears to be a promising job opportunity often is another way many of these companies lure customers into parting with their cash.

## *Be Sure You Get the Company's Performance Track Record*

Get as much information as possible about the firm's or individual's performance record on behalf of other clients. You should be aware, however, that it may be difficult or impossible to do so, or to verify the information you receive. While firms and individuals are not required to provide this information, you should be wary of any person who is not willing to do so or who provides you with incomplete information. However, keep in mind, even if you do receive a glossy brochure or sophisticated-looking charts, that the information they contain might be false.

## *Don't Deal with Anyone Who Won't Give You Their Background*

Plan to do a lot of checking of any information you receive to be sure that the company is and does exactly what it says.

Get the background of the persons running or promoting the company, if possible. Do not rely solely on oral statements or promises from the firm's employees. Ask for all information in written form.

If you cannot satisfy yourself that the persons with whom you are dealing are completely legitimate and above-board, the wisest course of action is to avoid trading foreign currencies through those companies.

## *Warning Signs of Commodity "Come-Ons"*

If you are solicited by a company to purchase commodities, watch for the warning signs listed below:

- Avoid any company that predicts or guarantees large profits with little or no financial risk.

- Be wary of high-pressure tactics to convince you to send or transfer cash immediately to the firm, via overnight delivery companies, the internet, by mail, or otherwise.

- Be skeptical about unsolicited phone calls about investments from offshore salespersons or companies with which you are unfamiliar.

Prior to purchasing:

- Contact the CFTC (see the information below).

- Visit the CFTC's forex fraud webpage at http://www.cftc.gov/enf/enfforex.htm.

- Contact the National Futures Association to see whether the company is registered with the CFTC or is a member of the National Futures Association (NFA). You can do this easily by calling the NFA (800-621-3570 or 800-676-4NFA) or by checking the NFA's registration and membership information on its website at http://www.nfa.futures.org/basicnet. While registration may not be required, you might want to confirm the status and disciplinary record of a particular company or salesperson.

- Get in touch with other authorities, including your state's securities commissioner (you can identify the appropriate office for your state by checking with the North American Securities Administrators Association website at http://www.nasaa.org), Attorney General's consumer protection bureau (contact the National Association of Attorneys General at http://www.naag.org), the Better Business Bureau (http://www.bbb.org) and the National Futures Association (www.nfa.futures.org).

- Be sure you get all information about the company and verify that data, if possible. If you can, check the company's materials with someone whose financial advice you trust.

- Learn all possible information about fees charged, and the basis for each of these charges.

- If in doubt, don't invest. If you can't get solid information about the company, the salesperson, and the investment, you may not want to risk your money.

## More Information

- Questions concerning this advisory may be addressed to the CFTC's Office of Public Affairs at 202-418-5080. You can also write to:

Commodity Futures Trading Commission
Three LaFayette Centre
1155 21st Street, N.W.
Washington, DC 20581

# Part Five

# Additional Help and Information

# Chapter 66

# *Glossary of Investment Terms*

**annual report:** A report that public companies are required to file annually which describes the preceding year's financial results and plans for the upcoming year. Annual reports include information about a company's assets, liabilities, earnings, profits, and other year-end statistics.[1]

**annuity:** A contract by which an insurance company agrees to make regular payments to someone for life or for a fixed period in exchange for a lump sum or periodic deposits.[1]

**asset:** An asset is anything that is owned by an individual. With respect to saving and investing, assets are generally categorized as liquid (cash) assets and capital (investment) assets.[2]

**asset allocation:** The placement of a certain percentage of investment capital within different types of assets (for example, 50% in stock, 30% in bonds, and 20% in cash).[1]

**asset allocation fund:** Mutual fund that holds varying percentages of stock, bonds, and cash within its portfolio.[1]

---

Terms marked 1 were excerpted from "Investing for Your Future," © 2006 Rutgers Cooperative Research and Extension. Reprinted with permission, www.investing.rutgers.edu. Terms marked 2 were excerpted from "National Standards in Personal Finance," Second Edition, 2002, with permission from Jump$tart Coalition for Personal Financial Literacy, www.jumpstart.org.

**automatic investment plan:** An arrangement where investors agree to have money automatically withdrawn from a bank account on a regular basis to purchase stock or mutual fund shares.[1]

**automatic reinvestment:** An option available to stock and mutual fund investors where fund dividends and capital gains distributions are automatically reinvested to buy additional shares and thereby increase holdings.[1]

**average annual return:** The rate of return on investments averaged over a specific period of time (for example, the last 20 years). It is determined by adding together the rates of return for each year and dividing by the number of years in the calculation.[2]

**balanced fund:** A mutual fund that holds bonds and/or preferred stock in a certain proportion to common stock in order to obtain both current income and long-term growth of principal.[1]

**banks:** Corporations chartered by state or federal government to offer numerous financial services such as checking and savings accounts, loans, and safe deposit boxes. The Federal Deposit Insurance Corporation (FDIC) insures accounts in federally chartered banks.[2]

**bear market:** Term used to describe a prolonged period of declining stock prices.[1]

**before (pre)-tax dollars:** Money contributed to a tax-deferred savings plan that you do not have to pay income tax on until withdrawal at a future date.[1]

**beta:** A measure of a stock's volatility; the average beta for all stocks is +1.[1]

**blue-chip stock:** Term, derived from the most expensive chips in a poker game, used to indicate the stock of companies with long records of growth and profitability.[1]

**bond:** A debt instrument or IOU issued by corporations or units of government.[1]

**bond fund:** A mutual fund that holds mainly municipal, corporate, and/or government bonds.[1]

**broker:** A professional who transfers investors' orders to buy and sell securities to the market and generally provides some financial advice.[1]

**budget:** A financial plan that summarizes future income and expenditures over a period of time.[2]

**bull market:** Term used to describe a prolonged period of rising stock prices.[1]

**buy and hold:** A strategy of purchasing an investment and keeping it for a number of years.[1]

**capital appreciation:** An increase in market value of an investment (for example, stock).[1]

**capital gain:** A positive difference between an asset's price when bought and its price when or if sold; the opposite of capital loss.[2]

**capital gains distribution:** Payment to investors of profits realized upon the sale of securities.[1]

**capital loss:** A negative difference between an asset's price when bought and its price when or if sold; the opposite of capital gain.[2]

**capitalization:** The market value of a company, calculated by multiplying the number of shares outstanding by the price per share. Capitalization is often called "cap" for short in the names of specific investments (for example, ABC Small Cap Growth Fund).[1]

**cash-value life insurance:** Type of life insurance contract that pays benefits upon the death of the insured and also has a savings element that provides cash payments prior to death.[1]

**central registration depository (CRD):** A computerized system, which includes the employment, qualification, and disciplinary histories of more than 400,000 securities professionals who deal with the public. Consumers can get CRD information about a sales representative by calling (800)-289-9999 or visiting the website www.nasdr.com/2000.htm.[1]

**certificate of deposit (CD):** An insured bank product that pays a fixed rate of interest (for example, 5%) for a specified period of time.[1]

**churning:** When a broker excessively trades securities within an account for the purpose of increasing his or her commissions, rather than to further a client's investment goals.[1]

**class A shares:** Mutual fund shares that incur a front-end sales charge upon purchase.[1]

**class B shares:** Mutual fund shares that incur a back-end sales charge (also known as a contingent deferred sales charge or CDSC) if sold within five to six years of purchase.[1]

**class C shares:** Mutual fund shares that incur higher management and marketing fees than Classes A and B, but no sales or redemption charges upon purchase or sale.[1]

**closed-end fund:** An investment company that issues a limited number of shares that can be bought and sold on market exchanges.[1]

**cold calling:** A practice used by salespeople of making unsolicited phone calls to people they don't know in order to attract new business.[1]

**collectible:** An investment in tangible items such as coins, stamps, art, antiques, and autographs.[1]

**commission:** A fee to a third party for assisting a business transaction, such as buying or selling an asset.[2]

**commodities:** An investment in a contract to buy or sell products such as fuel oil, pork, grain, coffee, sugar, and other consumer staple items by a specified future date.[1]

**common stock:** Securities that represent a unit of ownership in a corporation.[1]

**compensation:** The total wage or salary and benefits that an employee receives.[2]

**composite indices:** Stock market indices comprised of stocks traded on major stock exchanges: New York Stock Exchange Composite (index of stocks traded on New York Stock Exchange); American Stock Exchange Composite (index of stocks traded on American Stock Exchange); NASDAQ Composite (index of stocks traded over the counter in the quotation system of the National Association of Securities Dealers).[1]

**compound interest:** Interest credited daily, monthly, quarterly, semi-annually, or annually on both principal and previously credited interest.[1,2]

**consumer:** A person who buys and/or uses a product.[2]

**convertible securities:** Bonds or preferred stock that can be exchanged for a fixed number of shares of common stock in the same corporation.[1]

**core holding:** The foundation of a portfolio (for example, a stock index fund) to which an investor might add additional securities.[1]

**corporate bonds:** Debt instruments issued by for-profit corporations.[1]

**credit laws:**[2]

- Equal Credit Opportunity Act (1975): Federal law that ensures that consumers are given an equal chance to receive credit. Prohibits discrimination on the basis of gender, race, marital status, religion, national origin, age, or receipt of public assistance. Lenders cannot ask about your plans for having children or refuse to consider consistently received alimony or child support payments as income. If you are denied credit, you have a legal right to know why.[2]

- Fair Credit and Charge Card Disclosure Act (1989): A part of the Truth in Lending Act that mandates a box on credit card applications that describes key features and costs (that is, APR [annual percentage rate], grace period for purchases, minimum finance charge, balance calculation method, annual fees, transaction fees for cash advances, and penalty fees such as over the limit fees and late payment fees).[2]

- Fair Credit Billing Act (1975): Federal law that covers credit card billing problems. It applies to all open-end credit accounts (for example, credit cards, overdraft checking). States that consumers should send a written billing error notice to the creditor within 60 days (after receipt of first bill containing an error); creditor must acknowledge in 30 days; creditor must investigate; and creditor may not damage a consumer's credit rating while a dispute is pending.[2]

- Fair Credit Reporting Act (1971): Federal law that covers the reporting of debt repayment information. It establishes when a credit reporting agency may provide a report to someone; states that obsolete information must be taken off (7 or 10 years); gives consumers the right to know what is in their credit report; requires that both a credit bureau and information provider (for example, department store) have an obligation to correct incorrect information; gives consumers the right to dispute inaccurate information and add a 100-word statement to their report to explain accurate negative information; and gives consumers the

533

right to know what credit bureau provided a report when they are turned down for credit.[2]

- Fair Debt Collection Practices Act (1978): Federal law that prohibits debt collectors from engaging in unfair, deceptive, or abusive practices when collecting debts. Collectors must send a written notice telling the amount owed and name of the creditor; collector may not contact consumer if he or she disputes in writing within 30 days (unless collector furnishes proof of the debt); collectors must identify themselves on the phone and can call only between 8 A.M. and 9 P.M. unless a consumer agrees to another time; and collectors cannot call consumers at work if they are told not to.[2]

- Truth in Lending Act (1969): Federal law that mandates disclosure of information about the cost of credit. Both the finance charge (that is, all charges to borrow money, including interest) and the annual percentage rate or APR (that is, the percentage cost of credit on a yearly basis) must be displayed prominently on forms and statements used by creditors. The law provides criminal penalties for willful violators, as well as civil remedies. It also protects you against unauthorized use of your credit card. If it is lost or stolen, the maximum amount you have to pay is $50.[2]

**credit unions:** Not-for-profit cooperatives of members with some type of common bond (for example, employer) that provide a wide array of financial services, often at a lower cost than banks.[2]

**deflation:** A broad, overall drop in the price of goods and services; the opposite of the more common inflation.[2]

**direct purchase plans (DPPs):** "No load" stocks where every share, including the first, can be sold or purchased directly from a company without a broker.[1]

**discount broker:** A broker that trades securities for a lower commission than a full-service broker.[1]

**disposable income:** Income remaining after income and payroll taxes are deducted from gross pay; income available to spend or save.[2]

**diversification:** The process of spreading assets among different investments to reduce the risk of a decline in value of an investor's total portfolio from a decline in any one investment.[2]

**dividend:** A payment to shareholders that a company's board of directors approves from earnings.[2]

**dividend reinvestment plans (DRIPs):** Plans that allow investors to automatically reinvest any dividends a stock pays into additional shares.[1]

**dollar-cost averaging:** Investing equal amounts of money (for example, $50) at a regular time interval (for example, quarterly) regardless of whether securities markets are moving up or down. This practice reduces average share costs to investors, who acquire more shares in periods of lower securities prices and fewer shares in periods of higher prices.[1]

**Dow Jones Industrial Average:** The most widely used gauge of stock market performance. Also know as "The Dow," it tracks 30 stocks in large well-established U.S. companies.[1]

**earned income:** Payment received for work, such as wages, salaries, commissions, and tips.[2]

**EDGAR (Electronic Data Gathering, Analysis, and Retrieval):** An electronic system developed by the U.S. Securities and Exchange Commission (SEC) that is used by companies to file documents required by the SEC for securities offerings and ongoing disclosure. EDGAR information is available to consumers on the internet at www.sec.gov, usually within 24 hours after filing by a company. EDGAR information is also available in the SEC's public reference room by calling 202-942-8090 or sending a fax to (202) 628-9001 or an e-mail to publicreference@sec.gov.[1]

**employee benefit:** Something of value that an employee receives in addition to a wage or salary. Examples include health insurance, life insurance, discounted childcare, and subsidized meals at the company cafeteria.[2]

**employer-sponsored retirement savings program:** Tax-deferred savings plans offered by employers that provide a federal tax deduction, tax-deferral of contributions and earnings, and, in some cases, employer matching. They include 401(k) plans for corporate employees, 403(b) plans for employees of schools and non-profit organizations, and Section 457 plans for state and local government employees.[2]

535

**employer-sponsored savings plan:** A government-approved program through which an employer can assist workers in building their personal retirement funds.[2]

**entrepreneur:** A person who starts a business.[2]

**equity investing:** Becoming an owner or partial owner of a company or a piece of property through the purchase of investments such as stock, growth mutual funds, and real estate.[1]

**expense:** The cost of a good or service.[2]

**Federal Deposit Insurance Corporation (FDIC):** Federal agency that insures bank deposits up to $100,000. Investments purchased at banks are not FDIC-insured.[1]

**FICA (Federal Insurance Contributions Act):** The legislation that funds Social Security.[2]

**financial goals:** Short-, intermediate-, and long-term goals that require money and guide a person's future plans and savings decisions.[2]

**financial plan:** A plan of action that allows a person to meet not only the immediate needs but also the long-term goals.[2]

**financial resources:** Financial assets that can be accessed when necessary.[2]

**fixed annuity:** An investment vehicle, often used for retirement accounts, that guarantees principal and a specified interest rate. Fixed annuity earnings grow tax-deferred until withdrawal.[1]

**403(b) plan:** Similar to a 401(k), a retirement savings plan for employees of a tax-exempt education or research organization or public school. Pretax dollars are contributed to an investment account until the employee retires or terminates employment.[1]

**401(k) plan:** A retirement savings plan sponsored by for-profit companies that allows an employee to contribute pretax dollars to a company investment vehicle until the employee retires or leaves the company.[1]

**fraud:** A seller's intentional deception of a buyer, which is illegal.[2]

**full-service broker:** A broker that charges commissions based on the type and amount of securities traded. Full-service brokers typically charge more than discount brokers but also provide more extensive services (for example, research and personalized advice).[1]

**GNMAs (Ginnie Maes):** An investment in a pool of mortgage securities backed by Government National Mortgage Association (GNMA)[1]

**government transfer payments:** Payments by governments, such as social security, veterans benefits, and welfare, to people who do not supply current goods, services, or labor in exchange for these payments.[2]

**grace period:** A time period during which a borrower can pay the full balance of credit due and not incur any finance charges.[2]

**growth fund:** Mutual fund that invests in stocks exhibiting potential for capital appreciation.[1]

**growth stocks:** Stock of companies that are expected to increase in value.[1]

**guaranteed investment contract (GIC):** Fixed-income investments, offered in many tax-deferred employer retirement plans, that guarantee a specific rate of return for a specific time period.[1]

**income fund:** A mutual fund that invests in stocks or bonds with a high potential for current income, either interest or dividends.[1]

**income:** Earnings from work or investment. (See compensation.)[2]

**income stocks:** Stock of companies that expect to pay regular and relatively high (compared to growth stocks) dividends.[1]

**index:** An unmanaged collection of securities whose overall performance is used as an indication of stock market trends. An example of an index is the widely quoted Dow Jones Industrial Average, which tracks the performance of 30 large company U.S. stocks.[1]

**index fund:** A mutual fund that attempts to match the performance of a specified stock or bond market index by purchasing some or all of the securities that comprise the index.[1]

**individual retirement account (IRA):** A retirement savings plan that allows individuals to save for retirement on a tax-deferred basis. Individuals may contribute up to $2,000 per year in an individual account. For spousal accounts, the limit is $4,000. [Note: Amounts are scheduled to change in 2008. Consult your tax advisor for current limits.] The amount that is tax deductible varies according to an individual's access to pension coverage, income tax filing status, and adjusted gross income.[1]

**inflation:** A broad, overall rise in the price of goods and services; the opposite of the less common deflation.[2]

**interest:** Money paid to savers and investors by financial institutions, government, or corporations for the use of their money (example: 5% interest on a certificate of deposit or 6% interest on a bond).[2]

**interest rate risk:** The risk that, as interest rates rise, the value of previously issued bonds will fall, resulting in a loss if they are sold prior to maturity.[1]

**investing:** The process of setting money aside to increase wealth over time and accumulate funds for long-term financial goals such as retirement.[2]

**investment clubs:** Organizations of investors who meet and contribute money regularly toward the purchase of securities.[1]

**investment grade bond:** Bond rated with one of the top four grades by a rating service like Moody's and Standard & Poor's, indicating a high level of creditworthiness.[1]

**investment objective:** The goal (for example, current income) of an investor or a mutual fund. Mutual fund objectives must be clearly stated in their prospectus.[1]

**investors:** People investing in securities, such as stock and bonds, to achieve long-term financial goals.[2]

**Keogh plan:** A qualified retirement plan for self-employed individuals and their employees to which tax-deductible contributions up to a specified yearly limit can be made if the plan meets certain requirements of the Internal Revenue Code.[1]

**limit order:** An order to buy or sell securities that specifies that a trade should be made only at a certain price or better.[1]

**liquidity:** The quality of an asset that permits it to be converted quickly into cash without a significant loss of value.[1,2]

**load:** A commission charged by the sponsor of a mutual fund upon the purchase or sale of shares.[1]

**loss:** The negative difference between total revenue from a business or investment minus total expense.[2]

**management fee:** The amount paid by mutual funds to their investment advisers.[1]

**marginal tax rate:** The rate you pay on the last (highest) dollar of personal or household (if married) earnings. Current federal marginal tax rates range from 15% to 39.6%.[1]

**market order:** An order to buy or sell a stated amount (for example, 100 shares) of a security at the best possible price at the time the order is received in the marketplace.[1]

**market value:** The current price of an asset, as indicated by the most recent price at which it traded on the open market. If the most recent trade in ABC stock was at $25 for example, the market value of the stock is $25.[1]

**maturity:** The date on which the principal amount of a bond, investment contract, or loan must be repaid.[1]

**microcap stock:** Low priced stocks issued by the smallest of companies. Companies with low or "micro" capitalization typically have limited assets and a small total market value. Many microcap stocks trade in small volumes in the "over the counter" (OTC) market, with prices quoted on the OTC Bulletin Board or "Pink Sheets."[1]

**money market mutual fund:** A highly liquid mutual fund that invests in short-term obligations such as commercial paper, government securities, and certificates of deposit.[1]

**Moody's Investors Service:** A rating agency that analyzes the credit quality of bonds and other securities.[1]

**mutual funds:** Investment companies that pool money from shareholders and invest in a variety of securities, including stocks, bonds, and short-term money market assets.[2]

**needs:** Those economic goods and services that are considered basic, such as food, clothing, and shelter.[2]

**net asset value:** The market value of a mutual fund's total assets, after deducting liabilities, divided by the number of shares outstanding.[1]

**net worth:** The dollar value remaining when liabilities (what you owe) are subtracted from assets (what you own). Example: $200,000 of assets - $125,000 of debt = a $75,000 net worth.[1]

**online investing:** The purchase of securities from brokerage firms via the internet using a computer and modem.[1]

**open-end fund:** An investment company that continually buys and sells shares to meet investor demand. It can have an unlimited number of investors or money in the fund.[1]

**opportunity cost:** The opportunity cost of a choice is the value of the best alternative given up.[2]

**payroll deduction:** An amount subtracted from a paycheck as the government requires or the employee requests. Mandatory deductions include various taxes. Voluntary deductions include loan payments or deposits into saving accounts.[2]

**penny stocks:** Stocks that sell for $5 per share or less.[1]

**portfolio:** The combined holding of stocks, bonds, cash equivalents, or other assets by an individual or household, investment club, or institutional investor (for example, mutual fund).[1]

**preferred stock:** A type of stock that offers no ownership or voting rights and generally pays a fixed dividend to investors.[1]

**price/earnings (P/E) ratio:** The price of a stock divided by its earnings per share (for example, $40 stock price divided by $2 of earnings per share = a P/E ratio of 20).[1]

**principal:** The original amount of money invested or borrowed, excluding any interest or dividends.[1]

**profit:** The positive difference between total revenue from a business or investment minus total expense.[2]

**prospectus:** An official booklet that describes a mutual fund. It contains information as required by the U.S. Securities and Exchange Commission on topics such as the fund's investment objectives, investment restrictions, purchase and redemption policies, fees, and performance history.[1]

**purchasing power:** A measurement of the relative value of money in terms of the quality and quantity of goods and services it can buy. Inflation decreases purchasing power; deflation increases it.[2]

**rate of return:** Also called the "yield," this is the return on an investment expressed as a percentage of its cost (for example, $3 annual return divided by $24 price per share = .125 or a 12.5% rate of return).[2]

**real estate:** Land, permanent structures on land, and accompanying rights and privileges, such as crop or mineral rights.[1]

**real estate investment trust (REIT):** A portfolio of real estate-related securities in which investors can purchase shares that trade on major stock exchanges.[1]

**real-time quotes:** A requirement that trades in a NASDAQ (over the counter market) security be reported within 90 seconds of execution. Thus, information is current up to 90 seconds of the market, rather than typical quotes which have a 15 or 20-minute delay.[1]

**reciprocal immunity:** A principle of taxation where state and local governments don't tax earnings on federal debt securities and the federal government doesn't tax earnings on state/local debt securities.[1]

**rent:** Periodic fee for the use of property.[2]

**risk:** Exposure to loss of investment capital due to a variety of causes such as business failure, stock market volatility, and interest rate changes. In business, the likelihood of loss or reduced profit.[2]

**risk management:** Actions taken (for example, purchase of insurance) to provide protection against catastrophic financial losses (for example, disability and liability). Risk management is an important investing prerequisite.[1] Procedures to minimize the adverse effect of a possible financial loss by: 1) identifying potential sources of loss; 2) measuring the financial consequences of a loss occurring; and 3) using controls to minimize actual losses or their financial consequences.[2]

**Rule of 72:** A quick way to calculate how long it will take to double a sum of money. Divide 72 by the expected interest rate to determine the number of years (example 72 divided by 8% = 9 years).[2]

**salary:** Payment for work, usually calculated in periods of a week or longer. Salary is usually tied to the completion of specific duties over a minimum but not maximum number of hours. (See wage.)[2]

**sales charge:** The amount charged to purchase mutual fund shares. The charge is added to the net asset value per share to determine the per share offering price.[1]

**savings:** The process of setting aside money until a future date instead of spending it today. The goal of saving is to provide funds for emergencies, short-term goals, and investments.[2]

**savings and loan associations (S&Ls):** Financial institutions that provide loans and interest-bearing accounts. Accounts in federally chartered S&Ls are federally insured.[2]

**savings accounts:** Accounts at financial institutions that allow regular deposits and withdrawals. The minimum required deposit, fees charged, and interest rate paid varies among providers.[2]

**savings bond:** A bond is a certificate representing a debt. A U.S. Savings Bond is a loan to the government. The government agrees to repay the amount borrowed, with interest, to the bondholder. Two types of savings bonds are Series EE and inflation-adjusted I bonds. Savings bonds are often purchased through payroll deduction or at financial institutions in denominations of $50 to $10,000.[2]

**Savings Incentive Match Plan for Employees (SIMPLE Plans):** A tax-deferred retirement plan for owners and employees of small businesses that provides matching funds by the employer.[1]

**securities:** A term used to refer to stocks and bonds in general.[1]

**Securities Investor Protection Corporation (SIPC):** A nonprofit corporation that insures investors against the failure of brokerage firms, similar to the way that the Federal Deposit Insurance Corporation (FDIC) insures bank deposits. Coverage is limited to a maximum of $500,000 per account, but only up to $100,000 in cash. SIPC does not insure against market risk, however.[1]

**simple interest:** Interest credited daily, monthly, quarterly, semiannually, or annually on principal only, not previously credited interest.[2]

**simplified employee pension (SEP):** A tax-deferred retirement plan for owners of small businesses and the self-employed.[1]

**Social Security:** A federal government program of transfer payments for retirement, disability, or the loss of income from a parent or guardian. Funds come from a tax on income, a payroll deduction labeled "FICA."[2]

**Standard and Poor's 500 Index:** An index that is widely replicated by stock index mutual funds. Also known as the S&P 500, it consists of 500 large U.S. companies.[1]

**Standard and Poor's Corporation:** A rating agency that analyzes the credit quality of bonds and other securities.[1]

**stock:** Security that represents a unit of ownership in a corporation.[1]

**substandard grade (also known as "junk") bond:** Bond rated below the top four grades by a rating service such as Moody's and Standard and Poor's. They generally provide a higher return than investment grade securities to compensate investors for an increased risk of default.[1]

**take-home pay:** Total wage or salary (plus bonuses) minus payroll deductions.[2]

**tax:** A government fee on business and individual income, activities, or products.[2]

**tax credit:** An amount that a taxpayer who meets certain criteria can subtract from tax owed. Examples include a credit for earned income below a certain limit and for qualified post-secondary school expenses. (See tax deduction, tax exemption.)[2]

**tax deduction:** An expense that a taxpayer can subtract from taxable income. Examples include deductions for home mortgage interest and for charitable gifts. (See tax credit, tax exemption.)[2]

**tax deferral:** Investments where taxes due on the amount invested and/or its earnings are postponed until funds are withdrawn, usually at retirement.[1]

**tax-exempt (tax-free):** Investments (for example, municipal bonds) whose earnings are free from tax liability.[2]

**tax exemption:** An amount that a taxpayer who meets certain criteria can subtract from taxable income. Examples include exemptions for each dependent or for life insurance proceeds. (See tax credit, tax deduction.)[2]

**taxable income:** Income subject to tax; total income adjusted for deductions, exemptions, and credits.[2]

**time value of money:** Comparison of a lump sum of money, or a series of equal payments, between two different time periods (for example, present and future), assuming a specified interest rate and time period. (Reference: *The Time Value of Money* by Clayton and Spivey.)[2]

**tip:** An amount paid beyond what's required, usually to express satisfaction with service quality; also known as a gratuity.[2]

**total return:** The return on an investment including all current income (interest and dividends), plus any change (gain or loss) in the value of the asset.[1]

**transfer payments:** *See* government transfer payments.[2]

**12(b)1 fee:** A marketing fee levied on mutual fund shareholders to pay for advertising and distribution costs, as well as broker compensation.[1]

**unearned income:** Money received for which no exchange was made, such as a gift.[2]

**unit investment trust (UIT):** An unmanaged portfolio of professionally selected securities that are held for a specified period of time.[1]

**U.S. Securities and Exchange Commission (SEC):** Federal agency created to administer the Securities Act of 1933. Statues administered by the SEC are designed to promote full public disclosure about investments and protect the investing public against fraudulent and manipulative practices in the securities markets.[1]

**U.S. Treasury securities:** Debt instruments issued by the federal government with varying maturities (bills, notes, and bonds).[1]

**value stock:** A stock with a relatively low price compared to its historical earnings and the value of the issuing company's assets.[1]

**variable annuity:** An annuity where the value fluctuates based on the market performance of its underlying securities portfolio.[1]

**volatility:** The degree of price fluctuation associated with a given investment, interest rate, or market index. The more price fluctuation that is experienced, the greater the volatility.[1]

**wage:** Payment for work, usually as calculated in periods of an hour rather than longer. (*See also* salary.)[2]

**wants:** Desires for economic goods or services, not necessarily accompanied by the power to satisfy them.[2]

**wealth:** Accumulated assets such as money and/or possessions, often as a result of saving and investing.[2]

**zero-coupon bonds:** Debt instruments issued by government or corporations at a steep discount from face value. Interest accrues each year but is not paid out until maturity.[1]

# Chapter 67

# A Directory of Finance Information Resources

## Information about Finances and Financial Planning

**Actuarial Foundation**
475 North Martingale
Schaumburg, IL 60173
Phone: 847-706-3535
Website: http://
www.actuarialfoundation.org

**American Association of Individual Investors**
625 N. Michigan Ave.
Chicago, IL 60611
Toll-Free: 800-428-2244
Phone: 312-280-0170
Fax: 312-280-9883
Website: http://www.aaii.com

**American College of Trust and Estate Counsel**
3415 South Sepulveda
Boulevard, Suite 330
Los Angeles, CA 90034
Phone: 310-398-1888
Website: http://www.actec.org

**American Council of Life Insurers**
101 Constitution Ave. NW
Suite 700
Washington, DC 20001-2133
Phone: 202-624-2000
Toll free: 800-942-4242
Fax: 202-624-2319
Website: http:www.acli.com

---

Information in this chapter was compiled from many sources deemed accurate. All contact information was verified in May 2007. This list does not serve to recommend or endorse any particular source of information and there is no implication associated with omission.

## American Institute of Certified Public Accountants

Personal Financial Planning Division
1211 Avenue of the Americas
New York, NY 10036
Toll-Free: 888-999-9256
Website: http://www.aicpa.org
Website: http://
www.360financialliteracy.org

## American Savings Education Council

2121 K Street NW, Suite 600
Washington, DC 20037-1896
Phone: 202-659-0670
Fax: 202-775-6312
Website: http://www.asec.org

## Certified Financial Planner Board of Standards

Communication and Consumer Services
1670 Broadway, Suite 600
Denver, CO 80202-4809
Toll-Free: 888-237-6275
Phone: 303-830-7500
Fax: 303-860-7388
Website: www.CFP-Board.org
E-mail: mail@cfp-board.org

## Choose To Save

Employee Benefit Research Institute (EBRI)
2121 K Street, NW, Suite 600
Washington, DC 20037-1896
Phone: 202-659-0670
Fax: 202-775-6312
Website: http://
www.choosetosave.org
E-mail: info@choosetosave.org

## Consumer Federation of America

1620 I Street, NW, Suite 200
Washington, DC 20006
Phone: 202-387-6121
Fax: 202-265-7989
Website: http://
www.consumerfed.org

## Credit Union National Association

P.O. Box 431
Madison, WI 53701-0431
Toll-Free: 800-356-9655
Fax: 608-231-4263
Website: http://www.cuna.org

## Employee Benefits Security Administration

Department of Labor
Rm. S2524
200 Constitution Ave., NW
Washington, DC 20210
Toll-Free: 866-444-3272
or 866-275-7922
TTY Toll-Free: 877-899-5627
Website: www.dol.gov/ebsa

## Federal Deposit Insurance Corporation (FDIC)

Division of Supervision and Consumer Protection
550 17th St., NW
Washington, DC 20429
Toll-Free: 877-ASK-FDIC
(877-275-3342)
TDD Toll-Free: 800-925-4618
Phone: 703-562-2222
Website: http://www.fdic.gov

### Federal Trade Commission
Consumer Response Center
Attention CRC-240
Washington, DC 20580
Toll-Free: 877-FTC-HELP
(877-382-4357)
TDD/TTY: 866-653-4261
Website: http://www.ftc.gov

### Financial Planning Association
4100 E. Mississippi Ave.
Suite 400
Denver, CO 80246-3053
Toll free: 800-647-6340
or 800-322-4237
Fax: 303-759-0749
Website: http://www.fpanet.org
E-mail: fpa@fpanet.org

### Foundation for Investor Education
120 Broadway, 35th Floor
New York, NY 10271
Fax: 212-968-0743
Website: http://www.foundation
forinvestoreducation.org
Website: http://
www.pathtoinvesting.org
E-mail:
foundation@foundationforinvestor
education.org

### Insurance Information Institute
Consumer Affairs
110 William St., 24th Floor
New York, NY 10038
212-346-5500
Toll free: 800-331-9146
Website: http://www.iii.org

### Investing for Your Future
Rutgers Cooperative Extension
Website: http://
www.investing.rutgers.edu

### Investment Company Institute
1401 H Street NW
Washington, DC 20005
Phone: 202-326-5800
Website: http://www.ici.org

### Iowa State University Cooperative Extension
2150 Beardshear Hall
Ames, IA 50011-2046
Phone: 515-294-6675
Fax: 515-294-4715
Website: http://
www.extension.iastate.edu/
finances

### Jump$tart Coalition for Personal Financial Literacy
919 18th St., NW, Suite 300
Washington, DC 20006
Toll-Free: 888-45-EDUCATE
Fax: 202-223-0321
Website: http://
www.jumpstart.org
E-mail:
info@jumpstartcoalition.org

### Motley Fool
2000 Duke St., Fourth Floor
Alexandria, VA 22314
Phone: 703-838-3665
Fax: 703-254-1999
Website: http://www.fool.com

### National Association for Variable Annuities
11710 Plaza America Drive, Suite 100
Reston, VA 20190
Phone: 703-707-8830
Fax: 703-707-8831
Website: http://www.navanet.org

### National Association of Investors Corporation
711 W. 13 Mile Rd.
Madison Heights, MI 48071
Toll-Free: 877-275-6242
Phone: 248-583-6242
Fax: 248-583-4880
Website: http://www.better-investing.org

### National Association of Personal Financial Advisors
3250 North Arlington Heights Road, Suite 109
Arlington Heights, IL 60004
Toll-Free: 800-366-2732
Website: http://www.napfa.org

### National Endowment for Financial Education
5299 DTC Boulevard, Suite 1300
Greenwood Village, CO 80111
Phone: 303-741-6333
Website: http://www.nefe.org

### Profit Sharing/401(k) Society of America
20 N. Wacker Dr., Suite 3700
Chicago, IL 60606
Phone: 312-419-1863
Website: http://www.401k.org

### Social Security Administration
Office of Public Inquiries
Windsor Park Bldg.
6401 Security Blvd.
Baltimore, MD 21235
Toll-Free: 800-772-1213
Website: http://www.socialsecurity.gov

### Society of Financial Service Professionals
17 Campus Boulevard
Suite 201
Newtown Square, PA 19073-3230
Toll-Free: 888-243-2258
Phone: 610-526-2500
Fax: 610-527-1499
Website: http://www.financialpro.org

### Sudden Money Institute
10 Huntly Circle
Palm Beach Gardens, FL 33418
Toll-Free: 888-838-9446
Website: http://www.suddenmoney.com

### Women's Institute for a Secure Retirement
1725 K Street, NW, Suite 201
Washington, DC 20006
Phone: 202-393-5452
Fax: 202-393-5890
Website: http://www.wiserwomen.org

## Securities Information

### American Stock Exchange, LLC
86 Trinity Place
New York, NY 10006
Toll-Free: 800-THE-AMEX
Phone: 212-306-1000
Website: http://www.amex.com

### Boston Stock Exchange, Inc.
100 Franklin St.
Boston, MA 02110
Phone: 617-235-2000
Fax: 617-235-2283
Website: http://
www.bostonstock.com

### Bureau of the Public Debt
Marketing Office
P.O. Box 7015
Parkersburg, WV 26106-7015
Toll free: 800-4US-BOND (for recorded bond information)
Website: http://
www.publicdebt.treas.gov

### Chicago Board Options Exchange, Inc.
400 South LaSalle Street
Chicago, IL 60605
Toll-Free: 877-THE-CBOE
Phone: 312-786-5600
Website: http://www.cboe.com

### Chicago Stock Exchange, Inc.
One Financial Place
440 South LaSalle Street
Chicago, IL 60605
Phone: 312-663-2222
Website: http://www.chx.com
E-mail: info@chx.com

### Commodity Futures Trading Commission
Lafayette Center
1155 21st St., NW
Washington, DC 20581
Phone: 202-418-5080
or 202-418-5000
Fax: 202-418-5525
Website: http://www.cftc.gov
E-mail: oea@cftc.gov

### International Securities Exchange
60 Broad Street, 26th Floor
New York, NY 10004
Phone: 212-943-2400
Website: http://
www.iseoptions.com

### National Association of Real Estate Investment Trusts
1875 I Street, NW
Suite 600
Washington DC 20006
Toll-Free: 800-3-NAREIT
Phone: 202-739-9400
Fax: 202-739-9401
Website: http://www.nareit.com

### National Association of Securities Dealers
Phone: 301-590-6500
Website: http://www.nasd.org

**National Futures Association**
200 West Madison Street
Suite 1600
Chicago, IL 60606-3447
Toll-Free: 800-621-3570
Website: http://
www.nfa.futures.org

**National Stock Exchange**
440 South LaSalle Street
Suite 2600
Chicago, IL 60605
Phone: 312-786-8803
Fax: 312-939-7239
Website: http://www.nsx.com

**New York Stock Exchange, Inc.**
11 Wall Street
New York, NY 10005
Phone: 212-656-3000

**North American Securities Administrators Association**
750 First Street, NE, Suite 1140
Washington, DC 20002
Phone: 202-737-0900
Fax: 202-783-3571
Website: http://www.nasaa.org

**Options Clearing Corporation**
One North Wacker Drive
Suite 500
Chicago, IL 60606
Toll-Free: 800-537-4258
Phone: 312-322-6200
Website: http://
www.optionsclearing.com

**Options Industry Council**
One North Wacker Dr.
Suite 500
Chicago, IL 60606
Toll-Free: 888-OPTIONS
Website: http://
www.888options.com

**Philadelphia Stock Exchange, Inc.**
1900 Market Street
Philadelphia, PA 19103
Toll-Free: 800-THE-PHLX
Phone: 215-496-5000
Website: http://www.phlx.com

**Securities Industry and Financial Markets Association (SIFMA)**
120 Broadway, 35th Floor
New York, NY 10271-0080
Phone: 212-608-1500
Fax: 212-968-0703
Website: http://www.sifma.org
Website: http://
www.investinginbonds.com

**U.S. Securities and Exchange Commission**
Office of Investor Education
and Assistance
100 F Street, NE
Washington, DC 20549-0213
Toll-Free: 800-SEC-0330
Phone: 202-551-6551
Fax: 202-942-9634
Website: http://www.sec.gov
Website: http://www.sec
.gov/investor.shtml (Investor
Information)

## Business and Financial Information

### Bloomberg News Service
Phone: 212-318-2000
Fax: 917-369-5000
Website: http://www.bloomberg.com

### Dominion Bond Rating Service (DBRS)
DBRS Tower
181 University Avenue
Suite 700
Toronto, ON M5H 3M7
Phone: 416-593-5577
Fax: 416-593-8432
Website: http://www.dbrs.com

### Dun and Bradstreet (D&B)
103 JFK Parkway
Short Hills, NJ 07078
Toll-Free: 800-234-3867
Website: http://www.dnb.com

### Fitch Ratings
Phone: 212-908-0500
Website: http://www.fitchratings.com

### Hoover's, Inc.
5800 Airport Blvd.
Austin, TX 78752
Phone: 512-374-4500
Fax: 512-374-4501
Website: http://www.hoovers.com

### Kiplinger Washington Editors
1729 H Street NW
Washington, DC 20006
Toll-Free: 800-544-0155 (for subscription information)
Website: http://www.kiplinger.com

### Moody's Investors Services
99 Church Street
New York, NY 10007
Phone: 212-553-0300
Website: http://www.moodys.com

### Morningstar
Phone: 312 384-4000
Website: http://www.morningstar.com

### OTC Bulletin Board
Phone: 301-978-8263
Website: http://www.otcbb.com

### Pink Sheets, LLC
304 Hudson Street, 2nd Floor
New York, NY 10013
Phone: 212-896-4400
Fax: 212-868-3848
Website: http://www.pinksheets.com

### Standard and Poor's
55 Water Street
New York, NY 10041
Phone: 212-438-1000
or 212-438-2000
Website: http://www.standardandpoors.com

Chapter 68

# A Directory of Investor Protection Services Agencies

## Anti-Fraud and Investor Support

### Alliance Against Fraud in Telemarketing and Electronic Commerce

National Consumers League
1701 K St., NW
Suite 1200
Washington, DC 20006
Phone: 202-835-3323
Fax: 202-835-0747
Website: http://www.fraud.org/
aaft/aaftinfo.htm
E-mail: info@nclnet.org

---

This list of regulatory, fraud prevention, and advocacy organizations and agencies was compiled from many sources deemed accurate; inclusion does not constitute endorsement and there is no implication associated with omission. All contact information was verified in May 2007.

### American Institute of Certified Public Accountants

Professional Ethics Division
Harborside Financial Center
220 Leigh Farm Road
Durham, NC 27707
Toll free: 888-777-7077 (Ethics Hotline)
Website: http://www.aicpa.org
E-mail: ethics@aicpa.org

### Coalition Against Insurance Fraud

1012 14th St. NW
Suite 200
Washington, DC 20005
Phone: 202-393-7330
Fax: 202-393-7329
Website: http://
www.InsuranceFraud.org
E-mail: info@insurancefraud.org

### Federal Communications Commission

Consumer and Governmental Affairs Bureau
Consumer Inquiries and Complaints Division
445 12th Street, SW
Washington, DC 20554
Toll-Free: 888-CALL-FCC (888-225-5322)
TTY: 888-TELL-FCC (888-835-5322)
Website: http://www.fcc.gov

### Federal Trade Commission

Consumer Response Center
Attention CRC-240
Washington, DC 20580
Toll-Free: 877-FTC-HELP (877-382-4357)
TDD/TTY: 866-653-4261
Website: http://www.ftc.gov

### National Association of Insurance Commissioners

Government Relations
444 N. Capitol St., NW Suite 701
Washington, DC 20001
Phone: 202-624-7790
Fax: 202-624-8579
Website: http://www.naic.org

### National Fraud Information Center/Internet Fraud Watch

1701 K St., NW, Suite 1200
Washington, DC 20006
Toll-Free: 800-876-7060
TDD/TTY: 202-835-0778
Fax: 202-835-0767
Website: http://www.fraud.org

### Pension Benefit Guaranty Corporation

1200 K St., NW
Washington, DC 20005-4026
Phone: 202-326-4100
Toll-Free: 800-400-PBGC (7242)
Fax: 202-326-4047
Website: http://www.pbgc.gov

## Federal Banking Regulators

### Comptroller of the Currency

Office of the Ombudsman
Customer Assistance Group
1301 McKinney Street
Suite 3450
Houston, TX 77010
Toll-Free: 800-613-6743
Website: http://www.occ.treas.gov

### Federal Deposit Insurance Corporation (FDIC)

Division of Supervision and Consumer Protection
550 17th St., NW
Washington, DC 20429
Toll-Free: 877-ASK-FDIC (877-275-3342)
TDD Toll-Free: 800-925-4618
Phone: 703-562-2222
Website: http://www.fdic.gov

### Federal Reserve System Board of Governors

20th and C Streets, NW
Washington, DC 20551
Website: http://www.federalreserve.gov

## National Credit Union Administration

Consumer Complaints Specialist
1775 Duke Street
Alexandria, VA 22314
Phone: 703-518-6330
Website: http://www.ncua.gov

## Office of Thrift Supervision

U.S. Department of the Treasury
1700 G St., NW
Washington, DC 20552
Toll-Free: 800-842-6929
Website: http://
www.ots.treas.gov

## Broker and Securities Regulation and Oversight

## Federal Financial Institutions Examination Council

3501 Fairfax Drive
Room D8073a
Arlington, VA 22226
Website: http://www.ffiec.gov

## International Organisation of Securities Commissions

C/ Oquendo 12
28006 Madrid
SPAIN
Phone: (34) 91 417 55 49
Fax: (34) 91 555 93 68
Website: http://www.iosco.org
E-mail: mail@oicv.iosco.org

## Municipal Securities Rulemaking Board

1900 Duke Street, Suite 600
Alexandria, VA 22314
Phone: 703-797-6600
Website: http://www.msrb.org

## National Association of Securities Dealers

Office of Dispute Resolution
165 Broadway, 27th Floor
New York, NY 10006
Toll-Free: 800-289-9999
Phone: 212-858-4400
Website: http://www.nasdr.com

## National Futures Association

200 West Madison St.
16th Floor
Chicago, IL 60606-3447
Toll-Free:
800-621-3570 (outside IL)
Phone: 312-781-1300
Fax: 312-781-1467
Website: http://
www.nfa.futures.org
E-mail:
information@nfa.futures.org

## North American Securities Administrators Association, Inc.

750 First St., NE, Suite 1140
Washington, DC 20002
Phone: 202-737-0900
Fax: 202-783-3571
Website: http://www.nasaa.org
E-mail: info@nasaa.org

### Securities Investor Protection Corporation

805 15th Street, NW, Suite 800
Washington, DC 20005-2215
Phone: 202-371-8300
Fax: 202-371-6728
Website: http://www.sipc.org
E-mail: asksipc@sipc.org

### U.S. Securities and Exchange Commission

Office of Investor Education
and Assistance
100 F Street, NE
Washington, DC 20549-0213
Toll-Free: 800-SEC-0330
Phone: 202-551-6551
Fax: 202-942-9634
Website: http://www.sec.gov
Complaints: http://www.sec.gov/complaint.shtml

## State Securities Administrators

### Alabama

Securities Commission
770 Washington Ave., Suite 570
Montgomery, AL 36130-4700
Toll-Free: 800-222-1253 (AL)
Phone: 334-242-2984
Fax: 334-242-0240
E-mail: asc@asc.alabama.gov
Website: http://www.asc.state.al.us

### Alaska

Division of Banking and
Securities
Department of Commerce,
Community and Economic
Development
P.O. Box 11807
150 3rd Street, Suite 217
Juneau, AK 99811-0807
Toll-Free: 888-925-2521
Phone: 907-465-2521
Fax: 907-465-1230
Website: http://www.commerce.state.ak.us

### Arizona

Securities Division
Arizona Corporation
Commission
1300 West Washington
3rd Floor
Phoenix, AZ 85007
Phone: 602-542-4242
Fax: 602-594-7470
Website: http://www.cc.state.az.us
E-mail: info@azinvestor.gov

### Arkansas

Securities Division
Heritage West Bldg., Suite 300
201 East Markham
Little Rock, AR 72201
Toll-Free: 800-981-4429
Phone: 501-324-9260
Fax: 501-324-9268
Website: http://www.securities.arkansas.gov

### California
Department of Corporations
1515 K St., Suite 200
Sacramento, CA 95814-4052
Phone: 916-445-7205
Toll-Free: 866-275-2677
Website: http://www.corp.ca.gov

### Colorado
Department of Regulatory
Agencies
1560 Broadway, Suite 900
Denver, CO 80202
Phone: 303-894-2320
Fax: 303-861-2126
Website: http://
www.dora.state.co.us/securities
E-mail:
securities@dora.state.co.us

### Connecticut
Department of Banking
Government Relations and
Consumer Affairs
260 Constitution Plaza
Hartford, CT 06103-1800
Toll-Free: 800-831-7225
Phone: 860-240-8299
Fax: 860-240-8178
Website: http://www.ct.gov/dob
E-mail:
banking.complaints@ct.gov

### Delaware
Department of Justice
State Office Bldg.
820 North French St., 5th Floor
Wilmington, DE 19801
Phone: 302-577-8424
Fax: 302-577-6987
Website: http://www.state.de.us/
securities

### District of Columbia
Dept. of Insurance, Securities
and Banking
810 First St., NE, Suite 701
Washington, DC 20002
Phone: 202-727-8000
Fax: 202-535-1196
Website: http://www.disb.dc.gov

### Florida
Department of Financial
Services
200 East Gaines St.
Tallahassee, FL 32399-0370
Toll-Free: 800-342-2762 (FL)
Website: http://www.fldfs.com
E-mail: fldbf@dfs.state.fl.us

### Georgia
Division of Securities and
Business Regulation
Office of the Secretary of State
2 MLK Jr. Dr. SE
Suite 802, West Tower
Atlanta, GA 30334
Toll-Free: 888-733-7427
Phone: 404-656-3920
Fax: 404-657-8410
Website: http://
www.sos.state.ga.us
E-mail:
securities@sos.state.ga.us

### Hawaii
Department of Commerce and
Consumer Affairs
335 Merchant St., Room 201
Honolulu, HI 96813
Phone: 808-586-2744
Fax: 808-586-2733
Website: http://www.hawaii.gov

## Idaho

Department of Finance
800 Park Blvd., Suite 200
Boise, ID 83712
Toll-Free: 888-346-3378 (ID)
Phone: 208-332-8000
Website: http://finance.idaho.gov

## Illinois

Secretary of State
300 W. Jefferson St., Suite 300A
Springfield, IL 62702
Toll-Free: 800-628-7937 (IL)
Phone: 217-782-2256
Fax: 217-782-8876
Website: http://
www.sos.state.il.us

## Indiana

Securities Division
Office of the Secretary of State
201 Statehouse
Indianapolis, IN 46204
Toll-Free: 800-223-8791 (IN)
Phone: 317-232-6531
Website: http://www.state.in.us/
sos

## Iowa

340 Maple St.
Des Moines, IA 50319-0066
Phone: 515-281-4441
Toll-Free: 877-955-1212 (IA)
Fax: 515-281-3059
Website: http://
www.iid.state.ia.us
E-mail: iowasec@iid.state.ia.us

## Kansas

Office of the Securities
Commissioner
618 South Kansas Ave., 2nd Floor
Topeka, KS 66603-3804
Toll-Free: 800-232-9580 (KS)
Phone: 785-296-3307
Fax: 785-296-6872
Website: http:www.ksc.ks.gov
E-mail: ksecom@cjnetworks.com

## Kentucky

Department of Financial
Institutions
1025 Capitol Center Dr., Suite 200
Frankfort, KY 40601-3868
Toll-Free: 800-223-2579
Phone: 502-573-3390
Fax: 502-573-0086
Website: http://www.kfi.ky.gov

## Louisiana

Securities Division
Office of Financial Institutions
8660 United Plaza Blvd.
2nd Floor
Baton Rouge, LA 70809
Phone: 225-925-4660
Fax: 225-925-4548
Website: http://
www.ofi.state.la.us

## Maine

Office of Securities
121 State House Station
Augusta, ME 04333-0121
Toll-Free: 877-624-8551 (ME)
Phone: 207-624-8551
Fax: 207-624-8590
Website: http://
www.investors.maine.gov

## Maryland
Securities Division
Office of the Attorney General
200 Saint Paul Place
Baltimore, MD 21202-2020
Toll-Free: 888-743-0023 (MD)
Phone: 410-576-6360
Fax: 410-576-6532
Website: http://
www.oag.state.md.us
E-mail:
securities@oag.state.md.us

## Massachusetts
Securities Division
One Ashburton Place
17th Floor, Room 1701
Boston, MA 02108
Toll-Free: 800-269-5428 (MA)
Phone: 617-727-3548
Fax: 617-248-0177
Website: http://
www.sec.state.ma.us/sct
E-mail:
securities@sec.state.ma.us

## Michigan
Office of Financial and
Insurance Services
611 W. Ottawa St., 3rd Floor
P.O. Box 30220
Lansing, MI 48909
Toll-Free: 877-999-6442
Phone: 517-373-0220
Fax: 517-241-3991
Website: http://
www.michigan.gov/ofis

## Minnesota
Department of Commerce
85 Seventh Place East, Suite 500
St. Paul, MN 55101
Phone: 651-296-4026
Fax: 651-297-1959
Website: http://
www.commerce.state.mn.us

## Mississippi
Business Regulation and
Enforcement
Secretary of State's Office
401 Mississippi St.
P.O. Box 136 (Zip 39205)
Jackson, MS 39201
Toll-Free: 800-256-3494
Phone: 601-359-1350
Fax: 601-359-1499
Website: http://
www.sos.state.ms.us

## Missouri
Consumer Protection Division
P.O. Box 1276
Jefferson City, MO 65102
Toll-Free: 800-721-7996 (MO)
Phone: 573-751-4136
Fax: 573-526-3124
Website: http://sos.mo.gov

## Montana
Securities Division
State Auditor
840 Helena Ave.
Helena, MT 59601
Toll-Free: 800-332-6148 (MT)
Phone: 406-444-2040
Fax: 406-444-3497
Website: http://
www.sao.state.mt.us

## Nebraska

Bureau of Securities
P.O. Box 95006
Lincoln, NE 68509-5006
Phone: 402-471-3445
Website: http://www.ndbf.org

## Nevada

Securities Division
Office of the Secretary of State
555 East Washington Ave.
Suite 4000
Las Vegas, NV 89101
Phone: 702-486-2880
Fax: 702-486-2888
Website: http://
www.sos.state.nv.us
or sercetaryofstate.biz
E-mail: nvsec@sos.nv.gov

## New Hampshire

Department of State
107 N. Main Street
State House, Room 204
Concord, NH 03301-4989
Phone: 603-271-1463
Fax: 603-271-7933
Website: http://www.sos.nh.gov/
securities

## New Jersey

Bureau of Securities
Department of Law and Public
Safety
P.O. Box 47029 (Zip 07101)
153 Halsey St., 6th Floor
Newark, NJ 07102
Phone: 973-504-3600
Fax: 973-504-3601
Website: http://
www.njsecurities.gov

## New Mexico

Regulation & Licensing
Department
2550 Cerrillos Road
Santa Fe, NM 87505
Toll-Free: 800-704-5533 (NM)
Phone: 505-476-4580
Fax: 505-984-0617
Website: http://
www.rld.state.nm.us

## New York

Bureau of Investor Protection
and Securities
Office of the Attorney General
120 Broadway
New York, NY 10271
Website: http://
www.oag.state.ny.us

## North Carolina

Secretary of State
2 South Salisbury St.
Raleigh, NC 27601
Toll-Free: 800-688-4507
(Investor Hotline)
Phone: 919-733-3924
Fax: 919-821-0818
Website: http://www.sosnc.com

## North Dakota

Securities Department
State Capitol, 5th Floor
600 E. Boulevard Ave.
Bismarck, ND 58505-0510
Toll-Free: 800-297-5124 (ND)
Phone: 701-328-2910
Fax: 701-328-2946
Website: http://
www.ndsecurities.com
E-mail: ndsecurities@state.nd.us

### Ohio

Securities Division
77 South High St.
22nd Floor
Columbus, OH 43215-6131
Toll-Free: 800-788-1194
(Investor Protection Hotline)
Phone: 614-644-7381
Fax: 614-466-3316
Website: http://
www.securities.state.oh.us

### Oklahoma

Department of Securities
First National Center
120 North Robinson
Suite 860
Oklahoma City, OK 73102
Phone: 405-280-7700
Fax: 405-280-7742
Website: http://
www.securities.state.ok.us

### Oregon

Division of Finance and
Corporate Securities
350 Winter St., NE
P.O. Box 14480
Salem, OR 97309-0405
Toll-Free: 866-814-9710
Phone: 503-378-4140
Fax: 503-947-7862
Website: http://dcbs.oregon.gov
E-mail: dcbs.fcsmail@state.or.us

### Pennsylvania

Securities Commission
Office of Secretary
Eastgate Office Building
2nd Floor
1010 North 7th St.
Harrisburg, PA 17102-1410
Toll-Free: 800-600-0007 (PA)
Phone: 717-787-8062
Fax: 717-783-5122
Website: http://
www.psc.state.pa.us

### Puerto Rico

Oficina del Comisionado de
Instituciones Financieras
Centro-Europa Building
Suite 600
1492 Ponce de Leon Avenue
P.O. Box 11855
San Juan, PR 00910-3855
Toll-Free: 800-981-7711
(Español)
Phone: 787-723-8445 (Español)
Fax: 787-723-4225
Website: http://www.cif.gov.pr

### Rhode Island

Securities Division
233 Richmond St., Suite 232
Providence, RI 02903-4232
Phone: 401-222-3048
Fax: 401-222-5629
Website: http://
www.dbr.state.ri.us

## South Carolina

Securities Division
Office of the Attorney General
P.O. Box 11549
Columbia, SC 29211-1549
Phone: 803-734-9916
Fax: 803-734-4323
Website: http://
www.scattorneygeneral.org

## South Dakota

Division of Securities
445 East Capitol Ave.
Pierre, SD 57501-3185
Phone: 605-773-4823
Fax: 605-773-5953
Website: http://www.state.sd.us/
dcr/securities

## Tennessee

Department of Commerce and
Insurance
Davy Crockett Tower, Suite 680
500 James Robertson Pkwy.
Nashville, TN 37243
Toll-Free: 800-863-9117 (TN)
Phone: 615-741-2241
Website: http://www.state.tn.us/
commerce

## Texas

State Securities Board
P.O. Box 13167 (zip 78711-3167)
208 East 10th Street, 5th Floor
Austin, TX 78701
Phone: 512-305-8300
Fax: 512-305-8310
Website: http://
www.ssb.state.tx.us

## Utah

Department of Commerce
160 East 300 South, 2nd Floor
P.O. Box 146760
Salt Lake City, UT 84114-6760
Toll-Free: 800-721-7233 (UT)
Phone: 801-530-6600
Fax: 801-530-6980
Website: http://
www.securities.utah.gov
E-mail: securities@utah.gov

## Vermont

Department of Banking,
Insurance, Securities, & Health
Care Administration
89 Main St., Drawer 20
Montpelier, VT 05620-3101
Phone: 802-828-3420
Fax: 802-828-2896
Website: http://
www.bishca.state.vt.us/
SecuritiesDiv

## Virginia

State Corporation Commission
P.O. Box 1197
Richmond, VA 23218
Toll-Free: 800-552-7945 (VA)
Phone: 804-371-9051
Fax: 804-371-9911
Website: http://
www.scc.virginia.gov/division/srf

## Washington
Securities Division
Department of Financial
Institutions
P.O. Box 9033
Olympia, WA 98507-9033
Toll-Free: 877-746-4334
Phone: 360-902-8700
Fax: 360-586-5068
Website: http://www.dfi.wa.gov

## West Virginia
State Auditor's Office
State Capitol Bldg. 1
Room W100
Charleston, WV 25305
Phone: 304-558-2257
Toll-Free: 888-368-9507
Fax: 304-558-4211
Website: http://www.wvsao.gov
E-mail: securities@wvsao.gov

## Wisconsin
Division of Securities
Department of Financial
Institutions
P.O. Box 1768
Madison, WI 53701-1768
Toll-Free: 800-47-CHECK (WI)
Phone: 608-266-1064
Fax: 608-264-7979
Website: http://www.wdfi.org

## Wyoming
Office of the Secretary of State
State Capitol Bldg.
200 West 24th St.
Cheyenne, WY 82002-0020
Website: http://soswy.state.wy.us
E-mail: securities@state.wy.us

# *Index*

# Index